BOOKS,

BRICKS

&BYTES

Edited by
Stephen R. Graubard
& Paul LeClerc

BOOKS,

BRICKS

&BYTES

LIBRARIES IN THE TWENTY-FIRST CENTURY

Transaction Publishers
New Brunswick (U.S.A.) and London (U.K.)

Second printing 1999
Copyright © 1999 by Transaction Publishers, New Brunswick, New Jersey.
Augmented version of a special issue of *Daedalus,* Fall 1996, "Books, Bricks
and Bytes," Volume 125, Number 4, of the *Proceedings of the American
Academy of Arts and Sciences,* copyright © 1996 by the American Academy
of Arts and Sciences

This book is printed on acid-free paper that meets the American National
Standard for Permanence of Paper for Printed Library Materials.

Library of Congress Catalog Number: 97-22113
ISBN: 1-56000-986-1
Printed in the United States of America

Library of Congress Cataloging-in-Publication Data

Books, bricks, and bytes : libraries in the twenty-first century / edited by
    Stephen R. Graubard and Paul LeClerc.
        p. cm.
    Includes bibliographical references (p.   ).
    ISBN 1-56000-986-1 (pbk : alk. paper)
    1. Library science. 2. Library science—United States. 3. Libraries—
Data Processing. 4. Libraries—United States—Data processing. 5. Digital
libraries. 6. Digital libraries—United States. I. Graubard, Stephen Richards.
II. LeClerc, Paul O.
Z665.B698   1997
020—dc21   97-22113
                                                                     CIP

020
B724
C.1

Contents

Preface

THIS BOOK CELEBRATES a centennial, that of the New York Public Library, one of the world's largest and most distinguished libraries. It owes a very great deal to two presidents of that institution, the late Father Timothy Healy, who first discussed the possibility of such a book with the Editor, recognizing its importance for the many publics that rely on and make use of libraries, and Paul LeClerc, who did so much during a very busy time to make certain that the book came to fruition. It is a distinct pleasure to acknowledge the debt that the American Academy of Arts and Sciences owes to both these men.

Libraries are today experiencing a technological revolution that goes well beyond anything that has existed since the invention of printing. It is not at all surprising that the digital library, with all that it portends for the future of the book and the periodical, but also with all that it implies for the kinds of information that will be collected and disseminated, for the new publics that will make use of the data collected, for the problems of copyright, access, and costs that will necessarily preoccupy those responsible for the libraries of the twenty-first century, should figure conspicuously in this book. Nor is it surprising that this book is truly international, concerned with libraries in North America and Europe, but also in Africa, Asia, and Latin America.

In 1896, as for most of the twentieth century, a library defined itself by its holdings. The pride that American colleges and universities took in their libraries was generally expressed in some statement about the number of books that they could claim to own. Indeed, the greatest of the world's libraries were judged by the number of their cataloged items. The three greatest libraries were all European, the largest being the Bibliothèque Nationale with its purported 2,700,000 volumes. The other two great European libraries were the British Museum and the Imperial Library of St. Petersburg, each with holdings of more than one million. The Royal Libraries in Munich and Berlin followed very closely behind, as did the Library of Congress, the largest in the United States, claiming 690,000 volumes; the Boston Public Library's collections were larger than those of the New York Public Library, and university libraries like Harvard and Heidelberg had collections that numbered some 400,000 volumes. Such data was thought immensely significant at the time. It is this kind of data, vastly changed in the collections formed since on both sides of the Atlantic but also in other parts of the world, that still gives certain institutions a sense of pride and indeed of confidence about the state of their scholarly patrimony. Yet, as will be obvious to anyone who reads this book, the factor of proprietorship is no longer as governing as it was in a pre-computer age.

The cooperation between institutions, the novel ways of gaining access to information—indeed, the centrality of that vastly expanded and transformed commodity that goes under the name of information—makes the library of the late twentieth century a very different place from what it was even a few decades ago. It would be easy to believe that everything has changed. It has not. If this is a time of library building, on a scale virtually unprecedented in any previous decade, if bricks and concrete remain vitally important, if books continue to be printed in numbers inconceivable even half a century ago, if many of these libraries are avowedly national, emphasizing that fact even more in their names than in their holdings, if the digital is invading everywhere, it is in fact a time of continuity as well as novelty. As will become apparent to those who read this book, the profession of librarianship is changing dramatically. If certain libraries are seeking to bring the ideals of the Andrew Carnegie era into a new century, appealing to new publics, providing new services, making for greater access, scholarship is itself also being transformed. The kinds of research pursued today do not always resemble what passed for scholarly inquiry some decades ago. Those who came in search of archival materials a century ago imagined they knew what an archive should be, what materials it ought to contain. This is much less obvious today. If, for some, the library remains a "place of memories," national and even civilizational, though the latter term carries a certain pejorative meaning in some quarters, it exists to keep alive the record of the past, what some are not afraid to call the nation's cultural inheritance. The library is also, and not only in the newly developing nations of the world, a place of education— of the young certainly, but also of adult populations, those seeking to become literate in ways that involve more than learning one's letters. All these tasks remain central, and they are increasingly supplemented by all the tasks that reflect the interests of corporate groups that are heavily dependent on the kinds of information that only a well-staffed library can provide access to.

Whether or not one believes in the reality of the so-called information revolution that is overtaking the world, whether or not one believes that a good deal of it is "hype" of a crass, commercial kind, it is obvious that the libraries being built today do not resemble those marble sanctuaries constructed in the late Victorian age or early in this century. They are not "refuges" from the world outside, but they continue to reflect values, intellectual and social, that are not simply those of the marketplace. They aspire to be public places, open to a vastly larger public, to individuals and groups who would not have thought to consult their resources some decades ago. The libraries of the world are changing, responding to new technologies, but also to new social and economic demands. Institutions that seemed very stable and unchanging only a few decades ago, with clearly defined responsibilities and agendas, are today being transformed, accommodating the demands of educated men and women in a great variety of ways, seeking to serve democratic institutions in ways that would not have been thought necessary in a pre-twentieth-century world. Libraries, quite as much as universities and museums, reflect the culture of their specific societies and perceive their roles differently. The uniformity of their technology—where it exists—ought not to delude us into believing that they are apolitical institutions, divorced from the specific educational and cultural purposes of their societies. They inevitably reflect the values and conflicts of their respective societies. They are acted upon by public and private interests.

If they are obliged to adopt new technologies, and do so willingly, if they have an obligation to instruct in the use of specific machines that provide access to information that would have once been unavailable, and if these machines are as useful for businessmen as for lawyers, for physicians as for social workers, for politicians as for civil servants, they have another obligation, no less essential. It is to consider their commitment to scholarship and learning, to what some would have called the "republic of letters," to what those who founded the American Academy of Arts and Sciences in 1780 called "the Arts and Sciences...the foundation and support of agriculture, manufactures, and commerce." If these were, in the words of the original charter of the Academy, "necessary to the wealth, peace, independence, and happiness of a people as they essentially promote the honor and dignity of the government which patronizes them," that objective remains no less central today. Libraries are national treasures, but they exist today in an international framework, serving multifarious purposes that would have been largely inconceivable even a few decades ago. This book is intended to pay tribute to the institutions and those who serve them but also those who see the need to support them, not least in these times when there are so many other demands for public and private funds.

The New York Public Library provided the financial support that made the planning and realization of this book possible. We are immensely grateful for that help. Also, thanks need to be given to The Andrew W. Mellon Foundation for its assistance in making it possible for us to make this an international book, concerned with more than just the conditions that obtain in the United States and the European Union.

Stephen R. Graubard

Introduction

A S IS AMPLY EVIDENT IN THE ESSAYS contained in this book, the last decade of our century is proving to be one of the most thrilling—and challenging—of times to be involved in the governance, the support, the building or rebuilding, and the management of libraries.

Libraries have been a fixed element in organized societies, have been engines of cultural and economic production, for well over two thousand years. To name a great center of learning is, inevitably, to name the library or libraries that helped make it so.

Libraries have enjoyed what is arguably the simplest and most enduring set of organizing principles of any cultural enterprise. Simply put, libraries have had, since their origins, only three basic functions: to acquire materials; to store and preserve these acquisitions; and to make them available for inspection. These are the rock-bottom, fundamental characteristics of any library, anywhere in the world, at any time in history.

What differentiates one library from another is the attitude its proprietors adopt in relation to the traditional functions of acquisition, conservation, and access. What sets the present era apart from virtually all others in the history of libraries is the rapid—

indeed revolutionary—ways in which information technology is transforming each of these core functions. It is in the management of this change that lies, in my estimation, the thrill of directing a library today.

ACQUISITIONS

The actual physical possession of texts—whether inscribed on cuneiform tablets, papyrus, vellum, or paper—has, until the very recent past, been at the very heart of the library business. A library was what it owned, and the general imperative was to expand the domain of ownership in either benign ways—through purchase or gift—or through more brutal means: confiscation, seizure, pillage, or theft.

Precisely what kinds of things a library owned, in which subject fields, and in what scope or scale, gave collection-building a necessary focus and gave an individual library a particular—and at times a peculiar if not eccentric—identity. The founders and directors of the legendary library of Alexandria, for example, sought to amass an authentically global collection. And they did, even if it meant resorting to outright theft, as was the case of the manuscript copies of the works of Aeschylus, Sophocles, and Euripides, borrowed from the state archives in Athens and never returned. Ultimately, the collections in Alexandria numbered close to a million scrolls and became the model for collecting on a truly massive scale, one that continues today at institutions such as The New York Public Library, although admittedly in a more law-abiding fashion.

Library collections need neither be immense nor global, however, to be brilliant. Samuel Pepys, the celebrated seventeenth-century diarist, had a very clear sense of how to impose limits on his library's growth. This library is, of course, the famous Bibliotheca Pepysiana of Magdalene College, Cambridge, one of the glories of a glorious university. Pepys believed firmly that a gentleman's private library should contain precisely three thousand volumes, no more and no less. He collected for forty years, discarding books as he acquired new ones so as to never exceed his three-thousand-volume limit.

Restrictions other than size have, of course, long been used to determine an institution's collections. Collegiate and university libraries, public libraries, research libraries, national libraries, those of schools of divinity, law, and medicine, and specialized libraries of every kind will each adapt different criteria in their acquisition policies. But the very act of acquiring, of bringing physical objects into ownership, has been the central activity of virtually all libraries, from their origins in antiquity until the present day.

This paradigm—that a library is what it owns—has come under the powerful influence of information technology within the last decade. As a consequence of the production, primarily by the commercial sector, of electronic data bases, available through CD-ROMs or servers, a library can suddenly bring its readers into contact with abundant information in products that it either may not or cannot purchase. These products may reside physically anywhere in the world—mounted on servers in Shanghai, Singapore, or Seattle, for example—yet their content is instantly available to patrons in library reading rooms through global telecommunications networks.

If the library's function is to satisfy the curiosity of its patrons, doing so by placing them at electronic gateways that take them to information dispersed globally but retrievable locally through a computer network, is no less valid a function than putting books, journals, and manuscripts from our physical collections in their hands in reading rooms. Increasingly, and inevitably, the acquisition budgets of libraries will be used not only to purchase hard copies but also to secure access to electronically-formatted information whose ownership remains in the hands of others. At The New York Public Library, we will devote 5 percent of the Research Libraries' acquisitions budget this year—$400,000 out of $8 million—to give our readers access to electronic data bases owned by others. We anticipate that this share of the acquisitions budget will grow to 10 percent by the year 2000.

ACCESS

If collections are the point of origin of a library's identity, then access to these collections is a necessary corollary. For more than two millennia, using a library collection meant at least two things:

first, going physically to the library itself, often at considerable cost and inconvenience; and second, actually getting into the reading rooms to use its materials. The first part, the trip, offered no guarantee of succeeding in the second part: getting one's hands on the books and manuscripts. I shall always remember, and not with fondness, my own experience of being turned away from the doors of the Bibliothèque de l'Institut de France in Paris on a sweltering summer day, not because I did not have the requisite letters of introduction but because I was not wearing a tie and suit coat.

Most libraries are, and always have been, closed collections, providing access only to a select readership. The royal and monastic libraries of pre-revolutionary Europe, college and university libraries and research libraries today, and even some national libraries, are closed to the general public. In still other cases, access may be fee-based or may require proof of identity, reader cards, or justification for seeing the collections.

Despite these traditional, sometimes centuries-old, limitations on physical access, we find that information technology is also altering this realm of the library's function in dramatic ways. Virtually all major libraries in developed countries are now committed to creating on-line catalogs of their holdings and retrospective conversions of their printed or card catalogs. Thanks to the initial support of The Andrew W. Mellon Foundation, The New York Public Library committed two years ago to spend $10 million for the retrospective conversion of its monumental, eight-hundred-volume, printed catalog. When completed in 2000, this project will, for the first time, permit us to open to a truly global audience the immense bibliographical record of the research collections.

As important as it is to provide the curious of the world with the ability to search our bibliographical records electronically, it is through digitizing collections and making their content available on-line that we see technology's greatest power to transform libraries. The leadership given by the Librarian of Congress to the American digitization effort, the creation within the United States of the National Digital Library Federation, and the sponsorship by the U.S. National Science Foundation of its Digital Library Initiative have all clearly placed before us the opportunities to bring otherwise inaccessible portions of our collections to readers nationally and internationally. These efforts have also served a salutary, cautionary purpose. They have reminded us of how costly, and how complicated, regional and national digital projects can become, with issues such as intellectual property, archiving, and technical architecture requiring resolution prior to the advent of an authentic digital library, even on a limited scale.

The final aspect of access that deserves mention is the reverse side of the digital library coin. That is, in addition to providing content, many libraries are now actively committed to providing our readers with access to the outside world of information from library buildings. Public, free access to the Internet is rapidly becoming a reality within the American library community. The New York Public Library's four Research Libraries and eighty-four Branch Libraries give the public broad and free access to the Internet at one thousand terminals spread through the Library's eighty-eight facilities. Internet use by the public has been overwhelming, justifying our decision to double the size of the network to two thousand public terminals by the year 2000. Every terminal with Internet accessibility is being used by the public at full capacity and every terminal that we add is immediately used at full capacity.

The access paradigm within the library is therefore now characterized by considerable change. While no one should ever assume that the public will stop frequenting libraries and their hard-copy collections in a physical sense, readers will henceforth be able to supplement their searches for information through the intermediary agency of telecommunications networks.

PRESERVATION

The third and final organizing principle of libraries is the storage and preservation of materials. Here we can divide the world of libraries into basically two categories: those committed to keeping their collections virtually forever; and those libraries that routinely move old materials out to make way for the new. Research libraries like The New York Public Library, the Morgan, the Vatican, or the Bodleian belong to the first category: institutions that make a conscious decision in acquiring a book or manuscript to keep it for as long as the library endures or as long as the artifact endures.

Circulating libraries and most college and university libraries belong to the other group, where weeding the collections of material deemed inessential or irrelevant takes place routinely.

Whether a library's policy to keep an item is for centuries or merely for a few years, its acquisition is usually accompanied by an explicit understanding that there will be an institutional commitment, of greater or lesser magnitude, to its preservation. For large-scale institutions, this will mean an investment in conservation and restoration activities, often carried out in library-based conservation laboratories staffed by highly specialized technicians.

The creation of microfilm versions of brittle or otherwise endangered materials has served as an important adjunct to conservation activities for at least four decades. Microfilming, however, should not be seen as a general substitute for preserving actual documents, particularly rare and unique items. In intervening to save these materials, we can, happily, rely on decades of experience in conservation. We can deacidify, splice, patch, or otherwise mend paper and membrane-based materials in ways that are wholly reassuring from a library management point of view. What confounds us is the magnitude of the preservation task before us, not any deficiency in our knowledge of how to preserve hard-copy materials. In other words, fulfilling our preservation responsibilities to collections is now basically a matter of economics—primarily where to find the resources to render stable the vast quantities of material printed on acid-laced paper that are being consumed by "slow fires"—not one of technique or technology.

As in the case of acquisitions and access, the paradigm of preservation is being significantly altered by the advent of electronically-formatted information. In this case, however, our accommodation to technology is less confident than in the other two. Does the rapidity with which hardware and software evolve—not to mention the uncertainties surrounding our ability to keep data sets intact for decades and even centuries—jeopardize our traditional commitment to preserve library materials? What is the appropriate locus of responsibility for preserving electronic information? Does it lie with the library, which may have never acquired data in a proprietary sense but only access to it, or rather with the commercial producer? And what are we to make of our responsibility to preserve the electronic version of literary manuscripts formerly on paper? Will the poets and novelists writing on computers today be able to rely on libraries to preserve for generations to come the modern, computer-based equivalents of Virginia Wolfe's journals or Keats's odes? We lack as yet satisfactory answers to such questions.

CONCLUSION

These thoughts on the information revolution's transformation of library functions are not, admittedly, universally applicable. They tend more to characterize the situation of well-financed institutions in economically and technologically advanced societies rather than the majority of libraries in our world. Any dispassionate assessment of the library situation worldwide will inevitably conclude, I believe, that technology is doing far more than revolutionizing our traditional notions of acquisitions, access, and preservation. It is also sundering the global community of libraries into separate enclaves of the privileged and not-so-privileged, where the defining characteristic is the capital—or lack of it—to buy and maintain computer-based information systems and Internet access.

Financial inequalities have always existed among libraries; and they always will. And yet the disparities between libraries in the electronic era are sharpening the divide between the information "have's" and "have-nots" in ways that are as unprecedented as they are ominous. In a time when competitiveness is based on access to current and valid information, the electronic aspect of the library can be the key to individual success, and even economic survival. Thus the recent investment by The New York Public Library of $100 million to create a new Science, Industry, and Business Library (SIBL), run along the lines of a public library even though, by charter and by funding source, it is a private one.

SIBL's success is illustrative of the drawing power of an information center that joins a massive print collection to a ubiquitous and powerful technology platform. In its first ten months of operation, SIBL has attracted over half a million reader-visits and has rapidly fulfilled our intentions of being a new and essential force in the New York region's economy. At the same time, it must be acknowledged that SIBL's very existence is due to private-sector support on a scale unimaginable in most other parts of the world:

fully 75 percent of the $100 million cost is being borne by the private sector—individuals, corporations, and foundations. The costs of SIBL's annual operations are also shared by the public and private sectors, but with the private side assuming 67 percent of the burden.

The New York Public Library model of massive private support to maintain a library that is open to all without charge is, admittedly, not easily exportable. The cultures and tax laws of other countries do not encourage philanthropy on the scale that has been essential to The New York Public Library's growth for a century, and it would be fatally naive to assume that the private sector alone will bear the financial burden of library modernization and computerization elsewhere in the world, particularly in developing countries. Hence the dilemma facing the international library community: how to alleviate the disparity in resources, particularly those based on or devoted to technology, that separates advanced libraries from struggling ones? Technology itself may well provide the answer ultimately, but not within the near term and not without the commitment of First World nations and institutions to assist in modernizing less economically favored societies and their libraries.

Paul LeClerc

Peter Lyman

What is a Digital Library? Technology, Intellectual Property, and the Public Interest

W HAT IS A DIGITAL LIBRARY? In attaching the adjective "digital" to the noun "library" the future seems to be reconciled with the past. Over the last century the United States has built a marketplace of ideas upon three institutions—libraries, publishing, and copyright law. Will "digital libraries," "electronic publishing," and "information highways" constitute the marketplace of ideas for an information society? Futurist tropes like these are reassuring because they suggest an institutional continuity between past and future, yet if technological innovation generally begins by imitating the past, it is not new tools that constitute innovation but new institutions. But futurist tropes often conceal the latent tensions between digital technology and the institutions of an industrial society, tensions that lead to important questions about the nature of the digital library. Highways carry manufactured commodities across the country, but information is an immaterial electronic signal traveling on a global digital network. What are the consequences of this difference in the nature of printed and digital artifacts? Publishers today manufacture and distribute printed books and journals, but network technology enables every writer to create and personally distribute digital documents worldwide. How will the new relationships between writer and text change our sense of authorship, literature,

Peter Lyman is University Librarian and Professor in the School of Information Management and Systems at the University of California, Berkeley.

1

and library collections? A library is a distinctive kind of public place, a place that defines the center of a community and polity, but cyberspace is cosmopolitan, encompassing the globe. Is it possible to create public institutions in cyberspace?

The concept of an "information society" is also a futurist trope, for we do not yet know the impact of information technologies on our social life and, by extension, on the dynamics of organizations and institutions that use digital communication. Print technologies were a revolutionary innovation because they preserved knowledge by shaping it into a literature and reproduced and distributed it on a mass scale, making possible new social institutions such as science and the nation-state. The print revolution, as described by Lucien Febvre, was about

> something other than the history of a technique. It has to do with the effect on European culture of a new means of communicating ideas within a society that was essentially aristocratic, a society that accepted and was long to accept a culture and a tradition of learning which was restricted to certain social groups. . . . How did the printed book facilitate the rule and activity of these men?. . . Conversely, how successful was the book as an agent for the propagation of the new ideas, which we classify sometimes under the name Renaissance, sometimes under that of Humanism?[1]

Today the politics of information policy is focused on controlling access to markets for knowledge in an emerging information society, but it is not yet clear what ideas, traditions of learning, or elites the new media will empower. It is not too soon to go beyond political rhetoric—to begin to explore the first research findings about the computer revolution—and ask: What kinds of social relations can exist in cyberspace, using "information" as an organizational glue? Even more intriguing, given the emergence of a global network information infrastructure that has already become the foundation of global credit markets and media, can the information policies of a nation-state regulate something that far transcends its scope and powers?

Libraries in America are situated on the boundary between the market and the polity, in a liminal space that provides free access to knowledge in order to fulfill the public interest in education and democratic participation. The public quality of libraries derives from a nonmarket principle of free and equal access to knowledge; this, indeed, is the essence of the library as both a place and an institution. National information policy is now focused on a different principle, not only postulating that universal access to the digital library is a precondition for the development of a robust digital market, but asking whether a market mechanism for the distribution of information is sufficient to serve the public interest. Even a preliminary exploration reveals the emergence of a new kind of political realm in cyberspace, a new realm of free speech, innovative new forms of political association, and an unprecedented kind of freedom of the press that will command the protection of the First Amendment. How might a digital library balance the needs of the market and the polity, intellectual property and the public interest?

For the first time since the Constitutional Convention, information technology has provoked a fundamental debate about the structures of our national information policy. This discussion is not only about the digital library; it may shape the future of the print library as well. A library is more than its collections or buildings; it is part of a social strategy to create "progress in the Sciences and Useful Arts," in the words of the Constitution. How might a digital library support the new kinds of research and creativity of an information society? Can free public access to information in a digital library be made compatible with a robust information market—one capable of generating investment in research, education, and publishing—in an economy in which knowledge is a kind of capital? And how will the digital library fulfill the traditional role of the library as a public institution, supporting the public interest in learning as well as facilitating the democratic debate about ideas?

Given that nearly all predictions regarding technology have been wrong in the past, the attempt to assert political control over cyberspace tells us more about the information politics of the present than those of the future. If the future is to be understood with metaphors from the past, perhaps the best way to predict the shape of the digital library would be to compare it with the first stages of the most important technological innovation in history, namely, print itself, in order to interpret the emerging signs of the new kinds of digital documents and the social communication in cyberspace. The concept of *electronic publishing* can be explored by comparing printed and digital documents as published artifacts since they are different media for writing and reading, and ultimately for public forms of knowledge. An *information society* will be built upon the kinds of social relationships that are emerging in cyberspace. The structure of commerce suggested by the concept of an *information highway* is based on industrial society being regulated by national copyright policy, but digital commerce implies far different modes of production and government regulation. And, finally, the definition of the *digital library* will require an understanding of the role and nature of public institutions in a postindustrial society.

WHAT IS ELECTRONIC PUBLISHING?

The computer will not replace the book any more than the book has replaced speech. Oral, print, and digital media are not alternatives; rather, it is the interrelationship of these modes of communication that is significant in shaping public knowledge. The print revolution did not change public knowledge from speech to print, but from script to print, both of which were part of a culture of public discourse. In that transitional period, according to Elizabeth Eisenstein, "literary compositions were 'published' by being read aloud, even 'book' learning was governed by reliance on the spoken word—producing a hybrid half-oral, half-literate culture that has no precise counterpart today."[2] Ethnographers of reading describe the interrelationship of print and oral cultures as "living textuality," characterized by collective rather than individual recitation: religious communities and legal discourse are contemporary examples of living textuality, and multimedia Web pages may be distinctive new forms of living textuality as well.[3]

Technical artifacts containing knowledge must always be interpreted in the social contexts within which they are published and read. While the design of digital knowledge artifacts will be the foundation of any new system of public discourse, in practice a new public realm must inevitably combine speech, print, and digital expression. The silent reading of modern print cultures has obscured the way that printed texts tacitly occupy space within the context of public forms of knowledge; to read a scientific journal, for example, is to participate in the literature of a profession, which is authoritative by virtue of standard editorial rules and rhetorical practices.

If the social function of publishing is to make knowledge public, then the physical characteristics of the artifacts within which knowledge is contained, whether books or computers, will shape the dynamics of reading and writing, and therefore intellectual property markets, and ultimately the shared modes of learning and knowledge that define the public realm. Clearly a book and a digital document are different kinds of knowledge artifacts, and those differences will have consequences for the way ideas are written and read, but they are not opposites. Today, discussions of the digital library often oppose "print" with "digital," arguing that the civilization of the book is either threatened or made obsolete by "technology." But binary pairs of singular nouns like "print and computer" or "analog and digital" conceal significant variations within print and digital. Print is not a homogeneous medium of communication; newspapers and books are significantly different kinds of knowledge artifacts, using different rhetorical forms and having very different social uses. So too are electronic mail and data bases. Moreover, "print," meaning the print revolution, was not one innovation but many. The invention of movable type, which could reproduce multiple copies of manuscripts by mechanical means, was a response to the introduction of paper, a new medium for the preservation and distribution of knowledge. Similarly, it is not the computer alone that makes the digital library possible, but digital networks like the Internet, which can reproduce and distribute texts around the globe almost instantly and for little incremental cost.

While the expressions of ideas are published by becoming instantiated within technical objects like books and computers, in practice they are consumed by a skilled performance of literacy that uses knowledge artifacts like musical instruments. Reading, or literacy of any kind, is above all an aesthetic performance that only becomes tacit when it is masterful. Only then can there exist a pure experience of play; in this way reading recapitulates the spontaneity of ideas themselves and of membership in a community of speakers. Although reading may be experienced as an abstract mental activity, it is also a skilled performance employing a knowledge artifact. The physical relationship to the printed work in the act of reading is described by Stanley Fish: "The availability of a book to the hand, its presence on a shelf, its listing in a library catalog—all of these encourage us to think of it as a stationary object. Somehow when we put a book down, we forget that while we were reading, it was moving (pages turning, lines receding into the past) and forget too that we were moving with it."[4] If the solitude of reading is an intensely private experience, which might be objectively described as an eye-hand relationship, it is also often experienced internally as an intense dialogue between reader and author. The computer user is no more isolated than is the book reader, although the computer is a far different kind of knowledge artifact. Digital texts evoke a different kind of sociability and sense of public space.

One of the most important findings of the sociology of technology is that computers are knowledge artifacts that evoke genuine social responses; people respond to computers as an *other*, if not exactly as a person.[5] Although books and computers both contain texts, an important phenomenological difference is that digital texts often seem to have the direct impact of speech, creating a sense of social engagement and dialogue. This may be due to the malleability of computer signals that makes possible the interactivity of digital texts, evoking a sense of intimacy that is experienced as responsiveness. This engagement seems to be characteristic of all interactive digital texts, even though new media texts still are written within relatively primitive rhetorical forms with limited capacity for expressive nuance.

Although knowledge artifacts evoke dialogical responses, their quality as objects is critical to the nature of publishing; the characteristic facticity of knowledge artifacts brings continuity and structure to ideas, making possible the authoritative voice of the author, the structure and continuity of a literature, and ultimately institutional life itself.[6] The most significant difference between print and digital publications is a consequence of the facticity of print, its form as a fixed material commodity, compared to the immaterial and therefore malleable quality of digital information. The facticity of print creates an authority that transforms the writer into an author; printed texts are authoritative because the author and publisher control the context of information for the reader. In digital documents, the reader is given the power to reformat and reorganize the text and thereby the context within which the information appears; thus authority is replaced by provenance. The name given to the reader of digital documents, "user," reminds us that the computer reader does not have perfect freedom, since all of these choices are given by the technical structures designed by the programmer.

Nor are digital documents like broadcast media, although both are electronic signals and not artifacts. Television and radio are mass media; their content is centrally controlled by the broadcaster, as regulated by the government. They constitute a public realm by virtue of their ubiquity, but they define the individual as a consumer, not a citizen, free to choose only between standard programming. Digital documents are published by being placed in a public domain from which they may be copied and transferred to the reader; they are selected and "pulled in" by the reader. The reader passively "watches" the media; the digital reader actively composes the text. This distinction was crucial in a recent court decision concerning pornography on the Internet. The digital reader may be described as exercising civil rights—engaging in freedom of speech, press, and political association—in a way that a television watcher is not, and perhaps even more directly than a book reader.

Although both printed and digital documents contain texts, it should not necessarily be assumed that there is an epistemological continuity between analog texts and digital information. The provenance of digital texts is often dynamic, linked to software models and real-time information. Thus, analog and digital texts may differ fundamentally in their provenance, for what is simulated "is no longer the territory, an original substance or being, but a model of the real. . .from now on it is the map that precedes, and thus generates, the territory."[7] Compare, for example, the simulated and the photographed portions of the film *Jurassic Park,* and consider the very different kinds of literacy required to read these juxtaposed kinds of images with critical awareness of their provenance. Print and the computer screen seem to be similar because both contain alphanumeric symbols, but text and information constitute very different kinds of public knowledge.

Information

Information has no author; it is a style of reading in which data are organized by creating or changing the context. The prototypical digital document might be the spreadsheet, a tool that manages information within a data base, leaving the reader free to reshape the data to conform to different hypotheses or to visualize data in different ways, i.e., in numeric form or as graphic representations. Of course, it is always possible to read printed works as information—as in browsing a book, looking up a particular passage, or subjecting the text to content analysis—but generally print is given meaning by authors, by weaving words and sentences into a context. Computer design reflects the distinctive reading habits of the engineers who designed them; thus they are optimized for numeric analysis and the kind of reading that is useful for solving problems. For example, as Seymour Papert describes problem solving in programming, "the question to ask about the program is not whether it is right or wrong, but if it is fixable."[8] While it is interesting to analyze other kinds of texts with the tools created for science and engineering, the real challenge of electronic publishing is to design technologies that are compatible with other kinds of rhetorical strategies and traditions of reading and writing.

Knowledge always has a social context, although it may be tacit and is often concealed by the social prestige of artifacts like books and computers. In the printed book, context and meaning are created by the page designer and printer as well as by the author, but all of the tacit ways in which the medium becomes the message typically disappear in the play of reading. Every digital text has multiple designers in addition to the traditional author. It has, therefore, multiple cultures and ultimately multiple levels of intellectual property rights: that of the electrical engineer who designed the chip and network; the systems scientist who designed the operating system; the programmer who designed the application; the writers of the texts; and, finally, the new authority of the user to shape both the form and content of the message. Yet all must work within a common technical structure derived from military, engineering, and scientific uses of information. Technical reading has shaped the standards and practices of the network, making electrical engineering into the dominant public culture of cyberspace. Print, on the other hand, has many genres and rhetorical strategies that have been designed for different kinds of messages and social relations.

Yet even within this restricted domain new and unique forms of communication are evolving, that is, new modes of reading and writing that could not have occurred in print or broadcast media. Electronic mail (e-mail) makes it possible to send brief printed texts from person to person all around the world; unlike the telephone, e-mail is an asynchronous medium, so the exchange of messages does not require coordination in time. Even so, it is clear that e-mail is a type of speech, a form of living textuality. However, since it lacks the synchronous dialogical quality of a telephone conversation and the emotional context and nuances of meaning that are communicated by tone of voice and speaking patterns, e-mail communication is best restricted to the exchange of messages. Attempts to resolve conflict or negotiate differences often deteriorate into an emotional confrontation called "flaming," unless those writing and reading e-mail are members of a very disciplined community of speakers that requires rational communication and values group consensus more than individual expression.

Flaming might be explained by the relative novelty of the medium, or perhaps it reflects the everyday speech habits of the young men who dominate computer communication, but more likely it is a consequence of the design of the medium: e-mail reduces the social context cues that enable us to interpret the emotional valence of messages.[9] It is not only that electronic mail communication is conducted by strangers, although that is not unusual, but electronic mail has no rhetorical structure capable of moderating the consequences of its relatively limited range of expression even when used by people who know each other well. Compared to a printed page, an electronic mail message has no composition or layout, no choice of fonts or font styles, and few norms governing the presentation of ideas; text is treated as a kind of data that conforms to the space allowed, without norms for configuration appropriate to the message. And yet, for all of its limits, e-mail is a medium capable of sustaining social relationships and institutional life, and lacks only the development of software that will support more varied and sophisticated genres and rhetorical structures.

The creation of a rhetorical structure appropriate for digital texts might begin with systematic experimentation to discover the relationships between form and content, medium and message. In one study, for example, researchers compared readers' comprehension of the same text in the form of a printed book, as an unformatted ASCII file on a computer screen, and within hypertext, a program that enables the reader to organize the flow of information by jumping around the text to follow a theme of personal interest.[10] The researchers found that readers understood the information conveyed in print much better than the ASCII text, which scrolled by on the screen, but the readers' comprehension was the highest with hypertext. The printed book had a coherent structure that was superior to ASCII text, but hypertext was superior to print because it enabled the reader to create a customized, personal structure for the text, replacing the context provided by the author. It is significant that the book used for the research was a statistics text, the kind of book that might be read as a narrative but which is more likely to be read as a handbook when solving a problem in statistical analysis. Digital libraries thus far have been designed for this kind of reading, for finding information when context is provided by a question or a problem to be solved, and not by the structure of a narrative provided by an author.

Information, in this sense, might be defined as communication without social context cues or rhetorical structure. Digital information, of course, has a tacit social context for the engineers who invented digital technology. The first digital libraries included the kinds of shared information that were given social context by a shared professional culture; they contained e-mail messages, reference works, tools to manage data, and the forms of literature that build serial relationships through the shared hostility of games, jokes, and pornography. The original ARPAnet was restricted to those with Defense Department contracts; the Internet expanded network communications to the worldwide research community; and today the World Wide Web is used by millions of people who are essentially strangers. Thus far, cyberspace lacks the rhetorical structures that allow a common culture to be developed or sustained among strangers.

Digital Documents

Electronic publishing today is exploring the invention of rhetorical possibilities for a new medium in much the same way that print publishing did in its first century. Richard Lanham has compared modern hypertext to the rhetorical strategies and living textuality in medieval manuscripts and modern law.[11] Similarly, French historian Carla Hesse describes the similarities between

> the new electronic text and the modes of textuality invented and explored by the periodical press of the eighteenth-century: the free-play with formatting, the excitement about combining of image, music and text, the reassertion of the editorial over the authorial voice, the notion of the text as a bulletin board, and, alternatively, as a transparent network for the exchange of letters. . . . In 1789, Condorcet had the fantasy of using these new technologies of print and modes of textuality to, as he put it, "bring all of France into a dialogue with itself." And, in fact, he became a key player in the formation of a multimedia publishing group that experimented with all of these modes of publication and circulation.[12]

And the idea of using multimedia images to create a new public culture leads art historian Barbara Stafford to compare multimedia reading to public art in pre-Enlightenment oral-visual culture.[13] In these observations, historical context is brought to problems that computer science believes it has discovered for the first time, reasserting the historical continuity of culture against the view that the information age is the end of history.

The challenge of electronic publishing is to create new rhetorical forms that are appropriate to reading in cyberspace. To do so, a new kind of public culture will have to be created, or, as Barbara Stafford has commented about the possibility that multimedia might become a new public realm, "all forms of graphic display will have to be reassociated with common rituals and public concerns."[14] Multimedia is an innovative new kind of text that is made possible by digital technologies, but the juxtaposition of images and texts without context is only a technical achievement, not a new form of literature. The difference between information and a genuine visual culture is that cyberspace must rediscover or reinvent the social contexts of public life. Thus far, our dominant, public, visual culture consists of entertainment and mass media, rhetorical forms that require a passive surrender rather than active learning or participation, thus transforming the reader into a consumer, not a citizen.

Just as the print revolution began with the mechanical reproduction of manuscripts, so the digital library has begun with the imitation of print: digitizing thousands of printed books and articles. The ability to store digitized print documents and to send them wherever they are needed is of great significance because it will create unprecedented kinds of access to all published information anywhere in the world. Time and distance have created inequalities in access to printed publications, particularly time-sensitive scientific information, making the digitized library important, economically and educationally, to counties remote from the centers of research. Australia has built a national digital network to provide access to library resources from around the world to every remote village, and Singapore's national information policy is designed to create a new strategic port on the information trade routes of Asia.[15] However, as the study of readers' comprehension in hypertext suggests, on-line digitized texts are read as if they are reference works; they are not read in context. The digitized library can organize printed works into a universal library and provide access to it from anywhere in the world, but most likely it will be printed out again and read on paper. As important as access to printed information is, this new kind of access to information remains a theoretical possibility as long as the computer networks or workstations that are needed to read from the digitized library are not universally available.

Nor is there evidence that the digitized library is cheaper, given the cost of technology and the necessity to invest continuously in new technology. The digitized library has raised new problems for copyright enforcement, since much of this republication in a new form is unauthorized or raises new kinds of copyright questions that have not yet been answered. Finally, paper is a far more durable medium for the preservation of knowledge than is the computer. These are not unsolvable problems, but they suggest that even the most elementary kind of digital library will require more than an evolutionary change.

Ultimately the digital library will be defined by the creation of new forms of knowledge, which are uniquely possible only in digital environments, and so will create new kinds of public spaces. The network thus far has few original digital documents, but those that exist are significant. Electronic mail messaging is a fundamental innovation, allowing the coordination of organizations having worldwide scope without face-to-face management. The credit card is a digital document; data processing and management have created the credit structure and financial markets that enable us to charge purchases electronically anywhere in the world. The spreadsheet has made possible new ways of visualizing numeric data because it not only manages quantitative information in a new way but creates new modes of graphic display and answers new kinds of questions.

The physical, phenomenological, and epistemological differences between print and digital media have fundamental consequences for the nature of publishing. In print publishing, value is created by the author and the publisher through the reproduction of the mass-produced book in a standard form and format. The computer user, however, controls not only the creation of the text but also its reproduction and distribution through the network.[16] Digital media, therefore, imply new modes of production and consumption, new markets and regulatory forms. The publisher of digital documents will be similar to a merchant banker who invests in the development of intellectual property, a kind of capitalism far different from the publisher's traditional investment in the mechanical reproduction of the printing press and mass distribution of printed commodities. Publishing the digital document requires the invention of new kinds of knowledge and an awareness of a new relationship between the author and the reader. At the same time, it will require new forms of intellectual property, which may resemble the licensing mechanisms that govern the performing arts more so than the copyright mechanisms that are used today. Some publishers describe these new modes of electronic publishing as the digital library: they are ubiquitous, provide the reader with direct access to knowledge, and are customized to the needs of the individual.

WHAT IS AN INFORMATION SOCIETY?

What kind of society is possible in cyberspace? Can an institutional life be built upon the patterns of digital communication, and if so, would it resemble that which has been built upon print technologies? A sense of public place has been created by the social relations gathered and situated by library architecture. If networked information is everywhere, however, it might also by extension be said to be nowhere. Is the architecture of digital texts and virtual spaces capable of creating a sense of place that performs the functions of architecture in a public library? If so, what is the character of cyberspace as a public place within which participation in an intellectual community or civic life might be created and nurtured?

Cyberspace is not empty; it is a reflection of the nature of digital information itself, that is, of the possibility and limits of social control using technology. Norbert Wiener derived the term *cybernetics* from the Greek word for steersman, intending to point out the link between communication and power: "In giving the definition of Cybernetics. . .I classed communication and control together. When I control the actions of another person, I communicate a message to him, and although this message is in the imperative mood, the technique of communication does not differ from that of a message of fact."[17] Cyberspace cannot be defined in technological terms alone; it is a technology that was originally designed to use information as a means to assert social control. Thus, the social capacity of cyberspace is more a consequence of its history than the nature of technology itself.

While the history of cyberspace begins with hierarchical organizations like the military and business, which invented mainframe technology, it was in turn transformed by the egalitarian structure of scientific laboratories, which invented UNIX and client-server architecture. And later, again, it was transformed by the personal computer, a technology designed to serve the need for individual self-sufficiency by a new class of entrepreneurs and independent professionals; in turn, the merger of the personal computer culture and network technology has now evolved into the free play of independent publishers on the World Wide Web. The history of digital technology has not been linear; it might best be described as a process of metamorphosis, transformative change, as techniques and ideas have moved from one social context to another. Only recently has this process become political, as cyberspace has become the object of government regulation and a medium for international trade.

History and Cyberspace

Computer technology was originally invented by engineers to solve the specific problem of command and control. The technology of command and control initially addressed the relationship between humans and machines, as in aircraft control or ordnance, which required managing changing data in real time through computation. This computational function gave the "computer" its name, a name that became anachronistic as soon as the network connected the computational engines into a communications medium. It was when computers were used to create control over human labor in business organizations that computers came to be called "electronic brains," which is to say the computer was the brain to human brawn. While "electronic brains" were mainframe computers to which limited-function "terminals" were connected in order to strictly control the flow of information, the Web is based upon highly flexible client-server technologies developed for scientific laboratories—social structures built upon equal access to shared information. Without the recognition that technologies have a history, not a nature, cybernetic authority may be concealed within the prestige and facticity of a machine that might well be redesigned.

This is not to say that command and control is not a useful metaphor for the relationship between humans and information, but only to situate cyberspace within the social contexts for which computer technology was designed. For example, in data management the function of cyberspace is to manage and analyze information from, for instance, global financial markets or scientific instrumentation in real time. In a sense, cybernetic command and control is a specific concept of reading, one that is highly useful in managing quantitative data. The vestigial remnants of this evolution from military to economic authority are still apparent on the computer keyboard: we give "commands," a social relationship far from most literary cultures, using "control" keys; there are generally "break" and "escape" keys; and software often includes mnemonic commands like "control K" to "kill" text. This is military language but also the language of computer games, a distinctively masculine language of action emphasizing emotional control. This construction of computers is generally not technologically necessary or inevitable; it is sociological, derived from the problems that technology was built to solve, and reflects the masculine culture of its creators. Given the resources, every knowledge culture, every discipline or profession or group, might design a different computer.

Tacitly, then, the concept of cyberspace imposes the social and economic relationships of industrial culture upon Internet communication, which is an entirely new context for social relationships. Cybernetics was a solution to the problem of inventory control and transportation, of military material or market commodities; the Internet allows the transportation of information around the world at virtually no cost. The uses of cyberspace have included the logistic control of real-time numeric data for military, scientific, and technical research largely funded by the government and now, perhaps, to regulate the marketplace of intellectual property in cyberspace. With the evolution from the Defense Department's ARPAnet to the National Science Foundation's NSFnet to the Internet, which links universities and research labs, to the World Wide Web, the social world of cyberspace has grown and changed. Today the language of national information policy is industrial, returning to the language of cybernetics to exert control over a technology that has unexpectedly evolved from a computational machine into an unprecedented kind of communications medium. What is not being addressed in policy debates are the embryonic new social formations that are already developing in cyberspace; it is this new dimension that will shape our concept of the public sphere and the place of the library within it.

Sociability in Cyberspace

The technical definition of the Internet as the "network of networks" is useful because it states a problem that can be solved by engineering, namely, the need for technical standards that allows information in different networks to be exchanged. Internet protocols were designed to be tools for information management, including protocols for e-mail, file transfer protocol (FTP), and telnet; these are technical standards that allow readers to connect to information servers anywhere in the world and to exchange documents of any kind. In an evaluation in the early 1990s of NSFnet, the high-speed network that was designed to provide scientists access to national supercomputer centers for basic scientific and technical research, it was found that nearly two-thirds of the traffic on the network was actually used for information management, such as looking up information, exchanging papers, and organizing and analyzing data. These are clearly library activities, although a subset of library activities. As a medium for the literature of fields like engineering and high-energy physics, shared information can sustain a sense of community; professional communities have other resources to ensure social solidarity, such as the common culture built upon shared educational backgrounds and face-to-face relationships in professional meetings. But, in the absence of such social resources, can the network build and sustain something that reasonably might be called a community in the society of strangers in cyberspace?

The World Wide Web provides publishing tools that have been useful in addressing the problem of social solidarity in cyberspace. The Web was designed as a medium for creating multimedia hypertext documents (using hypertext markup language, HTML) to generate Web pages—in essence, self-published documents with worldwide distribution. Each page has an address (called a universal resource locator, or URL) that enables readers to navigate the information in cyberspace and to link one page to another, wherever it may be located on the network.

The Web is an unprecedented medium for individual publishing on a global scale, since anyone may distribute information, and today an estimated fifty million Web pages on untold numbers of topics are available to readers in cyberspace. In practice, however, as a consequence of the capacity to create hypertext links, the Web is a medium for group authoring, since every writer's document can be directly linked to information in any other document on the Web. Within this context, a digital document is very different from a printed text or a digitized version of a printed text. A digital document is dynamic, changing in real time, because it is given context by the actions of a reader; every digital document is potentially public, and any part of it is potentially part of another document. In this sense, the "Web" is an appropriate new metaphor for the network because it suggests a textile, sharing a Latin root with the word "text"; this is particularly useful because it suggests that we read the network as a text, or perhaps as a library of texts.[18]

The Web consists of more than pages; it is becoming a kind of literature for new types of social groups. New rhetorical strategies are creating patterns of communication that are gathered and situated by the architecture of computer software applications. These patterns of communication initially evolved using e-mail lists, which are more than random groups but less than communities in the traditional sense. One must join a listserv to receive its broadcasts of standard e-mail messages. The Web is multimedia, and both public and personal; that is, any part of a Web page can be read at any time, and it is the reader who chooses to create a link. Many new experimental forms of group reading are being built with these new technologies. Electronic journals, for example, are an experimental literature that take advantage of the dynamic qualities of digital documents to distribute texts quickly, or combine text with new modes of visualizing information, or use interactive discussions to simulate the research process itself. Collaborative laboratory software, *collaboratories,* enables groups of scientists to examine and discuss data together even though they may be physically located in places around the world; collaboratories are a kind of group discussion, a form of living textuality.[19]

Computer games have been at the leading edge of experimentation in creating new kinds of digital documents. One of the earliest forms of collaborative text on mainframes was "Adventure," a text-based mystery game similar to "Dungeons and Dragons." Game technology has now evolved into multi-user dungeons (MUDs) and more recently into MOOs (MUDs object-oriented) with interactive graphic illustrations of places and characters. MUDs and MOOs are texts that simulate social institutions, the most famous of which is Xerox PARC's *Lambda Moo* simulation of a boarding house. These are institutions of strangers, whose common culture is mediated by software that simulates places and situations through text-based conversational dialogues. What is most striking is that participants in collaborative digital environments experience them as genuine social relationships; people who have never met face-to-face experience an intense sense of community.[20] It is not incidental that collaborative software began in game technology or that games represent the largest computer software industry. The element of play is essential to the creation of a virtual world. Not surprisingly, games often (but not invariably) constitute social solidarity through shared hostility or aggression, or rely upon anonymity and the construction of fictitious personae to create a playful field for communication.

Just as the digital library has functioned very well as a public institution within the context of a profession like engineering or high energy physics, so the Web has performed the function of a public place containing the literature of social and political movements. Just as the facsimile became the medium of choice for publications by political exiles with access to telephone technology, so the Web has become a medium for political organizations of social movements that have no political voice, enabling those who feel isolated locally to reach out, to gain a sense of community or solidarity on a national or global scale. Within the United States, the Web is a medium for political movements whose message is not accepted by the established media, such as gays and lesbians or the militia movements that challenge government authority. Globally, environmental movements whose causes transcend nations, such as Greenpeace, use the Web as an organizing tool.[21] Unlike traditional communities, these groups do not depend upon a sense of place or face-to-face personal relationships but rather upon a communications medium that is personal enough to overcome isolation yet anonymous enough to encourage risk taking, interactive enough to create a sense of participation and membership, and able to create a collective memory through the collaborative production of a shared literature. Historically, the great public libraries have been public spaces serving immigrants and minorities. In Mary Ryan's words: "...the appropriation of the social spaces of everyday life is an essential precondition for the political empowerment of subordinated social groups."[22] In a sense, in serving as a resource for the organization of social movements, the digital library has inherited the great tradition of the public library as a place that provides a sense of community to the outsider.

Public and Private in Cyberspace

If cyberspace is a medium for social communication, it is not yet clear whether it achieves the stature of a *public* place, that is, a place that links individual participation to a sense of membership in an institution or polity. Cyberspace seems to foster intimate relationships that people experience as community; yet there is a problem of social scale that raises questions about the quality of this experience. In cyberspace, private communications have a fragmentary quality because they are broadcast on a global scale. Information has no quality control in cyberspace because there are no analogies to the publishing functions that manage the quality of print—the authority of the author and editorial discipline of the publisher, the highly specialized rhetorical structures of print and continuity of a literature. Thus, cyberspace is both an intimate and a mass medium, without the intermediary institutions that might link private expression to public concerns, create intellectual continuity by preserving the collective memory or literature of a group, or create the intellectual quality that public criticism and debate might provide. There are exchanges of information in cyberspace, but not conversations; there are documents, but not a literature; there are social movements and communities, but not institutions. The Internet is cosmopolitan, perhaps, but not yet a polity. A digital library must create this institutional infrastructure if it is to perform the social functions of the print library.

Recently, government information policy has adapted strategies from the print and broadcast sectors to begin to address these problems, extending copyright policy to support a market in networked information and creating new government regulations on the content of networked information similar to those that regulate broadcast media and interstate commerce. These are minimalist policies, designed only to define a space for information markets; in themselves they do not address the creation of public institutions, but they do begin to define the public interest in cyberspace as a social environment.

One strategy, developed by the Commerce Department, concerns new copyright policies that protect and regulate intellectual property in cyberspace in order to encourage market incentives for publishers to develop high-quality, on-line information.[23] The proposed amendment to the copyright law would extend the definition of copyright to include the "transmission" of intellectual property on the Internet. This extension of the definition of copying is an elegant and efficient way to adapt current copyright law to include networked information; however, it is not literally true that networked information is transmitted in the broadcasting sense—it is made public by giving others permission to make copies of it. New technologies have been developed to protect copyright in a digital medium in which the making of copies is essential to the structure of every computer chip: encryption technologies encode transmissions to protect them against unauthorized reading; digital watermarking technologies make it possible to trace the origin and use of digital information. The proposed amendments to the copyright law would also proscribe the development and distribution of technologies that would defeat these defenses.

A second mode of control has been legislation to regulate the content of information on the Internet, the "Communications Decency Act." The global scale of the Internet provides access to information that local communities may well find objectionable, since the 'Net currently enables anyone to publish every conceivable kind of information. Congress acted to establish regulatory control of publication on the Internet. It defined the "transmission" of a pornographic signal across state lines as interstate commerce and hence a criminal act.[24] This provision was ruled unconstitutional by a federal court for two reasons that go to the heart of the debate about the social nature of cyberspace. The court argued that the network is a medium for free speech; thus a network publication is protected speech. In considering the special situation at issue, that children might see pornographic images on the 'Net, the court rejected the argument that networked signals are transmitted like broadcast signals, recognizing that the computer reader must choose to see a given image; technology itself provides parents with the tools to regulate what their children see on the 'Net. While the Communications Decency Act makes it criminal to access networked information that is not illegal if read in a library book, it has been argued that a public library is precisely the kind of intermediary institution that can represent local community standards bypassed by the 'Net.

A third strategy relates to issues of security. Because of its global scope the Internet may raise issues of national security. It is axiomatic that there is neither privacy nor security in cyberspace; since by definition the Internet interconnects every computer, every signal can be monitored. There is always an *audience* in cyberspace, real or potential. Not only are digital documents designed to be collaborative, but nearly every tool that enables the reader to access and navigate the Web could also be used as surveillance technology. If there is no right to privacy in cyberspace, the use of encryption technologies to create privacy raises possible issues of national security. Thus, the government has proposed that an encryption chip, the Clipper chip, be installed in every computer, allowing national security agencies to monitor all networked communication.

Government policy, then, has resisted the definition of cyberspace as a communication medium equivalent to speech or print and therefore protected by the First Amendment. Rather, it has focused on the information-highway metaphor, the development of a market in cyberspace, and regulating communications that are pornographic or that raise security issues, that is, protecting the right of the local and national polities to regulate content. Between the extremes of economic and political interests, it is possible to design public institutions within the network, such as a digital library. For example, public libraries have begun to create network services that serve as points of access to social services for immigrant communities whose members will not go to city hall because they fear the police power of the state. On a larger scale, the *National Information Infrastructure: Agenda for Action* of 1993 defines four public interest goals for the National Information Infrastructure that resemble the historic functions of the public library: support of research, lifelong learning, civic participation and access to government information, and education and training of the work force.[25] The first and most dramatic step in the evolution of the digital library will be the conversion of the Government Printing Office from print to digital publications, which will potentially make every public government document available to every networked computer. The other goals of the National Information Infrastructure, which the public library has served in the past, may well be located within the domain of the information marketplace and not in a public digital library.

WHAT IS THE INFORMATION HIGHWAY?

The public library is a place where strangers can read next to one another; it is one of the few public places where social peace may transcend race, age, ethnicity, and social class. Public access to knowledge is of fundamental importance in a society where access to learning is subsidized in order to support a theory of social justice, which emphasizes equality of opportunity in the economy and democratic participation in the polity. The subsidy for learning includes direct taxation to support public institutions such as libraries, museums, and schools. But it also includes indirect subsidies in the form of fair use and the first-sale doctrine, which are exemptions to copyright law and therefore exceptions to the market mechanism that is the primary means for the distribution of intellectual property. The idea of an information highway emphasizes the commercial potential of the 'Net as a new medium for the distribution of intellectual property and thus is at odds with the idea of a digital library—a public institution that might provide the subsidies for learning that have characterized the public library.

Libraries have exemplified the public realm by fulfilling the constitutional interest in the promotion of learning and invention. Today, a debate about the future shape of the public interest in learning is tacit within the concept of a digital library, not only in legislative deliberations about the form that intellectual property should take in the information age, but in the *absence* of legislative interest in a national digital library. The dominance of the "information highway" metaphor is a signal that network policy is focused upon defining the network as a means for the *transmission* of private property; federal policy envisions the new information economy to be like a broadcast medium, a public space regulated by the government but whose content is created and sold on a global scale by corporations. Yet in previous telecommunications policies, part of the broadcast bandwidth has been reserved for public interest programming. What is the public-interest component of the national information policy?

Thus far, information policy in both the United States and Europe has defined the establishment of an information marketplace in cyberspace as a sufficient public good in itself; in the words of a European Community planning document, "The market will drive...the prime task of government is to safeguard competitive forces...."[26] If the 'Net is defined as a broadcast medium, the digital library consists of *universal access* to a commercial digital marketplace in which the needs of citizens are fulfilled through their role as consumers. The public interest in learning will be served through subsidized network connections to public institutions like schools, museums, and public libraries. A library, however, consists of collections. Is there a public interest in providing subsidized access to a national digital library collection, or to a medium that enables participation in the creation of knowledge as well as the consumption of commercial information commodities? National information policy discussions contain revolutionary possibilities, including the idea that market mechanisms can replace the public sector; for example, the discussion of fair use in cyberspace certainly includes consideration of the possibility that fair use should not exist for print.

An Industrial Policy for Cyberspace?

For over a century the three building blocks of our national information policy have encompassed 1) copyright and patent, encouraging investment in innovation and the dissemination of knowledge; 2) land-grant colleges, educating a skilled citizenry and producing socially useful research and innovation; and 3) public libraries, providing subsidized access to the resources for learning. Following from the Federalist version of Enlightenment philosophy, social policy assumed that knowledge was a public good because it led to invention and thereby social progress, but the *expression of knowledge* was a private good, protected by copyright and patent.

In an information society built upon digital technologies this pragmatic distinction between public good and private property has become ambiguous. Describing the role of knowledge in an information economy, Walter Wriston argues, "Intellectual capital is becoming relatively more important than physical capital. Indeed, the new source of wealth is not material, it is information, knowledge applied to work to create value. The pursuit of wealth is now largely the pursuit of information, and the application of information to the means of production."[27] If information has become the new kind of capital, the significance of intellectual property is fundamentally changed, and global economic forces will require every government to change its modes and purposes of regulation. And, if information is capital, the nature of work will be transformed and, by extension, so too will the way workers are educated. Like all digital documents, some part of the value of information will be created by the reader, as knowledge is applied to work to create value.

While Adam Smith described the source of national wealth as the technical division of labor in manufacturing, which requires workers to act as if they were extensions of the machine, workers in the digital workplace will be *readers*. Thus Shoshana Zuboff describes the new origin of wealth as the ability of workers to use information in a skilled way. She defines digital technologies as "an informating technology," that is, technologies that continuously create new knowledge that workers must read and understand in order to be able to manage the production process. In the digital age, labor implies reading and writing digital documents, not obedience to the authority of the industrial process.[28] The worker of the future merges mental and manual labor; here again there is a public interest in education, but in a new way that may well require a fundamental rethinking of the nature of both literacy and the digital library's social role in promoting literacy.

This vision of a knowledge economy is the end of industrial production in any sense that Adam Smith might have been able to imagine, and yet government information policies still emphasize industrial metaphors like "information highway" and "copyright"— metaphors explicitly built upon an industrial process of reproduction that no longer exists in cyberspace. The power of these metaphors is undoubtedly derived from the financial power of the interest groups that will benefit from their application. However, the immateriality and malleability of digital documents deprives copyright law of its primary mode of rights control and management and does not recognize the value that the reader brings to information management. Prior to the invention of computer networks, it was relatively easy to control the reproduction and distribution of print because the production process clearly differentiated the creation of knowledge from the process of copying and distribution, but that distinction is now becoming anachronistic.[29] Because intellectual property was always contained within a commodity form, it could be regulated by controlling the technology of reproduction—through copyright. But the computer is simultaneously a technology for the creation, reproduction, and distribution of texts; copying is intrinsic to the operation of computers and cannot be regulated. For this reason, commercial publishers and government policy initially focused on creating the technological equivalent of an information artifact that can be regulated like a commodity, preferring the physical package of the CD-ROM to the electronic signal of networked information and developing encryption containers for copyrighted information. Digital watermarking technologies that make surveillance of the misuse of information possible are the first sign of a new approach, one that recognizes that knowledge is now more like a performing art than a commodity and that intellectual property will focus more on the utility of information than the possession of it.

Gift and Market Exchange

In the American regime the relationship between polity and knowledge is founded upon Article I, Section 6 of the Constitution, which empowers Congress to pass laws to promote progress by developing science and the useful arts. Thus, the Constitution treats knowledge as a market commodity for *utilitarian* reasons and grants copyright in order to create material incentives to create and distribute knowledge. This is the rationale for copyright, but also for the two exceptions to copyright that have subsidized free public libraries. The first-sale doctrine allows libraries a limited right to loan books, which otherwise would only be accessible in the marketplace; while books are private property, in a library they are treated as if they are part of a gift economy. Fair use allows readers a limited right to copy private property in printed knowledge for personal and noncommercial educational purposes. Through these mechanisms, libraries have sustained the constitutional interest in invention by serving the needs not only of authors but also inventors (the copy machine was invented in the New York Public Library) and small businesses. The First Amendment tacitly contains a second justification for the public appropriation of private knowledge in libraries: public education and public access to information are a precondition of public discourse about political life.

Today's intellectual property debates challenge these two exceptions to copyright. At the philosophical level, copyright is now defended as *a natural right,* not a pragmatic policy. This return to a natural right, which the founders of a new undeveloped nation had originally rejected, is a recognition that the utilitarian argument may no longer hold. First, the utilitarian argument might well be used by today's undeveloped nations, who are now markets for intellectual property held by the United States. But secondly, when information was scarce, libraries had the function of preserving and centralizing collections of information that otherwise were dispersed and ephemeral. Today, the distribution of printed knowledge is nearly universal, and the network provides an effective means of giving access to knowledge. Electronic publishing, it might be argued, may well be the digital library that best serves the constitutional purpose.

From a sociological point of view, the relationship between knowledge and the economy is more complex than the copyright discussion allows; as important as they are, it is not market incentives alone that make a society creative. Nearly all knowledge is created and consumed within gift exchange systems, not markets—that is, by groups whose very social glue consists of sharing knowledge. If the expression of ideas is alienable, ideas themselves are inalienable. The inalienable substance of any group, whether community or corporation, consists of shared modes of learning, creating and sharing knowledge, and a sense of continuity that is derived from preserving knowledge of the past. In a digital world, an information policy must not only serve the publisher, it must nurture the author.

This is not to say that gift cultures and markets are opposites. The stark contrast between the market and gift relationships in libraries, the free use of information that is subsidized by the community, distorts the interdependence of these two forms of exchange.[30] Without economic incentives, the quality of social knowledge would be very low. During the French Revolution, copyright was abolished in the name of equality, resulting in the destruction of public access to printed works.[31] A balanced social policy must manage the relationship between gift cultures and the market, the liminal sphere occupied most notably by the library but also by every educational institution. And, in fact, the Internet may well fail as a public institution because it is entirely a gift culture and therefore suffers from poor-quality information. A creative information policy must define how the 'Net can combine both gift and market exchange. Even beyond an economic rationale, gift exchange in the library also serves the political interest of creating a social bond, called the public realm, which crosses the fault lines of the economy, especially the inequalities of class, race, and education. How will the commercial digital library serve the young, the poor, the immigrants?

Who Governs Cyberspace?

If the scope of political coordination is limited by the technology of communication, then it might be said that print made the creation of the nation-state possible and that the network—"the end of geography"—suggests the possibility of global political and economic institutions. Perhaps the network itself is the first example of a new kind of institution: decentralized yet personal, and structured more like a market than a political institution. Regulation takes the form of technical standards rather than the direct forms of control that have characterized print and telecommunications.

Cyberspace is cosmopolitan in scale and in some respects may well transcend the direct regulative powers of any particular state. If so, the most urgent agenda of an information policy may be the creation of a public culture for cyberspace, one that fulfills the criterion for public art, reassociating cyberspace with "common rituals and public concerns." Such a culture would have to be cosmopolitan, not only because the Web is cosmopolitan, but in recognition that so too is our nation's population and culture. Cyberspace is not only a medium for the organization of international political movements like Greenpeace; it is also a medium within which the diaspora of exiles and ethnic groups can find a community.

Walter Wriston concluded his argument in *The Twilight of Sovereignty* by saying, "the old political boundaries of nation-states are being made obsolete by an alliance of commerce and technology."[32] He pointed out that no nation-state can control the value of its currency in modern, global information markets. Thus, in a real sense global information systems are the new currency because they have the power to set the value of each national currency in the world market. Similarly, the emergence of the global economy has made the nation-state less and less able to control domestic economies. This argument suggests that there may be a fundamental difference between intellectual property rights in an industrial age in which nation-states were dominant and in the approaching digital age. In industrial nation-states, intellectual property was defined, regulated, and enforced by national legislation and litigation. In the digital age, if intellectual property is the primary content of world trade, intellectual property markets will be regulated by international trade agreements and treaties, not the normal political processes and values that now shape national policy. Thus, while each nation strives to define a national information policy, the true future of intellectual property will be defined by the Global Information Infrastructure (GII), which will be crafted by treaties among nations. The treaty process, unfortunately, is the least democratic form of government.

Government information policy has the goal of creating robust information markets, and yet these markets are certain to be global, not national. Third World nations already perceive that the nations that dominate world industrial markets intend, with these policies, to establish the same patterns of dependence in an information economy as existed in industrial economies.[33] Information policy for domestic markets must recognize that the digital library is a realm of free speech and association as well as an information marketplace. By extension, a global information policy might recognize that information is a powerful instrument for economic and social development in the Third World. A true information policy would include a global digital library that encompasses the programs of the World Bank and the Agency for International Development, understanding that information is not only the new form of capital investment but an essential component of human rights.

ENDNOTES

[1] Lucien Febvre and Henri-Jean Martin, *The Coming of the Book: The Impact of Printing 1450–1800*, trans. David Gerard (London: Verso Editions, 1984), 13.

[2] Elizabeth Eisenstein, *The Printing Press as an Agent of Change: Communications and Cultural Transformations in Early-Modern Europe* (Cambridge: Cambridge University Press, 1979). Although there are differences between oral and written cultures, both involve literacies that have overlapping characteristics. In his description of the different understandings of the Treaty of Waitangi to the print literate English and the orally literate Maori, D. F. McKenzie illustrated the distinctive intellectual problem of understanding the complex possibilities for cultural domination at the boundary between literacies. D. F. McKenzie, *Oral Culture, Literacy and Print in Early New Zealand: The Treaty of Waitangi*, Victoria University of Wellington (New Zealand: Victoria University Press, 1985).

[3] See *The Ethnography of Reading*, ed. Jonathan Boyarin (Berkeley, Calif.: The University of California Press, 1993).

[4] Stanley Fish, *Self-Consuming Artifacts* (Berkeley, Calif.: University of California Press, 1972), 401.

[5] Sherry Turkle, *The Second Self* (New York: Simon and Schuster, 1984).

[6] See Mihaly Csikszentmihalyi, "Why We Need Things," in *History From Things: Essays on Material Culture*, ed. Steven Lubar and W. David Kingery (Washington, D.C.: Smithsonian Institution Press, 1993), 23. "Artifacts help objectify the self. . .by demonstrating the owner's power, vital erotic energy and place in the social hierarchy. . .revealing the continuity of the self through time, by providing foci of involvement in the present, moments and souvenirs of the past, and signposts to future goals. . .and [giving] concrete evidence of one's place in a social network as symbols [literally, the joining together] of valued relationships. In these three ways things stabilize our sense of who we are, they give permanent shape to our views of ourselves that otherwise would quickly dissolve in the flux of consciousness."

[7] Frank Popper, *Art of the Electronic Age* (New York: Harry Abrams, 1993), 58.

[8] Seymour Papert, *Mindstorms: Children, Computers and Powerful Ideas* (New York: Basic Books, 1980), 23.

[9] Lee Sproull and Sara Kiesler, "Reducing Social Context Cues: The Case of Electronic Mail," *Management Science* 32 (1986): 1492–1512.

[10] D. E. Egan, J. R. Remde, T. K. Landauer, C. C. Lockbaum, and others, "Behavioral Evaluation and Analysis of a Hypertext Browser," Conference on Human Factors in Computing Systems (CHI 89), Austin, Tex., 30 April –4 May 1989. *SIGCHI Bulletin* (May 1989, special issue): 205–210.

[11] Richard A. Lanham, *The Electronic Word: Democracy, Technology and the Arts* (Chicago, Ill.: The University of Chicago Press, 1993).

[12] Carla Hesse, "The Book in Time," forthcoming in Geoffrey Nunberg, ed., *The Future of the Book* (Berkeley, Calif.: The University of California Press, 1996).

[13]Barbara Maria Stafford, *Artful Science: Enlightenment Entertainment and the Eclipse of Visual Education* (Cambridge, Mass.: MIT Press, 1984).

[14]Ibid., 311.

[15]*A Vision of an Intelligent Island: The IT 2000 Report*, National Computer Board, Singapore, March 1992. "Singapore, the Intelligent Island, will be among the first countries in the world with an advanced nation-wide information infrastructure. ... Too small to rely only on its own resources, Singapore has always plugged into the global networks. More Singapore companies are spreading their wings overseas. Complementary use of resources across borders is becoming the basis for global competitive advantage. Networking with other countries will generate mutual benefits and greater prosperity for all, as is being shown through the Growth Triangle. The NII has an important role in this strategic economic thrust. It will help turn Singapore into a highly efficient switching centre for goods, services, capital, information and people." Ibid., 20.

[16]Geoffrey Nunberg, "The Places of Books in the Age of Electronic Reproduction," *Representations* (42) (Spring 1993): 21.

[17]Norbert Wiener, *The Human Use of Human Beings: Cybernetics and Society* (New York: Avon Books, 1967), 23–24.

[18]D. F. McKenzie, *Bibliography and the Sociology of Texts: The Panizzi Lectures 1985* (London: The British Library, 1986). "I define 'texts' to include verbal, visual, oral and numeric data. ... We can find in the origins of the word 'text' itself some support for extending its meaning from manuscripts and print to other forms. It derives, of course, from the Latin texere, 'to weave,' and therefore refers not to any specific material as such, but to its woven state, the web or texture of the materials. Indeed, it was not restricted to the weaving of textiles, but might be applied equally well to the interlacing or entwining of any kind of material." Ibid., 5.

[19]The National Research Council, *National Collaboratories: Applying Information Technology for Scientific Research* (Washington, D.C.: National Academy Press, 1993), defines a collaboratory as "a center without walls, in which the nation's researchers can perform their research without regard to geographical location—interacting with colleagues, accessing instrumentation, sharing data and computational resources and accessing information in digital libraries." Ibid., 7. Cited in Thomas A. Finholt and Gary M. Olson, "From Laboratories to Collaboratories: A New Organizational Form for Scientific Collaboration," published on the World Wide Web at <http://www.sils.umich.edu/UARC/Labtocollab.html.>

[20]J. Dibble, "A Rape in Cyberspace," *The Village Voice*, 21 December 1993, 36–43. Xerox PARC's famous Lamda Moo may be explored directly by Telnet to the Lamda MOO site at <telnet://Lambda.parc.xerox.com:8888.> See also Jim Falk, "The Meaning of the Web," a paper exploring the meanings of community on the Web, published on the web at <http: www. scu.edu.au/ausweb95/Papers/Sociology/Falk.>

[21]The Greenpeace home page is located at <http://www.greenpeace.org.>

[22]Mary P. Ryan, *Women in Public between Banners and Ballots, 1925–1880* (Baltimore, Md.: The Johns Hopkins University Press, 1990), 92.

[23]*Intellectual Property and the National Information Infrastructure: The Report of the Working Group on Intellectual Property Rights* (Washington, D.C.: US Patent and Trademark Office, August 1995).

[24]The Communications Decency Act is Section 507 of the Telecommunications Bill, which amends Section 1462 of Title 18 of the US Code (Chapter 71) to add the phrase "interactive computer service" to the prohibition against interstate or foreign commerce concerning texts, graphics, or sounds that are lewd, lascivious or filthy; any information about how to obtain an abortion or how to obtain and make drugs; or obtaining or making anything that is for indecent and immoral use. On 12 June 1996, a three judge panel of the US District Court for the Eastern District of Pennsylvania found the Communications Decency Act unconstitutional. On 3 July 1996, the US Department of Justice stated that it will appeal to the US Supreme Court.

[25]Information Infrastructure Task Force, *The National Information Infrastructure: Agenda for Action,* 15 September 1993. This document develops the themes of Executive Order 12864 of 15 September 1993, establishing the United States Advisory Council on the National Information Infrastructure within the Commerce Department. "Presidential Documents," *The Federal Register* 58 (179) (17 September 1993): 48773.

[26]"Europe and the Global Information Society: Recommendations to the European Council," Brussels, 26 May 1994. As in the United States, the primary emphasis of the European policy is to encourage competitive forces in telecommunications, where state monopolies have dominated technology development and implementation. The recommendations include the following ten key applications to create an information society: *1)* teleworking; *2)* distance learning; *3)* a network for universities and research centers; *4)* telematic services for SMEs (firms with more than fifty employees); *5)* road traffic management; *6)* air traffic control; *7)* health-care networks; *8)* electronic tendering; *9)* trans-European public administration network; and *10)* city information highways (bringing the information society into the home).

[27]Walter Wriston, *The Twilight of Sovereignty* (New York: Charles Scribner's Sons, 1992), xii.

[28]Shoshana Zuboff, *In the Age of the Smart Machine* (New York: Basic Books, 1988). "An informating technology challenges the organization to recognize the skill demands associated with computer mediation and the redistributi of knowledge that intellective skill development implies. . . . Obedience has been the axial principle of task execution in the traditional environment of imperative control. When tasks require intellective effort, obedience can be dysfunctional and can impede the exploitation of information. Under such conditions, internal commitment and motivation replace obedience as the primary bond between the individual and the task. As the work that people do becomes more abstract, the need for positive motivation and internal commitment becomes all the more crucial." Ibid., 291.

[29]As Geoffrey Nunberg describes the difference: "Unlike mechanical antecedents like the printing press, the typewriter or the telegraph, the computer isn't restricted to a single role in production or diffusion. In fact, the technology tends to erase distinctions between the separate processes of creation, reproduction

and distribution that characterize the classical industrial model of print commodities." Nunberg, "The Places of Books in the Age of Electronic Reproduction," 21.

[30]Arjun Appadurai, "Commodities and the Politics of Value," *The Social Life of Things: Commodities in Cultural Perspective,* ed. Arjun Appadurai (Cambridge: Cambridge University Press, 1986). "Gifts, and the spirit of reciprocity, sociability, and spontaneity in which they are typically exchanged, usually are starkly opposed to the profit-oriented, self-centered, and calculated spirit that fires the circulation of commodities...this is a simplified and overdrawn series of contrasts...it is important to see the calculative dimension in all these forms of exchange, even if they vary in the form and intensity of sociality associated with them." Ibid., 11–13.

[31]Carla Hesse's study shows that the French revolutionary policy to destroy copyright in the name of social equality had the opposite impact: the quality of published works deteriorated. Carla Hesse, *Publishing and Cultural Politics in Revolutionary Paris, 1789–1810* (Berkeley, Calif.: The University of California Press, 1991).

[32]Wriston, *The Twilight of Sovereignty,* 11.

[33]See, for example, Peter Lor, "Information Dependence in Southern Africa: Global and Subregional Perspectives," *African Journal of Libraries, Archives and Information Science* 6 (1) (1996): 1–10.

We have all become modishly aware that the information environment, so to speak, of the late twentieth century individual is in the course of being transformed. News columns with titles that play neatly on the words *revolution, age, galaxy, shock,* appear monthly. But we remain prisoners still of an essentially Victorian idea of the requisite constituents of social change, in the sense that we tend to predicate the transformation upon the technology. We relate and chart development according to a measure of machinery, alongside the evolution of inventions. So numerous are the gadgets of the computer age (there goes an example of what is being criticized!) that the designated historic turning points—the number of "revolutions" per decade—are too numerous to absorb, their effects too shrilly predicted for easy listening. We are paralyzed by the dimensions of the transformation, partly because we have internalized a kind of Whiggian principle, by which machines "produce" social effects of a measurable or, at least, observable variety. The trouble is that technological and social history cannot be related in this way, since the extrapolated trends shoot off the graph every time. Consider the influence of the photocopier, the coaxial cable, television news, teleconferencing, and so on. There are no anchors to cast in each voyage of speculation; every trip rushes straight toward infinity.

We would be greatly helped in the present epoch of speculation if we had available some improved metaphors for social change, something less traumatic and less overworked than "revolution," something more intermingling of cause and effect, something that suggested less emphasis on technology and placed more pressure on social need as the starting point of technology.

Anthony Smith

From "Information Technology and the Myth of Abundance"
Dædalus 111 (4) (Fall 1982)

James H. Billington

Libraries, the Library of Congress, and the Information Age

N ORTHROP FRYE, the late brilliant Canadian critic, once said
that our only real crystal ball is a rearview mirror. If you
take that mirror and look back one century, you would
read in the newspaper of any major city in America that people
were concerned about violence in the cities, about social conflict,
about the growth of narcotics usage (opium was the drug of choice
in those days), about the breakdown of traditional American values, and about the impossibility of assimilating parts of the population into the mainstream of upward mobility promised in the
American dream. In short, you would be reading almost exactly
what you might read in any urban newspaper today.

What you would not read—and still do not read in history
textbooks—is who really made a difference in turning what many
people thought, as the twentieth century approached, would be
the collapse of America into what many have called the American
century. Certainly, the twentieth century has brought extraordinary growth and more progress and prosperity than many people
anticipated.

Among those names that are not in the history books, three are
worth remembering here. Justin Morrill, a quiet, remarkable United
States senator from Vermont, was perhaps more influential than
any president during his career in the late nineteenth century.
Through the Morrill Act, he created a system of land-grant universities centered on the library and the laboratory—on the idea that
knowledge is infinitely expandable. The purpose of university instruction became to expose people to a constantly expanding body

---

James H. Billington is the Librarian of Congress.

of knowledge rather than merely to transmit a fixed canon of ideas from the past.

Next is Andrew Carnegie, the philanthropist who started his career in the communications industry and who always had a fascination with how information and knowledge were conveyed from one place to another. As we all know, he built the great public library system in towns and cities across America. So, we had libraries embedded both in the expanding state university system and in the culture of our cities.

Finally, coming from the Boston Public Library, Herbert Putnam became the Librarian of Congress at the beginning of the twentieth century and was responsible for ensuring that the Library of Congress subsidized the cost of cataloging all the nation's libraries. As most librarians are aware, it costs more to catalog a book than it does to buy one. So, by absorbing cataloging as a central responsibility of the national library, a generous federal subsidy (of which many people are unaware) was built into the system. A connection was forged between the dynamic accumulation of knowledge in the universities and cities and the national government.

THE AMERICAN LIBRARY SYSTEM

The public library system in this country is unique among nations. As the first Librarian of Congress who is a specialist in foreign cultures, I may be more aware of the uniqueness of our system than many who take it for granted or assume that other countries do something similar. Universal accessibility to knowledge at the community level has been built into our system. At the Library of Congress we see a stream of visitors from the former communist countries of Eastern Europe, and they are amazed by the open access to knowledge that is available at the Library.

If you look at our public library system, each of its four distinctive features currently faces a unique threat. First, for democracy to be sustainable on a continental scale in a multicultural society, it must be based on the dynamic use of knowledge. The American library is a place for the common pursuit of truth at various levels in various ways by various people. Implicit in the institution is a shared commitment to the enterprise of turning knowledge into practical use for society. The Constitution itself recognizes the need "to promote science and useful arts," which is a key feature of our democracy.

Second, this knowledge must be *openly accessible* to all people. While not written into the Bill of Rights, it is one entitlement that is not negotiable in the various reexaminations of entitlements in our society. The Founding Fathers were not altogether sure that democracy would work, so they created a representative republic. We became a true democracy only in the course of the nineteenth and early twentieth centuries when we fully enfranchised all of our citizens. But it was always assumed that a free society had to be based on the dynamic use of knowledge that was broadly accessible.

Third, public libraries expressed the *growing pluralism* of American society. I like to call them temples of pluralism, places where a great diversity of people gathered. Individuals with conflicting points of view sat peacefully next to each other in the reading rooms just as books with conflicting points of view stood quietly next to each other on the shelves. If you look at pictures of the reading rooms of the Cleveland, New York, Boston, Baltimore, or any other large urban public library at the turn of the century, they reveal an ethnic festival. The faces and the clothes signal a heterogeneity far greater than that which you would find in other cultural institutions of those days.

Fourth, public libraries were, nevertheless, a *unifying force* in the communities where they existed. There might be six different churches, many competing enterprises, and even some variety in schools, but there was always a unifying library at the heart of any growing American community. The building itself often resembled a church. In fact, it was a kind of shrine, a communal tribute to the culture and values of the book, which have in many ways undergirded our democratic system.

Each of the four ideals that the public library system of this country stood for, still stands for, and must stand for is under serious threat today.

The idea of knowledge-based democracy is threatened, in a peculiar fashion, by the flood of information generated by new technologies, including the advances of the audiovisual, multimedia world. We talk about the information age, not the knowledge age; we talk about information centers rather than knowledge centers. The first outline of a proposal sent to me by a legislator several years ago talked about the need for forming "nodal points of local information dissemination"; I picked up the telephone and told him, "These things already exist—they happen to be called libraries."

I am haunted by the thought that all the miscellaneous, unsorted, unverified, constantly changing information on the Internet may inundate knowledge, may move us back down the evolutionary chain from knowledge to information, from information to raw data. We may be sinking down, rather than rising up to wisdom and creativity, those twin peaks that are the highest attainment of civilization. Instead of a knowledge-based democracy, we may end up with an information-inundated democracy. Information itself is becoming degraded into "infotainment," "infomercials," and various other crudities, raising the problem of whether we can go on creating—let alone making use of—knowledge.

The question of open access is threatened by the fact that this very flood of information has the unintended but inexorable effect of dividing us into information "haves" and "have-nots." This is a real and increasing threat, not because anyone is trying to monopolize access to information, but simply because the costs and constraints faced by public institutions are such that more and more people will have to buy highly-priced equipment and highly-priced private services to access important information.

The communal nature of a library is threatened by the growing notion that you can get everything you want in your own home, that you do not have to go anywhere to get anything. We already have the image of the lonely nerd sitting before the computer screen, slowly mutating from a normal human being into a kind of extension of the screen and the keyboard. With this notion, there is a deformation of the whole idea that there is a gathering place in a community where people of different backgrounds seeking different answers can still come together in a place that acquires meaning for the community as a whole. There is, in short, a threat to the concept of a library as a vital *place.*

Finally, the culture of television poses a long-term threat to the culture of the book. Even among the college-educated, television has already substituted a passive spectator habit for the activity of reading; it has substituted emotion for reason and imagination.

Libraries and librarians, it seems to me, have important things to say about all four of these threats. The flood of unsorted, unverified information will not replace knowledge in the country if librarians can transform themselves from information dispensers into knowledge navigators.

The very flood of unsorted information makes the librarians' role of sorting, dispensing, and serving as objective, informed navigators even more important. The excessive specialization and use of guild jargon in academia—combined with the deluge of unsorted, electronic information—increases the need for a special caste of discriminating knowledge navigators who will add the value of judgment and the warmth of human mediation to all this unintelligible material. Words, sounds, and images are being changed into zeroes and ones in the digitization process. These materials will, in a sense, be dehumanized even more unless they are rehumanized at the end of the terminal by the knowledge navigator.

Libraries must be sustained as places with individual identities in the future. On-the-spot human mediation will be needed that is suited to each particular location, and it will provide a shared and cost-efficient communal setting for meeting its special needs. But almost all libraries will need to link up-to-date, electronically available information with a storehouse of books and memory—and to mix all this in with the live human judgment of a knowledge navigator and the miscellaneous humanity of the community itself. The role of libraries as well as librarians becomes more, not less, important.

Accessibility and openness will be endangered not only by expensive delivery systems but also by encryption and various other instruments of exclusivity. It is extremely important that technology be used to make information accessible rather than to create privileged knowledge resources for paying customers. That is why the Library of Congress believes it is crucial to get out to everyone plain vanilla versions of our key materials that are as near to free as possible. As we see it, this is the extension in the electronic age of the whole philosophy of free access, of opening up public reading rooms.

THE EVOLUTION OF THE LIBRARY OF CONGRESS

Our new endeavors grow out of our own experience, our own peculiar role, and the expectations of Congress, other libraries, and the American people. As libraries move into the information age, it is instructive to consider the remarkably little-known history of the creation and growth of the Library of Congress, America's de facto national library.

The Library of Congress has played a quiet but important role in American history in four distinctive ways: *1)* by symbolizing and institutionalizing the idea that free, representative government must be based on knowledge; *2)* by establishing that knowledge should be inclusive and expansive and based on a universal collection; *3)* by facilitating and championing the broadest and most open access to knowledge; and *4)* by helping to set bibliographic standards and supplying bibliographic data that makes knowledge easier for other libraries and all Americans to use.

The first two features are directly connected to the ideals of Thomas Jefferson and the very creation of the United States. The Library of Congress was not the benefaction of a king or a prince or a dictator, but a totally new creation of the elected representatives of a new republic. Its expansion and growth over almost two hundred years reflects the ideals and ambitions of the entire American nation.

Reading was—along with work and worship—an essential activity for the leaders of the colonial states. It is appropriate that the first gatherings of both the Continental Congress in Philadelphia in 1774 and the Congress of the United States in New York in 1790 took place in libraries. As the fledgling legislature of the new American republic prepared to move to its new capital in the District of Columbia, a *tabula rasa* library was established. On April 24, 1800, President John Adams approved legislation appropriating $5,000 to purchase "such books as may be necessary for the use of Congress."[1] The first books, ordered from London, arrived in 1801 and were stored in the US Capitol, the Library's first home. The collection consisted of 740 volumes, mostly history, economics, and law, and included three maps.

On January 26, 1802, President Thomas Jefferson approved the first law defining the role and functions of the new institution.

This law established the position of the Librarian of Congress and created the first Joint Committee of the Congress so that both Houses of Congress could participate in establishing the Library's budget and its various regulations. From the beginning, however, the new institution was more than just a legislative library; the 1802 law made the Librarian's appointment a presidential responsibility—and permitted the president and vice president to borrow books, a privilege later extended to officials in both the executive branch and the judiciary.

This first Jeffersonian ideal—that legislation be linked to learning and libraries—was soon enriched by a second: that knowledge must be universal and continuously expanding. Jefferson was a pragmatic polymath with a restless intellectual curiosity. He declared that he could not live without books and took a keen interest in the Library of Congress while he was President from 1801 to 1809. He recommended books for the Library and appointed the first two Librarians of Congress.

During the War of 1812, the British occupied Washington and burned the Capitol, including the three-thousand-volume Library of Congress. Retired by then to Monticello, Jefferson offered to sell his personal library, the largest and best in America, to Congress to "recommence" its library. After some debate, Congress approved the purchase—6,487 volumes for $23,940—in 1815.

Jefferson's collection was not only bigger but far more wide-ranging than the collection burned by the British. It expanded the scope of the Library far beyond the bounds of a legislative library devoted primarily to legal, economic, and historical works. Jefferson was a man of encyclopedic interests—architecture, the arts, science, literature, and geography. His library included books in French, Spanish, German, Latin, Greek, and one three-volume statistical work in Russian. Anticipating the argument that his collection might be too comprehensive, he argued successfully that there was "no subject to which a member of Congress may not have occasion to refer."[2]

The Jeffersonian concept of universality became the rationale for the increasingly comprehensive collecting policies of the Library of Congress. Jefferson's belief in the power of knowledge and the direct link between knowledge and democracy shaped the Library's philosophy of sharing its collections and services as widely as possible. The man responsible for transforming the Library of Congress into an institution of national importance in the Jeffersonian spirit was Ainsworth Rand Spofford, a former Cincinnati bookseller and journalist, who served as the Librarian of Congress from 1865 until 1897. He assembled a comprehensive collection of Americana and built the Library's first permanent home, the magnificent Thomas Jefferson Building.

The copyright law of 1870 ensured that the Library of Congress would become the archives of American creativity. The law centralized copyright deposits and registrations in the Library and stipulated that two copies of every book, pamphlet, map, print, photograph, and piece of music registered for copyright be deposited in the Library. The international copyright law of 1891 brought deposits of foreign works into the Library for the first time.

By the time the Library moved from its overcrowded space in the Capitol to its new building in 1897, its collections ranked first among American libraries in both size and scope. More than 40 percent of its 840,000 volumes and at least 90 percent of its maps, music, and graphic arts collections had been acquired through copyright deposit—including Civil War photographs by Mathew Brady and the first motion pictures by Thomas Edison.

The new Library of Congress building both symbolized and facilitated open, democratic access to knowledge. Its Italian Renaissance architecture, distinctive dome, exuberant interior decoration, and grand main reading room created a national monument overnight. Frescoes and mosaics celebrated the unity and utility of all human knowledge, and open public reading rooms assured that the collections would be shared with all Americans because, as Spofford put it, the United States is a "Republic which rests upon the popular intelligence."[3]

If Spofford built the collections and opened them to the public, Herbert Putnam (1899–1939) helped to make knowledge more accessible to the American people outside of Washington by directly helping other libraries. He began substantial free interlibrary loans and the free National Library Service for the Blind and Physically Handicapped. And, most significantly, the Library began to supply both bibliographic standards and original cataloging at federal expense for the nation's libraries. In 1902, Congress authorized the sale and distribution of the Library's printed catalog cards to other libraries, signaling the beginning of the Library's role as a national resource.

Congress consistently gave bipartisan support to the expanding role of its library—and to the authority of the Librarians, who continued to serve through multiple administrations as part of the legislative branch of government. In 1914 Congress established the Library's Legislative Reference Service—the forerunner of the Congressional Research Service—as a nonpartisan "think tank" for Congress, basing it on models established during the Progressive Era in Wisconsin and other states.

Putnam's four successors served an average of twelve years each from 1939 to 1987, a period that saw the addition of two more library buildings on Capitol Hill: the Art-Deco Adams Building (1939) and the James Madison Building (1982), which is the third largest building in the Washington area (after the Pentagon and FBI headquarters). Even more space than this was needed; the Library has begun to build special warehouses at Fort Meade, Maryland, and already has a film preservation laboratory in Ohio and a storage warehouse in Landover, Maryland.

The world's intellectual productivity continues to increase. The Library's holdings of foreign materials now comprise 50 percent of the Library's books, in 450 languages. Since World War II, the Library has established six overseas acquisition offices (Moscow, Djakarta, Rio, Karachi, Cairo, and Nairobi) to acquire materials for itself and for sixty other American libraries in places where normal commercial channels are inadequate.

The Library modernized its service to other libraries by creating the Library of Congress MARC (Machine Readable Cataloging) format, which in 1973 became the international standard for communicating bibliographic data in machine-readable form. Soon after, the Library launched its long and costly quest for a process that would preserve books that were disintegrating because they were printed (as most have been since the mid-nineteenth century) on acidic paper. That quest has finally begun to pay off; approximately thirty-six thousand "brittle books" will go through a new commercial preservation process of deacidification this year.

In 1976, the Library created a small but dynamic Center for the Book, partly funded by private donors, which helps local libraries and hundreds of other groups promote reading and literacy and has helped in the creation of thirty affiliated state centers.

THE LIBRARY TODAY

Today, thanks to Congress, the Library is a sizable enterprise, with a 1996 budget of $352 million and a work force of approximately 4,500. It is doing more work with fewer people, having lost 435 staff positions since 1992.

It is sad to record that as the end of the century approaches, the Library of Congress, like other libraries, is operating in a changing culture, where respect for public property has eroded. After uncovering a rash of thefts and mutilations (three thieves were arrested), the Library closed access to its stacks in 1992 and began a series of costly, complicated security measures that have inconvenienced both patrons and staff. However, these measures have been generally recognized as necessary in order to safeguard the Library's unique collections for future generations.

The Library is also operating in a broader cultural and political environment where many apparently do not regard the continuing acquisition, preservation, and dissemination of the world's knowledge and of the nation's creative record as necessarily worthy of public support. The Library's myriad services tend to be taken for granted. Unlike other federal cultural institutions like the Smithsonian Institution or the National Gallery of Art, the Library has no board of trustees or regents to act as its advocate. The very variety of its users leaves it without a special-interest constituent support group. Moreover, a generation of lawmakers who have tirelessly supported the Library for three decades is retiring—notably Senators Claiborne Pell and Mark Hatfield.

It is not sufficiently appreciated that the Congress of the United States has, in fact, been the Library's largest and most consistent patron. No royal house, no Medici family, no private benefactor has created an institution as universal in its collection policy or as openly accessible and extensive in its service mission as the Library of Congress. By the same token, however, as a part of the legislative branch of government, the Library has necessarily been subjected to the increasing economic pressures to downsize that have been felt in recent years throughout the government, particularly within the legislative branch.

In this difficult fiscal environment, the Library has to face the need simultaneously to streamline management and to make up for long-deferred infrastructure maintenance while at the same time forging a transition to the totally new electronic environment. It is precisely the Library's efforts to exercise leadership in the emerging electronic environment that has attracted crucial congressional support and minimized the cuts inflicted on traditional core services and needs. Bipartisan interest in both Houses of Congress has generally accorded the Library fair treatment in recognition of the Library's broad national role. Digitization of the Library's catalogs, exhibits, and, more recently, its Americana collections has enjoyed particularly strong support from Speaker of the House Newt Gingrich and from Vice President Al Gore, who has spoken repeatedly of getting the Library of Congress into more American homes. President Clinton honored the entire library community recently by holding the signing ceremony for the Telecommunications Act of 1996 in the main reading room of the Library.

Since the Library decided in 1989 to share electronically its collections and services with the wider public, progress has been so rapid that the Library is now a major content provider on the Internet. Overall, the Library now records approximately one million electronic hits every working day. Starting in 1992, the Library has provided free access, via the Internet, to its massive bibliographic records. The Library now serves Congress and the public via its Internet-based systems that include three World Wide Web services (THOMAS, LC-Web, and CRS-Web), gopher services (LC-MARVEL), the Library of Congress Information System (LOCIS), and various file transfer options.

All this has provided a base for the Library's most ambitious effort, the National Digital Library program, aimed at supplying not only bibliographic data but the content of the Library's collections—and those of other great repositories—to schools, libraries, and the public across America. As we see it, electronics now make the Library's resources accessible everywhere—thus continuing the opening-up process that began a century ago with the creation of public reading rooms in the new Jefferson Building.

Like America's schools and other libraries, the Library of Congress faces the great challenge of bringing the new multimedia, audiovisual culture into harmony with the culture of the book. Television has arguably done more to distract the young from learning (and their elders from serious reading, or even thinking) than any other phenomenon of the twentieth century. It is extremely important that the new multimedia technology help the active mind, the active citizen, rather than feed the passive emotions and inactive spectatorism that television generally encourages.

We have faith that not only librarians and teachers but a critical mass of citizens and leaders in the public and private sectors share this concern about the direction of our culture and the possibilities of enrichment and renaissance latent in the new technology. And that is where the Library of Congress is hoping to make a distinctive contribution. We will soon be receiving as copyright deposits vast amounts of material in already digitized form: census data, films, music, scientific papers, legal documents, and much else. For preservation purposes, many periodicals and books will be available in digital as well as in paper formats. We have already begun to digitize our paper and film collections for dissemination to local schools and libraries. This effort, in which the private sector and local institutions play a key role, can reap enormous positive results over the long term.

In delivering library materials by electronic means, our purpose is to reinforce learning in the local communities. Public libraries are the heart of the information delivery system. They have deep ties in the community and special knowledge of the community's particular information needs. They are the keys to whether the idea of open access to knowledge and information will succeed or fail. They will need strong local support, of course, but also new sources of financial or in-kind support from the private sector— and probably some kind of federal matching help for hardware and training.

At the Library of Congress, we see our role as that of a kind of wholesaler to local institutions, retailing knowledge and information in a wide variety of ways. Our material will be integrated with what other institutions already have—and will contribute to the local initiatives they will be developing for students, teachers, the general public, and the private sector in their communities. Our National Digital Library program, begun in late 1994, is designed to provide high-value cargo for whatever form or varieties of forms the information superhighway will take.

This program builds on our American Memory project, which tested the use of our American history materials that were made electronically available at forty-four sites around the country over five years (1990–1994). We found that, contrary to popular belief, audiovisual primary material of American history and culture especially appealed to the young—and within inner cities and rural communities. In other words, it motivated youngsters who were not already plugged into reading and the educational system, which I see as a kind of escalator on which everyone has to rise in order to become a productive participant in our economy. American Memory materials on the computer screen activated their curiosity by stimulating the kinds of open questions that the hitherto inaccessible primary materials of our history inevitably raise. They went to books for most answers. The materials exposed the youngsters simultaneously to new technology and to old materials, to memory, to the values of the past. The American Memory materials—some 210,000 items on CD-ROM that are becoming rapidly available on-line—exposed students of all ages to historical sources rather than political correctness, to the good as well as the bad in our history, and thus to a heightened but mature sense of our complex yet common cultural legacy.

The content and programming of the National Digital Library are being developed in collaboration with both the private sector and other libraries and institutions. Last year, we joined with fourteen other repositories—including the National Archives, the New York Public Library, Harvard University, and Yale University—to collaborate in the digitization of American history materials. In addition to the mix of largely private funds supporting the National Digital Library, the Ameritech Corporation donated $2 million expressly to help other depositories digitize key elements of their Americana for addition to the National Digital Library.

Two-thirds of our collections are in nonbook formats: documents, films, prints and photographs, maps, sound recordings, and rare manuscripts. The new technology allows these often fragile and unique materials to be used without worries about preservation or theft. The Library has most of the papers of twenty-three Presidents of the United States, which include George Washington's surveyor drawings and Theodore Roosevelt's diary. Our two drafts of Lincoln's Gettysburg Address and a draft of Jefferson's Declaration of Independence were recently put on exhibit and are now available on-line. The rough draft of the Declaration contains changes by Ben Franklin, John Adams, and others—enabling young people to see the minds of the Founding Fathers at work. Ordinary citizens can now use a widening variety of such hitherto inaccessible materials. The Library's massive music collection—all the commercial sound recordings of Duke Ellington and Jelly Roll Morton, the entire archives of Irving Berlin, George and Ira Gershwin, and Leonard Bernstein—are in fragile or potentially endangered condition and would, in an earlier age, be available only to a very few scholars who are able to visit Washington.

Now digital versions will make it possible for most citizens anywhere to see the record of the American experience: drawings by Robert Fulton, the Wright brothers, and Alexander Bell. Most core material for the first stage of the National Digital Library program has been drawn from cartoons, photographs, almanacs, posters, sheet music, and unpublished American plays. We have some 250,000 unpublished plays from before World War I, including many ethnic and African-American plays.

The Library has identified two hundred multimedia collections relating to American history as candidates for digitization; six were presented last year on the World Wide Web. These include manuscripts *(Life Histories from the Folklore Project; WPA Federal Writer's Project, 1936–1939; and Notebooks of Walt Whitman)*, motion pictures *(Films of San Francisco Before and After the Earthquake and Fire, 1897–1907; Films of President William McKinley and the Pan-American Exposition, 1901; and Paper Print Films of New York City, 1897–1906)*, and photographs *(Photographs by William H. Jackson and the Detroit Publishing Co., ca. 1880–1920)*.

We live in an immensely creative country, but only a small portion of our creativity has ever been looked at, let alone studied. Almost all of our creativity is recorded on material that is rapidly deteriorating. Therefore, the digital revolution, among other things, has the capacity of preserving for future generations things that might otherwise disappear.

The National Digital Library program is a new expression of the old American library ideal of providing the widest possible access to knowledge and information. This program is fortunate in having the support of both the Vice President and the administration's National Information Infrastructure effort and Speaker Gingrich's and the Congress' interest in disseminating the materials of its library more broadly to the nation. The Library was given a specific grant in 1995 from the appropriations committees of Congress in support of this program, though most of the funds for the $60 million project will come from private-sector philanthropy. A variety of institutions will have to join with us in preparing and providing the materials. We hope that the final product will be comprehensive and inclusive enough to tell the story of America— both extremely diverse and yet having a common set of memories for most of us. The private sector will add value to much of this unembellished, archival material and distribute it in a variety of packages and delivery systems. Finally, as librarians and teachers both develop the skills and acquire the technology, the nation's fifteen thousand school districts and sixteen thousand public libraries will provide local access to the public—and may also repackage and use this material in a variety of ways that they themselves will determine.

By the year 2000, the end of the five-year launch period and the two hundredth anniversary of the Library of Congress, we hope to have up to five million American history items from the collections of the Library of Congress and other institutions accessible either on-line or on CD-ROM at schools and libraries across the country. The body of material will provide educational content for the Internet and, we hope, a learning model for digitizing and delivering other serious subject matter to advance American education and productivity. We will together be advancing the core library commitment to accessibility in the new electronic environment.

While we are working to supply the content, public libraries will be working to enhance their electronic delivery systems. Already, libraries in various state systems—Maryland, Utah, and Ohio, to mention a few—are being interconnected. According to the National Commission on Libraries and Information Science, some 45 percent of the nation's sixteen thousand public libraries are connected to the Internet, up from 21 percent two years ago. Service to users varies greatly, with large urban libraries leading the way in assisting patrons in accessing on-line materials; most small rural libraries are still unconnected. Roughly 35 percent of the nation's school libraries are linked to the Internet, but the students' use of the on-line materials varies greatly.

Problems remain with the cost of digitization, copyright issues, standards, and obsolescence, and they must be addressed not only by the library community but also by state and federal governments and by the private sector. For our part, we continue in Washington to emphasize the need to provide content for and links with libraries and schools across the country. Otherwise, the entire electronic enterprise will fall far short of its potential for educational renewal.

Our basic belief is that, like public libraries, the new electronic superhighways are a public good, merit public support, and must do more than offer entertainment and high-priced information on demand to the well-to-do at home or in the office. Few Americans now lack entertainment on television, but many lack inexpensive access to the knowledge that is necessary to learn, work, and prosper; and this, of course, is where local libraries come in. Suitably staffed and equipped, these local institutions will provide access for most Americans, rich or poor, to on-line services either free or at reduced fees negotiated by libraries, collectively with the providers.

Traditions of high-quality service, profound democratic instincts, and a firm belief in the importance of knowledge are deeply embedded in the library profession. It is essential that academic, philanthropic, business, and political leaders at all levels understand and endorse the idea that libraries must be sustained if we are going to maintain the link between democracy and access to information that has been so important to our society.

I believe that the new technology, properly employed, can spur learning and provide vital enrichment to previously isolated communities, libraries, and schools. This information superhighway can give us, through libraries, a new access to knowledge that will feed the intellectual curiosity, entrepreneurial energy, and civic spirit of Americans of all backgrounds in the twenty-first century.

The library profession has a historic opportunity not just to utilize but to humanize and to democratize this remarkable new technology.

It is of central importance that the new digitized knowledge be mixed in with the old books. The book, that most user-friendly communications medium, has a long life ahead of it. I do not believe that our great-grandchildren will be reading the plays of Shakespeare or *Moby Dick* on computer screens. We will keep supporting local literacy and reading promotion efforts through our own Center for the Book and will keep alive a memory bank in this present-minded city, a place for the pursuit of truth in a center of power.

Beyond all the data, information, and even the knowledge that we can accumulate and disseminate electronically lies the real payoff: those true peaks of *human* accomplishment on which the future of our civilization depends, namely, wisdom and creativity. Wisdom is the practical quality that grows up among people who live with and among books. Creativity is the capacity for unpredictable leaps that make innovation and renewal possible in this civilization. Both qualities are essential to the kind of open and self-correcting democracy that we cherish. Free democratic societies were born out of the book culture and may not survive without it. That is why we believe it is essential to integrate the new world of electronic knowledge and communication harmoniously into the traditional book culture of which librarians are the most dedicated and dependable custodians.

At the heart of the National Digital Library effort is something important to all libraries: the belief that old institutions, in order to survive, must embrace new technologies while maintaining old values. The secret of America has always been the ability to add without subtracting. New immigrants, new ideas, new books are added to the old ones, and we have been repeatedly enriched by the mix—rather than impoverished by discarding the old. In attempting radical innovation within an institution inherently resistant to change, the Library of Congress in recent years has been confronted with a kind of two-front war: a guerrilla war against introducing the new, and a thermonuclear threat from without to obliterate the old.

The guerrilla warfare against innovation results largely from the persistent tendency to think of electronics as a fad or an optional add-on to library equipment (like a new form of typewriter) rather than as an entirely new mode of generating and transmitting knowledge (like the invention of the printing press). The idea of sharing Library of Congress collections electronically with the broader library world emerged from ten forums that were held all around the nation during the early days of my tenure as the Librarian of Congress. It has required raising a large amount of private money—almost all of it from sources not hitherto seriously involved in supporting libraries. At times this has encouraged sniping, if not guerrilla warfare, against the project by those who resent either the phenomenon of a national institution seeking new private money, on the one hand, or any single institution assuming a leadership role that might ideally be played by some altogether new or collegial body on the other. (It seems to be part of the dyspepsia of our times that a project funded entirely by one institution and designed entirely to benefit other institutions is occasionally misrepresented as some kind of empire building.)

Within an institution that has the biases of a highly unionized federal bureaucracy with virtual lifetime tenure and very low turnover, there has been at times great resistance to innovation and in particular to networking new outside services. But the understandable concerns that accompany change have not generated anything like the challenge posed by the sudden intrusion of outside management consultants, who proposed that the Library discard its traditional artifactual collections altogether and enter into a total embrace of the new networked environment.

In the course of clearing massive deferred maintenance in our infrastructure and conducting many audits, we were recently confronted with a remarkable management study by Booz-Allen & Hamilton, Inc. It suggested that the Library consider a fundamentally new mission that would involve dispersing its massive collections and becoming, in effect, merely a giant switchboard to direct Congress and other users to sources of knowledge elsewhere. At a hearing of the Joint Committee on the Library on May 7, 1996, we received a ringing endorsement of the Library's historic mission of sustaining a universal collection. By sheer chance, that same evening, the entire congressional leadership appeared at a function in the Library and also endorsed the Library's historic mission of sustaining the vastness of its collections for the future health of America. They praised our effort to integrate electronic into traditional information and to share it more broadly with more of the American people. As Speaker Gingrich put it:

> I want to take this evening as a moment to state emphatically my disagreement with the effort of the management analysts who looked at the Library. They assumed that in a time of limited budgets as we entered the information age that this Congress should diminish and shrink and divide the greatest knowledge asset this country has. I believe just the opposite. . . . I believe that we should encourage the Library to boldly reach out, to seek, to expand, and grow as a repository of knowledge, and to seek, to spread even more widely.[4]

There will undoubtedly be many battles still ahead in ensuring that the Library of Congress can sustain its ambitious service mission to the nation—particularly now that it includes for the first time an educational as well as a government and scholarly service component.

The future will call for much more efficient and networked activity than ever before. The overall library system will continue to need the specialized materials and talents that only the Library of Congress will be able to provide. It is not at all certain that the scholarly and library communities are united and determined enough—or that future political leaders at all levels will be committed enough—to create and sustain a library system that will be far more networked than in the past, yet no less dependent on the strength and integrity of its individual institutions.

It seems certain to me, however, that without both embracing the new and sustaining the old, the Library of Congress will lose its historic mission and its future ability to serve the nation in ways we cannot even imagine today. The decline and fall of classical civilization resulted not just from barbarians at the gates but also from barbarism within. Contrary to common belief, the great library of Alexandria was not definitively destroyed by the famous fire at the time of Julius Caesar; rather, it vanished imperceptibly with the slow extinction of a sophisticated and cosmopolitan civilization that took its central institution for granted and did not fight hard enough to sustain it. With 110 million items in all languages and formats, the Library of Congress is a modern Alexandria that serves the entire library system. If we do not stoke the fires within the core institutions that keep wisdom and creativity alive in our society, our civilization will burn out from within even if it is not overtaken and destroyed from without.

ENDNOTES

[1] 2 Stat. 55 (24 April 1800). Cited in John Y. Cole, *Jefferson's Legacy: A Brief History of the Library of Congress* (Washington, D.C.: Government Printing Office, 1993), 12.

[2] Thomas Jefferson to Samuel H. Smith, 21 September 1814, Jefferson Papers, Library of Congress.

[3] Ainsworth Rand Spofford, "The Government Library at Washington," *International Review* 5 (November 1878): 769.

[4] Speaker Newt Gingrich, quoted in the *Library of Congress Information Bulletin* 55 (9) (13 May 1996): 176.

Ann Shumelda Okerson

Buy or Lease? Two Models for Scholarly Information at the End (or the Beginning) of an Era

Some say the world will end in fire,
Some say in ice.
From what I've tasted of desire
I hold with those who favor fire.
But if it had to perish twice,
I think I know enough of hate
To say that for destruction ice
Is also great
And would suffice.

> —*Robert Frost*
> *"Fire and Ice"*

W ITHIN LIVING MEMORY, our use of print (static) information has been governed by copyright law and the practices that have evolved around it. Enter electronic information, where publishers deliver it with licenses and new rules, a very different framework from copyright. In fact, the recent report of the US National Information Infrastructure Working Group on Copyright imagines a world that is increasingly governed by licenses (or contracts) rather than copyright. In order to understand these two different modes within the context of today's research and academic libraries, given the rapidly growing world of electronic information, I will discuss the concept of copyright—

Ann Shumelda Okerson is Associate University Librarian at Yale University.

what it is, how it works, and what it achieves—as well as contractual licensing and how it currently works. Since the publishing universe now contains both modes, with licensing rapidly on the rise, we need to imagine how the two kinds of regimes will interrelate and what the future may hold for academic research libraries whose mission for centuries has been to provide scholarly information for their patrons.

Poets and prognosticators from the earliest mythical times to Robert Frost have shown us a world imperiled from opposite extremes at once. At a time when settled ways of publishing and distributing the fruits of research are shaken up by new electronic technologies, it may seem that the prevalent economic models offered by copyright law and licensing agreements suggest threats as extreme as Frost's. This essay will look at both contexts—fire and ice—to see what unexpected middle ways might lie before us, suggesting that in fact there will be a middle ground if the copyright and information licensing worlds converge over time.

SYMBOLIC MONEY AND DE-MASSIFIED INFORMATION

In discussions during a recent meeting about the future of scholarly communication, a wise publisher of our time thought to express his uncertainty about the future of electronic information by wondering rhetorically whether people would be comfortable paying "real money" for networked electronic information, which by its nature does not supply them with the physical sense of possession that the printed book or even the CD-ROM can provide.[1] Under what future conditions, in other words, will the movement of information happen optimally, so that both prospective seekers of information and prospective distributors are content with the exchange and with the relationships that emerge?

If indeed we are to live in a postindustrial, information-based economy, few questions are of such practical, social, cultural, and economic moment. So it is a curiosity of fate that this particular question is one raised with surprising clarity and force in libraries—places not usually thought to be much roiled by forces of social change and certainly not often perceived as the setting for front-line confrontations or innovations. Few regard the collections development departments (not infrequently, cramped spaces hidden away off back corridors) of major research libraries as the center of paradigm shifts. But where the information is of high sophistication and urgently broad social value (affecting research and education across the full range of active disciplines), that is just where substantial economic decisions are made daily, through market encounters between those who have information to sell and those who would buy it; it is there that change is felt, seismically, disturbingly, long before the rest of society is aware of the issues.

Let us return for a moment to the publisher mentioned at the outset and his juxtaposition of "real money" and electronic networked information. The notion of the "reality" of money is worth lingering over. In earlier times, the reality of money was not an issue. A donkey might be swapped for two goats; a crop of corn might be swapped for a cow; or, one remove from direct barter, a laborer who tilled the corn (or built a barn) might be paid from the corn crop. But donkeys and corn were heavy and awkward to carry and soon became inadequate for the diverse and multiple transactions in which people wished to engage. So the reality of money next inhered in the value of the material from which currency was minted. That value was itself a bit precious, possibly in more ways than one, but it was firmly grounded in a market reality: more people wanted gold than there was gold to go around.

Most recently, and for a long time now, money has itself been virtual. Written bonds promising to pay "real money" are as ancient as literacy itself. Indeed, the remarkable thing is that precious metallic currency retained its real value as long as it did. But then there came a time when paper money began to stand as a surrogate for gold and silver hidden away in national vaults, followed by a time when direct relationships to that gold and silver eroded. The "realest" money today is itself a symbol of an abstractly constructed value, valuable itself because all have agreed to agree that it is valuable.

These days, only a tiny fraction (apparently well under 10 percent) of the money in daily use in the United States is the kind that folds or clinks.[2] Few consumers give much thought to what happens when they hand over a credit card to settle their restaurant check. At this moment, several closely related electronic transactions begin, completed perhaps a month later when the consumer sits down miles away to write a check and drops it in the mail, covering possibly dozens of diverse purchases and transactions. That check itself is turned from "real" paper (a surrogate for the donkey, the gold, and the paper cash) into electronic information as rapidly as possible. If the check is returned to the consumer with the monthly bank statement—and this is less and less the norm—it is only because customers are still irrationally attached to that previous transaction mode: the check, a physical artifact, itself a triumph of virtuality. Banks would probably prefer to throw away the canceled check the moment the electronic juice— the *real* money—has been sucked out of it.

Two important points should be taken away from this consideration. First, that the unreal, the virtual, the abstract—the purely mental—construct of a human culture becomes reality enough for its users in time, reality enough that they will cling to it and prefer it to other, seemingly less substantial constructions of later date or less broad acceptance. Second, if we return to the moment when we consider the curious seeker of information and the libraries with which we here began, we realize that what is at stake is not *precisely* an exchange of money for information, or reality for insubstantiality, but in fact a more complex interplay of information systems communicating with each other. If the formula for a complex polymer or a collection of Cyrillic characters appears on a computer screen, it will only be because the formula for one's bank account has made its way onto someone else's screen in a carefully scripted and understandable way.

Surely, a book is one thing, and a file of data bits scattered over multiple sectors of a multi-gigabyte hard drive hundreds or thousands of miles from a reader's desk is another. But the *value* of the book and of those data bits is in the way they are constructed to fit a given use. Once we recognize that, we are faced not with a shift from reality to virtuality but with a study in the history of virtual realities going back at least two hundred years.

OWNING THE EXPRESSION OF IDEAS

For convenience's sake, we may assign the rise of modern intellectual property law to the early eighteenth century.[3] That is when the idea of copyright took on tremendous power, shaping a marketplace for cultural products unlike any seen before. Today's authors, publishers, and readers have taken the assumptions of copyright for granted to a considerable extent, but it is easier to understand where electronic information transactions may be headed if we unpack those ideas and characterize their strengths, weaknesses, and influence. This is not merely an academic exercise in self-understanding. Society now faces what seems to be a powerful competitor for copyright's influence over the marketplace of cultural products, one that carries its own assumptions about what intellectual property is, how it is to be used, how it can be controlled, and what economic order can emerge as a result. The concept of the license (or detailed contract) for buying and using intellectual property is a comparatively new one, certainly new in its application to most of the products a librarian thinks about, and powerful in its own way.

The creation of the concept of copyright was an ingenious fiction. It abstracted from the covers of a book the words contained therein and turned them, no matter how many times multiplied by printing technologies, into a single piece of property governed according to strict rules. In its original form, copyright depended in two ways on the technologies of its time.

First, the capital costs of establishing and operating a printing press meant that those who used such presses to violate copyright (by printing and distributing what was not theirs to handle) were liable to confiscatory punishment at least commensurate with the injury done by the crime itself. The thought of losing what had been produced or the instruments of production themselves was enough to give one pause, and the likelihood that the printer could escape detection was relatively slight.[4]

Second, the power of copyright was enhanced by the development of high-speed printing presses that both increased the capital investment at risk and greatly multiplied the number of copies that could be produced of a given original (and thus lowered their price) so that an author could begin to realize financial rewards through signing over his copyright to a publisher. The publisher (generally becoming the new copyright owner to whom the creation was transferred), who had assumed the expense and risk of publication, stood to gain a substantial portion of the revenue earned by the publication.

The technologies themselves have, of course, been transformed over time. Publishers and authors concerned with protecting the intellectual property that is rightfully theirs have seen, beginning in the 1970s, the photocopying machine, the offshore knock-off artist, and most recently the personal computer dramatically increase the ease, cheapness, and accuracy with which intellectual property can be copied and distributed in great quantities and the relative certainty with which the perpetrator of such an offense can escape detection. The photocopier is still a large and expensive tool but not nearly as pricey as a printing press; it is ubiquitous in places of business and education (though not in the home). The personal computer, a tool for accomplishing many organizational, personal, and social activities, is an important growth industry. Nowadays even school children own PCs, as do most libraries, businesses, and other kinds of institutions. Gradually the offshore knock-off artist might be brought under control as the countries where he plies his trade develop an interest in protecting intellectual property of their own. The photocopier and the computer are less subject to such scrutiny.

In a modern society supposedly based on private property, copyright both exalts and undermines the integrity of property in telling ways. It grants to the person who has written a text (or created a picture, film, or dramatic work) an extraordinary power over that creation, though it may go to the ends of the earth—a power that lasts at least five decades beyond the author's death. Elvis Presley has already made more money dead than in all his career alive. At the same time, copyright means that those who have hundreds or thousands of books on their shelves do not quite own them the way it is possible to own a screwdriver or a piece of real estate. It is remarkable just how much of what humans own is constrained by property law of one kind or another—patent and trademark, if not copyright. But the likelihood that one would wish to create an exact copy of one's own, say, teddy bear is so slight that one does not feel constrained by the potential violation of patent, trademark, or copyright protection. With written material, the temptation to copy has always been great, and the technological possibility now in hand is greater than ever and thus far more tempting. It is no accident that the legal debates about copyright over the last generation have focused on ways to discourage people who own photocopiers or computers from doing with those machines things that the machines are eminently suited to do, that a reasonable and responsible person might very well want to do with them.

But for all the risks copyright holders face, the industry that has arisen around the market for intellectual property is vast and thriving. The great value of copyright continues to lie in linking authorship to reward; in a quintessentially capitalist way, it has given millions the incentive to labor away at articles, plays, and novels that will never be published and has prompted resourceful businesspeople to calculate precisely how best to create "products" that can be marketed. By the early 1990s, US copyright industries accounted for well over $200 billion in annual business, or about 3.6 percent of the gross national product.[5] Scholarly and literary publishing accounts for only about half a percent of that total, or perhaps $1 billion per year,[6] and public or government information, much of which is freely distributed, plays a small part in this market.

One of the growth areas in the intellectual property marketplace since World War II has been scholarly and, in particular, scientific publishing. The late Robert Maxwell, a buccaneer publishing tycoon, deserves much credit for the dubious achievement of "inventing" the large-scale, for-profit, commercially-published scientific journal. In the early 1950s, when his Pergamon Press first distributed such titles, they were a roaring success story precisely for academic producers and consumers of such information. By accessing a global marketplace, Maxwell brought significant capital into the scientific publishing food chain and assured wide distribution of a vast quantity of scientific literature of unprecedented sophistication and specialization.

It turns out, at least in the United States, that the last generation's boon is the bane of this generation of libraries and universities. The golden age of scientific research funding—driven by vast quantities of American defense and space dollars and buoyed precisely by the strength of what, it is now quaint to remember, was thought of as "the almighty dollar"—faded in the 1970s and 1980s, and with its fall from glory the commercial science journal became a heavier and heavier tax on the limited funding of research institutions. Research libraries are staggering under increasing costs; they cut back titles judiciously and manage to get by somehow.

Rising prices and spreading technologies have, to be sure, brought publishers and some users to quarrelsome intersections in recent years. Several high-profile legal cases have seen publishers taking legal action against a highly visible agency (the National Library of Medicine, New York University, Kinkos, the Texaco Corporation, and Michigan Document Services being some of the more prominent recent ones) on charges of illicit or excessive photocopying. From both the court decisions and the statutory legislation of our time, users (particularly institutions) have struggled to draw guidelines regarding the use of equipment whose natural and spontaneous use could undermine a piece of the intellectual property economy. The difficulty in such attempts for both courts and users is that it is always hard to measure real damage and to assess its importance. For example, software publishers know that some substantial percentage of users of popular products have not paid for the software they use in the way that the publishers wish, but that market remains robust. At most, software entrepreneurs could argue that the incentive for innovation at the margin is less than it could be, but it is an impossible argument to quantify.

THE US COPYRIGHT ACT

By law, copyright protection begins from the moment of creation, when the work is "fixed in a tangible medium of expression," which can be writing on a piece of paper, a recording on magnetic tape, keystrokes on a computer screen, or paint to canvas. Copyright can be transferred from the original creator to another entity; normally a publisher requires a full transfer or sufficient assignment of rights in order to bring the creations to market. The 1976 US Copyright Act protects creative works in general, including literature, music, drama, pantomime and choreographic works, pictorial, graphical, and sculptural works, motion pictures and other audiovisual works, sound recordings, and architectural works. Copyright law grants the owners of the expression of an idea five exclusive, or monopoly, rights: to reproduce copies of the work, prepare derivative works, distribute the work, perform it, or display it. In order to do any of these things, one must have the owner's permission.

At the same time, the law recognizes certain exceptions or limitations on the exclusive rights of owners. Those limitations include:

- Public domain: Works produced by federal government employees created on government time (Section 105); works past the copyright period (now, with some exceptions, the lifetime of the author plus fifty years); and those that are explicitly placed in the public domain by their owners (in practice, a minuscule proportion of created works).
- Fair use: The 1976 Copyright Act was the first to explicitly address the balance between copyright holders' rights and readers' rights by codifying fair use rights (Section 107). Fair use permits certain kinds of reproduction of copyrighted works without users having to pay or explicitly request owners' permissions, for purposes that include research, teaching, journalism, criticism, parody, and library activities. The primary beneficiaries of fair use are students, educators, researchers, and commentators. Fair use makes it possible for them to go about learning, teaching, engaging in scholarship, and being creative without needing to take the time to ask permission of copyright owners or pay a potentially significant price for using the materials. Fair use is said by many educators and public policy specialists to be the most vital piece of the law that fulfills copyright's constitutional mandate.
- Archival preservation and the operations of libraries: Section 108 permits libraries certain privileges to preserve rare or frail works for future readers or to lend books via interlibrary loan, so long as such activities do not systematically undermine owner's revenues. This section enables libraries to act as powerful consolidators of information and to serve a strong societal information mission.
- Additional definitions and limitations on specific media, formats, and delivery mechanisms are enumerated in Sections 109–120.

Thus, the copyright law protects ownership and at the same time places limitations on ownership to achieve a balance of interests that preserves the underlying purpose behind the US copyright law as embodied in the Constitution: "to promote the progress of science and useful arts."

CAN ELECTRONIC CREATIONS BE OWNED?

The Clinton-Gore campaign of 1992 may be responsible for having first placed the Internet before the general public's, or at least the popular journalist's, eye. This administration is extremely committed to rapid development of the National Information Infrastructure (NII) and determined to respond to industry and economic concerns. Part of that commitment arose from a passionate belief (well expressed by Vice President Gore, and more recently taken up in different terms by Speaker Gingrich) that electronic networks create an environment and a set of instruments vital to the overall economic growth of the United States.

In 1993, the Clinton-Gore administration created a number of super-agency committees to define problem areas (e.g., privacy, security, standards, libraries, copyright) and to make recommendations to assure full exploitation of the information superhighway. In mid-1994, the twenty-five-member NII Working Group on Copyright, chaired by Commissioner of Patents and Trademarks Bruce Lehman (and colloquially called the "Lehman Commission"), released a green paper or first draft report, put the draft into play, and actively solicited responses. In September 1995, the Working Group released the final white paper containing a legislative package intended to update the current Copyright Act for the cyber-nineties and beyond. As of the summer of 1996, this package is being debated in the appropriate House and Senate committees.

In short, the Working Group's commitment to the NII takes the form of a belief expressed thus: "The full potential of the NII will not be realized if the education, information and entertainment products protected by intellectual property laws are not protected effectively when disseminated via the NII."[7] The Working Group affirmed strong intellectual property protection in the NII and at the same time was at pains to insist that the recommendations it presented merely "tweak" the law. That characterization is accurate, in the sense that comparatively few sections of the act would be affected by wording additions, changes, or extensions, and its fundamental organization would remain intact. But in the eyes of many citizens and legal scholars, especially reader/user rights advocates, the Lehman Commission's proposed legislative changes overturn the balance that the current law maintains between the rights of copyright owners and users. The underlying concern is about the paper's unequivocal affirmation that any information alighting in a computer's memory, for any amount of time—however fleeting—is "fixed." The definition of fixation is important because the Copyright Act governs only those ideas "fixed in a tangible means of expression, when its embodiment. . .is sufficiently permanent or stable to permit it to be perceived, reproduced, or otherwise communicated for a period of more than transitory duration" (Section 101). By this reasoning, copying occurs each time information is transferred between computers. Therefore, the user who transfers copyrighted information between computers through a network without permission of the copyright owner is breaking the law.

If access to electronic materials without payment for every use is to be recognized, then fair use is the area in which bridges can be built between the rights of copyright owners and information users. Fair use may not be the *only* possible bridge, and perhaps it may be replaced one day with more effective concepts, but in the print information world, with its static documents and comparatively easily controlled bottlenecks (at the printing press and booksellers), fair use is where US society has achieved a great deal of the balance between users' and copyright owners' needs. Fair use concepts exist (though not identically) in the copyright laws of most Western nations.

ENTER THE ELECTRONIC LICENSE

One response to the anxieties of intellectual property owners in an age of electronic copying and transmission has been to seek to change the conditions under which "fixed" creations are protected. Actually, the concept of a license is old and fundamentally transparent. If one owns a piece of property and allows another to use it without transferring title, one may by law of contract stipulate whatever conditions one chooses; if the other party agrees to them, then a mutually agreeable deal has come into being. A similar transaction takes place in the case of performance rights for films and recordings. The owner of a movie theater rarely owns the cans of film delivered weekly to the cinema, holding them instead under strict conditions of use: so many showings, so much payment for each ticket sold, etc. As with the economic relationship between author and publisher that is sanctioned by copyright, with the right price such an arrangement can be extraordinarily fruitful. But in this type of license the relationships are driven entirely by contract law: the owner of such a piece of property is free to ask whatever price and set whatever conditions on use the market will bear.

Most of our academic contemporaries began to be parties to such license agreements when personal computer software appeared in the 1980s in shrink-wrap packages for the first time. Purchasers of such software may have read the fine print on the wrapper detailing the terms and conditions of use, but for the most part users either did not or have ceased to do so. The thrust of most such documents is simple: by opening the package, the purchaser has agreed to certain terms, terms that include limited rights of ownership and use of the item paid for. One may, perhaps, be allowed to make a copy for personal use or backup only, and if one resells the materials, any copies on the home computer must be deleted. (For a brief time, software producers even coded their disks so as to restrict the number of copies that could physically be made from one original, but sharp customer resistance, a genuine market force, caused them to withdraw those restrictions.)

If the contract created by shrink-wrap is a valid one,[8] it is also one where no evenhanded arbiter has set out the balance of rights and duties. The owner of the intellectual property, buffeted perhaps by market forces but at the same time often able to control (if rich and successful) some of those forces by his own acts, stipulates the terms on a "take it or leave it" basis. The user has the rights the owner decides to give; there is, on a personal level, no possible negotiation.

In recent years, the concept of the license has gradually extended from covering software to covering the even "softer" ware of content. As material that was traditionally sold in printed form

and distributed under the protection of the copyright statute becomes available in electronic form, particularly in networked electronic form, publishers seeking a return on their investment have
not been content to insist that their copyright privileges be recognized. This may be because such publishers sense that on-line text
can reproduce itself like the proverbial rabbit and that whatever
self-discipline readers of a print text might exercise can easily
disappear the moment that reader forwards a copy of an article to
an e-mail discussion list with multiple subscribers—in a flash, the
publisher fears, a substantial part of the academic market for a
given product could receive copies that had never been paid for.
Copyright prosecution, moreover, is difficult for a number of
reasons and needs to take into account the indisputable statutory
rights of users. Litigation under a license agreement, by comparison, is likely to be far simpler and far more favorable to the
copyright owner.

So it is that in 1996 the Internet is being inundated with publishers of standard reference works and journals offering electronic
versions of their wares on access terms that are strictly contractual. Often these terms appear to obviate all discussion of users'
statutory rights by specifying in detail the conditions under which
material may be used and copied. Few of the licenses offered to
libraries or academics seek to charge for every examination of the
published material, but that may be at least partly because as yet
no reliable, affordable technologies exist for charging and billing
such costs (though they may be expected to become available
soon). In the meantime, publishers are peddling their wares, usually both the print and electronic versions (it is worth keeping in
mind that such electronic versions rarely "push the envelope" of
what is possible in electronic publishing—as long as they are
yoked to a print version, they usually do little more than reproduce what the printed page has already offered), at prices that give
the user (or the user's library's collections development officer) no
economic advantage as a result of efficiencies of production and
distribution. Today, for the privilege of access to an electronic
version of the print information, libraries pay more rather than
less. It remains to be seen whether the boon of improved access
will sustain such prices in the market; it seems that if a publisher
were willing to forgo printing, binding, bundling, and shipping

costs, the same information might be distributed much more cheaply than before.[9]

So far, it is characteristic of electronic information that it rarely comes to libraries, when they pay for it, as free of "strings" as did print material. The concept of First Sale in the US Copyright Act of 1976 (Section 109, with the equivalent principles in other countries) has given libraries the ability to service and lend all the objects they buy. Book purchasers have the right to keep and preserve their books. Electronic information license agreements, on the other hand, tend to constrain rights in various ways.

- *Potential loss of knowledge.* Libraries generally do not own the material that they are paying for—they lease it for a limited time. If at the end of that time, they cease paying the lease price, prior investment may become worthless if the information is taken away.
- *License restrictions on use and users.* Not infrequently, libraries cannot let all and sundry make reasonable use of materials but rather must employ passwords and user IDs to restrict use to formal members of specified academic or scientific communities. Librarians who are used to defining institutional access policies acutely feel a loss of control at such a moment, a loss of the power to grant wide access to information for the good of our communities and society.
- *Limitations on users' rights.* In the world of license agreements the licensee generally begins with fewer rights to use information than in the world of print material, and further limitations are then added (the licensee is liable for misuse of the data and for preserving security, while the licenser may take only limited responsibility to assure that the resource performs as advertised). These agreements, indeed, seem to have been designed for commercial rather than educational customers.
- *Loss of browsing.* There are also signs that many producers will begin experimenting with "pay by the drink" systems of information access by electronic network, where every glimpse of the precious metal of information can have a price tag. The threat-

ened end of browsing and serendipity is a worrisome one for all concerned with the free flow of ideas and creativity in scientific and academic settings.

- *Cost.* In general, electronic licenses so far have cost on average one third more than print equivalents. This has been the experience, in any case, for indexing and abstracting services, and research libraries have attempted to find the funding to absorb these increased costs for such valuable bibliographic tools. Now, full text is imminent. For full text, many publishers also have the expectation that higher prices will be asked and should be paid. Publishers are setting surcharges of as much as 35 percent on electronic journals, and libraries simply do not have the capacity to pay such amounts without canceling a corresponding number of the print journals of that particular publisher or dipping into other publishers' journals.

- *The stability factor.* Full-text electronic access licenses offered to customers by publishers are experimental in many ways, and their longevity is far from secure. Many of these licenses are for trial projects. For these titles, libraries are partners in an important experiment with publishers. It is not readily within libraries' power either to cancel the print format altogether (the publisher may cease to maintain the electronic version or maintain it in a hard-to-use or obsolete technology) or to pay higher-than-print prices for such titles.

- *Other stumbling blocks* include prohibitions against using the electronic versions for interlibrary loans, significant liability matters for the institution (if a user infringes, for example), and confidentiality (terms of licenses are often labeled as confidential and are not supposed to be widely shared with colleagues, let alone other institutions).

Institutional licenses are generally negotiable, but negotiations are labor-intensive. Negotiation requires time, and time is a major cost here. How librarians can work together with publishers to encourage a more enlightened form of agreement, with a more equitable balance of rights and responsibilities, is an open question of the greatest importance.

On the positive side, both individual libraries and consortia of libraries have reported negotiating electronic content licenses with a number of publishers who have been particularly understanding of research library needs. In general, academic publishers are proving to be willing to give and take on license language and terms, provided that the licensees know what terms are important to them. In many cases, librarians ask that the publisher reinstate the "public good" clauses of the Copyright Act into the electronic content license, allowing fair use copying or downloading, interlibrary loan, and archiving for the institutional licensee and its customers.

The comparatively new phenomenon of institutional licensing has evolved in a short time. Initially (perhaps twenty years ago), academic and research libraries began accessing electronic information, at that time primarily indexing and abstracting services, through intermediaries such as Dialog. Different data bases levied different per-hour charges, and for the most part libraries established running accounts to which these searches were charged. Libraries accepted the terms of such services, which were in general nonnegotiable. Next, a number of the indexing and abstracting service publishers, along with others, offered electronic products of their own directly to libraries via CD-ROM or through dial-up, and it was at this point that institutional licenses became recognized as a means to information acquisition or access. Initially there was little back and forth negotiation between providers and libraries, but now, particularly with the advent of consortia (institutions that band together to buy electronic access or content for group prices and enhanced terms), negotiating the content license is a part of library life. As a rule, the consortial license takes longer than the individual license to negotiate, but the economies of scale can be helpful to both publishers and institutional customers.

FUTURE SCENARIOS: A LONG-TERM PROGNOSIS FOR THE
ELECTRONIC LICENSE

To clarify the issues and give the reader some ways to move forward along the trajectories suggested here, we conclude with a discussion of two possible outcomes for the information future of libraries under an electronic licensing scheme and the implications of these scenarios. Reality is always messier than any scenario, but the issues libraries are likely to face will almost certainly emerge along the polarity that links the scenarios described below.

First, consider this extrapolation. Currently, publishers of scientific and scholarly information are actively encouraging and cooperating not only with individual libraries but, lately and enthusiastically, with libraries that gather together in consortia to obtain cost-effective bulk pricing "deals" for the purchase of on-line versions of existing journals and other data bases. A typical negotiation, for example, may involve a number of sizable colleges and universities aggregating all the current subscription dollars paid to a particular journal publisher, counting at the same time to see how many of that publisher's journals are subscribed to by one or another of all the libraries. For example, an interesting on-line network access arrangement being offered lately to research library consortia by one large publisher of nearly two hundred scholarly journals asks for a price equaling 110 percent of what each member library (of the consortium) now pays for the print journals it takes. For the 110 percent, each library in the consortium will continue to receive its current print subscription and will also have electronic access to *all* the publisher's journals via the World Wide Web. Because no single library is likely to subscribe to more than two-thirds of that publisher's list in print form, this is potentially a 50 percent increase in information purchased for only a 10 percent surcharge; on the other hand, the journals not taken at each university are items that have been considered and deemed of lesser value to that community. Currently, then, the mix of benefit and cost for the library customers in this particular arrangement remains unclear even as it and others like it seem to be interesting ones to explore. Meanwhile, the publisher is making a best guess as to the costs of providing the electronic version.

What can we expect next under such arrangements, particularly when they increase in scale to multiple consortia dealing thus with many publishers? We would have a collectivity of subscribers, carefully scrutinizing each others' journal holdings from each publisher, discussing among themselves the terms of agreement under which they would continue to take the journals when the time comes for annual renewal of the license. This begins to look like a combination of institutional economic interests working together where before there has been disunity. Certainly one weakness of the traditional library faced with publishers' price lists has been the isolation of the individual subscribing library, coupled with antitrust restrictions placed on library associations to prevent consumer boycotts, and the like. But now the buying power of a number of large and influential customers is being aggregated. Will such an aggregation bring with it a shift of power from the producer to the licensees?

Take this further example. Some publishers are advocating what they call a "national site license"—a single fee that is paid to them by the research-funding authorities of a given country (in the United States, this is more likely to be a "state" site license, and a number of such state-wide library consortia are rapidly emerging), in return for which all patrons in that country (or state) have free access to the electronic publishing output of the publisher with whom the wide area site license has been arranged. Such a national or state-wide relationship suddenly seems like a boon to all the students, faculty, and researchers in a given jurisdiction. The information becomes akin to a public good, and it certainly betokens a simplified way to do business for the publisher: one price, one server, no hassles, and an assured income stream.

Extend such a wide-area licensing scenario five years into the future, and then imagine that research funds, for some reason, become tight; a new government has taken office and is squeezing the spigots wherever possible. Users in the meantime have become accustomed to accessing various publishers' wares as a kind of common good. The publishers have become beneficiaries of state subsidy and then the subsidy is threatened. By that time, will certain players in the publishing industry have found themselves subtly transformed into a dependent arm of the state? Instead of a cutback in local institutional subscriptions, as would happen in today's print and copyright regime—selectively, prudently, based on real need for information but discouraged by researchers' outrage at the loss of precious material—might there instead be a draconian 15 percent cut to deal with? How might the affected publishers respond to such a situation? Would they cut prices? Cut back on their offerings? Go out of business? Who benefits? Who loses? Who manages the outcomes?

It is too early for answers to such questions, but they need to be pondered if they are eventually to be addressed. The point here is to highlight some of the positive characteristics of our *present* system of publishing, for example, its decentralized, research-driven nature and distributed funding, which thus follows research and use but does not dictate to it. The larger the scale on which licensing takes place, the more control shifts to those who fund publication: in practice, libraries and their funding sources. On the one hand, both researchers *and* publishers may object to such an outcome. On the other, the potential for good should not be underestimated. A fundamental criticism of current ways and means of publishing is that there is little disincentive to a proliferation of publishing outlets and published articles—too much published, insufficient material of significant value. Could the large-scale license, then, become the thin end of a wedge that will leave in place the valued freedoms of inquiry and information but allow some form of more rational assessment of needs and abilities, or will it forever alter publishing as we have known it?

Let us now take a second tack. What licensing agreements have in common with copyright is that both accept the fundamental underlying idea of the nature of intellectual property inherent in a given work of authorship. Where they differ is only in the vehicle by which they seek to balance users' rights and authors' (and, to be sure and of greater economic importance here, publishers') rights and to regulate the economy that springs up around those rights. Copyright represents a set of regulations negotiated through statutory enactment, where the power of concentrated economic interests has been modulated by the original constitutional objective of copyright (to promote progress in science and the useful arts) and the voices of various interests in legislative lobbies and before committees. Licenses, on the other hand, represent a market-driven approach to this regulation. The marketplace is imperfect, especially where a fairly small number of large publishers based in one economic environment (for example, the European Union) face a diverse number of customers based in another (for example, the United States), but it is still a place where interests meet, deals are struck, and working arrangements between parties are negotiated and revised over time. In fact, it is possible for libraries and publishers to negotiate licenses that incorporate the precepts of copyright (such as fair use) in the agreement.

The confrontation between the models that copyright and license offer, moreover,[10] further changes the imperfect market relationship in a way that potentially gives users some advantages. Users know what their rights are under copyright statute, and that puts them in a relatively stronger position to negotiate license deals. Users (their institutional aggregators being the libraries) already have *something,* so what they seek from publishers is an incentive to transcend statutory obligations and privileges in a different relationship. One way publishers can seek to influence this negotiation, of course, is by pursuing litigation to enforce their own copyright privileges in a way that encourages the public to think of copyright as a restricted and less advantageous umbrella compared to what a possible license agreement might provide.

This is one underlying explanation for the ongoing series of copyright court cases by which some representatives of the scholarly publishing communities seek to define "fair use" with restrictive interpretations. One need not be a legal soothsayer and foresee how these cases and their successors will play out in order to identify the economic incentives that both readers and publishers will have when they negotiate license agreements.

It is surely not unreasonable to suggest that the gap between the two ways of doing business (copyright-governed and license-governed) will narrow over time in a kind of dialectical relationship. If they seem at odds at the moment, the true interpretation is that legal and market forces are still scrambling to keep up with the changes in users' habits driven by empowering new technologies. It would not be reasonable to expect such great changes in media to arise without consequent disruptions in long-stable patterns of economic and legal relationships.

The lesson to be drawn from these meditations is perhaps no more elaborate than this: that in a time of rapidly changing technologies and uses of technologies, haste in the prescriptive reconstruction of legal and economic relationships is inappropriate. Room needs to be left for experimentation and exploration. Both publishers and academic libraries understandably have real fears about the security of their economic livelihood in the short term—and the larger they are, the more fears they are likely to have. Both groups are relatively vulnerable to the risks of short-term fluctuations in what they can expect from the other, but both—in a curious kind of prisoner's game—may be less vulnerable if together they work pragmatically towards mid-term, modest solutions to pressing difficulties, leaving ambitious reengineering to a later time.

Our greatest need is to sustain and, where possible, enhance the truly remarkable system of communication that we have built up over the centuries. Ezra Pound wrote, "Properly, we should read for power. Man reading should be man intensely alive. The book should be a ball of light in one's hand." We should think of how bright that light can be if we understand copyright on the way to doing our licensing work well. Fire and ice both have the power to dazzle and thwart our vision.

ENDNOTES

[1] Colin Day, Director of the University of Michigan Press, after his presentation on "Cost Recovery in an Electronic Publishing Environment: Issues and Perspectives," at the Association of Research Libraries/Association of American University Presses' symposium, *Scholarly Publishing on the Electronic Networks; Filling the Pipeline and Paying the Piper,* Washington, D.C., 5–7 November 1994.

[2] James Gleick, "Dead as a Dollar," *New York Times Magazine,* 16 June 1996, 26ff. Gleick shows that electronic cash is already seriously in play, traces the history of money, and speculates on its next instantiation.

[3] Mark Rose, *Authors and Owners; The Invention of Copyright* (Cambridge, Mass.: Harvard University Press, 1993).

[4] Lynn Hunt, ed., *The Invention of Pornography: Obscenity and the Origins of Modernity, 1500–1800* (New York and Cambridge: Zone Books, 1993). Hunt shows just how far one could, with great difficulty, conceal responsibility for a printed book, but only when the offended party was merely public taste and decency, not an outraged competitor.

[5] Ann Okerson, "Who Owns Digital Works?" *Scientific American* (July 1996): 80–84. The electronic version of this essay can be found on the World Wide Web at URL: <http://www.sciam.com/WEB/0796issue/0796okerson.html.>

[6] Estimate by Joseph J. Esposito, President of *Encyclopaedia Britannica,* in the Flair Conference at the Humanities Research Center, University of Texas, November 1994. These remarks were subsequently published in both the conference proceedings and in *ARL: A Bimonthly Newsletter of Research Library Issues and Actions,* January 1995, p. 1–2.

[7] *Intellectual Property and the National Information Infrastructure: The Report of the Working Group on Intellectual Property Rights,* September 1995. Available on the World Wide Web at URL: <http://www.uspto.gov/web/ipnii.>

[8]In the recent decision (20 June 1996) in *ProCD v Zeidenberg*, the Seventh Circuit responded to the question, "Must buyers of computer software obey the terms of shrink-wrap licenses?" The judges overturned the ruling of the lower court by answering the question in the affirmative. Part of their rationale was that the purchaser could read the license upon opening the box and if the terms were unacceptable, the merchandise could be returned. Additionally they commented that copyright and licenses are very different: copyright is "a right against the world. . .contracts, by contrast, generally affect only their parties." This decision can be found on the World Wide Web at URL: <http://www.sgpdlaw.com/case/procd_op.html.>

[9]*Scholarly Journals at the Crossroads: A Subversive Proposal for Electronic Publishing. An Internet Discussion about Scientific and Scholarly Journals and Their Future*, ed. Ann Shumelda Okerson and James J. O'Donnell (Washington, D.C.: Association of Research Libraries, June 1995). This volume presents the diverse points of view of scientists, librarians, and publishers on the following topic: Can the costs of scholarly journal publication be significantly reduced (by as much as 70 percent) by fully employing the capabilities of electronic authoring and distribution?

[10]Copyright lawyers and those who are interested enough to discuss copyright electronically on lists such as cni-copyright@cni.org from time to time raised the important topic of whether a license that disallows provisions of the Copyright Act (such as, say, fair use) can be preempted by the Act itself. For a sound introduction to this particular question, see Trotter Hardy, "Contracts, Copyright and Preemption in a Digital World," *Richmond Journal of Law & Technology* (17 April 1995). This electronic journal can be found on the World Wide Web at the URL: <http://www.urich.edu/~jolt/v1i1/hardy.html.>

Kenneth E. Carpenter

A Library Historian Looks at Librarianship

A MERICAN LIBRARIES HAVE THE REPUTATION of being the best in the world—easy to use and with collections appropriate to their purpose. Some are also among the largest in the world. In fact, three of the five largest libraries, exclusive of those in Russia, are in the United States. One of these, Harvard University's, has millions of books in open stacks. The holdings of other American libraries are also highly accessible, for American librarians have long emphasized access to materials in addition to other services for their clientele, whether it be the general public, specialized professionals, students, or scholars.

Despite the reputation of American libraries, most American librarians feel that they are unappreciated and in fact seem to be so.[1] A sign of this is that the greatest of our libraries—those on which we fundamentally depend for the preservation of the written record of our civilization and for access to it, namely, the Library of Congress, the New York Public Library, the Harvard University Library—have as their senior officer a non-librarian. So, too, do a number of other libraries that are also crucial in preserving the written record, such as the Morgan Library, the Newberry Library, and the Library Company of Philadelphia. Abroad, this pattern also applies: one of the great contemporary historians recently led the Bibliothèque Nationale and, moreover, the chief executive of the British Library is an anthropologist.

Kenneth E. Carpenter is Assistant Director for Research Resources at the Harvard University Library.

Exceptions do exist: the American Antiquarian Society and, most recently, the Huntington Library have appointed librarians as their heads, but it should be noted that the governing structure of the American Antiquarian Society is such that the public voice, at least much of the time, is that of a non-librarian. No one would argue, of course, that the positions of Andrew W. Mellon Director of the Research Libraries (at the New York Public Library) or the Roy E. Larsen Librarian of Harvard College are unimportant. Quite the contrary; occupants of such positions may exert more influence over the well-being of the institution than the person who heads it, but those librarians, while they have a powerful voice among other librarians, are not the primary public voice. That belongs to non-librarians—people who are seen as better able to articulate the purposes of the institution and gain for it the necessary support.

Even Melvil Dewey suggested, in 1886, that libraries ought not necessarily to be under the control of trained librarians. In an address before the Association of Collegiate Alumnae, he stated:

> The great element of success [for a library] is the earnest moving spirit which supplies to the institution its life. This should be the librarian, though often the one who bears that name is little more than a clerk and the real librarian will be found among the active members of the trustees or the committee, or possibly not officially connected with the library.[2]

It is understandable that what Dewey described was often the case at a time when librarianship was just emerging as a field of work requiring special preparation. But why today are non-librarians chosen to lead these great libraries? Specifically, why do the directorships go to scholars in the traditional academic disciplines? Or, these questions could better be phrased, "Why are there no librarians deemed to be appropriate to lead these institutions?" That there are none is a symptom of a malaise in librarianship.

Another symptom of the malaise is represented by a series of essays under the general heading of "Significance of Primary Records," which was published recently in *Profession*.[3] These are the results of a debate in the Modern Language Association (MLA) about the preservation of originals. What is striking here is that not a single librarian is among the essayists and that no librarian was invited to participate in the debate within the MLA at a stage when it could have mattered. Behind these omissions must lie the perception that librarians are a group lacking the ability to deal with complex issues on a theoretical level.[4]

This essay will attempt to explain why those libraries that are particularly important cultural institutions are not entrusted to librarians, and why a learned society did not involve librarians in so crucial an issue as the preservation of its source material.[5]

One factor is the emphasis in librarianship on practice. That librarianship has been historically a woman's profession is important, in part because society has devalued women's work. Until recently, though, a dual structure of librarianship existed—elite males and female subordinates. This has furthered in libraries a concentration of power in the hands of the head librarian, which in turn has inhibited the display of individual initiative as well as the discussion and debate that is crucial to developing librarians who can be cultural leaders. Very important in diminishing the status of librarians has been society's high valuation of knowledge creation—research—and its low estimation of knowledge dissemination. Furthermore, librarians have not been a countervailing force against this because of the emphasis on technique. It has led to a too-narrow definition of service that has lessened the capacity of librarians to serve as purveyors of information as opposed to providers of books, i.e., librarians have emphasized a passive rather than active service. Moreover, the American Library Association (ALA) has not helped, for it has focused on organizational imperatives at the expense of crucial support to libraries and librarians.[6]

There is thus a reinforcing pattern with interlocking parts. Although this essay will suggest that a new set of factors may be emerging, it is not another in a long series directed to librarians about how librarians can attain higher status. Librarians as a group would benefit from change, but the goal behind encouraging it must always be the good of society, not of librarians. The irony is that librarians' focus on the status of librarians must always be self-defeating; true status comes only through being a community that, along with being devoted to the common good, is able to communicate with the public, scholars, and policymakers—to not just reiterate but thoughtfully address the new issues and conditions that every generation faces.

* * *

Librarianship as a definable occupational category began in the fourth quarter of the nineteenth century. The two crucial dates and events are 1876, the year that the American Library Association was founded, and 1887, the year that the first library school, at Columbia University, officially opened. This was also the era during which Americans developed an "obsession with disseminating the printed page."[7] A historian of professionalization argues that the profusion of reading matter fostered confusion, self-doubt, and mistrust that prompted Americans to turn to professionals for guidance. He refers to Noah Porter's *Books and Reading,* whose first of many editions was published in 1870, as well as to Charles William Eliot's "Five-Foot Book-Shelf," also known as the Harvard Classics, a publishing success that far exceeded expectations. Other presidents of institutions of higher education also produced reading guides: Alice Freeman Palmer of Wellesley and G. Stanley Hall of Clark.

Librarians also produced reading guides, but not for the public. Instead, librarians emphasized indexes or buying tools for librarians. The most famous was the American Library Association's 1893 catalog of the five-thousand-volume model library that it had on display at the Chicago World's Fair. This catalog was received so favorably that it immediately led to other listings of librarian-recommended best books.[8] Whereas the 1893 catalog was directed primarily at librarians and secondarily at the public, others tended to be solely for librarians. One of the first such, *Best 25 Books of 1894,* published by the New York Library Association in 1895, aimed to provide a list of the twenty-five best books for a "village" library. The list was produced by asking librarians to vote on 232 "leading books," and 156 librarians participated in this popularity contest.

The New York Library Association's list is not an isolated example of library publishing for librarians, especially for librarians of small libraries. That library associations focused inwardly— not on the public at large, but on small, public libraries—is not surprising since education for librarianship did likewise. The first library school, Melvil Dewey's at Columbia University, which was established in the 1880s and later reincarnated at Albany,[9] emphasized this practice. In the prospectus of the Columbia School, Dewey spelled out that instruction would be in the practical:

> The course will include little of the antiquarian or historical except when necessary to illustrate or enforce modern methods. Its aim is entirely practical; to give the best obtainable advice, with specific suggestions on each of the hundreds of questions that rise from the time a library is decided to be valuable till it is in perfect working order including its administration.[10]

In devoting his school to practice, Dewey was fulfilling a need expressed in 1871 in the American Social Science Association's *Free Public Libraries: Suggestions on Their Foundation and Administration*. This work, whose object was to "help the growth of free public libraries, to suggest their planting where they do not exist, and to favor their development where they do," met with sufficient demand for two editions to be published in 1871. A prefatory note to both editions quotes from Justin Winsor's 1869 Boston Public Library annual report:

> We have no schools of bibliographical and bibliothecal training whose graduates can guide the formation of and assume management within the fast-increasing libraries of our country; and the demand may perhaps never warrant their establishment: but every library with a fair experience can afford inestimable instruction to another in its novitiate; and there have been no duties of my office to which I have given more hearty attention than those that have led to the granting of what we could from our experience to the representatives of other libraries, whether coming with inquiries fitting a collection as large as Cincinnati is to establish, or merely seeking such matters as concern the establishment of a village library. It is much to be hoped that during the coming year there will be instituted an organized medium for such intercommunication, under the direction of the American Social Science Association.[11]

The subtext of this message is that Winsor was besieged by queries and visitors from throughout the country. In an era in which the number of newly founded public libraries continued to increase, the situation could only get worse for those in a position to offer practical, specific advice.

Yet another factor that led to practical education was the battle against patronage appointments, especially by machine politicians.[12]

Practical education could be an indisputable qualification, whereas a more theoretical education would have lacked the same clout. In other words, the emphasis on practice served then to keep out non-librarians, although a resulting side effect was that it furthered insularity among librarians.

At the end of the nineteenth century and the beginning of the twentieth, practical education that would serve one-man or one-woman libraries and that would deter patronage was exactly what was needed; the fault lies not with Dewey. It is also not surprising that change subsequently has been so difficult, especially since graduates of Dewey's New York State Library School and of Columbia became powerful in librarianship. During the period from 1913 to 1917, 39 percent of the members of the ALA Executive Board were from those schools,[13] and the human tendency is to esteem most highly our own talents and background.

Another aspect of librarianship that has been seen as central and as beginning with Dewey is the opening up of librarianship to women, which ultimately led to a "female-intensive" occupation.[14] The argument, as put forward by Harris in her thoughtful and provocative book, is that a correlation exists between librarianship being a female-intensive occupation and the low status of librarianship. This low status is not inherent in it being female-intensive, she argues, but rather stems from society's devaluing of "women's work," above all, service to others. In other words, if society highly valued service to others, it would value women's work, and consequently the status of librarianship would be elevated.

Harris's conclusion seems indisputable, particularly since it fits as well with female-intensive occupations other than librarianship. But it is only part of the story. Librarianship was, in fact, a low-status occupation before women began to work in libraries. To read the rules of the membership libraries of the eighteenth and nineteenth centuries is to see that the librarian's function was clerical: recording books loaned and returned, accounting for fines, copying out brief records for catalogs, and the like. From the mid-nineteenth century on, some librarians—a very few—were scholars of stature, but, as the chapter title of a work on academic librarianship puts it, librarians have traditionally had "neither power nor dignity."[15] Thus, there was not a golden age of male librarianship that the entry of women brought to an end.

For men, though, the entry of women brought about a shinier, even if not golden, era, since it created a two-tiered structure in libraries: an elite, comprised of males, and their female subordinates. When women entered the low-status occupation of librarianship they did so at the lowest level. They were not even heads of small libraries, positions in which there is inevitably some degree of independence. The first women employees of libraries were hired to do low-level work in institutions headed by men. The first library to hire women was, it seems, the Boston Athenaeum (in 1857), and Harvard followed not long after, in 1859, apparently shortly after the Boston Public Library had also begun to employ women. The motivation was, of course, not altruistic, nor did it have anything to do with feminism. Quite the contrary. Inexpensive labor was needed at Harvard to copy off lists of books to be ordered under an expanded acquisitions program, and the women were so satisfactory that they were engaged to produce from scratch the public card catalog that was needed to record those books after receipt.[16]

The entry of significant numbers of women into librarianship to do the low-level work of the institution, work that was particularly susceptible to management, virtually required a hierarchical library organization given the nineteenth-century mentality, and the gender difference must have contributed to a great gap between the "library assistants" and senior management or "the boss." What began in the nineteenth century has continued. In fact, a European observer of American libraries in 1936 found a striking contrast in this respect between libraries in this country and those in Europe.[17] Allen Veaner, the author of a recent book on academic library administration, describes these organizations as follows:

> As recently as the 1930s the academic library was still virtually autonomous and highly self-sufficient, in some ways resembling a feudal barony, or manor house. An early example of vertical integration, a manor had everything it needed to sustain itself completely, and, for stability, a rigidly hierarchical system of governance. The lord of the manor presided over all.[18]

After quoting from Henri Fayol, the influential French management theorist from early in this century, Veaner describes libraries as places in which "management knows all and commands all" and in which "it is the duty of subordinates, like children, to know their places and to obey." Although Veaner places the "manor" in the past, he also argues that it is difficult in an academic setting to build loyalty through teamwork and to promote high regard for all levels of employees, since the college or university in which the library functions is itself highly stratified and elitist.[19]

The historian can flesh out Veaner's broadly drawn picture. When Justin Winsor came to Harvard in 1877 from the Boston Public Library, he began a book in which he listed "orders" for those who worked in the library; this asserted his full control over hours of work and absences and seemed above all aimed at making sure that women did not gossip during working hours.[20] Twenty-five years later, in 1902, the same mind-set that had led to Winsor's rules still existed at Harvard, and the rules were looked upon so favorably that they were deemed worthy of widespread dissemination, as William H. Tillinghast, assistant librarian at Harvard, did in "Some General Rules and Suggestions for a Library Staff" in *Library Journal*.[21] His first general rule was: "Begin work promptly, avoid interruption so far as possible, stop promptly at the closing hour. The entries on the time card are to be the times of actually beginning and quitting work, not the times of entering or leaving the building."

All of this is, in a sense, unexceptionable. After all, it is desirable that one avoid interruption, and there is nothing wrong with beginning work promptly, but the tone suggests male administrators controlling female subordinates—and, indeed, the subordinates were female. Moreover, a rule about stopping work "promptly" shows that the library assistants were certainly not professional, not even in the nation's largest academic library. Shiflett points out that Harvard was not alone.[22]

The crucial mechanism, therefore, through which the presence of women has lowered the stature of librarianship may not be society's devaluation of women's work—though no one could deny its role—as much as the fact that the presence of women led to the development and long continuation of organizations in which the power of the head librarian was enhanced and made more "natural" by the gender difference between the managers and those being managed. And further, that organizational pattern has worked in symbiosis with the historic deprivation of a voice for women to produce an occupational group that focused on the task at hand, carried out the rules and policies of others, and did not assert its role in the wider communities in which it existed. The introduction of innovation, public discussion of the overall direction of the library, entering into dialogue with the library's public—all of these were the role of the chief librarian and an assistant or two. As Veaner noted, the feudal lord wants obedience.

The argument put forth here—that hierarchical organizations have limited the role of most librarians and have been crucial to the low status of librarianship—is different from Harris's view. It is also more optimistic, for though it seems difficult, it may be easier to change organizational patterns than society's values. That, however, is not the reason for adopting it: the evidence is. Service has not historically been denigrated in librarianship as women's work. In fact, service was well rooted in librarianship before large numbers of librarians were women.

The tradition of service developed in American libraries in part because some types of libraries had to provide service if they were to survive. This was true of the membership libraries that flourished from the late eighteenth century to the latter part of the nineteenth. These were libraries in which one bought shares and paid an annual fee, or to which one subscribed annually. These included, among others, athenaeums, mercantile libraries, young men's libraries, mechanics' libraries, and apprentices' libraries.[23] To survive it was necessary to provide the books that were wanted and give easy access to them. The very short hours of academic libraries were not typical. For example, in 1820 the Athenaeum of Philadelphia was open from 8 A.M. to 10 P.M., from the first of November to the first of May, and from the first of May to the first of November from 7 A.M. to 10 P.M., every day of the week except Sunday.[24] To be sure, libraries generally did not have the financial means to be open such long hours, but this example illustrates the desire.

When publicly-financed libraries began in the second half of the nineteenth century, they competed with the membership libraries, not for public funding but for readers and, ultimately, for the continued support of the community. That the nature of the existing institutions was crucial is evident by comparison with France. There, after the Revolution, the *dépôts* of confiscated books became the various municipal libraries. Not only were these institutions without competitors and without pressure to attract readers, their existence formed an obstacle to the formation of another kind of publicly-financed library, i.e., popular libraries.[25]

The ideology behind the formation of the new kind of library, the publicly-financed library, also led to a service orientation. Public libraries were seen to be, variously, a means of elevating the lower classes through good reading and by providing sources of information that would help the working man in his trade, of keeping peace between the classes, of inculcating democratic values in immigrants, of promoting civic virtue, and the like.[26] Such are important reasons for libraries to exist, sufficiently so that those responsible for the libraries could see themselves to be missionaries with a special calling.

These missionaries, these people who struggled to find ever more creative ways to be of service to the community as a whole—and to individuals—included Theresa Hubbell West, Minerva Amanda Sanders, and Mary Salome Cutler; but among the number were also William Eaton Foster, Frederic Beecher Perkins, James Mascarene Hubbard, Frederick Morgan Crunden, Sam Walter Foss, and Samuel Swett Green, the last remembered as a pioneer in providing library service to children.[27] To be sure, women provided the service, but men were also imbued with the missionary spirit that lay behind library service to various constituencies.

Men could also recognize that the actual provision of service began with the little things and with the right attitude. Here, for example, is the conclusion to an address delivered in 1884 by Moses Coit Tyler, professor of American history at Cornell University:

> And that public library is never a complete success, in which is not present in the officers a spirit of courtesy toward readers, of sympathy, of cheerfulness, of patience, even of helpfulness. Don't permit your library ever to be a dismal, bibliographical cave, in charge of a dragon. Let it always be a bright and winsome place, hospitable to all orderly people; a place where even those ill-informed about books will not be made embarrassed, but encouraged. Let it be one

of the most attractive places in town; let it outshine in attractiveness the vulgar and harmful attractions of the bar-room and the gambling den; let it grow up into the best life of the community, a place resorted to by all, loved by all, a blessing to all.[28]

The ideal of service is pervasive, moreover, not just among public librarians. It is also present, sometimes to a greater or lesser degree but present nonetheless, in libraries in institutions of higher education, in rare book collections, in the Library of Congress, in independent research libraries, and in historical societies. What began as a public library ideal moved over into these other kinds of libraries. Clearly important in this process was Justin Winsor, who in 1877 came from the Boston Public Library to Harvard and very quickly increased its circulation significantly. It can be argued, therefore, that American librarians of all varieties have been united by a fundamental value.

That the ideal of service is a female value, that society does not esteem female values, and that therein is the source of the low status of librarians—this line of reasoning, put forward so well by Roma Harris, is perhaps relevant to librarianship today, but it does not fit the days of the "public library movement." The ideal was not then gender-based, and still librarians were concerned with status.

It is not service per se that has been at the root of librarians' low status. Rather, it is the devaluing of a particular kind of knowledge work—the dissemination of knowledge. The creation of knowledge has over the last 100 to 150 years come to be the most esteemed aspect of knowledge work. This can be seen in the fact that American institutions of higher education have been transformed from institutions whose function was solely to pass on, i.e., disseminate, knowledge to ones whose claim to importance lies primarily in the creation of knowledge, the more "pure," the more highly esteemed. Of course, the transformation entailed some conflict within academe. As Bledstein put it: "Academics themselves obstructed progress toward greater professionalization and higher standards. Mediocre professors in American colleges preferred to view their efforts as administrative and supervisory rather than intellectual."[29] The battle to transform the college into the research university necessarily entailed denigrating dissemination, and an occupation focused on dissemination found itself allied with the loser.[30] Dissemination was not even the worst of it. Furnishing a means of entertainment through provision of fiction was, of course, even lower on the scale of values.

The denigration of knowledge dissemination is historically conditioned; as a value, it is not inherently inferior to knowledge creation. Librarians' emphasis on practice and technique has, however, worked to reinforce the sense that knowledge dissemination is inferior to knowledge creation, for it has limited the librarian's role in knowledge dissemination. Just as there are different methods of knowledge creation, so can there be different sorts of knowledge dissemination. Throughout most of this century librarians have basically been passive in disseminating knowledge. To be sure, librarians have carried out all sorts of campaigns to attract people to libraries and to books, but librarians have not pursued an active, intellectual role in providing access to the contents of material. What is meant by this can be clarified by looking at proposals by two individuals who have publicly called for a knowledge-based librarianship.

One of the first to call for librarians to be active partners of the scholar and student was Herbert Baxter Adams, professor of history at Johns Hopkins, who in 1887, in a paper delivered to librarians at the ALA's Thousand Islands conference, pointed out that at Columbia "there is a special librarian of the historical and political sciences, who gives an annual course of lectures upon the bibliography of his department to members of the School of Political Science, thus teaching students the ways and means of inquiry in their particular field. This librarian is stationed at the entrance to the political science section of the main library, and there serves as an efficient mediator between men and books."[31] Note that Adams is calling here for a true specialist librarian. He also states: "It is not enough that a great library should be able to deliver on call a single book.... That ideal is good so far as it goes. It is a good thing to be able to find the needle in the haystack; but it is a much finer thing to be able to gather quickly all the needle-guns from a great armory and equip a band of trained men instantly with all that they need for the advancement of science."[32] He seemed to have in mind that librarians would do this, and he quite accurately perceived that librarians generally have seen their role as providing access to individual books rather than to content.

Adams also holds up for public librarians the ideal of a similar kind of service, and in doing so he points to the essential unity of librarianship:

My plea to American librarians is to popularize the seminary method. Set apart special rooms where classes and clubs can meet under competent direction for the special use of books. Convert your library into a popular laboratory. . . . It is not enough to connect public libraries with the work of public schools. You must connect your institutions with the educational wants of the people. There should be in every great community organized instruction, through public libraries, for the graduates of public schools, for persons past the school age, for mechanics and the working classes in general.[33]

Another proposal, one of the most carefully reasoned and written works in the entirety of library literature, is by William S. Learned, an official of the Carnegie Corporation. His *The American Public Library and the Diffusion of Knowledge*[34] may also be the work that most challenges librarians.[35] Learned begins by stating that it is "often largely a matter of one's social philosophy or temperament as to which [advancement or diffusion] is considered to be of the greater importance" and that in many respects diffusion is the "more difficult function." It is also highly important, for a programmatic diffusion of knowledge can "secure solidarity of thought and action through the general inculcation of a set of common ideas." Learned seems to take for granted that this goal will meet with universal approval, though in our day it is controversial. More modern sounding is his belief that the masses of information make "imperative some means of selection, digest, or abridgment whereby any one who needs them may gain possession of essential facts without delay and without discouraging or prohibitive effort." Although he speaks here of "facts" as being neutral, he emphasizes that knowledge must be adapted to the needs of the recipient. Without that, there is not effective consumption of knowledge, and, consequently, "the daily losses in energy and material that result from sheer ignorance on the part of otherwise intelligent persons of how to avail themselves of the contents of books must be colossal beyond all calculation." What is needed is a "Community Intelligence Service," a "conspicuous and indispensable feature of [which]. . .is a well-specialized personal service. . . ." It must supply "just the information required in the form in which it can best be utilized by the person in question and in a manner that invites repetition." Doing so "is a task for an expert possessing personal tact, quick intellectual sympathies and appreciation, a thorough knowledge of a certain field of material, precision and discrimination of thought, and the power promptly to organize results." Learned believed that "public servants of this quality and capacity would soon hold an exceptional place in any community" and that serving in such a capacity "could not fail to appeal powerfully to capable men and women."

Learned recognized that "in the great majority of cases the existing library service is. . .a totally different phenomenon," but he advocated that the ALA, "through the simple extension of its editorial and publishing function alone, [could] become supremely useful to America's vast system of libraries and other educational institutions by supplying an intelligent agency for organizing their printed materials. It should have a staff qualified to take a mass of important verified fact, say from child-welfare organizations, and as a result of its experience, to advise as to the forms of presentation best calculated to reach the largest possible public. It should have funds wherewith to command the services of the leaders in literature, art, science, and public life for such authoritative and convincing treatment of books or groups of books as would charge reading with powerful interest. . . ." Learned believed that such work "could be done as well by no other institution" than the ALA. It would produce materials that help libraries to carry out the personal teaching, for the "free library, as a civic unit, is fitted, beyond any other institution that we possess, to undertake that task." He goes on to state that the "essential factor in enabling a library to perform this greater function is an adequately large and competent personnel" and that all education requires "sufficient personal direction."

Learned envisioned a crucial role for the American Library Association; it did not take him up on it. That would have taken a significant shift in an organization whose energies have been devoted to a very considerable extent to the politics of librarianship. The very title of Wiegand's previously-cited book, *The Politics of an Emerging Profession,* suggests this. In fact, Wiegand's beautifully detailed work is full of maneuvering by various constituencies for influence within the ALA: Western librarians versus Eastern, public librarians versus academic, rural librarians versus urban librarians; while at the same time the ALA has struggled to be the umbrella organization for all librarians.

Sometimes this has actually required that debate be stifled. For instance, at the ALA conference of 1898 Dewey used his position as secretary to allocate five minutes to each speaker and to keep them within that limit. At the same time more section meetings were deliberately planned in order to keep specialized interests under the ALA umbrella, thus making for sidelined debate.[36] To give another example, before the Atlanta conference of 1899, the question was raised about the possibility of a session on the library's role in educating African Americans, and W. E. B. Du Bois was even suggested as a speaker, but the idea died for fear of controversy.[37]

Some would argue that the ALA is not much different today, that organizational imperatives serve to stifle or marginalize debate. Cronin, cited earlier, would go even further: "It is nothing short of ludicrous that the organization's meager resources should be squandered on patently pyrrhic efforts to shape social and political issues."[38] In fact, there is so little readily available information that it is difficult to determine where resources go. In the journal of the ALA, *American Libraries,* almost no financial information is present.

The past continues to play itself out in the present, both with respect to the ALA, as Blaise Cronin suggests, and in other ways as well. Librarianship is, in a sense, being ever more closely coupled with technique, as can be judged by the *Chronicle of Higher Education.* The advertisements for vacancies show that in institution after institution one person is wanted to head both the library and computing services. This clearly offers university administrators a way to balance budgets by draining off resources from the library, but it links librarianship with a field in which the majority of people, though highly skilled, focus on narrow tasks.[39]

The continuing closing of library schools, fourteen between 1978 and 1991, also limits the opportunities to develop intellectual leaders.[40] As Blaise Cronin argues: "the annual production of doctoral graduates is so tiny that the field lacks genetic variety and, historically at least, is prone to inbreeding. The problem, in other words, is not a shortage of substantive topics or research issues, nor, indeed, lack of demand for library and information science graduates, but the lack of a *cadre* of first-rate faculty to address these issues, and exploit the field's comparative advantage."[41] No reason exists to doubt his view that the closings will have a cumulative effect in the long run. One of them may well be "the progressive decoupling of librarianship programs from information science/information management programs, leading, eventually, to a two-tier educational system."[42]

Information science and librarianship ought not to be decoupled. To look through the *Journal of the American Society for Information Science* is to see that the methodologies and insights of those who term themselves information scientists should have an important role in the management of libraries. Indeed, it is the price of the journal, nearly $700, that serves to limit the influence of an approach having much to offer. Information science is, however, practical in its focus. In fact, a leading theoretician of information science, Pertti Vakkari, emphasizes the practical goal of information science: "Information science has been characterized from the outset as being purpose minded. Although its name has been changed through documentation from library science to information science, its raison d'être has always rested on the support it provides for certain practical activity."[43]

Here still today is the emphasis on practice and on science—knowledge creation or research—but the term "information science" is problematic. Not only is the term an attempt to gain respectability in the research university, it is suspect and for that reason is likely to fail in that aim. Just as there is not a science of libraries any more than there is a science of hospitals, the study of information, however mathematical and theoretical it may be, is not science in the classical sense. In fact, in the essay cited above, Vakkari considers another work that gets around this by the claim that information science is postmodern science, that it is not "about the nature of things but strategies to deal with problems."[44] A broader term that would further inclusion rather than exclusion would be "information studies." It could then encompass scholarship in the burgeoning field of the history of the book, a growing aspect of which is the study of reading.[45]

* * *

This account does not reveal a list of culprits. We cannot put the blame on Dewey. Accordingly, a recent article in *American Libraries* errs when it states in a sectional head that "Dewey led us astray."[46] Similarly, it would have been absolutely extraordinary if the hierarchical structure of libraries had been avoided. And as for the ALA, its leadership certainly did face the possibility of the fragmentation of librarianship into specialist and regional groups. Moreover, librarians themselves are not to blame and certainly are not responsible for the fact that society has valued knowledge creation over knowledge dissemination.

Rather than culprits, this account shows a variety of factors that combined to produce an occupational group whose isolation and focus on technique has kept it from producing people deemed to be capable of heading the major cultural institutions that are our greatest libraries. The question is whether the mix can be turned around or perhaps is actually changing.

One positive sign is that library administrators are now calling for a broader education, if a recent meeting of Boston-area practicing librarians and Professor Jerry Miller of the Simmons College School of Library and Information Science is representative. At the meeting, which took place in early March 1996, the practicing librarians, taking library skills for granted, called for the development of analytical skills, an understanding of the interrelatedness of every decision in today's complex libraries, an awareness of the import of financial constraints, attitudes that will enable today's graduates to be teachers of the faculty, an awareness of the whole, and the inculcation of professional attitudes, including furtherance of the desire to provide service. What these library administrators want cannot be termed theory over practice, but it certainly is a step in the direction of forming librarians with broad understanding. This is a characteristic that is essential to institutional change.

Librarians are also questioning the hierarchical institutions that libraries have been. Notable is the library of the University of Arizona-Tucson, where senior management has taken the initiative of moving "away from a staff performing narrow tasks within tightly defined job descriptions, according to prescribed policies and procedures, to one empowered to make the daily decisions about what work to do and how to do it in a way that resulted in delighted customers, the elimination of unnecessary tasks, constantly improving processes, and the fulfillment of library strategic objectives." To accomplish this requires organizational change:

> The roles of the director, assistant directors, and department heads must change from managers, controllers, directors of activities, deciders, and evaluators to leaders, coaches, and facilitators. All these administrators must be willing to give up a great deal of decision-making authority and become much more comfortable with being challenged, having to explain, not having the last say, and living with ambiguity and uncertainty. They will no longer be experts and have sole control of information.[47]

Even if libraries do not generally go the way of the University of Arizona-Tucson—or go so far in its direction of thoroughly undergoing fundamental transformation—change may be coming, though the threat of downsizing and "reengineering" is a countervailing force to wider adoption of the Arizona model. The Arizona model was much discussed at the conference "Finding Common Ground," which was held at Harvard on March 30 and 31, 1996. Interest in participation in that conference, and the reaction to it, exceeded expectations, which is a sign that librarians want more opportunities for substantial discussion than they are getting from the American Library Association. Regardless of whether the ALA will change or whether there will be further extra-ALA conferences, the desire is present for intense exploration of the important issues facing librarianship.

Another positive sign is that librarianship is continuing to attract large numbers of talented individuals. In the past librarianship drew individuals of a higher quality than the status and rewards justified, and this is a major reason why American libraries have been institutions to be praised. In writing this, I am referring especially to the large numbers of talented women. That librarianship attracted such people is clearly stated in the concluding chapter of Alice I. Bryan's book, *The Public Librarian*,[48] one of the volumes of the report of the Public Library Inquiry:

> It [librarianship] was one of the first occupations requiring formal higher education and technical skill in which women could rise unhampered to the top executive posts. Historically, the high quality

of library service. . .may be due in large part to the real opportunities for advancement and administrative leadership that librarianship offered women as compared with other occupations open to them.[49]

Personal observation indicates that the women's movement has continued to bring talented women into librarianship. Because so many other occupations are open to women—and provide greater financial rewards—one might wonder whether this will continue. That it has is perhaps a sign that libraries are changing and that the nature of the work is becoming ever more complex and challenging.

The technology that can bring increasing quantities of information into every study, office, and home is at the same time heightening the complexity of research. It may be that the distinction between knowledge production and knowledge dissemination, never as clear in practice as in terms of values, is breaking down. At the very least the complexity of supplying the needed information is clear.

This may be one reason why Harvard faculty members at the "Finding Common Ground" conference called for a closer alliance between faculty and librarians. The historical antagonism between scholars and librarians may also be breaking down.[50] When it does, faculty tend to become proponents of an intellectually-based librarianship, just as Adams and Learned were.

Similarly, when the traditional antagonism diminishes, librarians are freed up to advocate for a more intellectual staff. In fact, one of the greatest librarians of this century, Keyes D. Metcalf, a library school graduate who was director of the Harvard University Library from 1937 to 1955, recognized the need for an intellectually-based librarianship. On January 8, 1938, Metcalf wrote to Charles Warren, chairman of the Visiting Committee of the Board of Overseers, who was questioning Metcalf's wish to appoint William A. Jackson both as a professor and as a librarian in charge of the rare books of the Harvard College Library:

> Your letter asks specifically about the need for a new professorship. The Library staff should include, as it has in the past, at least one man with professorial rank as part of his title (later there should be several of these positions). This is in connection with my effort to knit the library and the faculty together so that the latter will take

full advantage of the resources of the former. The Library, to perform its proper function in the University, should be the best possible service organization, and should also take its place as a productive unit. Without men of faculty rank and calibre on its staff, this will not result. In my opinion university libraries in general, in spite of their much advertised claims of being the heart of their respective universities, have been mediocre in character, this being largely due to their not having employed first-rate men to help open their doors to the faculty and students who are doing distinctive work.[51]

Metcalf appointed Jackson. His broader hope was not realized, yet this letter clearly articulates the need and a means of accomplishing it. Note that Metcalf did not write about improving the status of librarians. Instead, his goal was to have libraries that fulfill their functions fully by means of being institutions of high quality and having librarians of high caliber.

Having a large cadre of librarians who are functioning in creative and intellectual ways must continue to be the goal. The fact that our major libraries are not entrusted to librarians shows that it has not been met.

* * *

I would like to conclude on a personal note, for I am well aware that my essay is shaped by my career. In fact, its title might just as well have been "A Practicing Librarian Looks at Librarianship." In 1959 I began library work as an attendant in the reading room and the stacks of the Houghton Library at Harvard, and a couple of years later I attended library school at the urging of William A. Jackson, Houghton's librarian. For most of the years since then I have been employed by or at Harvard in various of its libraries. From the first, in Houghton, I have been keenly conscious of the possibilities of an intellectually-based librarianship, and colleagues in other Harvard libraries have only reinforced this.

One is Lorna M. Daniells of Baker Library at the Harvard Business School, now retired, who has served librarians, business school students and faculty, and perhaps even practicing businessmen throughout the country with her *Business Information Sources*.[52] Another example is Charles Berlin, Lee M. Friedman Bibliographer in Judaica and Head of the Judaica Division. His contribution is different from that of Lorna Daniells's in that it lies in building a collection—in his case, on Israel, with such insight that the result may be the most complete documentation in existence of a culture. A last example—though there could be others—is Cheryl LaGuardia, Coordinator of the Electronic Teaching Center in the Harvard College Library. This relatively new colleague regularly displays in *Library Journal* her virtuosity in navigating and evaluating new CD-ROMs, and her writings have no doubt improved the quality of products in this medium.

In giving these examples, I seek to demonstrate concretely that this essay is not simply about the need for librarians to produce scholarly papers in learned journals in the traditional academic disciplines, though personally I am well aware that doing so has helped to shape my work as a librarian. All kinds of paths exist for an intellectually-based librarianship, and they certainly include colleagues such as Michael Kaplan, whose work on catalogers' workstations is bearing fruit at Harvard and elsewhere.

These examples ought not to lull us into complacently thinking that the historical obstacles have been overcome. Instead, I mention these individuals to suggest possibilities for librarians to contribute in intellectual ways to the dissemination of knowledge outside their local institution—and to urge that ways be found to populate our libraries with such individuals and increase their number.

Today's changes in technology and society make the need for such librarians greater than ever. But librarians, however much they need to debate and struggle among themselves to meet society's needs for knowledge dissemination, must also welcome, nondefensively, the participation of non-librarians. All of society has a stake in such matters, and the good of society must be the goal. Only with that focus—not the status of librarians—will librarians better contribute to filling those needs. At the same time, perhaps only then will no parent have a daughter at work on a college application turn and say, "Daddy, do I have to put down that you're a librarian?" She might even aspire to follow in her father's steps.

ENDNOTES

[1] The large literature on the status of librarians demonstrates these points. Two authors who describe reasons for the low status of American librarians and outline strategies to cope with or improve their status are George E. Bennett, *Librarians in Search of Science and Identity: The Elusive Profession* (Metuchen, N.J.: Scarecrow Press, Inc., 1988), and Roma M. Harris, *Librarianship: The Erosion of a Woman's Profession* (Norwood, N.J.: Ablex Publishing Corporation, 1992). Essays in periodicals continue to come out, including, as of this writing, Bill Crowley, "Redefining the Status of the Librarian in Higher Education," *College & Research Libraries* 57 (2) (March 1996): 113–121.

[2] Melvil Dewey, *Librarianship as a Profession for College-Bred Women* (Boston, Mass.: Library Bureau, 1886), 10, quoted in Orvin Lee Shiflett, *Origins of American Academic Librarianship* (Norwood, N.J.: Ablex Publishing Corporation, 1981), 254.

[3] "Significance of Primary Records," *Professions* 95 (1995): 27–50.

[4] A reason for optimism is that some librarians did seek involvement, and there was a panel of librarians at the MLA, though too late to affect the statement. A reason for lack of optimism is that since publication of the MLA statement, no discussion of it has appeared, it seems, in the library literature. This "stony silence" is reminiscent of a statement in the preface to Roma Harris's work already cited: "Whenever I have spoken about the undervaluing of library work being a product of its gender nature, I am greeted, as often as not, by stony silence. . . . At my own peril, perhaps, I have decided to ignore those who will, no doubt, disapprove of feminist analysis of library work." What is striking about this statement are the phrases "stony silence," "at my own peril," and "feminist analysis." In other words, Harris finds that librarians often erect a wall within librarianship against an analysis that they do not like and that to breach the defense entails danger.

[5] A more extensive list of symptoms of the malaise in librarianship was put forth in the keynote presentation at the Association of Library and Information Science Education in February 1995 by Blaise Cronin, dean of the School of Library and Information Science at Indiana University: "Fundamentalism, inertia, resistance to change, fetishism, inbreeding, feminization, censorship, social activism, clutching at straws, and intimations of xenophobia constitute the principal elements in a dispiritingly self-critical catalog of what is awry in the LIS [Library and Information Science] field." See Blaise Cronin, "Shibboleth and Substance in North American Library and Information Science Education," *Libri* 45 (1995): 55.

[6] It may well be that librarianship has not commonly attracted individuals with the intellectual and social capacities to lead important cultural institutions, whereas the essay focuses on other structural and societal factors that prevent such leadership from developing within librarianship or from being perceived as existing.

[7] Burton J. Bledstein, *The Culture of Professionalism: The Middle Class and the Development of Higher Education in America* (New York: W. W. Norton & Co., 1978), 77. See the section "Words and the Communications Revolution," 65–79, esp. 78–79.

[8]See Wayne Wiegand, "Catalog of 'A.L.A.' Library (1893): Origins of a Genre," in *For the Good of the Order: Essays in Honor of Edward G. Holley,* ed. Delmus E. Williams, John M. Budd and others (Greenwich, Conn.: JAI Press Inc., 1994), 237–254.

[9]A most illuminating account can be found in Wayne Wiegand, *Irrepressible Reformer: A Biography of Melvil Dewey* (Chicago, Ill.: American Library Association, 1996); unfortunately, this book was not available for use in writing this essay. Useful works are Sarah K. Vann, *Training for Librarianship Before 1923* (Chicago, Ill.: American Library Association, 1961), and Carl M. White, *A Historical Introduction to Library Education: Problems and Progress to 1951* (Metuchen, N.J.: The Scarecrow Press, Inc., 1976).

[10]Columbia College, Library, School of Library Economy, "Circular of Information, 18986–7," in *School of Library Economy of Columbia College 1887–1889: Documents for a History* (New York: Columbia University, School of Library Service, 1937), 99, as quoted in Shiflett, *Origins of American Academic Librarianship,* 183. Shiflett notes that Dewey devoted an hour to discussing fountain pens. Ibid., 186.

[11]"Report of the Superintendent," in *Seventeenth Annual Report of the Trustees of the Public Library,* Boston, 1869, p. 28. The American Social Science Association's transcription is not totally accurate.

[12]Vann, *Training for Librarianship Before 1923,* 8–9.

[13]Wayne Wiegand, *The Politics of an Emerging Profession: The American Library Association, 1876–1917* (New York and Westport, Conn.: Greenwood Press, 1986), 242.

[14]Harris, *Librarianship: The Erosion of a Woman's Profession,* uses this term throughout her work.

[15]Shiflett, *Origins of American Academic Librarianship,* chap. 5, 221–269. Shiflett, in his well-researched and written work, describes academic librarianship as he sees it, rather than as he and academic librarians wish it were.

[16]A paper by Barbara A. Mitchell, forthcoming in the *Harvard Library Bulletin,* will recount in detail the early history of women at the Harvard Library.

[17]"The Staff," in Wilhelm Munthe, *American Librarianship from a European Angle: An Attempt at an Evaluation of Policies and Activities* (Chicago, Ill.: American Library Association, 1939), 161–173. Munthe describes the American library as resembling a "large retail store with an army of young clerks and shopgirls and a relatively small group of 'floorwalkers' and 'heads.'" Ibid., 162. He also uses the term "boss" to refer to the head librarian. The expression "library assistants" is employed here because of its prevalence in Jessie Sargent McNiece, *The Library and Its Workers* (New York: H. W. Wilson Company, 1929), Classics of American Librarianship, 7. It should be noted that the American style of organization has permitted the "leadership" (Munthe points out that the quality of leadership is more widely written about in the United States) to act with great freedom, which can be highly positive.

[18]Allen B. Veaner, *Academic Librarianship in a Transformational Age: Program, Politics, and Personnel* (Boston, Mass.: G. K. Hall, 1990), 3.

[19]Ibid., see esp. 331.

[20]See Kenneth E. Carpenter, *The First 350 Years of the Harvard University Library* (Cambridge, Mass.: Harvard University Library, 1986), 105; also Joseph Alfred Borome, "The Life and Letters of Justin Winsor," dissertation, Columbia University, 1950, 265, 364–367, as cited in Shiflett, *Origins of American Academic Librarianship*, 224, 265.

[21]Tillinghast's essay appeared in *Library Journal* 27 (1902): 871–875. This essay is reprinted in McNiece, *The Library and Its Workers*, 211–226. See also Shiflett, *Origins of American Academic Librarianship*, 225.

[22]Shiflett, *Origins of American Academic Librarianship*, 225–226.

[23]On these libraries, see Jesse Shera, *Foundations of the Public Library* (Chicago, Ill.: University of Chicago Press, 1949).

[24]Athenaeum of Philadelphia, "Rules and Regulations" and "Of the Rooms," in *Charter and By-Laws of the Athenaeum of Philadelphia. . .Together with a Catalogue of the Books, Maps, &c.* (Philadelphia, Pa.: W. Fry, 1820), 17–18.

[25]Laure Léveillé, "Fascinations étrangères et naissance de la lecture publique," in *Histoire des bibliothèques françaises: Les bibliothèques au XXe siècle, 1914–1990* (Paris: Promodis-Editions du Cercle de la Librairie, 1992), 155–177. The difference is also made clear by the fact that a French library association was formed in 1906 (Association des bibliothécaires français), but it was felt necessary to form in 1936 another association for what in the French context has to be called "popular" libraries, as opposed to "public" libraries (Association pour le développement de la lecture publique).

[26]It is not necessary here to wade into the debate of the 1970s between Dee Garrison, Michael Harris, and others over the real motives behind establishing public libraries. Whether altruistic or hegemonic, those who supported public libraries wanted them used.

[27]The individuals cited here all had papers reprinted in *The Library and Society*, ed. Arthur E. Bostwick (New York: H. W. Wilson Co., 1920), Classics of American Librarianship.

[28]Moses Coit Tyler, "The Historical Evolution of the Free Public Library in America and Its True Function in the Community," in Bostwick, *The Library and Society*, 32. This was an address delivered at the dedication of the Sage Library at West Bay City, Michigan.

[29]Bledstein, *The Culture of Professionalism: The Middle Class and the Development of Higher Education in America*, 283.

[30]Ironically, the claim that librarians teach and should consequently have faculty status actually reinforces librarians' identification with the "inferior" aspect of the professoriat.

[31]Herbert Baxter Adams, "Seminary Libraries and University Extension," in *Seminary Libraries and University Extension*, Johns Hopkins University Studies in Historical and Political Science, 5th series, XI (Baltimore, Md.: Johns Hopkins University, 1887), 17. Other essays are included under the general title. By "seminary," Adams refers to what we today call "seminar."

[32]Ibid., 19–20.

[33]Adams, "Seminary Libraries for the People," in Ibid., 21.

[34]William S. Learned, *The American Public Library and the Diffusion of Knowledge* (New York: Harcourt, Brace and Co., 1924).

[35]Carl M. White, *A Historical Introduction to Library Education: Problems and Progress to 1951* (Metuchen, N.J.: Scarecrow Press, Inc., 1976), 168, notes that Learned's work played a role in the Carnegie Foundation's investment in library education, and, indeed, Learned advocated, among various specific steps, adequate support for the professional preparation of librarians and for the training of library staffs.

[36]Wiegand, *The Politics of an Emerging Profession*, 102–104.

[37]Ibid., 109.

[38]Cronin, "Shibboleth and Substance in North American Library and Information Science Education," 50.

[39]To have the librarian in charge of computing is preferable to the reverse, to be sure, for then the librarian has control over the means by which information will increasingly be delivered. What now appears to be contrary to an intellectual librarianship may not be so in the long run.

[40]For a detailed analysis of the elements involved in closing the library schools, see Marion Paris, Herbert S. White, Margaret F. Stieg, Daniel D. Barron, Kathleen M. Heim, J. Keith Ostertag, and Jeffrey Katzer, "Perspectives on the Elimination of Graduate Programs in Library and Information Studies: A Symposium," *Library Quarterly* 61 (1991): 259–292.

[41]Cronin, "Shibboleth and Substance in North American Library and Information Science Education," 54–55.

[42]Ibid., 60.

[43]See Pertti Vakkari, "Library and Information Science: Its Content and Scope," *Advances in Librarianship* 18 (1994): 1–55.

[44]Ibid., 46. The work referred to by Vakkari is "Information Science and Theory: A Weaver Bird's Perspective," in *Conceptions of Library and Information Science,* ed. P. Vakkari and B. Cronin (London and Los Angeles, Calif.: Graham Taylor, 1992), 201–217.

[45]Vakkari is wrong in asserting that "the number of scholars doing research on book and library history has decreased considerably." Vakkari, "Library and Information Science," 15. For example, the Society for the History of Authorship, Reading & Publishing has become so successful that it is beginning a journal. Multi-volume histories of the book and of libraries are being undertaken in countries around the world, and the scholarship of such figures as Roger Chartier, Robert Darnton, and Natalie Zemon Davis is translated and widely disseminated. The number of college courses on the history of the book seem also to be on the rise.

[46]Larry J. Oastler and Therrin C. Dahlin, "Library Education: Setting or Rising Sun?," *American Libraries* (July/August 1995): 683–684.

[47]Carla J. Stoffle, Robert Renaud, and Jerilyn R. Veldof, "Choosing Our Futures," *College & Research Libraries* 57 (1996): 223. Susan Lee, Bonnie Juergens, and Richard Hume Werking, "Commentaries on Choosing Our Futures," was also published in the same issue.

[48]Alice I. Bryan, *The Public Librarian* (New York: Columbia University Press, 1952), 436–437.

[49]The omitted phrase is "in relation to very modest salary rewards." It is possible that the same could be said about gays and lesbians whose opportunities were less in the pre-Stonewall days.

[50]For essays on this topic, see R. H. Logsdon, "The Librarian and the Scholar: Eternal Enemies," *Library Journal* 95 (1970): 2871–2874, and Mary Biggs, "Sources of Tension and Conflict between Librarians and Faculty," *Journal of Higher Education* 52 (1981): 182–201.

[51]*Records of a Bibliographer: Selected Papers of William Alexander Jackson,* edited with an Introduction and Bibliography by William H. Bond (Cambridge, Mass.: The Belknap Press of Harvard University Press, 1967), 1–2 (from the Introduction).

[52]Lorna M. Daniells, *Business Information Sources* (Berkeley, Calif.: University of California Press, 1st ed., 1976; 3d ed., 1993).

Peter R. Young

Librarianship: A Changing Profession

QUESTIONS ABOUT THE FUTURE OF LIBRARIES AND LIBRARIANSHIP

L IKE MANY LIBRARIANS TODAY, I view recent technological developments in information and telecommunication technologies with a mixture of excitement, nervous anxiety,
and paranoia.[1] In 1968, when I graduated from Columbia
University's library school and began working in my first professional position, library managers focused on matters related to
bibliographic control, acquisition of printed resources, and library
collection development. As a graduate student, I took no courses
in information systems retrieval, digital media, or network information infrastructure. In short, I entered librarianship before the
advent of the electronic frontier.

However, my Columbia experience did include lessons about
change. In the spring of 1968, student protesters shut down the
university. Ardent struggles between student radicals, the New
York City Police Department, and campus authorities created an
environment of revolutionary ferment, fanatic change, and passionate struggle. Although these lessons were not part of my graduate
library degree course work, my introduction to librarianship included the challenge, excitement, and exhilaration of witnessing
revolutionary change.

Today, almost three decades after graduating from Columbia, I
continue to confront revolutionary change in my profession. For

Peter R. Young is Executive Director of the US National Commission on Libraries and Information Science.

librarianship and libraries, the pervasive influence of digital computing is transforming the expression and communication of shared ideas and knowledge. When I completed my library school studies three decades ago, computers were just beginning to find their way into the orderly world of libraries. Today, it is almost impossible to identify a library or a librarian that is not affected by computers, digital information, and the electronic network infrastructure. Columbia's library school was unable to successfully manage change, closing its doors a few years ago. Librarians everywhere are concerned about their libraries suffering the same fate.

Unlike my introduction to librarianship, today's library-school graduates encounter an economic and technological landscape where information and communication concerns are intertwined with more traditional library-related issues. Consequently, librarians discuss the changing role of the library in the cultural, social, and economic structure of society. They express concern that the essential nature, values, and practice of librarianship are threatened by change. Increasingly, soft distinctions among library services, interactive media, and information communication networks raise concerns about the roles of libraries in the future.

The popular old-fashioned image of the librarian is of someone who is behind-the-times and far from business-like. Even today, the general public's view of librarians is that we are more concerned about collections than providing services with new information technology. But many librarians have sensed the ground shifting under their sensible shoes. Articles about reforming, reinventing, revising, and restructuring libraries, librarianship, and information studies are common in the professional literature. Even popular media articles are appearing about "Librarians Surfing the 'Net." Librarianship is caught in a sea of dynamic change; preservation, control, and dissemination of recorded knowledge appear to be at risk in a world where uncertainty, contingency, and the transforming nature of electronic media are increasingly dominant.

To some in the field the dynamic pace of change serves as an energizing motivation. These new-age librarian/information specialists embrace new technologies (often with little thought for preserving the past) and are more readily associated with Silicon Valley than with the dusty volumes shelved in many of our oldest and richest collections. I believe that libraries are entering into a challenging new stage of development characterized by an extended transition toward an increasingly electronic information future. Over the next decade librarians will encounter the twin challenges of managing buildings and print collections while simultaneously developing policies, tools, and support for digital collections and network information services. Not all libraries will succeed in meeting these challenges.

Are libraries, librarians, books, and reading in danger of being replaced with the digital confusion of cyberspace? Or will libraries successfully integrate new electronic formats and interactive media? The situation for me is captured by a picture hanging on the wall near the desktop computer I use at my office. To rest my eyes from long hours in front of the glaring screen, I look up at a photograph of my father working at the Library of Congress in the early 1940s. In the picture, my father is standing in the Orientalia Division book stacks, consulting two volumes for his work compiling a biographical dictionary of eminent Chinese.

The choice of professional work involving daily contact with books and other printed resources was a strong motivation for both my father and me in selecting our careers. However, over the past decade, I have spent less time with books and more time with keyboards and computer workstations, utilizing the information technology tools needed to access and download files from information networks, to communicate electronically with colleagues, to reformat files, and to manipulate digital resources. Despite the absence of books in my work, I am comfortable describing myself as a librarian. I sometimes see myself, however, in stark contrast to the photograph of my father at the Library of Congress, surrounded by printed text, quietly consulting ancient Chinese source material. The differences between my own library experience and his make me wonder about the library of the future. Will librarians of the future also have historic reminders displayed in their offices? Will these be books? Will technological change make the past more or less accessible to them than it is to our generation? Will they even be aware of the concerns of earlier generations of librarians?

While these concerns are based on personal experience, similar concerns about the future of libraries in a digital age are reflected in current information policy issues. A few of the doubts and uncertainties that trouble librarians are summarized by the following:

- The impact of recently enacted telecommunications laws on libraries and library users is uncertain, prompting questions about censorship, intellectual freedom, and liability. Will librarians be required to censor patron use of computer networks?
- Librarians and publishers disagree about protecting the copyright of works transmitted digitally and about what constitutes fair use of copyrighted materials. Will library users be charged directly for accessing electronic networked information?
- Congress is planning for the electronic dissemination of government information. Questions about access to print and digital public resources arise: Will printed copies of public documents continue to be available for library patron use?
- Federal grants for the construction of libraries are being redirected for libraries to acquire information technology, and there is concern about future support for library facilities. Will libraries become virtual places, and will librarians be replaced by navigators of cyberspace?

Explorations of the changing role of information in society and the impact of change on the concept of a library are part of an uneven and protracted transition to a future that is increasingly dominated by the fast pace of change set by the electronic information technology industries. Our serious consideration of the future direction and shape of librarianship and of libraries in the postmodern society of the twenty-first century raises fundamental and troubling questions. The following are typical:

- Do libraries have a future? Will they survive the rush to the digital information age? What will libraries look like in the future, and how will they be used?
- How are libraries responding to electronic information technologies? Do recent technological trends threaten libraries?
- How are the changes brought about by electronic information technology restructuring the concept of a library and the role of librarians?

- What forces are changing librarianship? Who are the librarians of the postmodern future and what sort of work will they perform? Are the historic values and principles of the field of librarianship changing?
- Why do we need libraries and librarians in a digital, interactive, multimedia cyberculture of the future where broader bandwidth and exponentially increasing technological change are reshaping the postmodern information-age landscape?

THE EMERGENCE OF A NEW INFORMATION SERVICE PARADIGM

One need not be a librarian to recognize that the emerging electronic frontier presents revolutionary challenges for libraries and librarianship. The traditional relationship between the user and the library involves individuals studying individual works within organized collections. Many of the traditional library tools are designed to guide individual library readers to published works of interest. However, innovative developments in commercial information network services are creating a flood of new information media and service offerings designed to meet the needs of the individual without the assistance or guidance of a librarian.

The inherent nature of digital and interactive network technologies makes analogies to the traditional library paradigm difficult. The introduction of each new interactive electronic information service designed to be used easily and intuitively by customers raises questions about the traditional library mission of facilitating information access and delivery of individual works to individual readers. Who needs a library (or a librarian) if one can access vast information resources with a computer, a modem, and a telephone line? But as experienced users of network information services have found, electronic information is not always as constant or reliable as published text in printed editions. Successive generations of retrieval software, browsers, and new operating system releases, as well as a constant flux of new features and functions, mean that a new paradigm of electronic information has evolved in which concerns about the validity and authenticity of information sources become critical.

The argument goes, however, if commercial on-line services provide seamless, instantaneous access to an increasingly vast array of global digital information resources capable of being accessed and downloaded by individuals for home use, why should libraries continue to serve as repositories for the world's storehouse of knowledge? Why would patrons continue to need librarians to interpret and guide them through collections and library resources? If access to information resources is made simple by dynamic and intelligent software "agents" functioning as knowledge guides, what need is there for librarians in an information age?

Indeed, if you believe corporate claims from the interactive online services industry, networks will soon be able to satisfy any information- or entertainment-access need. If realized, this capability will transform the information-services paradigm. Major shifts in the roles of libraries and librarians are fueled by a transition to a fluid new world of dynamic interactive services available directly from the commercial sector to users. These new information-service offerings are generating a sense of confusion, uncertainty, and crisis in the library and information-services communities. The situation reflects a fundamental reshaping of the basic conceptions about the nature and practice of librarianship. This accounts in part for that feeling of "losing control" that many librarians have about new electronic information services and technologies.

Few would deny that the information world is undergoing a paradigm shift. The current national climate is focused on greater privatization and the development of marketplace solutions to society's changing needs. The federal government is being downsized, consolidated, and reinvented. At the same time, government and industries increasingly demand efficiency in knowledge production and more effective means of information access. Few explanations for shrinking budgets address the need for more timely and comprehensive information to successfully manage the downsizing of information-based organizations. New challenges confront the established structures and familiar assumptions about libraries' roles and how information is generated, transferred, and used.

Numerous recent articles, cartoons, pamphlets, posters, monographs, editorials, and even bumper stickers extol the opportunities created from the confluence of computing and communications technologies. This technological cross-fertilization, it is argued, is responsible for the explosive growth of the global Internet and the World Wide Web, and is fueling a radical social transformation brought on by computer-mediated communications and networked information services. Further, rampant consolidation of media industries and segments by mergers, cross-industry alliances, and complex investment strategies promise to change the nature of the media and information services upon which libraries depend. Even the traditionally minded *New York Times* now devotes a portion of the business section to covering the information media scene, following the example of *Newsweek*'s "cyberspace" column.

Despite recent popularity and hype about the electronic information media's impending transformation of society into a virtual, interactive, multimedia, digital culture, disturbing questions arise about the implications of rapid technological change on the future of libraries and librarianship. For example: How can responsible librarians and library users address the serious underlying issues affecting their institutions and their futures? What transitional strategies are needed for libraries to chart a course from past missions to an uncertain future?

LIBRARIES AND CHANGE: THE CONTEXT

General forces of change confront libraries and society at large in the transition toward global digital information services. Within these general trends, subtle changes are occurring in the nature of information and the expression of knowledge and ideas. These subtle changes provide the subject for sociologists, anthropologists, and ethnographers studying the effects of technology on human behavior, social structures, and institutions.

Understanding the cumulative impact that technological tools are having on our intellectual behavior, our rational skills, and our understanding of the relations between events is a subject of increasingly intense study and debate. I find Sven Birkerts particularly cogent in discussing the fate of reading in an electronic age. Writing in *The Gutenberg Elegies* he notes that:

The advent of the computer and the astonishing sophistication achieved by our electronic communications media have together turned a range of isolated changes into something systemic. The way that people experience the world has altered more in the last fifty years than in the many centuries preceding ours. The eruptions in the early part of our century—the time of world wars and emergent modernity—were premonitions of a sort. Since World War II we have stepped, collectively, out of an ancient and familiar solitude and into an enormous web of imponderable linkages. We have created the technology that not only enables us to change our basic nature, but that is making such changes all but inevitable.[2]

Birkerts argues that adoption of information technology evokes inevitable change not only in information-based institutions like libraries, but in our basic nature. If the scope of these changes is as fundamental as Birkerts maintains, the consequences for libraries may well be more revolutionary than the invention of the printing press, although some may see Birkerts exaggerating in his characterization of electronic technologies as a cultural metamorphosis.

However, Birkerts's alarming observations resonate with my concerns about libraries and the nature of learning. From my work in the information industry and with national information-policy issues, I see the tremendously exciting technological potential of improved access to information. But I also have a healthy appreciation for the consequences that electronic information technology can produce. The influence of the US interstate highway system on transportation is an example of these consequences. Few would argue with the idea that automobiles have influenced the economic, cultural, and demographic life of America in the last three decades. By adopting policies to support the commercialization of technology-based services and products, whether the internal combustion engine or electronic network communication infrastructures, we change basic human behavior and expectations.

Sven Birkerts is not alone in his concern about the systemic nature of change brought about by the advent of information technology. John Perry Barlow, a founder of the Electronic Frontier Foundation, a group formed to protect civil liberties in cyberspace, is quoted in an interview that appeared in *Harper's Magazine* as saying:

...with the development of the Internet, and with the increasing pervasiveness of communication between networked computers, we are in the middle of the most transforming technological event since the capture of fire. I used to think that it was just the biggest thing since Gutenberg, but now I think you have to go back farther. . . . I don't think it's a matter about which we have much choice. It is coming, whether we like it or not.[3]

It certainly is provocative to view the advent of digital information networks as equivalent to the impact that the discovery of fire had on human existence. If the changes affecting libraries are of this magnitude, then all the future of communication is in an extremely precarious position. Is this all exaggerated hype, or have Barlow and Birkerts identified something of importance for the future of libraries? Certainly, Birkerts shares a perspective on the pervasiveness of the changes we are experiencing in moving toward the electronic frontier:

We have, perhaps without noticing, slipped over a crucial threshold. We have rather abruptly replaced our time-honored and slow-to-evolve modes of communication and interaction with new modes. We have in significant ways surmounted the constraints imposed by nature, in the process altering our relation to time, space, and to each other. We have scarcely begun to assess the impact of these transformations—that will be the work of generations. . . . [S]ome of our fundamental assumptions about identity and subjective meaning need to be examined carefully. For, by moving from the order of print to the electronic, we risk the loss of the sense of obstacle as well as the feel of the particular that have characterized our experience over millennia. We are poised at the brink of what may prove to be a kind of species mutation. We had better consider carefully what this means.[4]

Few of my friends and colleagues in the library field would agree that libraries' provision of electronic information services constitutes a species mutation. However, few library managers today would deny that new electronic services are requiring radically different approaches to library budgeting, to the skills required by librarians, and to the policies related to accessing information.

I believe that those experiences and insights that we gain through reading, studying, learning, and experiencing the thoughts and ideas of others are influenced by the medium by which these are communicated. Change the medium and the message changes. Alter the nature of the media in fundamental ways and the consequences are clearly evident. By adopting and integrating electronic media into communication channels, commercial concerns are seeking business revenues. However, for libraries to similarly accommodate these newer electronic media, they must redefine basic procedures, services, structures, and principles that reflect postmodern culture.

POSTMODERN TRENDS

Careful consideration of the meaning of the shift from print to electronic media is, indeed, needed to understand the changes that are influencing the future of librarianship. However, instead of turning to technologists, economists, futurists, or librarians for enlightenment about the social and human impact of changes in communications and information media and the possible influence of these trends on information and librarianship, it is instructive to study the work of selected anthropologists and sociologists who are directing attention to the ways that technology is affecting the fabric of our social and cultural lives.

With the advent of artificial intelligence and advances in the field of virtual reality, some are predicting the arrival of a science-fiction age characterized by a posthuman universe presided over by godlike human-machine hybrids. While this may seem far-fetched, cyberculture-induced scenarios can be seen growing from the increasingly blurred distinctions between human capacities and computers. These shifting boundaries between humans and machines are reflected in Birkerts's concern about "species mutation." Symptoms of an obsessive preoccupation with the insufficiency of the human body are becoming prevalent.

The range of human physical and mental activities seems to require extension through technological means, just as mobility has been extended through ubiquitous motorized transportation. Science fiction predicts that humans of the future will have computer implants giving superhuman capabilities to average people; cyberpunk performance artists proclaim that they seek a human-machine hybrid. Reflections of this are to be found in images included in *Wired,* a magazine where an unaltered photograph is a rarity. Altered or "morphed" images of humans dominate our media-saturated world. From television to movies the message seems to be that people need intelligent machines integrated into their internal environments to participate fully in the postmodern society of the future.

The term "postmodern" is increasingly used to describe a mind-reordering shift in the ways that people think about themselves and their world, a change in our concepts of "reality" and "self." This shift has important consequences for communication and information processes. In *Life on the Screen,* Sherry Turkle, a sociology professor at the Massachusetts Institute of Technology, discusses the psychological impact of the personal computer, especially in our use of the computer as a metaphor for personal identity.

The advent of technology on society in the form of the computer and, more specifically, through interactive computer-information networks is having a profound impact on the identity of self, according to Turkle, who has recently observed:

> In terms of technologies that have really changed people's deepest conceptions of self, we've had a long run with print.... Print has been a transparent medium for expression of unitary self.... But we're in the beginning of a profound shake-up of that sense of what a self is.... When you can embody your ideas in a machine [and] when you can have an instantiation of your body on a computer— this is new.[5]

Symptoms of postmodernist trends in society include rising public interest in virtual reality and "cyberculture," where computers transform our material and emotional lives. Similarly, advances in robotics and artificial intelligence are beginning to blur distinctions between human thought and "intelligent" machines. Our ordinary lives are increasingly dependent on structures established by electronic systems that define our financial, legal, medical, and communications-related activities. Electronic banking, self-check retail shopping, e-mail, and remote-user searches of on-line data bases are just a few of the unmediated digital services that structure time and define our activities.

We are increasingly dependent on digital information technologies to define meaning and provide a contextual framework for our activities and our identities. In this growing dependence, our cultural shifts from the linear, logical, and hierarchical world are noticeable. We seem to be hurtling towards a postmodernism characterized by this decentered, fragmented, fluid, opaque, and nonlinear cultural context. And in the rush towards the future, librarians are among the first to witness the destabilization of the old print order through the wholesale adoption of the electronic media by wide segments of the population.

For Turkle, social and cultural structures associated with a modern era are rapidly giving way to a postmodern society. These changes can be characterized as a transition from a modern era to a postmodern age:

Modern:	Postmodern:
linear	interactive
intelligent	intuitive
fixed rules and clearly defined truth	provisional paths
printed text	multimedia
unique identity	relationships
concern for history and preservation	hypertext
permanence	flexibility
independence	contingency
characterization	multiple on-line identities
clear definitions	adaptability and ambiguity
national	global
formal	informal
calculation	simulation

For example, modernist birthday parties have traditional cakes, candles, presents, guests, and games. In contrast, guests at postmodern birthday parties watch and comment on the videos shot and shown during the course of the party; a media abstraction of the event provides the substance for the party itself. The transition from modern culture to the postmodern results from the application of technological information and communication developments to personal and corporate activities. Perhaps the cultural and socio-logical impact of these shifts to a postmodern era is nowhere more pervasive than in the library and information fields. The postmodern library is as much of a reality for habitual Internet users as card catalogs were for modern library patrons. The chaos and confu-sion of the networked information world will not, I fear, be tamed by traditional librarian attempts to organize and control information resources. The postmodern information environment is too fluid, volatile, and dynamic for the traditional librarian to control. But the very interactive nature of the digital networked information/communications process requires new approaches in which librarians team with network service providers, software designers, and media specialists to forge a new paradigm for librarianship.

I do not intend for this essay to analyze the metaphysical nature of the changes brought about by the introduction of electronic communication technologies into human society—that is beyond the scope of this piece. But it is instructive for those in the library community to appreciate and understand the radical nature of the technological and social transformations that I believe are currently underway. A careful consideration of the meaning of these new modes of communication and interaction from the perspective of the library community indicates the following trend shifts from the modern to the postmodern library:

From:	To:
fixed, permanent, formatted text collections	fluid and transient multimedia resources
static library facilities with fixed stacks	free, flexible, and virtual information spaces
uniform sources, citations, references	customized annotations/transient works
services provided to individual readers	tailored services to collaborative teams
standard reference services	personalized consulting and analysis
professionally provided services	integrated service provision
locally owned permanent collections	holistic, integrated networked systems
centralized collections and services	distributed, decentralized global access
hierarchical organizational structures	participative and collegial relationships
discipline specialization	inter-, multi-, cross-disciplinary studies
generic user service offerings	user-/use-specific relevant services
formal publication acquisition	integration of informal with formal

These shifts in the paradigm of library and information service may not fully reflect the fundamental shift in the crucial threshold that Birkerts claims, nor, perhaps, the trend towards a postmodern culture that Turkle has identified, but the shifts from permanence to transience, from generic to customized services, and from local to global resource access have important consequences for library planning and for the development of the field of librarianship.

An interesting observation in Birkerts's study is that technology is affecting the nature of the human species. These changes, he maintains, are inevitable and unavoidable. The perception of loss of control and regression amidst the current electronic transition reflects the feelings of many within the library community, including myself. Especially within the library field, this perception underscores the importance of understanding the nature of the transition to an information age of the future. It becomes imperative that librarians comprehend the meaning of the species mutation brought on by embracing technological change. If librarians hope to have a future on the electronic frontier, they must develop an understanding of the impact of electronic media and learn to formulate strategies appropriate to the evolution and revision of libraries' institutional structures; this is essential in a future dominated by both digital media and more familiar printed information resources.

The choices librarians are confronting have important consequences for libraries and library users. Birkerts addresses this point in general terms by providing a comparison of gains and losses involved with what he terms the "systemic changes affecting the culture at every level." He writes:

> We are at a watershed point. One way of processing information is yielding to another. Bound up with each is a huge array of attitudes, assumptions, and understandings about the world.
>
> We can think of the matter in terms of gains and losses. The gains of electronic postmodernity could be said to include, for individuals, (a) an increased awareness of the "big picture," a global perspective that admits the extraordinary complexity of interrelations; (b) an expanded neural capacity, an ability to accommodate a broad range of stimuli simultaneously; (c) a relativistic comprehension of situations that promotes the erosion of old biases and often expresses itself as tolerance; and (d) a matter-of-fact and unencumbered sort of readiness, a willingness to try new situations and arrangements.

In the loss column, meanwhile, are (a) a fragmented sense of time and a loss of the so-called duration experience, that depth phenomenon we associate with reverie; (b) a reduced attention span and a general impatience with sustained inquiry; (c) a shattered faith in institutions and in the explanatory narratives that formerly gave shape to subjective experience; (d) a divorce from the past, from a vital sense of history as a cumulative or organic process; and (e) an absence of any strong vision of a personal or collective future.[6]

It is instructive to view current technological change from the perspective of World War II because much of modern librarianship assumed its current principles and ethos from this era. During the summer of 1995, events around the world marked the fiftieth anniversary of the end of World War II, a war that has been characterized as the defining event of the century. Certainly, America's involvement in it was of enormous importance to this nation. Few events in our national history have left more of a mark on our culture. The war effort fueled an industrial realignment and technological change of unprecedented magnitude. And the conclusion of World War II simultaneously signaled the beginning of the atomic age and the start of the Cold War.

World War II and the current electronic information revolution both reflect tremendous technological advancement and development. Indeed, the innovation and discoveries that fueled America's industrial and technological infrastructure development during the war era provided the basis for continued research and development investments; these led to advances in computing and communications that prompted the current information and media revolution. The challenge facing librarians today, however, is to develop fundamental strategies to guide the application of new electronic communication technologies for the peaceful advancement of civilization and knowledge.

There is agitation today, as there was fifty years ago, to motivate and mobilize the nation. Indeed, the successful transition to a peacetime economy and a nondefense-oriented national industrial sector depends on redirecting national policies and priorities that are distinctly different from those that have guided the nation since the commencement of hostilities over fifty years ago.

We often feel uneasy when confronted with new situations that do not conform easily to our conceptual models. This is especially true for librarians who find security in consistency and permanence. So it is particularly disturbing for a library community with traditional concerns related to bibliographic control and carefully defined index and classification schema to address uncertainties related to new electronic media. Problems arise in attempting to apply traditional approaches to more elusive digital media. Librarians are troubled when old solutions do not fit new challenges, such as:

- What information should the catalog record for an electronic journal contain? What information should be included as a standard citation for an e-mail message?
- What about the citation to a comment on a listserv?
- How can one project the building and shelving needs for a university library collection over the next two decades?
- What portion of the library's budget will telecommunications charges assume in the next five years?
- Will universities be held liable for suits filed against student hackers?
- What licensing arrangements will scholarly publishers impose on academic libraries to protect digitally accessible works from use by multiple libraries?
- How much risk should libraries assume by investing in new information technology rather than in the acquisition of collections?

At times, the advent of the information and communications technology revolution, together with a host of recent megamergers of global media conglomerates and cross-industry alliances between cable, telephone, software, and computing companies, threatens to overwhelm librarians' ability to manage the social structures and institutions established to define, house, and control the wonderfully diverse, tremendously creative, and incredibly rich output of human ingenuity and imagination.

This sense is expressed in the following passage from Richard Lanham's 1993 work, *The Electronic Word: Democracy, Technology, and the Arts*:

> The library world feels dépaysé today.... Both of its physical entities, the buildings and the books they contain, can no longer form

the basis for planning. And the curatorial function has metamorphosed...."from curatorial to interpretive." Librarians of electronic information find their job now a radically rhetorical one—they must consciously construct human attention-structures rather than assemble a collection of books according to commonly accepted rules. They have, perhaps unwillingly, found themselves transported from the ancillary margin of the human sciences to their center. If this is so—and can it be doubted?—how should we train librarians, much less plan the buildings where they will work?[7]

How are we to conceptualize and develop roles, training, skills, guidelines, competencies, values, and judgment that address the needs of libraries, schools, governments, communities, industries, researchers, artists, authors, and other citizens of a postmodern information age? What are the new catalogs, indexes, authority structures, knowledge structures, and organizational and access tools that librarians will need to serve the increasingly bifurcated world of paper and digital resources? Where are Lanham's "human attention-structures" to be found?

POSTMODERN LIBRARIANSHIP

With the glut of claims and assurances about the opportunities and improvements to come with the advent of the information technology age, there is clear evidence of a backlash responding to oversold claims about the promises of information networking and communications technology to solve problems related to productivity, education, and social inequities. The technological promise for linking large numbers of individuals and institutions to one another and to an unprecedented array of information and services is very real, as is the Internet's potential to be the most significant asset in the knowledge-based economy of the coming century. Information technology has the potential to improve the quality of life and transform the way people work, learn, and live. It can create new opportunities for individuals to communicate, provide, and receive information of all kinds, and to more actively participate in the political process.[8]

However, the truth is that those same social, economic, and cultural issues that librarians confront daily are showing up in the newer electronic media. The hard reality of cyberspace presents librarians with challenges that are just as significant as those faced in the preceding print-based culture. We cannot escape the difficult questions of intellectual freedom, censorship, freedom of speech, security, privacy, crime, useless information, open access, economic discrimination, and cultural bias just because we are hooking libraries up to a postmodern future.

The Internet, that "seamless web of communications networks, computers, databases, and consumer electronics that will put vast amounts of information at users' fingertips,"[9] requires that we address the fundamental issues of librarianship, whether our concern is with traditional printed textual materials or with the postmodern digital environment.

Whether librarians accept the changes or not, the public's perceptions of the "information superhighway" will have a fundamental impact on its relationship with and expectations of libraries. Visions of electronic or virtual libraries do not necessarily depend upon the concept of an information infrastructure within the social context of a public communications architecture. The metaphor of the Internet as an electronic highway is useful for articulating this distinction. The Internet has been compared to "a blisteringly fast, multilane roadway where the vehicles are traveling in at least three dimensions at once, the directional signage changes all the time, and there are no rest stops."[10]

An "information infrastructure" implies a conceptual analogy that incorporates all facets and aspects of transportation systems and the structures supporting these systems, regardless of the specific mode of transportation. Thus the information infrastructure analogy cannot be confined to the national interstate highway system. The US Office of Technology Assessment (OTA) has been explicit in defining the "communications infrastructure" as "the underlying structure of technical facilities and institutional arrangements that supports communication via telecommunication, broadcasting, film, audio and video recording, cable, print, and mail."[11] Similarly, the Clinton administration assigns an expansive meaning to the phrase "information infrastructure," characterizing it to include:

A wide range and ever-expanding range of equipment including cameras, scanners, keyboards, telephones, fax machines, computers, switches, compact discs, video and audio tape, cable, wire, satellites, optical fiber transmission lines, microwave nets, switches, televisions, monitors, printers, and much more.[12]

A national information infrastructure is seen to integrate and interconnect physical components to provide an advanced technological foundation for living in the information age and to make these technological advances useful to the public, libraries, business, and other nongovernmental entities. The value of this information infrastructure to users thus depends on the quality of the information; the ease of the applications and access software; the effective functioning of network standards and transmission codes; and the work of those who create the information and construct the facilities, applications, and services. We are moving away from the information highway towards a broader concentration on communications infrastructure. Similarly, in the terms of the "information superhighway" analogy, our attention is shifting from the lanes of the roadbed to the impact of networking technologies on the nature of social interaction within the global community.

Postmodern librarianship is concerned with the changing nature of information and the evolution of new forms of the information experience. The computer-mediated digital information environment yields altogether distinctly new characteristics—an informal, formless, interactive, subjective experience of multimedia. This is distinct from the private, internal, objective, sequential, solitary, and personal experience that characterizes involvement with printed textual resources. The postmodern librarian faces distinctions between the world of print and the postmodern digital world. These distinctions involve resources, services, facilities, patrons, and the human resources and skills associated with the profession of librarianship.

Resources

Printed resources are primarily textual materials that constitute fixed permanent collections purchased and owned by an institution. Printed works are objective, normalized, and standard. They are organized and arranged to provide centralized services from collections stored locally, based on standardized bibliographic catalogs and indexes that guide readers to desired materials through uniform standard citations, references, and conventions. Print libraries depend on bibliographic control assumptions that identify unique works of authorship and differentiate variant editions by distinguishing features. Printed works are represented in permanently established editions from recognized publishing sources.

Digital resources are likely to involve fluid structures and are characterized by multimedia. Their provenance is not easily established, and access may involve opening encrypted files and documents. Digital works depend on customized or subjectively determined assemblages from a variety of digital and print resources. They are not static and permanent but instead are subject to change and variance. Digital systems are distributed and available for access through globally decentralized structures. Digital libraries involve personalized or custom services for accessing, assembling, and analyzing information resources from a variety of diverse sources in many different formats. Digital information resource-based services require integrative skills and often add value to the individual works involved.

Services

Print-based library services involve the acquisition of permanent and formal publications through a payment transaction or a subscription arrangement. Libraries providing services based on printed or textual collections offer generic user-services for circulation, reference, and interlibrary loan, which depend on standard resources and references to provide generic links to published works. Print-based libraries offer professional services to patrons within the library service area.

Digital information services often require the integration of formal and informal publications and resources through flexible services and systems that blend customized interpretive services with standard service offerings. Digital services are offered by integrated technical/professional specialist teams within an informal service staffing structure, often to multiple, simultaneous users. Digital information services require the development of customized pay-per-use consultancies that can interpret multiple digital information resources for specific user-defined needs.

Facilities

Print library facilities are static buildings and shelving stacks that are constructed by capital investments and maintained through recurring physical plant budgets. Growing print collections require continual expansion of space facilities in order to maintain local ownership and control over physical collection resources. Maintenance of facilities and collections are human-intensive and require conservation, protection, and preservation. Hierarchic structures for collections and organizations are static and change slowly over time, if at all. Local, regional, state, and national print resource collections assume universal availability, but researchers often are required to be physically present in order to use unique collections and resources.

Digital library facilities are fluid and flexible, and they may not involve local physical structures or investments. Digital information infrastructures are electronic and dependent upon consistent, dependable, and uniform supports. Communications technology and digital processing storage systems constitute the digital information infrastructure facilities; fragile and complex software links to digital resources and systems underlie a global networked architecture. Multiple simultaneous users are often involved with digital information facilities and services in private linkages to intangible resources. Digital libraries provide facilities to support specific relevant information services that are customized to the needs of an individual user.

Patrons

Patrons of print-based libraries are individuals who are physically present at the facility and are usually visiting for a specific purpose within a known discipline or speciality. They come to the library to browse physical printed textual materials, often with little need for staff assistance or service. Patrons of traditional print collection libraries assume that their personal privacy is protected— borrowing records or browsing activities are private matters for patrons. Patrons are known to the library through registration procedures that identify them as being within the service area or as part of the community served by the library.

Patrons or users of digital information services are often participants in a interactive consultant activity involving other patrons, library staff, and various digital and printed resource materials. Digital library patrons may involve inter-, multi-, or cross-disciplinary studies and information requirements using published, unpublished, or informal materials in whole or in part. Digital information users may be physically present or only electronically present. They may be remote and anonymous or they may be local and registered users/borrowers. Digital information patrons may not have assured privacy in their use of library resources.

Human Resources and Skills of Librarianship

Libraries involving printed textual materials have professionally trained librarians providing management and services. These libraries have collections, services, and patrons that are divided by type: academic, school, special, and public. Print-based libraries have organizational structures that distinguish between technical and public-service operations. Service subdivisions are typically specialized by function or format: acquisitions, collection development, circulation, cataloging, reference, microform, documents, multimedia, systems, and administration. Distinctions also separate professional from support staff.

Digital information libraries have human resource requirements that are only now beginning to become clear. Although librarians have traditionally engaged in the organization and arrangement of information collections, digital collections and services call for librarians to function as knowledge navigators or, as some have suggested, as cyberspace organizers. The nature of digital information resources also requires digital librarians to be resource integrators and to offer users customized consultation and interpretation services. The new digital information environment requires that librarians add value to the use of information. Librarians working in digital information structures are creators of information through the assembly, organization, and generation of new knowledge. The authentication and validation of knowledge resources presents new opportunities to the postmodern librarian.

The volatile and pervasive nature of technological change presents libraries and librarianship with unprecedented challenges. At the same time, some in the field view these changes as opportunities. While ownership of print collections is yielding to access and customized delivery of relevant ideas and information in an increasingly electronic information environment, those librarians who embrace change and chance risk are likely to evolve a new customized information paradigm for librarianship. It is time for the new postmodern information profession.

ENDNOTES

¹The views and opinions expressed in this essay are those of the author and do not necessarily reflect the policies or positions of the US National Commission on Libraries and Information Science or the US government.

²Sven Birkerts, *The Gutenberg Elegies: The Fate of Reading in an Electronic Age* (Boston, Mass.: Faber & Faber, 1994), 15.

³"Forum: What Are We Doing On-Line?," *Harper's Magazine* (August 1995): 36.

⁴Birkerts, *The Gutenberg Elegies: The Fate of Reading in an Electronic Age,* 31.

⁵Sherry Turkle, quoted in Pamela McCorduck, "Sex, Lies, and Avatars," *Wired* (April 1996): 108.

⁶Birkerts, *The Gutenberg Elegies: The Fate of Reading in an Electronic Age,* 27.

⁷Richard A. Lanham, *The Electronic Word: Democracy, Technology, and the Arts* (Chicago, Ill.: University of Chicago Press, 1993), 134.

⁸National Information Infrastructure Advisory Council, *Common Ground: Fundamental Principles for the National Information Infrastructure* (Washington, D.C.: US Department of Commerce, March 1995).

⁹Information Infrastructure Task Force, *The National Information Infrastructure: Agenda for Action,* Washington, D.C., 15 September 1993, p. 1.

¹⁰Jeane Polly and Steve Cisler, "Connecting to the Global Internet," *Library Journal* 119 (1) (January 1994): 38.

¹¹US Congress, Office of Technology Assessment, *Critical Connections: Communication for the Future,* OTA-CIT-407 (Washington, D.C.: US Government Printing Office, January 1990).

¹²Information Infrastructure Task Force, *The National Information Infrastructure: Agenda for Action,* 5.

Thus we have sought to show how, within less than three decades, the digital logic machine has altered the ways and means of scientific discovery. Only now are generations of new students and teachers arising who will use these means fully and extend the reach of new thought with their help. Dr. George Stibitz, creator of the first electrical digital computer (based on the logic of telephone relay switches), said in describing his work beginning in 1937, "I had observed the similarity between the circuit paths through relays and the binary notation for numbers and had an idea I wanted to work out." Thus began a new path in science. In his endeavors, and those of Aiken, Eckert and Mauchly, von Neumann, Shannon, Wiener, and the others, began a fateful chapter of empowering the reach of the mind. Already the scientific concepts of our age—quantum theory and the wave mechanics, the structure patterns of molecules and crystals, and indeed the whole vast sweep of inorganic, organic, and social science which is surveyed in this volume—are peculiarly matched to a need for massive computation and logical manipulation.

Likewise, the applications of science for the benefit of man through industry and government increasingly depend on the conception and design of large interacting systems, in which many of the elegant uses of computers that we have sampled must be combined in the most ingenious ways. Far from seeing a plateau or decline in the rate of progress in a golden age of science and technology, I see boundless opportunities through the use of logic machine systems to resolve the puzzles of cosmology, of life, and of the society of man. And, above all, I see that automation, once viewed as an ominous, Frankensteinlike threat to personalism and humaneness, turns out to augment especially the bold individualism of new thought.

W. O. Baker

From "Computers As Information-Processing
Machines in Modern Science"
Dædalus 99 (4) (Fall 1970)

Donald S. Lamm

Libraries and Publishers: A Partnership at Risk

*People in general do not willingly read, if they can
have anything else to amuse them.*
—Samuel Johnson

T HE YEAR WAS 1979. At a preliminary planning meeting in
Albany for the White House Conference on Libraries and
Information Services, session after session appeared on the
agenda devoted to such subjects as security, literacy training, community service, networking, and access to information for ethnic
and other minority groups. A delegate appointed by the book
publishers association to attend the conference found himself at
sea; books went largely unmentioned. Perhaps two hours in the
course of three days were earmarked for the discussion of developing and maintaining a book collection suited to user needs, whether
in suburbs or cities, campuses or corporations.

Small wonder, then, that the Report of the Conference issued in
the wake of the national meeting in Washington was almost silent
on the matter of books. Sifting through that document one discovers new forms of technology crowding out traditional print matter. Even in 1980, when the Report was published, the electronic
genie was out of the bottle. Several key resolutions make that
clear. The library community is urged to "evaluate the economic,

Donald S. Lamm is Chairman of W. W. Norton & Company.

social, and political consequences of information and data processing technology so that public and private efforts can use this technology for the benefit of all," and also to "encourage cooperation among institutions for the efficient delivery of information technology, especially computer and communications technology, in the exchange and delivery of information. And to develop the necessary software packages to achieve these goals."

These recommendations date back to a time when personal computers and interoffice networks were in their infancy, exploring the Internet was largely limited to Defense Department operatives, and e-mail was far beyond the electronic horizon. The library of the future was to be reinvented as a center for the collection and dispatch of information, perhaps to overcome "the low profile" that the institution was reputed to hold "in communities across the United States."[1]

There was, fortunately, one voice in the wilderness crying on behalf of the book. Toward the end of the conference, Daniel Boorstin, the Librarian of Congress, had this to say:

> We too easily forget that the printed book...was a triumph of technology.... Books became the carriers and the record—also the catalyst and the incentive—for most of the knowledge, the amusement, and the sacred visions of the human race. The printed book has given all humanity its inexpensive, speedy, reliable vehicles across the centuries. Books have conquered time.[2]

The delegates may have applauded those words. Some may even have agreed with them. But while the word "information" courses through the conference report, only in Professor Boorstin's address and a few other stray remarks is there mention of "books" or "knowledge."

To a considerable extent book publishers were to blame for this neglect. Failing to grasp the political implications of the conference, the publishing community had no show of force in attendance and, as a consequence, had little impact on the final report. By way of contrast, representatives of new technologies actively promoted their interests, creating, in effect, a library-industrial complex that left producers of print materials as bit players when they should have commanded center stage.

Seventeen years after the White House conference, libraries have found far more to distract them from their historic role as repositories of printed material. Electronic means of creating, storing, transmitting, receiving, and retrieving information have spread like a prairie fire in high winds. Even under tight budget constraints, libraries have brought computers into play for activities ranging from the electronic card catalog to on-line journal subscriptions to preservation efforts. Beyond the diversion of funds away from book purchases, these activities do not generate open conflict with publishers. But an innocuous-sounding item, the full-text data base, may become the ground on which the interests of librarians and publishers eventually clash. By accessing this data base, a high-tech synonym for a book, a distant user linked by computer terminal to a library has the means not only to call up the entire content of a book but, with appropriate equipment, to download it. The full-text data base, thus, stands to transform the library into an electronic copy shop and thereby undermine the control of printed material implicit in the grant of copyright. As I soon will explain, the publisher's arsenal for defending copyright has yet to be retrofitted to protect material sent into cyberspace.

Meanwhile, in less startling ways, the mutual dependency of libraries and publishers may be weakening. Although precise dollar amounts are difficult to tease out from the rather shaky array of statistics on library operating costs, the book evidently commands a diminishing share of total library expenditures; in 1989 collection expenditures (meaning "books and serial volumes, audio materials, films, video materials, and current serial subscriptions") amounted to $592 million, or 16 percent of public libraries' total operating expenditures.[3] By 1994 collection expenditures had risen in dollar terms, largely a reflection of sharp price increases for all print matter, but dropped to 15 percent of the public libraries' total operating expenditures.[4] That is not a deep plunge, but intuitively one senses that there is more to the story. Given the antigovernment spending fever prevalent around the nation, the worst is yet to come in regard to funding public libraries along with other tax-supported institutions.

A glance at publishers' own data underscores the trend. Library purchases dwindled from 9 percent of publishers' total revenues in 1982 to 8.5 percent a decade later, and there are indications that the percentage has dropped more steeply since 1992, with no reversal in sight.

Cultural critics who decry the excessive production of books will be comforted to discover that with the library prop knocked out, at least a third of the roughly fifty thousand books now published annually would likely be eliminated before the century's end, and even that estimate may be low. The sour attitude of the public toward government spending has, to date, mainly been manifested at the federal level. It should be remembered, though, that the tax revolt that gave rise to antigovernment fever had its origins at the state level—in California in 1978 with Proposition 13, the movement to curtail the upward spiral in local property taxes. If, as the late Speaker of the House "Tip" O'Neill put it, "all politics is local," then the tax-cut juggernaut will make its way largely unobstructed from the United States Congress back to the states and municipalities.

In 1970, as the largest-ever federal windfall to libraries, some $60 million, was coming to an end, the director of the Princeton University Press wrote, "Libraries are very sensitive to the state of the economy generally [given] the vagaries and variations of local taxes and the uncertainties of Congressional support for national programs."[5] Twenty-six years later, the likelihood of public libraries receiving bounties at any level of government would appear restricted to upscale suburbs; even there, support for a public library may be expressed through fund drives rather than increases in the library allocation in town budgets.

As libraries decline in relative importance to trade publishers, that is, publishers of books for the general reader, efforts to reach the library market necessarily become less vigorous. Historically, only the largest publishers have mounted all-out sales promotions to libraries, utilizing representatives who are assigned to contact the major library systems, region by region. Other publishers resort to less costly sales strategies. Seasonal catalogs are mailed to public libraries in communities with budgets for new acquisitions exceeding $10,000 per year; more specialized libraries may receive brochures describing major new reference works or packs of index cards containing concise descriptions of forthcoming works. When it comes to actual ordering, all but the most extensive library systems rely on book wholesalers. That many of the wholesalers who specialize as library jobbers have come on hard times—with quite a few going out of business altogether—is a further indication of a market in decline.

The situation in academic libraries is no less bleak for publishers. Here the danger is both clear and present. Early signs of trouble brewing could be spotted over a decade ago. While the price of books increased at or slightly below the inflation rate, the costs of subscriptions to academic journals began to double and redouble. Yet in the competition among print materials for primacy in academic library budgets, relative price increases were not at issue. Journals invariably won out over books; they still do. Thus, in 1992, libraries at five hundred doctoral-granting institutions spent nearly twice as much on current serial subscriptions ($467 million) as books ($253 million).[6] The librarian at a preeminent research university explained to me that the process by which his subject-specialist librarians selected titles had not changed significantly in the face of budgetary stringencies. What had changed was the number of copies purchased of a given title. Whereas in the 1980s and earlier, multiple copies might be ordered to provision each of several libraries on the campus, now one copy must serve all on an interlibrary loan basis. And generally, he added, books faced sterner tests than before for purchase in the first place. The same stringencies, however, do not apply to periodicals. (American academic libraries are not unique either in favoring journals over books or, recently, in limiting book purchases. Five years ago, libraries in Germany reportedly lowered their expenditures on books by nearly 50 percent. Similar cutbacks, though not as deep, occurred in France and the United Kingdom.)

FOR WHAT THE BELL TOLLS

Almost certainly the books most vulnerable to a slump in public library purchases are adult trade, that is, novels, biographies, histories, nontechnical works in science, politics, and economics, poetry, and other books written for those who are sometimes lumped under the rubric "the common reader." Since libraries must be responsive to community demand, they cannot ignore best-sellers or other books that have been prominently reviewed in print or discussed on radio and television. The big losers with purchasing cutbacks are the books that need library sales the most, what the late Marshall Best of the Viking Press called in an earlier *Dædalus* issue "marginal books." In employing the term "marginal," Best was not making a value judgment, for the category included "the book of great literary distinction or real originality of thought, too experimental to be ready for a large public; the book whose subject matter will interest only specialists, or whose language or method makes demands on the reader which necessarily restrict it to an elite."[7] Ordered in limited quantities by retail bookstores, such books depend for their existence on library purchases.

Most at risk among the marginal books is literary fiction by authors without an established following. And by far the most vulnerable in this category is the first novel, usually the work of a writer whose previous appearance in print has been limited to a few short stories in literary quarterlies. The initial barrier the new novelist must overcome is the slush pile, an inelegant term for the repository where unsolicited manuscripts reside until someone at the publishing house, often an intern, happens to liberate the work. I once calculated that the chances of a blind submission, an "over the transom" manuscript, becoming a book under the aegis of a mainstream publisher are one in six thousand. For fiction, one in nine thousand may be closer to the mark.

First novels are chancy propositions for the publisher, given the absence of a track record that might help gauge an author's appeal. By extension first novels are also chancy propositions for the bookstores that have little more to go on before placing their orders than the publisher's catalog blurb, a sales representative's pitch, the dust jacket of the book, and very occasionally a bound proof. A small bookstore cannot allocate much of its limited shelf space to books by unestablished writers; some combination of the buyer's personal taste, ecstatic reviews, and word of mouth are usually necessary to make room for first novels in such stores. By sheer dint of their size, the book superstores can do more by way of stocking first novels. One of the large superstore chains has a "Discover" program where, for a deeper than standard discount, publishers may place a promising first novel in a section of the store reserved for previously unpublished novelists. Placement in that section raises a novel's visibility. It improves the odds of the novel selling slightly more than the routine three or four thousand copies. Readings or signings at selected bookstores may give the author a lift and also boost sales, but the revenues from the copies sold at such events rarely cover the publisher's expense of ferrying the author to the stores.

Despite the changing face of retail bookselling, the library remains an indispensable venue for all but the most-heralded (or hyped) first novels as well as for novels by seasoned authors whose writings appeal to a coterie audience. Reviews in *Library Journal* and recommendations from book wholesalers plus the taste of library staffs may prompt just enough orders to raise income from a novel to the publisher's break-even point. Put differently, remove the library sale, and the book almost certainly ends up in the loss column.

One can safely estimate that two-thirds of all novels would never appear without the publisher calculating on sales to the library market. Extending this scenario, it is not unreasonable to forecast further deep declines in library support imperiling the literary novel. Perhaps hypertext fiction on the computer screen will attract the next wave of readers. Or maybe the current vogue of purse-size fiction—"short shorts," as some dub the genre—will survive past the novelty stage. But format has not proved the salvation of the literary novel in recent years.

From time to time, individual publishers have attempted to overcome buyer resistance to literary fiction by issuing novels as paperback originals. Editors point to an occasional success in this format, such as Jay McInerney's *Bright Lights, Big City,* and solemnly pronounce the arrival of a new day in publishing, only later to realize that such exceptions prove no rule. Hard experience causes the small independent bookseller confronting the notoriously thin profit margins of the trade to adopt a variant of Mr. Micawber's equations:

> One copy ordered, one copy sold equals happiness
> Five copies ordered, four copies sold equals misery.

These equations hold, even though unsold copies can be returned to the publisher for full credit.

In the aggregate, bookstore buying patterns fuel the best-seller lists, and those lists, in turn, attest to the indifference that most literary fiction faces at the sales counter. The runaway success of a half-dozen romances or thrillers each season gives the false impression that the novel can get along without library support.

Ian Watt has written, "Literary traditionalism was first and most fully challenged by the novel, whose primary criterion was truth to individual experience—individual experience which is always unique and therefore new."[8] It happens that insipid works on the order of *The Bridges of Madison County* may reflect individual experience, but often that experience comes in recipe form, out of a writer's manual. Such books are not a reader's stepping-stone to literary fiction. Their popularity merely suggests that deep in the wellsprings of the culture a gradual shift may be occurring away from the individualist to the conformist, a shift that bodes ill for the novel as a genre.

The hard-pressed category of literary fiction has its counterparts in the subcategories of serious nonfiction, which account for more than three-quarters of the trade titles published annually. In areas such as history and biography that once formed the backbone of many publishers' lists, marginal books are beginning to outnumber the profit makers. What has happened to the so-called serious book can be inferred from a recent, and quite typical, *New York Times* Best Seller list that had these titles as nonfiction leaders: *Rush Limbaugh Is a Big Fat Idiot, My Point and I Do Have One,* and *Enter Whining,* all three accounts by TV semi-celebrities. Those looking for richer fare could find high on the list *You'll Never Make Love in This Town Again,* reminiscences of four Hollywood prostitutes.

Although the new book superstores carry inventories of one hundred thousand titles or more, their shelves contain many staple stock items—the hardy perennials of the book business such as cookbooks, nature books, gardening books, home-repair manuals, travel books, and the vast assortment of "how-to" books that promise to provide the customer with the best things in life, whether it be thin thighs in thirty days or fat investment gains on Wall Street. When it comes to current nonfiction titles—trade books that are not destined for bestsellerdom—the superstores are no bulwark for publishers against a weakening of the library market. For an intoxicating month or six weeks, those books may be on display, most often shelved spine out. But a high percentage make a round trip back to the publisher's warehouse, confirming with a vengeance Alfred Knopf's oft-quoted maxim on book returns: "Gone today, here tomorrow."

Children's books form a second broad class of books dependent on library purchases, even more so, in fact, than adult trade. In many families children's books are hand-me-downs from generation to generation. The books read in our own childhood tend to be the ones that we give to our children. Thus such staples as *Winnie the Pooh, Peter Rabbit,* and *Mary Poppins* can reliably be stocked by bookstores. So, too, can newer titles that bear the gold medal designating a Caldicott or Newbery award winner. The larger bookstores, including the superstores, imitate the popular library practice of weekend or early evening readings in the children's section, turning that section into a romper room with books, a haven for parents wilting under repeated assaults of young animal spirits. For all their inviting fittings, however, these bookstores together with the mega-toy stores such as Toys 'R Us will not pick up a major slack in library purchases. There seems no eradicating a stubborn fact: somewhere between three-fifths and two-thirds of children's books annually are purchased by libraries, including, importantly, elementary and high school libraries.

One should add another category of books that rests on a foundation of library sales: reference works. Even the smallest community libraries must maintain at least a basic holding of dictionaries, encyclopedias, and atlases. And while retail booksellers may find individual purchasers for desk and collegiate dictionaries and the briefer encyclopedias, specialized reference works are library-dependent. A complete set of the twenty-volume *Grove's Dictionary of Music and Musicians,* for instance, would sit undisturbed on the typical bookstore's shelf.

Evidence abounds that the decline of the library as a place of books has already forced changes in publishing programs of nearly every stripe. Few leading trade publishers talk anymore about expanding their lists; instead, discussions center on altering the mix of titles, a polite form of advocating a shift away from the marginal book toward the potential blockbuster. Children's book publishers, aware that the "baby boomlet" produced by the baby boomer generation is over, now speak of an overpublished juvenile book market.

THE MOST ENDANGERED SPECIES

Trade books overall will survive, though diminished in number, variety, and, for the most part, in sales. There is another species of book under extreme pressure that is facing possible extinction as libraries reconfigure their expenditures to cope with an electronic present. Its departure in book form may be mourned by few; even the publishers primarily responsible for its appearance will avoid its last rites. I refer to the academic monograph or a subspecies of the same, the dissertation that goes into print with its dense prose and still denser footnotes intact. There is little that the publisher can do to disguise the origins of such works other than to remove the telltale statement "submitted in partial fulfillment..." from the title page of the manuscript. No amount of line editing is likely to alter the grim fact that the monograph will be read only by a handful of scholars and researchers intent on fleshing out bibliographies. (Editors at university presses may pray that the morning's mail will bring a dissertation that can be transformed into an influential, readable work. That occasionally happens, but not as often as an ugly duckling turns into a swan.)

An academic custom of long standing decrees that the publication of a dissertation is a major step on the road to tenure. Few universities, however, consider the limited demand facing a publisher who is willing to bolster the fledgling scholar's career. Other than the author and his admiring relatives, the dissertation has but one reliable source of sales: the university library. Yet with new technology straining university libraries' resources to the breaking point, sales of monographs—never robust—have gone into a freefall, from an average of approximately fifteen hundred copies a decade ago to six hundred or seven hundred copies now.

Some of what technology takes away with one hand it delivers with the other, though in meager recompense. Short print runs, that is, any quantity under fifteen hundred copies on press at a time, were shunned by all but a few specialty printers until the recent advent of equipment that scans and digitally stores a text and then provides for its retrieval on a screen or even its reproduction in book form. Of immense value in the preservation of the so-called brittle books, that is, books printed in the period roughly spanning 1880 through 1950 when publishers relied on paper with high acid content, this new machinery permits the publisher to print in small batches without incurring exorbitant costs. Still a large question remains. Even if economically feasible, does it make sense to publish works where demand is limited to six hundred copies or so when the very same document might be digitally stored and easily circulated on an electronic network? In the past a scholarly work could be given extended life in the form of a microfilm copy of the original typescript. The new technology makes archival status far easier to achieve. But old practices die hard in the university. It remains to be seen whether the committees that determine tenure and academic advancement in general will consider a digitized version of a manuscript, approved for "publication," the equivalent of a published work. This is terrain strewn with land mines that an outsider to the academy enters with peril.

Contingency plans, if not concrete directives, are in place at leading university presses to cut severely the output of titles for which scant demand can be expected. Directors at these presses are hard-bitten realists; they recognize that the typical academic library will continue to tilt its limited budget for print materials toward serial publications.

THE LAST DAYS OF THE TRADITIONAL LIBRARY?

The convergence of diminished funding for libraries with increasing reliance on computer-delivered information hastens the onset of the library without shelves. An all-electronic library or, as some would have it, a virtual library is something I would prefer to leave to the visionaries of Silicon Valley. Yet a virtual library site already exists on the World Wide Web, so we cannot simply consign the notion of a library without shelves to the far-off future, when, as Lord Keynes observed, we will all be dead. And with educators and politicians, up to and including President Clinton, determined to connect classrooms with the Internet, the time is fast approaching when students may routinely bypass libraries altogether. A few keystrokes on their computers will enable them to capture data without resorting to hefty reference tomes or a search of the card catalog. Those of us bred in the print culture, who look on books as more than dehydrated collections of facts, can only hope that even the most ardent 'Net surfers might occasionally want to explore ideas in depth. If so, traditional libraries presumably will have some utility as filling stations along the information super-highway.

Among the more ominous signs that the traditional library has already lost ground is the disappearance of schools of library science. Some have closed down without replacement; others have metamorphosed into institutions with but a trace memory of their earlier existence. In the second category is the newfangled School of Information Management and Systems at the University of California at Berkeley. Its mission statement opens with this observation:

> The information revolution has created the need for a new kind of professional: someone who is skilled in locating, organizing, manipulating, filtering, and presenting information.

This new professional, dubbed an information manager, "must be familiar with the technology used to store, organize, and retrieve information in business, government, libraries, and academic settings." What is missing in this picture? The book.

Yet Hal R. Varian, dean of this new school, sees the traditional library coexisting with the virtual library. The provision of information may not be its principal function but, in his view, its archival role will remain and perhaps expand since there are limits to what can and should be scanned for digital storage. Community service and the training of expert assistants for research, Varian asserts, almost certainly will be continuing functions of the public library.

Much has been written about the screening or gatekeeping role of publishers. That role is a direct consequence of the high expense of preparing and producing books—selecting, editing, designing, printing, binding, marketing, and storing. Nothing comparable in the way of a filtering system exists in cyberspace. But Varian envisages a rating system, "better bit bureaus" not unlike the

Zagat restaurant guides, where frequent users of an information cluster will rate material, advising Internet users and others on what is worth investigating. Quality control may thus be possible, although the sheer mass of material sent into cyberspace is likely to overwhelm the best-intentioned reviewers.

Even if Varian and some others at the frontier of information management value the traditional library, any rush of optimism must be tempered by the scarcity of funds that have any chance of gravitating to libraries, whether public or academic, while the anti-tax, anti-spend mood persists in the nation.

THE FALTERING WILL TO READ

Beyond money there is something corrosive in the culture that may be sapping the foundations of libraries and the publishing business writ large, newspapers and magazines as well as books. In order for printed matter in any form to thrive, there must be a will to read in the culture. Yet in almost all spheres of American life, reading is being reduced to its most elemental form, whether in various digest publications, executive summaries, abstracts of articles, or Cliff's Notes and their ilk (the immensely popular college reviews or cram books pitched at students determined to earn course credits the easy way). Although I am unaware that any magazine recently has adopted the practice of the defunct Colliers by posting "reading time" at the top of each article, a rage for brevity has transformed the length of articles in journals spanning the spectrum of reader interest from the *New Yorker* to *Foreign Affairs*. Some evidence from late Victorian England suggests that fin de siècle anxiety may foster a sense that time is at a premium. "The impatience of the age will not tolerate expansiveness in books," exclaimed the Publishers' Circular in 1890, but that comment must be weighed against contradictory data, such as the 4,239,000 volumes of Dickens' works sold in the twelve-year period from his death to 1882.[9]

The situation a century later seems less transient. There is, I am convinced, a retreat from reading that may be behind the notion of a technological fix for our educational deficiencies. Symptoms of the "dumbing down" of higher education can be detected not merely in the proliferation of courses designed for "scholar-athletes" but in the readily documented fact that at elite and run-of-the-mill institutions alike, professors have trimmed their reading lists to approximately half of the assignments given a decade ago. If further evidence is needed, college bookstores routinely report that a third of the students do not purchase the assigned texts for their courses, while books that are recommended but not required might as well not be stocked at all.

To make matters worse, many professors are undermining the book by the process of custom publishing. The course pack, a made-to-order textbook, consists of chapters taken from books or journal articles, photocopied (or retrieved from digital storage) and bound by the college bookstore. The course pack not only destroys sustained reading from longer works, it also deadens whatever impulse students once had for library research. And it will ultimately force publishers to declare scores of titles out-of-print that have existed as paperback reprints solely because they have been sustained by course adoptions. While course packs may, in the aggregate, provide a tidy profit to the local copy shop and sometimes a royalty to the professors who compile the volumes for their own use, the economic loss to the original creators of the material, authors and publishers, is substantial. Permissions fees for the right to reproduce passages and chapters from books throw off paltry sums; often, academics frustrated by the permissions process simply overlook copyright restrictions altogether in assembling their customized texts. (That some book publishers encourage the proliferation of course packs by setting up their own custom publishing divisions indicates that even in the book business a fifth column may be on the move.)

Book publishers individually and collectively lack the resources to police all the photocopying of copyrighted materials that takes place on the nation's campuses and corporations. Still, I would argue that there are greater damages than economic losses to authors and publishers caused by the course pack. Habits of mind become ingrained wherein the germ of an argument, not its full unfolding, becomes all-important. Already primed in their exams to seek the correct answer to multiple choice questions rather than reason the way to a conclusion in essay form, students are now being provided with shortcuts in their reading. Cumulatively, these potted and abbreviated assignments contribute to the spread inside and outside the educational system of what two Librarians of Congress have termed "aliteracy": the ability to read but the failure to exercise that skill.

THE PHOTOTROPIC GENERATION

At the Exploratorium, a museum of science and technology in San Francisco, there is an exhibit that holds an eerie fascination for me. In a cylindrical tank filled with salt water and illuminated at the top, thousands of brine shrimp float about, blissful no doubt that they lack arteries that would harden in the saline solution. Curiously, their purposeless movements all appear to be in one direction, upwards. But push a switch so that the light now shines at the bottom of the tank, and, like an aqueous corps de ballet, the tiny creatures turn almost in unison downwards toward the new light source.

The biological phenomenon taking place is phototropism. While this mindless, even fatal attraction to light may be prewired in relatively uncomplex creatures like brine shrimp, human beings obviously have other behavioral options. And yet, when one considers the hours that college-age individuals have daily spent in front of light-emitting sources, whether television or computer screens, can anyone doubt that the first generation of phototropic humans has made its way through the educational system? I predict that this generation and its successors will become even more phototropic now that virtual reality is merely a headphone and goggles away.[10]

I am not versed in the educationist's literature bearing on television or, for that matter, on computer learning. Nonetheless, I will go out on a short limb by surmising that the educational payoff from classroom television has been far less than its advocates contended it would be. As for computers, they are instruments of great instructional power that permit, for example, remarkable simulations of scientific phenomena and arrays of data that, in their absence, might require tedious, uninstructive hours of hand calculation. B. F. Skinner and his acolytes who promoted step-by-step, or programmed, learning three decades ago would no doubt be driving the bandwagon in favor of interactive, computer-based learning today. Yet when it comes to understanding an intricate web of ideas, stimulus-response learning seems to me no substitute for sustained reading. And bringing judgment into play demands experience in the linkage or assembly of information, not merely in its display. Books still do that best.

Paradoxically, the computer as an educational device has taken on one aspect of the book that has caused teachers some frustration in the classroom. It instills an absolute certainty in students that what appears on the screen must, by its mere existence in electronic form, be accurate. Teachers have long been accustomed to railing against errors in books, because no matter how hard they try to correct those errors in class, students regard the book as the Higher Authority. Now computer infallibility may be the mind-set that must be overcome.

INTELLECTUAL PROPERTY RIGHTS AND WRONGS

The ideal of the free public library providing reading matter without charge to its users is deeply embedded in this nation's history. In Europe and elsewhere, library patrons pay a modest fee when borrowing a book, a charge that comes under the rubric "public lending right." The monies collected for such charges are then rebated to publishers who treat this income as a form of royalty to their authors. I am not the least bit hopeful that the notion of a public lending right will ever gain acceptance in this country even though, according to Ernest Seeman, "the majority opinion is that libraries reduce book sales [even if] nobody has proffered any hard evidence as to the magnitude of this reduction."[11] For want of such evidence, American publishers have never campaigned for fee-based library usage of books.

But publishers' attitudes may be stiffening when it comes to electronic transmission of copyrighted material. Especially galling to publishers is copying that takes place not out of a library's own holdings but through electronic library loans from distant collections. No longer is this merely a hypothetical issue; some libraries have already converted parts of their collections through scanning into digital form for storage and retrieval. There is, for example, a program in development at the library of the University of Colorado at Boulder that will transmit scanned images from computer to computer, although it is not actually in use yet.

In a position paper on scanning's threat to book publication, the publishers' trade association notes that "scanned text may be readily printed out in highly polished and reformatted presentations, indistinguishable from high quality typeset presentations, thus competing directly with the originals, without diminution of quality, content or appearance."

Sensitivity on the part of the library community to the publishers' concerns may exist, but it is nowhere to be found in a "working document" of the Association of Research Libraries, issued on January 18, 1995. That document, one hopes, is not actually working, for it asserts that nonprofit libraries should be able, among other activities, to provide copyrighted materials as part of electronic interlibrary loan service.

It is perhaps best to leave with lawyers the murky task of defining "fair use," based on the 1976 Copyright Law and the substantial case law that it has spawned. To a publisher *unfair* use may follow in the spirit of Justice Potter Stewart's dictum on pornography, "I may not be able to define it but I know it when I see it." The trouble with the research libraries' position is two-fold: it accelerates "resource sharing" to the point where a single copy of a book might now serve several hundred libraries, eroding the all too tenuous marginal revenue for the marginal book, and it casts the library in the role of the sorcerer's apprentice, that is, the library may unwittingly become an agency for individuals seeking to download material from electronic to print format for the purpose of manufacturing a pirated edition. One indication that the second point is more than publisher's paranoia can be found in the working document's insistence that "libraries, on behalf of their clientele, should be able to avoid liability, after posting appropriate copyright notices, for the unsupervised actions of their users." Given the spirit of the working document, I confess to worrying, too, about the *supervised* actions of their users. At the same time, I cannot envisage any device that publishers might persuade libraries to install, which, like the Club that impedes car hijacking, might stop copyright infringers in their tracks.

Thefts of copyrighted material placed on the Internet are occurring with increasing frequency, with publishers unable to mount an effective defense against these depredations. For librarians to disclaim any responsibility for illicit use of their computer facilities smacks of Tom Lehrer's unforgettable ditty on a well-known rocket scientist:

When the missiles go up, who cares where they come down
That's not my department, says Werner von Braun.

A PARTNERSHIP RESTORED?

Having devoted so much space to worrying about matters that divide libraries and publishers, I should point out what should be a cause for common concern: the enemy of the book is already at the gates. According to Nicholas Negroponte, founding director of the Media Lab at the Massachusetts Institute of Technology, the book has outlived its usefulness. It is ripe for replacement by hypermedia. Unlike the printed book where "sentences, paragraphs, pages, and chapters follow in an order determined not only by the author but by the physical and sequential construct of the book," in hypermedia "chunks of information can be re-ordered, sentences expanded, and words given definitions on the spot." If Negroponte were not conceiving all this activity taking place on-line, with the possibility of the text being mixed with pictures and sound, one man's hypermedia-ist would be another man's editor.

Ultimately, in this construct, the past retains dubious value. Indeed, Simone Weil's admonition that "the destruction of the past is perhaps the greatest of all crimes"[12] stands a pole apart from Negroponte's insistence that "the access, the mobility, and the ability to effect change" in virtual reality promises "new hope and dignity where very little existed before."[13] Having confessed that he is "someone who does not like to read," perhaps Negroponte may have been library-deprived in his youth. But he is far from alone among the cybernauts in his obsessive concern for the present and the future.

In his *Anti-Intellectualism in American Life,* Richard Hofstadter makes a distinction between intelligence, "an excellence of mind employed within a fairly narrow, immediate, and predictable range," and intellect, "the critical, creative, and contemplative side of mind." In support of this dichotomy he dwells on the forces within American culture, including the educational system, that drive a wedge between intelligence and intellect, forces that favor the "manipulative, adjustive, unfailing practical quality" of intelligence.[14] Hofstadter failed to identify the library as one place where instruments could be found that meet the needs both of the problem solver and the free-range intellectual; those instruments are books. To the extent that librarians become transfixed with the sheer quantity of information that can be tapped electronically, they ally themselves unwittingly with those who measure the worth of ideas by their applicability. Once it is no longer book-centered, the library becomes a fringe institution in the intellectual life of the nation.

To the query, "Why do you rob banks?" the dapper Willie Sutton replied, "'Cause that's where the money is." If someday my grandchildren ask me, "Why do you go to the library?" I still hope to reply, "'Cause that's where the books are."

ENDNOTES

[1]Summary, *The White House Conference on Library and Information Services, 1979* (Washington, D.C.: Government Printing Office, 1980).

[2]Daniel Boorstin, *The Republic of Letters* (Washington, D.C.: Library of Congress, 1989), 45.

[3]National Center for Educational Statistics, US Department of Education, *Public Libraries in 50 States and the District of Columbia, 1989* (Washington, D.C.: US Department of Education, April 1991.)

[4]Catherine Barr, ed., *The 1995 Bowker Annual* (New Providence, N.J.: R. R. Bowker, 1995).

[5]Herbert S. Bailey, Jr., *The Art and Science of Book Publishing* (New York: Harper and Row, 1970).

[6]Barr, ed., *The 1995 Bowker Annual,* 125.

[7]Marshall Best, "In Books They Call It a Revolution," *Dædalus* 92 (1) (Winter 1963).

[8]Ian Watt, *The Rise of the Novel* (Berkeley, Calif.: University of California Press, 1957), 13.

[9]Richard D. Altick, *The English Common Reader* (Chicago, Ill.: University of Chicago Press, 1957), 369.

[10]These observations are based on my Phi Beta Kappa lecture, "Is it Real? Does It Matter?," at Yale University, February 1994.

[11]Ernest A. Seeman, "A Comparative Look at Public Lending Rights from the USA," in Seeman et al., *Public Lending Rights* (Amsterdam: Kluwer, 1977).

[12]Simone Weil, *The Need for Roots* (London: Routledge, Chapman and Hall, 1979).

[13]Nicholas Negroponte, *Being Digital* (New York: Knopf, 1995).

[14]Richard Hofstadter, *Anti-Intellectualism in American Life* (New York: Knopf, 1979), 24–25.

Jamie Frederic Metzl

Searching for the Catalog of Catalogs

A LIBRARY IS A HOME FOR BOOKS, a storehouse of collective knowledge, a connection to past generations, and a mental passageway to new worlds.

For me, however, these are second degree realizations. My primary experience of libraries, the starting point of my deep love for them, begins in the predawn of thought, in the realm of the senses. It is my senses that first draw me into the library and form the passageway to the universe of the mind. Before I open a single volume, I am struck by the sheer physicality of the sculpture-like rows of books bound in varying sizes, shapes, and colors.

In addition to its particular form, each book has its own smell. It is a perfect smell, a smell that gives physical life to thoughts and ideas through the interaction of paper and ink. As the book takes in the oils on its users' hands, its readers' perfume, the amalgamated scents of neighboring works, it changes over time.

The unique physical forms of books announce ideas; they embody what was at some time the most pressing issue of someone's life, its author's response to being, his or her reason for perhaps neglecting an "understanding" spouse and children in the name of posterity. In the library, this magical place, the voices of these authors great and small reach a communion with the congregation of readers whose identities are whispered by an archaeology of wrinkled pages, illegal pencil marks, and disordered stamps of return dates long since past. It is the chorus of humanity's greatest aspiration, the challenge of the past to wisely, intelligently, and thoughtfully construct the future.

Jamie Frederic Metzl is a third year student at Harvard Law School.

The library is a shrine to these aspirations, and I have explored as a supplicant two of the world's great libraries—the Bodleian at Oxford and Widener at Harvard. Both are holy sites of literary humanity, containing busts of great writers and engraved names of literary virtuosi. Both post guards at their doors who strictly check the credentials of those who go in and meticulously search the bags of those who go out. While the Widener stacks are open to those with proper identification, the Bodleian does not allow such a mingling of the sacred and the profane. There, books must be ordered on small slips of paper and retrieved a few hours later in chapel-like reading rooms. It is a religious experience that brings my earlier education to mind.

In the Jewish tradition, the congregation stands when the ark is opened and the Torah, the most sacred of texts, is revealed. While the "real" Torah must be housed in the ark, the same words are available in books that are stored in holders traditionally found on the back of each seat. The "real" Torah is not meant to be touched directly by human hands, but these books are meant to be handled, carried, and used to exhaustion. Though the congregation had been standing when the closed scroll was displayed, they sit when the scroll is opened and the reading of its content begins. The object of the Torah, therefore, has acquired a meaning separate from and in some respects greater than the words it contains. The worshippers stand in awe before an object, a literary work whose content establishes meaning but whose sacredness is only fully bestowed by two wooden rollers, anointed parchment, and meticulously handcrafted letters. It is a similar appreciation of the physical presence of books separate from their content that colors my interaction with the Oxford and Harvard libraries. Receiving a book in the Bodleian is like standing while the ark is opened. Wandering the Widener stacks is more like stepping up to the ark.

Within this ark are so many mysteries, a labyrinth of hidden treasures. As I set out to find a specific citation, each book I pass announces a potential personal discovery, an unexpected inroad to an unexplored self. In those moments when I encounter such new surprises, I feel the sense-driven decision to pick up a certain book and begin a journey toward a new self that may in the future seem inevitable and axiomatic. My serial epiphanies become me as I interact with ideas, but also with ideas embodied in the particular form of the book.

Delving deep into the treasures of these libraries of old, however, my experience reveals glimpses of the new libraries, the libraries that are changing and will change my experience of books, of being in the library, and of being in the world. Even in the ancient Bodleian, one can feel this transformation.

The Bodleian's catalogs are a biblio-archaeologist's dream, where the passage of time and the rise of new technology can be traced in time-sequenced layers of cataloging. A reader looking for the library's older books must search the gargantuan, elegantly leather-bound tomes that contain listings glued onto thickly textured paper. Books published in the 1960s and 1970s are listed in wooden card catalogs, and works from the 1980s onward can be found through the on-line computer network. All of these systems are located in the same area, and there is a constant buzz of researchers shuffling to and fro.

As a member of a generation reared on books and card catalogs, who reluctantly accepted computer word processing to save time in college and fought off exploring e-mail and the Internet when doing graduate work in England (where a fellow doctoral candidate boasted to me that he was writing his entire dissertation by hand) only to later dive headfirst into cyberspace while in law school, the Bodleian's odd demarcation of time seemed to match the course of my own development. The bound volumes seemed the weightiest, the most time-honored, like the thick encyclopedias I had consulted as a child—uniquely appropriate to the imposing titles of old such as Gibbon's and Macaulay's. The card catalogs were the next step, reflecting a more conscious ordering of books, a manipulation for convenience's sake that was hard to imagine in my earliest childhood. The terminals paralleled my efficient, modern self, with access to the four corners of the world. They seemed to match the exploding number of books I had watched march from the best-seller list to the dollar store with seasonal regularity.

In contrast, something about the catalog rooms at Harvard seemed disharmonious to me. Harvard has invested heavily in updating its catalogs, and most materials are now on-line. As a result, the computer terminal room pulsates with the busy sounds of clicking keys and rhythmically-gliding printer jets. It is an efficient, corporate space. In contrast, the long rows of mahogany card cabinets languish, antique-like, in a completely silent and almost always empty room nearby. As I march towards the computers, I reflect that the wooden shelves seem closer cousins to the books—perhaps because they have no other function than to serve them—than do the multipurpose, ubiquitous computers. I miss leafing through the cards, following with my fingers the paths of so many before me.

At the keyboard, however, my physical reality changes. The fingers that searched back and forth in the card catalog become a thousand fingers connected to arms reaching in seemingly infinite directions. I skip around frenetically and search across subjects by combining key words or by specifying languages or certain dates of publication. I search all ninety libraries in the university, doing in five minutes what might otherwise have taken an hour or longer. Instead of scribbling call numbers on a scrap of paper, I print out the relevant information. I am the picture of efficiency as I cut across layers and levels of the library to pinpoint the exact targets of my search. I am the captain at the controls, and with a printout in hand I head into the stacks, but now with a clear target in mind. Of course, I am often sidetracked, but now that visiting the library is something I can do with twenty free minutes between classes, I map out a course and make a beeline to the books I have selected. I have the books in my bag as I sit down to my next class. I am on time and have even picked up a decaf latte to go on the way. But how do we know, I later ask myself, of potential epiphanies that we might have had but did not?

When I have less time, or when I have planned ahead, I search the computer catalog from home after checking my e-mail before bed. In my few free moments the next day, I rush in and pick up my books. This process gives me a glimpse of what seems sure to come. If I can search for the books at home, and the computer keeps track of which books are on the shelves and which are out, it seems unnecessary, inefficient, and economically wasteful for me to fetch the books personally and check them out from a student on work-study. It would make more sense to request the book on-line, order the computer to retrieve it from a storage facility and check it out to me, and pick it up by inserting my ID into a card reader at a take-out window. If the Denver International Airport with its modern automated baggage system has become one of the most efficient airports in the world, is it not inevitable that libraries will soon shift to the Denver system, one whose main functionaries require no health benefits or sick days? Even this high-tech system seems largely transitional, as it is based on the physical book model—a model that will remain prominent until sufficient percentages of old books are scanned, new books are accessibly placed on-line, and computer terminals are made more comfortable to use. In an electronic environment, I do not need to go to the books as a supplicant before the ark; the books, or rather the words that exist within them, come to me.

In my two years at Harvard Law School, I have searched cases at the law library, one of the world's great legal libraries, perhaps five times. Most everything I have needed was more easily, conveniently, and quickly available on Westlaw, a private on-line information service. When I need to cite a case, I can call it up on my home computer in a second and seek all references to it in other opinions or law articles. I can search all major newspapers or any of the thousands of data bases on a wide variety of topics. I can look for any of these materials by targeting key words whose frequency of occurrence will be revealed to me in materials listed in order of applicability. I can access today's articles on the situation in Bosnia as well as information on where to find the best croissant in Paris. Sure, the law library is still a nice quiet place to read casebooks and write letters, to visit the thick volumes that comprise the background of great justices' photographs, but the library that I really use and find most useful is the cyberlibrary I access in my pajamas.

Westlaw has surpassed the law library for my classmates and me so quickly and made such deep inroads into the legal community because it is efficient and effective for its users and profitable to its providers. Although offered free to law students, Westlaw charges firms about three hundred dollars an hour, a cost justified to the firms because it lets a lawyer accomplish in one hour on-line what otherwise might have taken a day.

Just as economic forces are pushing the electronification of the relevant legal library, so too are they transforming other shelves of the traditional library. In the electronic world, a particular text can be copied an infinite number of times for a virtually negligible cost (except for that of creating the original). According to simple supply and demand economics, a system of such easy copying, where copyright law becomes increasingly difficult to apply, could drive down the cost of the text dramatically. As more materials are placed on-line and people become more accustomed to searching on-line for the information they desire, this will challenge traditional sales models for physical books.

A large percentage of the works on Westlaw, with the notable exception of cases and other government documents, are permission-granted copyrighted materials. Westlaw pays the newspapers and journals whose materials are posted based on the amount of time users spend with each newspaper or journal article on their screen. It seems almost certain that publishers will do the same in the future, even if some works are initially embargoed in the electronic format so as not to compete with early sales of a physical book. This would be similar to the current movie market, where a film makes money first from a relatively small number of people paying seven dollars for a movie ticket and later from a larger number paying two dollars to rent a video. While nostalgic or specialty publishers may cling to traditional practices and sell entire works for a one-off fixed price, an increasing number of others will follow the Westlaw model and charge users in micro-charges of fractions of cents for time spent actually using a text.

Because illegal copies will thus threaten to cut substantially into an electronic publisher's profits, publishers will have an incentive to encrypt each text so that it cannot be transferred or copied onto a network. They will also want to make sure that no organizations, including libraries, are exempt from copying restrictions because one copy can generate an infinite number of others. Like everybody else, libraries would have to pay for time spent using a copyrighted work on-line. As more books go on-line, the aggregate costs of making these payments will grow, and libraries without unlimited budgets will find themselves having to balance money spent purchasing physical books and money spent paying for on-line services. As new books come out electronically and older books are scanned, this balance will invariably tip in favor of the on-line materials. Slowly, the percentage of on-line books will increase relative to their aging pulp cousins. With the help of computer networks and the Internet, this will create a global virtual library.

This virtual library will be a miracle of access. It will open the doors of the Bodleian and Widener not only to students wanting to work at home, but to aspiring Mongolian academics, Namibian journalists, and anybody else with the proper equipment and a little money. I realized the potential of this miracle on a recent visit to Cambodia, where I had lived for two years as a UN human rights worker. The libraries of Cambodia were decimated during the three and a half years of Khmer Rouge rule, as clearly evidenced in the "bibliotheque" of the Cambodian National Assembly in Phnom Penh. As I stepped into the small room, I was struck by how pathetic it was. The newly built shelves housed only about ten law books, and a few papers were piled on the floor. The librarian told me that the library had just opened and there was not much of a budget for books. The old law books had been destroyed or lost, she said, and new ones were too expensive to acquire. If ever there was an argument for an electronic library, I thought to myself, this was it. Cambodia was Internet-ready, and with one hookup in this library, the world's laws, access to legislators across the globe, and an endless stream of legal materials would instantly become available. Electronic media promised to bring Widener and the law library to my home but also here, to this remote place with no chance of building a physical library of its own.

As was clear to me in Cambodia, the virtual library that information technology creates has the tremendous potential to democratize access to knowledge, the most precious human commodity, and provide a forum for cross-cultural communication. In short, it stands to universalize the local mission of the library. As the walls of the library expand, however, what we have known as the library moves closer towards becoming what we know as information. Our perceptions and experience of books and libraries will undoubtedly change as a result. It will transform the individual act of reading, the social space of the library, and important aspects of the physical world around us.

I begin gathering materials on Westlaw by listing the key words that I want searched. If I want to examine articles on the best croissants in Paris, I can type "croissant /P Paris /P best," which will retrieve articles that contain those three words in any of their paragraphs. I can access the full texts of the listed articles in any order I choose. Once I call up a text, I can go directly to the specific paragraph containing the words without having to read any other part of the article.

While I did not read every word of every book listed in the bibliography of my doctoral dissertation, I did at least try to understand the perspective and basic argument of each author. The computer-facilitated ability to search so quickly and directly for so precise a piece of information seems, in contrast, inherently threatening to the idea of the book as an integrated whole. It is not that an on-line user does not have the opportunity to read an on-line work in its entirety, but rather that I feel myself being conditioned to think of articles and books less as integrated narratives and more as groupings of small bits of information that can be accessed independently. This partial change in my own temperament is even more apparent to me in the younger generation. My younger brother, ten years my junior, can barely make it through a book straight from beginning to end and requires six compact discs loaded at all times, switching incessantly from one to another. These are exciting and lively qualities; they are not, however, scholarly. A literary world is divided into books, an information world into bits. Books take time and patience. They need hidden corners of the Bodleian.

While both books and bits are central to my thinking life, new ways of accessing information have forced me to divide my experience of the two. For the pieces of information I use to fill footnotes and build the scaffolding around my ideas, I turn on my computer and flash like a semioticist between floating bits of information. To think through ideas, to process my life through the nightly installment of my current novel, I take out "real" books, lovingly feeling the pages that I turn. It is my split personality as a cross-generational reader. As comfortable as this feels, however, I recognize that the special feel of books and the world they create for me is not instinctive but learned—and the younger generation is learning it less. For them, a computer screen may seem more natural than a newspaper, and curling up in bed with a pocket monitor may feel just as familiar as curling up with a novel does to me.

In addition to changing popular conceptions of the book, the virtual literary world will alter the social space of the library. Libraries, in some ways quite uniquely, offer privacy in the most public of fora. Searching the stacks and retreating to a carrel are intensely individual activities; they are the background to private dreams and musings. They occur, however, in a public space where all of the materials—the books, the tables, the chairs—are shared. All of this dissolves when I bring the library home to my solely private world. From the private space of my home, I reach the transnational virtual community of private and electronic spaces. I can search the catalogs of libraries in Moscow, Cairo, or Mexico City and meet others with interests similar to mine in offices and homes across the globe. After connecting with someone at a Southeast Asian studies think tank in Singapore, for example, I was asked to write an article for the center's journal. I attached my article to an e-mail file that went directly into the center's word processor. When I was missing a citation for another article I was working on, I instantly found a listing in Bangkok's Chulalongkorn University Library.

This public international community, however, is very different from the community of human beings who together construct the physical reality of the traditional library. The traditional library, like the salon or the university, is a forum for human communication. Scholars naturally meet and discuss in libraries, but more important is the shared intellectual space that the library helps create, a meeting space between humans and ideas. While the library is not the only space where this can happen, it is an extremely important one. Its demise would not be without cost, even if it was slowly displaced by its virtual cousin.

The transformation of the traditional library and of the book culture into an electronic one changes the physical realities of our lives. Nostalgically observing the frayed prayer books in the background of an old photograph of yeshiva students, Yale computer scientist David Gelernter reflected,

A religious community creates a spiritual landscape. The landscape includes physical objects. The objects are shaped by the faithful and shape them in turn. They tend to live longer than people, so they connect generations; they absorb one generation's emotions and radiate them to the next. The things don't last forever, of course; each generation introduces some new ones and retires some old ones. But the spiritual landscape changes slowly relative to a human life span.[1]

"Retiring" books means much more than just changing their form. It means altering, at least in part, the spiritual landscape that we have constructed for ourselves. It means altering our perception and experience of the physical object of a book.

When the electronic revolution removes literary content from the exclusive domain of books, what remains is the book as an object, a pure form given life and meaning by its words but also by its sheer physicality—its touch, its feel, its smell, the way it fits in our hands. It is a carrier of content that in itself becomes a new form of content, an object containing meaning (words) that enters the physical landscape of our lives as a corporeal presence of meaning itself.

Curiously, this advance of modernity entails a return to a world before the printing press, when literary works like the Torah and Christian illuminated manuscripts took on meanings additional to their verbal composition. Gutenberg's world of books as content gives way to the biblical and postmodern world of books as sacred objects.

My desire to join the sacred literary community was very much in my mind as I read through the contract my publisher sent for my first book. The publisher was targeting the book at libraries and had therefore decided on a small print run at a high price. At almost sixty dollars a book, I doubted whether many would buy it except for my grandparents in Miami Beach and my most loyal friends. If the only people who would see it were those with access to libraries, I thought, would it not just be better to put the book on-line and send it out for the world to read? My paltry royalties offered little counterargument. It was an exciting prospect. The more I thought about it, the more depressed I became.

Like Gelernter's yeshiva students, books have charted the land-scape of my development. The books in my old room in my parents' house speak of the younger me grappling with new ideas. Piled on top of them are the types of books that I read in college as I tried on identities like hats in a thrift shop. Beside my desk in my current home are the special books that have made it through all of the selections. There is the thick volume of *Remembrance of Things Past*—the final half pound removed from my crate in order to fit my UN shipping allowance when returning from Cambodia. Though I had already read the book, I hand-carried it through China rather than leave it behind. Sure, I could have bought another book for twenty dollars, but this book was mine. These were the very madeleines I had thought of as I lay sweating in bed, reading through another power outage with my dying flashlight. There are my intimate books by Mishima and Yehudah Amichai that had helped me through painful and passionate times and now existed as objects testifying to the self of such extremes. My book, the ideas I had expressed as well as the physical object of the book, the connection of paper and ink, was destined to take its place among these physical signposts of my life—these constant reminders that I lived and had lived, that I was on a journey going somewhere, somewhere from where I would look back at the present moment. The book was more than an idea, it was an idea incorporated. I would send it with notes of gratitude to past mentors and think of my great-grandchildren finding it in an old rotten box, seeing their last name, reading it and wondering who the old man in the photographs had been, why he wrote such things.

The alternative hardly looked as appealing. With no filter, no publisher deciding what should and should not be published, no careful editors guiding the work, my book would be mixed with a million other works of greater and lesser quality. Yes, I would be on the same system as Shakespeare, but my work would more likely be confused with term papers from Cal State Fullerton and memoirs of obscure accountants. People searching through these vast stores of material would zoom from one piece of information to another without realizing how carefully and deliberately I had crafted my argument. They would pick apart pieces of information from my book like mechanics at an automobile salvage yard. As time passed, the pre-programmed "intelligence agents" that determine which works make it to the top of a computer-generated search list would send my work into obscurity. No, I thought, I wanted my name pasted into a leather book in the Bodleian. I wanted to smell the new book and visit it in the library. I wanted to experience my ideas as an object.

I knew, however, that I was a hypocrite. I also wanted to access other people's books at three o'clock in the morning. I wanted people in far corners of the earth to read my work and think thoughts that grew out of mine. When a spin-off article from the book was accepted by an obscure international law journal, it did not bother me a bit that the journal was not well known. I knew that in an electronic age, people search by subject and that to the computer all journals are equal. Even if the journal had two subscribers, my article would come up before articles in the most prestigious of journals to those who inputted the right keywords in their search request. If my love of books represented the future of the old libraries, my realization of these truths reminded me of how fast those libraries were changing. The libraries of the twentieth century were perfect for holding the books of the twentieth century. They would not, I knew, be suited for many of the literary works of the next generation.

At a recent dinner party I debated the future of the book with the wife of a former professor who now heads a book publishing company. She maintained that there would never be a market for an electronic novel because a novel requires character development that does not happen on the computer. It is just too easy to move back and forth on-line, to shuttle from one experience to another like my little brother choosing between CDs. I thought about this, and it made sense. The novels I had read were mostly linear, progressing through the development of characters to a predetermined denouement. Putting this type of novel on-line would just transfer the same thing to a new medium, like putting a lively concert on tape or a rousing lecture on paper. Perhaps, I then thought, the electronic novel is not about character but about possibility.

In the hypertext novel of the future, the reader will navigate through an interlinked series of options offered by an author, all embedded in a central text. The course of the reader's personal selections will become the novel, which will be different each time the text is interactively read. This electronic novel, like human life itself, did not know its own future. It contained a range of possibilities for each character to experience one life or another, to muddle through a series of improvisations that together become a life, to not know where life is going but only to be able to look back at previous choices to know from where it has come. Perhaps the novel of the future was not one entity to be filed away on a shelf but many that needed the vast infinity of cyberspace for its realization. And I wondered who would be the historians of this infinite space.

If the library is the repository of our collective past, where would we place the physical memory of our electronic future? As the amounts of information, filtered and unfiltered, expanded exponentially, I wondered how we would ever track the past literary trajectory to the present and where the ark would be that our children and descendants might want to approach to consult the wisdom of past generations. The library had become the universe and the universe the library, and there were no leather-bound Bodleian volumes to keep track of it all. Perhaps the walls of the library were not wide enough to hold the vast universe of information.

And I thought of Jorge Borges, who tells of his search for the catalog of catalogs in the "The Library of Babel." "The universe," he states,

> (which others call the library) is composed of an indefinite and perhaps infinite number of hexagonal galleries with vast air shafts between, surrounded by very low railings. From any of the hexagons one can see, interminably, the upper and lower floors. . .through here passes a spiral stairway which sinks abysmally and soars upwards to remote distances. In the hallway there is a mirror which faithfully duplicates all appearances. Men usually infer from this mirror that the Library is not infinite. . . . I prefer to dream that its polished surfaces represent and promise the infinite.[2]

Borges's library, like the library of the electronic future and the dreams of the physical past, reaches out of the spacial and the linear, out of the corporeal and the profane. Libraries have never been large enough to contain such aspirations. They will have to grow in new ways to track our collective journey as we seek the catalog of catalogs we will never find.

ENDNOTES

[1]David Gelernter, "The Dark Side of Jews in Cyberspace," *Sh'ma* 25 (483) (9 December 1994): 1–2.

[2]Jorge Luis Borges, "The Library of Libraries," in *Labyrinths* (New York: New Directions, 1964), 51.

Marilyn Gell Mason

The Yin and Yang of Knowing

I NFORMATION THEORISTS AND PRACTITIONERS have announced the information revolution. They tell us that computer and communications technologies will transform every aspect of our lives, from the way we know what we know to how we choose to govern ourselves. They predict the overthrow of print as a communications medium in favor of digitized information, consumed screen by screen from a computer attached electronically to the Internet. They contend that libraries will vanish from the earth, an anachronism in an electronic age.

There is no question that computer and communications technologies will play a role in our lives; they already do. The issue is whether the operative metaphor is the invention of the automobile, with its displacement of the horse and buggy, or something more akin to the invention of the television, a device that coexists with the radio, movies, and now videos as each fills a part of the information/entertainment spectrum. In short, will electronic technologies displace the printed page and revolutionize the way we make sense of the world, or will they work with existing ones, each occupying its own niche? Let us look at some of the basic questions.

IS IT A REVOLUTION?

The human spirit longs to live in revolutionary times, times loaded with meaning, pregnant with anticipation, full of promise for the future. Previous generations amplified their lives through religion,

Marilyn Gell Mason is Director of the Cleveland Public Library.

a system of belief that embodied social value and promised life everlasting to the true believer who followed certain rules. With the growing devaluation of religion, the need for value and hope has found its way into new systems of belief that many embrace with the intensity and commitment previously reserved for matters of divine revelation.

These new systems of belief are often cast as revolutions, since they predict massive change throughout society, but are often based on a limited set of observations and have a bias toward a specific set of actions. Some examples: In the post-World War II era we believed that science would bring us peace, prosperity, and at least a modicum of stability. As a nation we pursued the secret of the atom and the challenge of walking on the moon. As the baby boomer generation came of age, sex replaced science, and we came to believe that "all you need is love." Grown up and disillusioned, the idealism of the flower children gave way to money as a measure of value, and many believed—or acted as if they believed—that "the one who dies with the most toys wins," a slogan based on the belief that winning was the goal and spending the way to achieve it.

Ironically, the most revolutionary development of the past fifty years in the United States was not seen as a revolution at the time. It became a revolution gradually, as millions of Americans changed the conditions of their lives. It was the suburbanization of America, a revolution that finds its roots in the invention of the automobile, the passage of the GI Bill, and the enactment of the Civil Rights Act. Flowing from the desire for home ownership, the forces of government subsidy, mobility, and empowerment led to a de facto caste society where people sort themselves by race, ethnicity, and wealth. This, in turn, led to the current problems of isolation and urban decay, conditions that have created a vast underclass of people who are unable to participate in the information revolution because they are unable to read. It is hard to imagine electronic technologies transforming the lives of the 50 to 60 percent of urban public school students who fail to graduate, are unable to get and hold a job, and live on the margins of society. There may be a revolution here, but it is not an information revolution. If there is a transforming effect at all, it is among the educational elite.

For them, information theorists make extravagant promises of a perfect life in cyberspace, a new democracy where every man and woman can pursue his or her heart's desire in the pale glow of a computer, a virtual community where everyone has access to all recorded knowledge at the click of a mouse. New words have entered the language: Internet, World Wide Web, Netscape, user group. We surf the 'Net, travel the information highway, and interface with other like-minded souls.

Postmodernists like Sherry Turkle, professor of Sociology of Science at the Massachusetts Institute of Technology, claim that in this new, revolutionary information age "no unitary truth resides anywhere. There is only local knowledge, contingent and provisional. . . . The surface is what matters, to be explored by navigation. . . . Postmodernism celebrates this time, this place; and it celebrates adaptability, contingency, diversity, flexibility, sophistication, and relationships—with the self and with the community." Computers and the Internet, she claims, are postmodern because they foster "the precedence of surface over depth, of simulation over the real, of play over seriousness."[1] Or, to put it another way, nothing is true in or of itself; truth is only an artifact of social negotiation.

Other writers predict "the displacement of the page by the screen,"[2] and that "hypertext" will remove "the limitations of the printed page."[3] Turkle notes that "we've had a long run with print," and that "print has been a transparent medium for expressing a unitary self."[4] She believes that computers and computing networks are more in line with what she sees as a new, integrated reality.

These and other writers suggest that screens will replace books, that everyone will have access to everything electronically, and that the electronic media will significantly change—"revolutionize"—the way we know what we know and how we interact with each other on the basis of that knowledge. In short, they are predicting the death of books, the end of libraries, the abandonment of organized knowledge. Knowledge gives way to information and data—more data, faster data, information and data without bounds.

While these ideas are not really new (Marshall McLuhan concluded that the medium is the message more than twenty-five years ago, and Pierre Teilhard de Chardin was developing his theory of the Omega point in the 1940s), they do take on new meaning with the proliferation of personal computers and the enunciation of a national goal to wire America (first the United States, then the world). But are they revolutionary? If by revolution we mean a sudden, radical change affecting a large percentage of our society, the conclusion would have to be no, based on the alarming, and growing, portion of the population who cannot afford a computer and could not read the digitized text if they had one. If by revolution we mean a sudden, radical change in the way the rest of us get and use information, we must examine other questions.

WILL BOOKS GO THE WAY OF THE HORSE AND BUGGY?

To understand the relationship between the printed and digitized word (or image) we must first understand the difference between knowledge and information. While information may be thought of as a simple data point, knowledge requires data collection, contemplation, and the integration of new principles into an existing fabric of knowledge. While information may be random and dissociated, knowledge requires organization of some type and implies value. Knowledge answers the basic question: What does it mean? A reporter, for instance, may announce that the war in Bosnia is heating up. From an epistemological perspective this statement already implies an understanding of the concepts of war and nationalism, but beyond this most basic organization, the statement might be considered information. If the listener also knows where Bosnia is and something about its history, he or she adds the additional information about war to the preexisting base of knowledge, and his or her understanding is richer.

While it is clear that information and knowledge are interdependent, information tends to be more postmodern, to use the words of Turkle and others, while knowledge still has something of an old-fashioned flavor about it. While information may be contingent, knowledge requires context. Information may be fast; knowledge often comes more slowly.

Claims for the revolutionary nature of digitized information are often based on assumptions that everyone will have access to everything quickly and at a cost that is trivial. In fact, we are far from having all information digitized. Some experts estimate that less than 1 percent of all information is now available digitally. Nor is everyone on-line. In the United States fewer than 10 percent of households have Internet access. Finally, while it is undeniable that the cost to access and retrieve digitized information is falling and that the Internet is the most efficient way to get some information, it is also true that surfing the 'Net can become a very time-intensive and inefficient way to get other information.

If the claim that everyone will have access to everything quickly and efficiently is not now true, the question remains, if it were true, would it be desirable? From a practical perspective, does it make sense to invest the massive resources necessary to convert the remaining 99 percent of existing information into a digital format?

Some distinctions are in order. For very specific information, like the latest stock market quotations or a recipe for vegetable lasagna, there is nothing better than the Internet, especially with the graphic capability of the World Wide Web. Less precise questions may, however, yield hundreds or even thousands of sites of dubious origin that may or may not contain accurate information. For still other material, usually of a more conceptual nature like history, philosophy, or fiction, print may in fact be the most efficient delivery system. Books are still pretty handy packages, and people often behave in ways that are not strictly logical. Some may borrow a book from the library before deciding to buy it. Others, especially frequent travelers, may choose to purchase a paperback over a hard cover because of weight.

This bias toward print for some documents was acknowledged by Bill Gates in a recent speech at Harvard University.[5] Gates noted that even at Microsoft, when a document runs to three or four screens, people tend to print it out rather than read and use it in a digitized format. This suggests that in some instances the Internet merely becomes a faster distribution system for what is still a conventional information package.

There are reasons people prefer print for some documents and a computer screen for others. A printed document is essentially different from an electronic one. Digital information is, as Turkle says, postmodern. It is present, contingent, two-dimensional, and value-free. On the screen everything has equal weight, equal value. Nothing is more or less important than anything else. And everything is fast. That means that information arrives quickly, it is (or can be) current, and users tend to bring a short attention span to the task, with behavior that is more like that of skipping from one television program to another than it is like that of reading a book.

Information that is better in digitized form includes items that benefit from the characteristics of the electronic media: speed in access, currency, and the ability to skip from screen to screen. Some examples of this type of information include: data (statistics, lists, stock market quotations, preliminary findings of ongoing research; anything that is immediate, changing, hard to keep up with in print, and does not require sustained thought), information specific to one person or institution (home pages that provide more localized information about individuals or institutions than would be economical to print and distribute widely), and articles now published in scholarly journals. An additional type of document that benefits from the ability of the electronic technology to multiply and enhance distribution is primary source material that is now unavailable to casual researchers or students because of the fragile nature of the material or the remoteness of the holdings.

There is a distinction between information that remains digital and is manipulated on the screen and documents that are simply transmitted digitally because of the speed and ease of distribution but are printed out at the receiving end and used as one would any printed document. In the first instance, information that changes quickly, such as a stock market quotation, is treated as something instant, contingent, of limited continuing usefulness. In the second instance, when documents like journal articles or primary source material are printed out, the Internet functions as a very large, omnipresent copying machine, and it is hard to maintain the preeminence of the screen over print.

If the bookshelves in the local bookstore or library are any indication, one might even argue that computer and communications technologies have done more to encourage conventional publishing that they have to replace it. *Wired,* a graphically flamboyant publication with an electronic sibling called *Hot Wired,* is a magazine devoted to the finer points of the electronic revolution. Although *Wired* is as hip and trendy as any magazine, it recently launched its own publishing company, *Hard Wired,* that will publish, surprisingly, books. Such important revolutionary gurus as

Nicholas Negroponte, Bill Gates, and Sherry Turkle have also chosen a very old-fashioned format to carry the message of the revolution.

Why? It may be, as Nicholas Negroponte suggests, that the technology has not yet achieved enough market penetration to reach everyone that one wants to reach, but it may also be that books simply do something different. Negroponte himself hints at this when he explains: "Interactive multimedia leaves very little to the imagination. . . . By contrast, the written word sparks images and evokes metaphors that get much of their meaning from the reader's imagination and experiences. When you read a novel, much of the color, sound, and motion come from you."[6]

This is true, of course, but there is more to it. Books are different from digital documents, and for that reason they are unlikely to disappear. Books have substance. They take up space. They present us with a past, a present, and a future. As you read or thumb through them you are aware of how much has come before and how much is yet to be discovered. That in itself provides a context for the instant message, a frame that helps to understand where you are in relation to the material at hand. This context provides its own value system, its own set of assumptions and beliefs. You the reader are free to accept or reject those beliefs and values, but at least you know, or can know, what they are. In a hypertext world where you are propelled by your mouse from one screen to another, these contexts disappear, making it difficult for the reader (or viewer) to know if a term used in one document even means the same thing in another. While this is no problem with data, where we can make some assumptions about meaning, it may present difficulties in highly conceptual material like history, philosophy, and literature.

If digital information speeds things up, books slow things down. If digital information encourages us to get more information faster, books encourage us to linger awhile and contemplate what we have read, to think about the meaning of history or the beauty and subtlety of the language. If the electronic media revs us up by offering the world at our fingertips, books calm us down, encouraging us to think about what we have read, to understand what we have learned. There is more to knowledge, to life, than speed. Milan Kundera points out, "Speed is the form of ecstasy the technical revolution has bestowed on man."[7] He explains: "In existential mathematics, that experience takes the form of two basic equations: the degree of slowness is directly proportional to the intensity of memory; the degree of speed is directly proportional to the intensity of forgetting."[8] If Kundera is correct, digital information may give us more facts faster, but books help us become wiser.

WHAT ABOUT LIBRARIES?

Some maintain that the information revolution will make books and libraries obsolete. Others maintain that these new technologies will so transform libraries as to render them unrecognizable as the institution so many cherish. While technically and theoretically we can conceive of the entire Library of Congress on a compact disc the size of a quarter, the likelihood of such a development occurring in the near future is remote. Reasons for this include the cost of conversion from print to digital storage, the bias toward print for documents longer than a few pages, the continued existence of legal impediments contained in copyright law, and the role of the library in providing context.

Although contemporary documents and other media are regularly produced digitally, conversion of existing documents is limited by the size and scope of the undertaking. To give one example, the Library of Congress has embarked on a program to digitize some of its one hundred million item collection at the rate of roughly a million items a year. At that rate, if the Library adds nothing new, it will take one hundred years to complete the conversion and cost over a billion dollars. While costs will surely come down, and it is conceivable that libraries might jointly undertake such a project, one question remains: Should we?

The overwhelming preference for print has already been discussed. Additionally, libraries have some experience with this phenomenon. Some libraries, like the Cleveland Public Library, have been offering Internet access to the public for several years and have found that instead of replacing the conventional use of the library, electronic access (even to full text) has stimulated book borrowing, browsing, and use of printed reference material. It appears that electronic libraries not only provide information directly, but also advertise the existence of documents available in print and the vast store of resources in all media available at libraries individually and collectively. The fact is that with the dawn of the information age libraries are being used more than ever before.

The meaning of copyright in an electronic environment is cloudy. Publishers fear that if their titles were available on-line people would download a book in its entirety to read on the screen at their leisure. If the experience of libraries is any indication, it is more likely that the ability to browse electronically will stimulate, rather than replace, book sales. Most people would prefer to read a long document in print, and a printed book is a more convenient (and cheaper) package than a stack of paper printed at home or in an office. Nevertheless, fear of wholesale copying has led publishers to take a strong stand on copyright. They believe that the fair-use doctrine has no place on the Internet and that royalties should be paid for every electronic "hit." Issues of copyright in an electronic environment are complex and unlikely to be resolved anytime soon. Meanwhile, copyright is a much larger impediment to the electronic transmission of documents than technological or economic obstacles.

Libraries do many things. They collect, organize, and preserve; they make knowledge accessible—not books, but knowledge. Knowledge requires organization, context. Many argue that the Internet and the Web have created a new paradigm, that a new organization will emerge out of chaos, that systematic classification of knowledge is outmoded, and that Boolean search capabilities, hypertext, expert systems, and their offspring will revolutionize the way we think, the way we know. Yet the more there is on the Web, the harder it becomes to find. Even simple searches yield many hundreds of hits, many of them irrelevant. Microsoft, Sun Microsystems, and others are now developing indexing systems that seem like something out of Star Wars, although the structure is closer to Dewey or the Library of Congress classification schemes. If we assume that print and electronic information will coexist for the foreseeable future, it would make sense to use existing classification schemes and apply them to all types of information, print and digital alike, thereby facilitating the use of both in a complementary fashion.

If a book provides context for a document, a library provides context for all of human knowledge, knowledge that may be found in many documents and all types of information. If a book provides a sense of history of what came before and what is likely to come after the page being read, libraries provide a history of civilization. By their existence they imply that there is more to the study of philosophy than a book by Kant, more to the study of science than an article on geophysics, more to literature than *The Divine Comedy*. By their space and substance they provide a sensory understanding that knowledge is broader than any one subject field, that biography is related to history, that science owes much to mathematics.

It is this sensory understanding that we often forget when we discuss information. Humans are more than a collection of electrical impulses. Learning, knowing, takes place on many levels. There are things we know intellectually, and there are other things we know physically; there are even times we know something both intellectually and physically. There is something we know about knowledge when we walk in a library that we do not know when we sit at a computer terminal.

It is not surprising that as some announce the death of libraries, citizens across the country and around the world are investing billions of dollars, pounds, marks, and francs in rebuilding major national and urban libraries. In the United States alone, cities like Los Angeles, San Francisco, Denver, Phoenix, San Antonio, Chicago, and Cleveland have built or are building libraries. Libraries have become a national obsession. Could it be that we intuitively recognize the need for context? Or perhaps the reason is simpler. Perhaps libraries are a symbol of upward mobility and represent the possibility of a future better than the past or the present. Or maybe the reason is simpler still. Maybe people need to be near one another, in a safe place, where they can pursue knowledge in the company of others. There are, no doubt, practical, economic, philosophical, and symbolic reasons for the public's commitment to libraries, and the evidence of that commitment is all around us.

For libraries there is no choice between providing documents in print and information on a screen; they must offer both. Together they are the yin and yang of knowing: the male and the female, the active and the passive, the dark and the light, the sun and the moon. Both are needed, with each occupying a special niche and performing the task it does best.

In a recent book entitled *Longitude,* Dava Sobel describes the centuries-long search for the discovery of a mechanism that would correctly measure longitude, the lines that run from pole to pole. Latitude—the parallels that circle the earth—were established by observing the apparent transit of the sun over the earth, with the sun appearing to pass directly overhead at the equator and with the Tropic of Cancer and the Tropic of Capricorn marking the northern and southern limits of the sun's apparent transit over the course of the year. Sobel concludes: "Here lies the real, hard-core difference between latitude and longitude—beyond the superficial difference in line direction that any child can see: The zero-degree parallel of latitude is fixed by the laws of nature, while the zero-degree meridian of longitude shifts like the sands of time."[9]

To find our way in the contemporary world of knowledge, we need the latitude and the longitude, the yin and the yang, the book and the screen. Digital information is not a revolution but a development, albeit a fast one, and information is only part of what it takes to achieve knowledge. In the end it is not the speed of the information or even the information itself that will give our lives meaning. It is still what we do with it that matters most.

ENDNOTES

[1]Sherry Turkle, quoted in Pamela McCorduck, "Sex, Lies, & Avatars," *Wired* (April 1996).

[2]Sven Birkerts, *The Gutenberg Elegies* (Boston, Mass.: Faber and Faber, 1994), 3.

[3]Nicholas Negroponte, *Being Digital* (New York: Knopf, 1995), 165.

[4]McCorduck, "Sex, Lies, & Avatars," 109.

[5]Harvard Conference on the Internet and Society, Harvard University, Cambridge, Massachusetts, 29 May 1996.

[6]Negroponte, *Being Digital,* 8.

[7]Milan Kundera, *Slowness* (New York: HarperCollins, 1996), 2.

[8]Ibid., 39.

[9]Dava Sobel, *Longitude* (New York: Walker, 1995), 4.

Modern aesthetics frequently forgot that the classical theory of art, from ancient Greece to the Middle Ages, was not so eager to stress a distinction between arts and crafts. The same term (*techne, ars*) was used to designate both the performance of a barber or a ship-builder, the work of a painter or a poet. The classical aesthetics was not so anxious for innovation at any cost: on the contrary, it frequently appreciated as "beautiful" the good tokens of an everlasting type. Even in those cases in which modern sensitivity enjoys the "revolution" performed by a classical artist, his contemporary enjoyed the opposite aspect of his work, that is, his respect for previous models.

This is the reason why modern aesthetics was so severe apropos the industrial-like products of the mass media. A popular song, a TV commercial, a comic strip, a detective novel, a Western movie were seen as more or less successful tokens of a given model or type. As such they were judged as pleasurable but non-artistic. Furthermore, this excess of pleasurability, repetition, lack of innovation, was felt as a commercial trick (the product had to meet the expectations of its audience), not as the provocative proposal of a new (and difficult to accept) world vision. The products of mass media were equated with the products of industry insofar as they were produced *in series,* and the "serial" production was considered as alien to the artistic invention.

Umberto Eco

From "Innovation and Repetition: Between Modern and Post-Modern Aesthetics"
Dædalus 114 (4) (Fall 1985)

Kenneth E. Dowlin and Eleanor Shapiro

The Centrality of Communities to the Future of Major Public Libraries

"Skate to where the puck's going to be, not to where it has been. Anticipate. Anticipate."
—Walter Gretzky (Wayne Gretzky's father)

M AJOR URBAN PUBLIC LIBRARIES in the United States are undergoing a renaissance. Dallas began dramatic renovation and expansion in 1982 under the leadership of Lillian Bradshaw, followed by Tulsa, then New York, Atlanta, Chicago, Sacramento, Los Angeles, Denver, Phoenix, San Antonio, San Francisco, Cleveland, and now Boston.

While the focus has been on main libraries, new branch libraries in those cities are also being built as older ones undergo renovation and expansion. Beyond the building walls, new information technology tools are dramatically expanding public access, fostering resource sharing, and providing new methodologies for preservation as well as increased access through facsimiles of rare and source documents.

Detractors of these projects bemoan what they call the "edifice complex" and the intrusion of new information formats and access channels. They overlook the fact that the community as a whole approves, supports, and even challenges the library to im-

Kenneth E. Dowlin is City Librarian at the San Francisco Public Library.
Eleanor Shapiro is Public Information Officer at the San Francisco Public Library.

173

prove. Community support is the key to making the public library the most significant public institution of the future.

Why is the public library succeeding when so many public-sector programs and institutions are being cut back or marginalized? Libraries help people achieve their dreams through exploring and learning, by solving problems with information. Although a degree of "edifice envy" and hype does exist, leading to new buildings and acquisition of the latest technology, there is real magic when a community is involved in creating and supporting the vision of this public institution. Public libraries are generally respected and trusted; they are staffed with people who believe in the service ethic. It naturally follows that the public considers a great library system to be an essential part of creating a great city.

We should congratulate ourselves, celebrate our success, thank our communities, and prepare for the future. The public expects us to continue our past successes—no matter how long ago they occurred—provide leadership based on our values, and work hand in hand with them to live up to their expectations.

In San Francisco, the initial dream of a handful of library advocates thirty years ago became real in April 1996 when we opened a new main library. While similar in many ways to other library renaissance projects, I would posit that ours has two unique elements: the way we reassessed and planned our organization, collections, and programs with reference to the building design and the extent to which the many communities in San Francisco were involved in this process. The result has created the most community-connected major library in the world.

It makes sense that such an institution would have been realized in San Francisco. Its unique history as the port to pots of gold attracted a social base that was more cosmopolitan than most other American cities. According to social historian Glenna Matthews, the mix of cultures from the time of the Gold Rush has influenced the city's politics as much as its arts. It is no coincidence, she points out, that it was the first big city in the country to elect mayors whose backgrounds were Irish, Italian, Jewish, or labor; the first to send an Irish- or Jewish-American woman to Congress; or the first to elect a gay supervisor.

In grappling with the problems of urban America, says Matthews, the politicians and citizens of San Francisco are "well-served by a vision of inclusiveness as generous as exists in the United States."[1] This has been borne out by the overwhelming enthusiasm that has greeted the new main library, with its innovative centers and spaces that celebrate gay and lesbian, African-American, Chinese, Filipino, Latino, and environmental interests, with room for more.

The building is designed to bring people into contact with each other as much as with librarians, information, and knowledge. It will be the city's real and virtual-community communications center as well as an access point to other communities in the region and around the globe. It works as a magnet, bringing in thousands of people who never thought of using a public library before. For countless others, the library is their first introduction to the new world of digital resources.

Structural metaphors, incidentally, also emphasize this link between people and through time. The architects incorporated the use of bridges for connections, the creation of centers for community celebration and involvement, the synthesis of modern and beaux arts architectural styles linking the past with the future, and the use of light to portray knowledge.

Our vision called for a space centered around people and communication that would meet community needs structurally as well as through technology. Public space increased significantly, for example, while the shelving space increased by nine miles. Spaces for an auditorium and meeting-room complex were included, as was space for a computer network and cable television studio for in-house and cable distribution.

The new main library also includes centers that celebrate different ethnic and interest communities, which grew out of the need to solicit the financial support of these communities. Located in intimate corner areas, they provide a contrast to the more massive space of the central atrium.

In the future, it is hoped that these centers will lead to ongoing partnerships with these different groups—a collaboration that, in general, reinforces the political support we have with The Library Foundation of San Francisco as well as with The Friends of the Library of San Francisco. The Library Foundation, incorporated in 1987, has raised more than $30 million in three years to support the furniture and equipment needs of the new main library, a phenomenal success story. The Friends of the Library has worked tirelessly to ensure that the library system has an adequate operational budget. Its efforts led to an amendment to the city's charter, increasing our budget by over 60 percent in one year and guaranteeing our base-level funding for fifteen years. In return, the library is required to keep all of the branch libraries open and extend their hours by 46 percent.

The convergence of vision, leadership, and the hopes and dreams of the various neighborhood, ethnic, and interest communities, involving tens of thousands of people, has led to the creation of the new library and the guarantee of its long-term future. This experience leads me to believe that the future of major urban libraries lies in an understanding of community, connectivity, and collaboration.

COMMUNITY

John Gardner, a former US cabinet official, contends that the amount and rapidity of change in our society is creating stress in our communities. He asserts that without the continuity of shared values that a community provides, freedom cannot survive. Intellectual freedom, human rights, and a democratic form of government, after all, are social constructs.

The key to the future of a democratic society rests with the ability of its citizens to recreate a sense of community with common social purposes. This holds true for neighborhoods and cities as well as communities that go beyond geographic boundaries, such as those formed on the Internet. A library that meets community needs and expectations will succeed.

CONNECTIVITY

The creation of stronger ethnic and neighborhood communities carries a risk that they may become isolated, and that isolation can lead to conflict. There must, therefore, be a mechanism to connect them with information, education, understanding, and the tools to build consensus on larger issues.

The library is the logical institution that can both strengthen communities and be this mechanism. Through generations of public service, it has won the public's trust; it is recognized universally as a neutral space that is accessible to everyone. Rather than claiming to be an arbiter of truth, its role is to offer a range of viewpoints through available communication resources. Its archives can serve as the institutional memory of all communities because the library protects these irreplaceable resources.

Its computer network system, already in place to catalog library information resources, puts it in the best position of any public institution to maintain electronic community resources. In San Francisco, for instance, we provide public access to an on-line catalog that lists human services and government information. We continually update a neighborhood association data base and, in association with the local AIDS Foundation, provide access to a comprehensive AIDS/HIV information file. These on-line resources are available to anyone, anywhere in the world.

As more and more libraries become automated for cataloging and indexing purposes, and as more resources become available on-line, the connections between libraries achieve an efficiency not possible in the traditional interlibrary loan world. A major pressure on the public library, as well as on most business and government functions, comes from the collapse of time frames demanded by customers or users. Waiting for weeks or months for books and other materials to be sent through the traditional system no longer meets their expectations and needs.

It is critical that our access and delivery systems function in real time (that is, in seconds as opposed to months). Technology for the individual is becoming more and more commonplace, but the networks are fragmented. They are not user friendly, do not ensure equitable access, and require training and human support.

On the other hand, the connection of computerized resources and catalogs in thousands of libraries throughout the world could lead to a "global village library network." The San Francisco Public Library is in a position not only to extend the access of the citizens of San Francisco to those resources but also, because of its support and management, to lead the evolution of library networking throughout the region and beyond. Our challenge now is to realize this vision. I believe that our success in providing leadership within the city provides a basis for future successes on a larger scale.

Individual and community access to this world of digitized resources depends on a number of factors, including the library's ability to achieve electronic access from the home, school, or office to the library's network; provide navigation tools that can locate other communities' electronic resources and link to them; ensure citizen access through contracts and public subsidy; and facilitate payment to the producers of the newly formatted content. In addition, the library must help lead the way in developing new community content in new formats, such as multimedia material, so that the content will best serve their informational and educational needs. In the near future, most schoolchildren as well as college students and other users of public libraries will have learned how to use on-line public access catalogs (OPACs). These OPACs may well become the norm for on-line search systems and provide the standard entry point to the electronic information highway.

COLLABORATION

Today's information and communication technology provides an unprecedented opportunity for collaboration. The Internet connects tens of millions of people throughout the world and continues to grow at a phenomenal rate, combining the utility of the telephone, broadcast media, and publishing. It permits individual messages, conferences, transmittal of documents, and access to countless sources of information.

What our library is doing on a local level—using our on-line capabilities to organize and provide the widest possible access to all sorts of public information resources—needs to be done on a national level as well.

VALUES

While there are differences in communities and thus in their libraries, common values have been developed over time within the profession. The professionalization of librarians has centered around the understanding, articulation, and advocacy of these values and their continuing relevance for the communities they serve.

Intellectual Freedom

A fundamental premise for libraries and librarians in the United States is intellectual freedom—the right to read, view, hear, and consider diverse opinions on a wide range of topics, many of which may not be mainstream or in favor with the community. Librarians, like faculty members, should be shielded from punishment for selecting material that may be unpopular. While a library should represent its community, it should not advocate any one particular view. Since this premise is often challenged, it is critical that librarians and libraries be supported in their quest for knowledge and information on all perspectives. Community input should help determine priorities, especially given limited financial resources.

Expanding use of the Internet presents a unique challenge to the librarian's ethic of intellectual freedom. With the potential for children to gain access to graphically explicit sexual content, the traditional role of a children's librarian to select materials has been compromised. It will take considerable debate by libraries and communities to resolve this issue.

Free and Equitable Access to Information, Knowledge, Independent Learning, and the Joys of Reading

While there has always been debate over whether the concept of free public libraries means that taxpayers should pay for every service desired by each individual, the argument has intensified with new technologies that collapse time and distance as well as make copying and access fast and easy, threatening intellectual property rights.

As all library service is subsidized, the issue is not whether every service is free, but rather what level of public subsidy is appropriate for each service. Determining that level is a political decision that should be made by public process. For instance, there may be a continuing argument concerning new services, such as expedited research service and delivery. Most libraries also charge for photocopying, to cover the cost and hopefully avoid liability for the copyright issue. A library must likewise charge for document delivery, as it is liable for the infringement of intellectual property rights.

By contending that a library can charge no fees, services may be limited to the lowest common denominator, i.e., those that can be provided to everyone regardless of cost or level of public financial support.

There needs to be a process for moving forward in this age of increasing global networks. Public libraries need flexibility to recover costs for convenience and for services rendered beyond the historic compact, as well as to deal with the need to retrieve payment for services rendered to users beyond the library's jurisdiction. Many patrons today also request that documents come directly to them as electronic technology facilitates delivery to the home, office, or school. Libraries must be prepared to pay copyright fees for documents delivered to the user.

Delivery of content to individuals changes the nature of the compact whereby the library purchases a book, adds it to the collection, and makes it available for loan to everyone. Likewise, patrons now request that the library provide research. Free service includes assistance in locating resources and tools for access. Few libraries, however, have sufficient funding to provide research on demand.

In addition, as libraries become more linked and offer more electronic resources, a mechanism must be developed to share the costs over a larger geographical area or charge them to the distant user. While local taxpayers have supported funding the traditional interlibrary loan policy, which is well defined and provides limits on consumption, they are not ready to subsidize wholesale copying and delivery to the entire country or the world.

The Library as a Community Asset

Major urban libraries have invested hundreds of millions of dollars in facilities, materials, collection organization, staffing, and technology. While this spending is nominal compared to what is spent on health, education, and security, it represents a significant public investment. The cities that have built new libraries take pride in their accomplishment. But they must realize that construction of a new main library is not the end of a process; rather, it is the beginning of building community awareness of the library and its programs.

Most communities have a long-standing tradition of valuing library service. The creation of new library facilities demonstrates that communities continue to view the buildings, collections, and services as a community asset. This has been particularly true in San Francisco, where the traditional support for the neighborhood branch libraries quickly turned to political action when branches were threatened with closure. That energy was drawn upon to build support for the new main library, working in conjunction with the Friends of the Library, the Library Foundation of San Francisco, the leadership of the library administration, and the library commission.

Advocacy for Literacy

Literacy is the bedrock of communication. Even in the age of mass media and electronic communication, those who cannot read rarely attain full participation in a democracy or reap its full economic benefits. Long a bastion of literacy efforts outside the education establishment, public libraries continue to expand their role in literacy education and advocacy. While literacy has its roots in reading, the concept needs to be extended to all media. Charles McClure of the University of Wisconsin contends that people now require the ability to understand computer, media, and network literacy in addition to having access to them.

Honoring Diversity while Creating an Overall Sense of the Larger Community

Major urban cities have the most diverse populations in the United States. This diversity is a strength and a special challenge. The new library is not only a metaphor for valuing this diversity; it is an institution that can shape future relationships. Special program centers that celebrate the diversity and provide an entry point to the resources of entire collections create attachments to, even passion for, the institution. However, the resources of the library should not be divided into cultural ghettos. The collections need to be organized and managed in a way that facilitates access to the totality of all the items, regardless of format and physical location.

Computer technology makes possible the management of large collections and provides navigation aides for the location of information and knowledge. The World Wide Web is a new and powerful tool and global standard for computer networked access. Libraries that master the Web methodology as the organizer, navigator, and access mechanism to local collections will be viewed as leaders. The Web not only helps to locate resources, it points the way for organizing diverse collections into an integrated whole. Its power lies in its utility as well as in the energy and intellect of millions of users. As the nervous system of the new library structure, it facilitates service in ways that we have only begun to tap.

ROLES

The public expects a major urban public library to continue its traditional role as a repository of knowledge and wisdom, providing access to information, knowledge, learning, and the joys of reading; continuing to engage people in reading and learning activities; providing a safe haven for nurturing small children and challenging older ones; and supporting literacy and literary programs.

Information and communications technology facilitates, however, an expansion into new formats and programs. The library should focus more on access and communication, and perhaps less on ownership. New libraries now often include community spaces to attract people, such as meeting rooms, auditoriums, and public spaces like cafes and galleries. The more forward-looking institutions include spaces and technology for communication, such as cable television, computer networks, and Internet access. The traditional archive role for community records now needs to be expanded to include technologies beyond print. Electronic preservation, archiving, and the organization of community information must be part of future library planning. There is little archiving of local electronic media; someone must collect and organize the content. The new world of the Web provides the potential for the library to incorporate content created by the television media, particularly the public broadcasting stations.

A strong symbiotic relationship can be developed with media for this purpose, which would allow public access to local productions that would otherwise be lost after the air date. Commercial broadcasters and cable television systems presently have little incentive to produce local content. I have proposed that our library create an Electronic Encyclopedia for San Francisco, accessible through the library's computer network, that would incorporate as much local electronic content as might be obtained. It will contain local data bases and content from KQED (the local PBS radio and television outlet), schools, and universities, as well as our own electronic archives. This encyclopedia, expanded throughout libraries on the Internet, would create a powerful repository of information and knowledge. The encyclopedia model provides organization in a way that most people understand.

The new tool for communication and information access is the Internet. A library's badge of success, therefore, is not acquiring their five millionth or twenty millionth book; it is receiving distinction as being listed as one of the top 5 percent of Web sites by independent evaluators. The Cleveland Public Library was one of the first libraries to achieve this award. The San Francisco Public Library received this distinction in March. The review specifically cited our excellent links to other Web sites in San Francisco, such as the newspapers and the data bases of local information resources created by the library's staff.

Another new role could be to serve as an incubator for future programs built around the use of information and communications technology. The centers within the new main library in San Francisco could lead to growth opportunities outside the building. The New York Public Library provides a futuristic model with its creation of the Schomburg Center, the Center for Performing Arts, and the new Science, Industry, and Business Library. Our Children's Electronic Discovery Center is a partner with the Children's Center at the Yerba Buena Cultural Center, which has yet to be built. The library's program will provide the resources to start their program. Any one of the San Francisco Public Library's center programs might eventually grow large enough for its own building.

As a "global village library" major urban public libraries can be the entry point for their community to the electronic world, the archives of community information and knowledge, and the electronic access point to the graphic resources of the library; they can serve as the gateway to the Internet world for their community's information and communication resources by providing organized navigation tools. The library can be the connection to the national information infrastructure.

Participating in the National Information Infrastructure

Fred W. Weingarten, the senior policy advisor at the American Library Association's Washington office, provides an excellent description of the potential roles for the public library as a participant in the National Information Infrastructure.[2]

On-ramp of first resort. There will always be a need for advanced services that require resources, equipment, access, and training that the average person will not have. As technology continues to evolve, the library can be a leader in providing access as well as promoting the development of the technology.

On-ramp of last resort. There will always be segments of the population without access to specific types of information technology. Many barriers impede access to every home, classroom, or business. The library must, therefore, provide a safety-net system to guarantee citizen access. As our society places an ever-greater premium on access to electronic information, the library will become the critical institution to ensure that access is universal. The computer and telecommunications industries, elected officials, and the media all support the library's efforts to assume this role.

Navigator/guide. The World Wide Web has been likened to a library where all the books have been collected and placed in random order with little sense for organization and access tools. The historic function of the public library in cataloging and organizing the shelf provides the basic knowledge and emerging methodology for creating a global library of all the resources on the Internet.

Archivist/depository/authenticator. Internet content is very volatile, as are the locations of access points. Its strength is that it allows individuals as well as institutions and agencies to create and make available their own content. On the other hand, there is no archiving. Libraries must develop the systems to archive and authenticate community information resources.

Organizer of the Public Information Space

The library can bring its traditional function of providing community meeting rooms into the electronic age. It is important that political communities be retained as part of the electronic landscape since government, economic, and educational institutions are still a vital factor in our societies.

The electronic tools that public libraries often adopt comparatively early increase the value of the library to local government agencies. In San Francisco, we continue to provide graphic collections, such as books and government documents, to support better public policy decisions; we also support city agencies with research. We provide telephone referral services, on-line data bases, an expedited reference service (Library Express) that provides support to city agencies as well as to the public, and the city archives—all of which makes us the most advanced city department in the use of information and communications technology.

STRATEGIC GOALS

Major urban public libraries need to move forward on several macro shifts in the way that they do business. These shifts focus on the need for collaboration, shifting the culture of the institution, becoming a neographic library, and managing the library in a focused, planned environment that is systemic in its implementation.

Creating a Collaborative Institution

In order to achieve the new vision, we must start with the assumption that the library must use the operative verb "with" instead of "to" or "for." The San Francisco Public Library has learned the value of enlisting community support through political action, fund-raising, and voter-driven funding. It has brought the library to the point of excellence. Our ability to extend and enhance current collaborations will determine the degree of excellence that we can achieve.

The San Francisco Public Library can become an outstanding library with a marginal increase in the resources expended so far by relying on collaboration. Community support will increase the talent and skill level of the institution as well as our funding resources.

An example is our effort to incorporate two new collections— the Dorothy Starr music collection that includes hundreds of thousands of pieces of music and the tremendous resources in the gay/

lesbian archives—into our system of preservation, organization, and access. Both will consume thousands of human hours and require skills that may not be present in the library staff. A similar investment would be needed to incorporate current materials, such as government documents, the San Francisco history archives, and a myriad of other information and knowledge resources, into the library's on-line access system. In addition, while the staff has done a magnificent job of inventorying and cataloging the 2.4 million books in the librarywide collection over the last two years, inventorying and cataloging the other sixteen million items in the collection is a staggering challenge. Only 16 percent of the library's collections are in book form. The community is willing to help in this effort, but the system must be developed on a grand scale.

Shifting the Culture of the Institution to a Real-Time World

The staff and systems must move into the real-time world and do so in a way that incorporates the community. Most librarians were trained to deal with a scarcity of resources. The basis of the public library tradition has been to create and nurture a collection of books for sharing with all of the community, relying on the librarian's professional judgment to acquire this collection in a knowledgeable, considered way. That worked when there were only a few thousand titles published in a year and books were considered the only validated resource.

It does not work as well in a world where there are not only sixty thousand new titles in the English language every year, but tens of thousands of books in other languages, plus hundreds of thousands of items in non-book form. It grows even more complicated when on-line networks give access to thousands of libraries as well as on-line information that may never appear in print. And the information available from electronic media, such as television and radio, also needs to be considered. Everyone involved with the library must regard education as a lifelong process. The library must offer leadership and opportunities for learning for all its staff, library supporters and users, and the community at large.

Creating the Neographic Institution

A central concept to all of this is the commitment of the library to deal with all relevant formats and resources available electronically in a manner that provides seamless access to the user. The basis of the public library has moved beyond the book to include magazines, microfilm, and other graphic representations of information and knowledge. Most libraries now also include audio CDs, videos, and other formats. But few extend the level of organization and access currently provided to the book to these other formats and to the new formats such as CD-ROM data bases, network access, and electronic full-text delivery. This situation recalls the days of the monastery librarian being surprised by the invention of the printing press. The Internet/World Wide Web world functions as a new medium that may be more powerful than all previous media. We must learn how to harness it. "Neographic" is coined by this author from the same concept of neoclassical, merging the best of the past with the best of the present.

Creating the Organization for Systemic Strategic Planning and Resource Management

Major urban public libraries are created and sustained by a political process. Decisions tend to be incremental, often crafted through compromise, composed of an accumulation of individuals viewing specific parts. My training in systems analysis and my teaching at the University of Denver lead me to believe that while it is important that decisions be made at the lowest possible level, there must be overall guidance, a template, to ensure that the institution meets its mission and goals and that decisions maximize resources. While many major urban public libraries have made tremendous strides in developing their resources, and more will come, there is a need for continuous expansion of the program to manage these resources efficiently and to focus them on community needs.

Some of those needs are as yet undefined and may change over time. But there are core programs that will outlast the individual. The institution is not just a main library with some branches, or a lot of branches with a main library. The library must be a system where all resources are deliverable in all locations, to all communities, regardless of format or language. This is the opportunity that technology brings. Technology also provides the opportunity to develop sophisticated management information to collect ongoing data on usage and needs. The system, however, must be approached as a whole, not as a group of parts, for its potential to be realized.

The concept of the Learning Organization as advanced by Peter Senge[3] suggests that learning to learn may be one of the most critical attributes of the successful organization. The opening of the new main branch of the San Francisco Public Library has made it necessary for the staff to learn a great deal about technological resources in a very short time. Ongoing training for both staff and patrons is essential in order to maximize the use of these resources.

Libraries also need specific goals, such as buildings that are safe, compliant with the American Disability Act, and inviting, as well as collection and resource management systems, housekeeping systems, staff development (in some cases total reorganization), and technology implementation. Staff education and credentials need to be a priority for the profession. Training and education in resources and technologies are critical. But it is also important that we not leave behind our professional values. The trend of library schools metamorphosing into schools of information technology is worrisome for those of us who believe that a major benefit of the professional degree is the inculcation of values such as intellectual freedom, public service, and the worth of books.

PROCESS

So what is the process that can lead these repositories of knowledge and wisdom as well as trivia into the next era? It involves vision based on environmental scanning—the use of polls and other feedback mechanisms. Then comes planning, with perhaps some reorganization, leading to the delivery of services and facilities to meet the community's expectations. The best strategy for increasing support for a library is by raising those expectations.

What are the professional issues that must be faced? Payment for the major urban public libraries must be broad enough to sustain a larger role beyond the local community. Local communities have invested hundreds of millions of dollars into infrastructure, facilities, collections, and staff. Electronic access will aggravate the "free rider" concept in economic terminology. There must therefore be state and national mechanisms to recompense major resource libraries for service to a wider, international audience.

To serve that audience, major public libraries must move their institutions forward collectively. Paul LeClerc, President of the New York Public Library, has taken this initiative with the summit of world library leaders held in New York City in April 1996. At that meeting, the need for a new agenda for American public libraries became clear. In the past thirty years, the vision of a public library accessible to every citizen has been articulated and realized through local, state, and national efforts. Today, communities all over the world want to emulate it. Our next step must be to tackle broader social issues with the information resources that we are in the best position of any public institution to provide.

Working with schools, museums, and the public media, libraries can facilitate networks that can make a significant impact on public awareness. As public institutions, they can function as scouts on the electronic frontier, exploring the new territory in a way that will continue to make access to digital resources easier.

Legislators in Congress are currently in the process of restructuring the Library Services and Construction Act, the thirty-year-old legislation that was key to the dramatic expansion of public libraries in the 1970s and 1980s. The new Library Services and Technology Act emphasizes the use of information and communications technology to increase access to library and information services.

This act would create a National Institute for Libraries and Museums that could significantly raise the level of planning and coordination within the profession with the help of the American Library Association, the Council of Research Libraries, the Center for the Book of the Library of Congress, the Library of Congress itself, and major public libraries. If properly implemented, such a center, based in Washington, D.C., would complement the strengths of the Library of Congress, other major resource libraries, and the National Commission on Library and Information Services by providing continuing education for library and information science professionals, on-site or on-line.

Perhaps more than any other time in history, the future of major public libraries can be determined by library leadership. Visionary leaders understand that while a strength of libraries is our historic compact with our citizens, they need to be receptive to, even supportive of, new directions that respond to new elements in the environment, such as information technology, the National Information Infrastructure, and the communication tools available today.

Our key to success, however, will still be the understanding that libraries are about people. If the facilities are people oriented and facilitate communications, they will be great institutions. Libraries otherwise will be trapped in a warehouse mentality. The paradigm shift in museums is instructive to libraries. Museums that understand that people are their business are thriving. The same is true of libraries.

ENDNOTES

[1]Glenna Matthews, "Born Cosmopolitan: California North of the Tehachapisk," in Michael Steiner and David Wrobel, eds., *Many Wests: Essays in Regional Consciousness* (University Press of Kansas, forthcoming).

[2]Fred W. Weingarten, "Superhighway Speed Limit Abolished; Information Policy Serves," *American Libraries* (January 1996): 16–17.

[3]Peter M. Senge, *The Fifth Discipline* (New York: Currency Doubleday, 1994).

Deanna B. Marcum

Redefining Community through the Public Library

T HE NEWS MEDIA PORTRAY AMERICAN communities in disarray. Robert Putnam describes how Americans have ceased to join one another in neighborhood activities.[1] Distrust, fear, and diversity have forced Americans to partake of solitary and independent events—a far cry from the society of "joiners" that Alexis de Tocqueville portrayed in *Democracy in America*.[2] Putnam claims that social capital—the networks and norms of a civil society—is collapsing. Instead of gathering with colleagues and neighbors in civic and social activities that are tied to communities, Americans are giving priority to nonplace-based activities. Influences such as television, the global economy, and two-career families are rendering obsolete the stock of social capital that we had built up at the turn of the century. Putnam suggests that a new style of reform—the equivalent of the Progressive Era that accompanied the Industrial Revolution—is needed to reinvent, to reconceptualize, new social organizations that will connect members of a community for the information age of the twenty-first century.

The American public library may be the prototype of the new social organization that builds a sense of community for the next century. Or, at least, it is a bridging organization that allows us to experiment with organizational forms for a new age.

Surely this is not a universally-held belief. For most people, the public library is that familiar institution in the center of town that

Deanna B. Marcum is President of the Council on Library Resources and the Commission on Preservation and Access in Washington, D.C.

has good books for children, is a great source for recreational reading, and is the place for finding answers to questions. The perception of the library is that it is a public good; every community should have one.

Librarians, however, have viewed libraries rather differently. They do not think of the library as a community center so much as an information resource. At a time when many other agencies and organizations are claiming that they are information sources, the library may appear to the public to be one of many information providers. Digital technology has shifted the ground on which all such organizations stand, and the result is a dramatic reshaping of one of our most familiar community landmarks.

TODAY'S PUBLIC LIBRARIES

It is ironic that the technology that has magnified the opportunities for gaining access to more information has also been responsible for making the boundaries of the public library less distinct, thereby raising questions about the necessity of such institutions, at best, and prompting refusals to pay for the services, at worst.

While most public libraries today are struggling with role identification, what has remained constant is the librarian's determination to provide a useful service to the community. At stake, though, is the fundamental question of what the library actually does within the community. What role does it play? What role should it play? If the interest lies in providing needed information to all citizens, are there not ways of doing that without establishing public libraries—ways that are less expensive, less bureaucratic? If the vision of some politicians—that every citizen will have access to the information superhighway—is realized, will not the many problems associated with keeping public libraries open and fully functioning simply disappear?

Changes are taking place in the library world almost faster than anyone can measure and certainly faster than anyone can predict. Dramatic developments are occurring in public libraries across the country—developments that are altering the ways that libraries deliver information to patrons and interact with their communities. As the information revolution gains momentum, nationally and internationally, public libraries have a unique opportunity to harness electronic technology for their own purposes and provide resources to patrons and users that were unimaginable only a few short years ago. The Internet and the World Wide Web have effected changes in the way that public libraries do business, but the power of technology and its ability to draw people and communities together goes beyond the 'Net or the Web. Communities are being linked together—and linked to the outside world—by wires, cables, and fiber optics, but in many places it is the public library that stands as the real information nexus within the community.

In taking on this role, public libraries have expanded their horizons and, as it turns out, multiplied the challenges they must face in our modern society. The Council on Library Resources, an operating foundation that has been involved for some forty years in identifying library issues and finding solutions, wanted to find out more about what is going on in public libraries and to understand better the problems those libraries are confronting as a result of the information revolution. At the same time, the W. K. Kellogg Foundation, through its Human Resources for Information Systems Management (HRISM) program, took a keen interest in the roles public libraries are playing in their communities and how public library leadership is being developed for the future. As a result, the Council and the Kellogg Foundation joined forces to look more closely at public libraries and determine the best and most useful avenues to follow for developing leaders, building networks with the library and information science communities, and strengthening the interaction among the people who use and support public libraries. Through a grant to the Council by the Kellogg Foundation, a program was established to inquire into the innovative uses of electronic technology in public libraries.

Working with an advisory committee made up of influential library directors from around the country, the Council's staff undertook an informal survey of public libraries. The first step involved mailing 3,400 letters to public library directors across the country, asking them to describe how they were using technology in their communities in new and innovative ways. From the three hundred responses received, the advisory committee reviewed the replies and selected twelve of what seemed to be the most interesting locations to receive on-site and in-depth treatment. The Council's staff visited each of the sites in teams, talked to directors, staff, and users of the library, and prepared a case study for each of the visits that would attempt to explain how these libraries are dealing with the new age of electronic information and how their communities are responding.

In traveling to these libraries, the Council's staff realized that there is no single answer about how technology can be used by public libraries to serve their communities or to provide greater public access to information resources. But one thing that all twelve of the libraries had in common was that the most vibrant public libraries look to the community at large and to partnerships with various individuals and organizations to determine the goals and objectives that are appropriate for their communities. There are other common attributes of these innovative libraries. In each example, these libraries have a leader with vision, funding (in relative terms) to create a new environment using digital technology, and community-centered strategies for making a transition into the increasingly digitized world of information. At the same time, the case studies also reveal a wide range of responses to the challenge of how to use technology innovatively and effectively.

FINDINGS FROM THE CASE STUDIES

The libraries chosen for the case studies are located in communities that range anywhere from fifteen thousand to 2.5 million people. Common to all is their commitment to their communities, not simply as organizations that provide information, but as cultural and educational centers. These are institutions that are transforming themselves to meet the needs of the future while keeping themselves grounded in traditional library services and practices. With the advent of digital technology, these institutions have seen an opportunity to provide services to members of the community in new ways, even though it has meant substantial investments in computers and telecommunications infrastructure, software and electronic publications, and training initiatives. Most of these libraries are forging alliances and partnerships with organizations that have not, up until now, been central in the lives of public libraries. The partnerships are making the new or enhanced services a reality. Whether large or small, urban or rural, these libraries are using technology to reach larger audiences and to create new coalitions within their communities.

The Need for Vision

Public libraries became ubiquitous features of the American landscape when Andrew Carnegie donated money to thousands of communities to construct library buildings throughout the country in the last years of the nineteenth century and the first fifteen years of the twentieth century. The deal he struck required local governments to cover the cost of books and staff. Carnegie believed access to books and education would provide opportunities for motivated workers to improve their minds and, in the process, their economic conditions.

What would be a comparable contribution to the American people today? If Carnegie were alive, would he connect every home to the information superhighway? Would he fund one virtual library, to which the nation could gain access through the Internet or the World Wide Web or their successors? Would he build branch libraries in neighborhoods to serve expanding urban and suburban populations? Would he invest in community-based networks or freenets? Would he give personal computers with CD-ROM drives to libraries and equip them with the software they need to gain access to electronic catalogs and full-text journals from terminals inside and outside the main library building? Or would he wire the old Carnegie libraries, many of which still stand in the center of many cities and towns, for tomorrow's technology? These questions are not as fanciful as they at first might sound; they are aimed at the very heart of the question about the role of the public library. Is a public library a community center or an information provider? Is it a place where information resides or is it a conduit for information?

It has been, and continues to be, all of these things—and more— but the debate about the public library's role is important because municipal or other local funding for public libraries is not likely to increase, at least not in the current political and economic climate. More and more, public libraries must make difficult choices or seek external funds to pay for new programs. And the financial requirements for connecting community members to the information superhighway are immense. As they seek resources, library directors are finding themselves in new and unprecedented relationships with public and private agencies of all kinds. Public libraries have to make a clear and direct case for themselves, and they must take the lead in articulating a vision for what a public library can be in the twenty-first century. The twelve directors of the public libraries we chose for close scrutiny share an important characteristic: they possess a vision and know precisely how to articulate it. Once articulated, the vision is implemented and refined by the library's staff, by community leaders and supporters, volunteers, and partners. These efforts have not been without conflict and a certain amount of pain, and the results are yet to be evaluated. But all of them began with a vision for the future.

Building on Strength

One great advantage of public libraries is their neutrality within communities. They are public spaces that offer a place to learn on one's own about any subject and without review by any kind of authority figure. The library staff need not be consulted or involved in the pursuit of knowledge, unless the patron wishes. Carnegie referred to the public library as the "people's university," and this conceptualization of the institution has continued in the public's mind over the years. The collections in libraries allow for anonymous and unfettered inquiries into all subjects, and, unlike a school, the library has no predetermined curriculum or pedagogy. Individual curiosity and time are the only limitations on the knowledge that can be acquired.

The neutral space has another advantage: it is available to individuals of any socioeconomic group or of any age. The no-questions-asked policy of public libraries makes it possible for anyone in the community to take advantage of the library's services. Community standards and budget limitations temper the ideal of neutrality, to be sure, but the principle has remained a steadfast conviction of the thousands of public libraries around the country. For the most part, all library services have been offered without charge to members of the community, but in those few instances where charges have been levied, the charges have been required equitably of one and all. This attitude has distinguished public library service in the United States for the last one hundred years.

The Challenge of Partnerships

Libraries have been serving multiple roles for many decades, but electronic information has increased the number and complexity of roles that the institution performs or is contemplating. Public libraries traditionally have assumed roles that made sense for the local community. Across the nation, these roles have included serving as research centers and offering activities such as independent learning. Librarians participating in the evolution of new forms of service through technology complain that the public has not understood the number or variety of roles that the library has played in the past, and they point with some frustration to the number of new roles that they will take on in the digital age. Library directors are concerned, generally, that the expectations of the community, as well as their expectations of themselves, are greater than the resources will accommodate. As a result, public libraries have turned to partnerships to help them broaden their resource base and reach more deeply into the community, where the strongest support for the library's services is to be found.

What has changed is the type of partnerships public libraries have entered into in the last several years. Instead of doing their work independently, libraries are collaborating with telecommunications and corporate partners, other libraries, community organizations and agencies, and others to provide new services, increase public access to information, and create community-based information resources. The collaborations have helped libraries establish new constituencies, build wider support, and, in some cases, broaden and diversify sources of funding.

The partnerships have been varied and dynamic, which is only to be expected among libraries of different sizes and locales. Some public libraries, for instance, have joined forces with their local telephone companies or cable television providers to take advantage of fiber optic networks being installed in communities or regions. Others have looked to nearby universities and colleges for technological expertise and networking experience. Many libraries have benefited from alliances with the local school systems. The possibilities are endless. Whatever form they take, these partnerships have proven to be advantageous for those public libraries that have pursued them with vigor and diligence and with a certain creative imagination.

Some librarians, not accustomed to forging alliances with the public sector in particular, have been somewhat anxious about the demands placed on them by their new partners. Most, however, have embraced the new alliances with enthusiasm and with the hope that the partnerships will increase the library's opportunities and programs. Several librarians have expressed concern that the digital library initiatives are usurping disproportionate resources when compared to the full range of services that the library provides. Other librarians, casting such concerns aside, embrace the future that the digital world seems to be promising. These evolving and contested areas of role, responsibility, and vision will challenge library directors and staff for many years to come. The issues facing public libraries are not easy, and as time passes they will become more sharply defined and more intensely emotional for those who must reckon with them. Partnerships, like other relationships, are never easy. They generally require more work than anyone ever forecasts or readily acknowledges. But in looking to the future, public libraries have identified partnerships as a proven way, despite all the uncertainties and risks, to begin the journey into the next century.

THE PUBLIC'S PERCEPTION

The Kellogg HRISM program involves a great deal more than looking at library innovation. The objectives of the HRISM library project are to determine the vision of library leaders for the future and for their profession, test public sentiment toward libraries as they move into the digital age, and examine the direction and relevance of current public policy proposals as they relate to public libraries.

Kellogg engaged Lake Research in a public opinion survey to gauge the general opinion of the roles of public libraries.[3] Among the survey's findings are:

• The public strongly supports public libraries and wants them to take a strong leadership role in providing access to computers and digital information. At the same time, the public wants the library to continue its traditional role of providing books, reference services, and programs for children.

- There is a strong correlation between those who use libraries, frequent bookstores, and use personal computers.
- Most Americans do not believe that libraries will become less important as personal computers become more commonplace.
- Although many library leaders express concern that current anti-government sentiment will hamper libraries' abilities to raise money to support digital and traditional collections, the public says it is willing to pay additional taxes and fees for these services.
- A majority of those polled preferred to pay taxes in order to allow the library to develop an information service that would be accessible to the user at home, rather than investing the same amount of money on digital resources for one's personal use.
- Families with children are much more likely to have computers at home—and to use their local public library.
- The public values the idea that librarians should take on responsibilities for assisting users who want to navigate the information superhighway.
- The library's role in providing computer access to adults and children who otherwise lack it is strongly supported by the public.
- Maintaining and building library buildings was ranked third among all the library functions listed in the poll, behind providing children's services and books.
- The public favors using libraries for community meetings, although this role was not ranked very highly.
- The public voices less enthusiasm than library leaders for setting up computers in remote locations such as shopping malls to ease access to library information.
- Americans are divided along demographic lines on some key issues. For example, the youngest Americans polled, those between the ages of eighteen and twenty-four, are the least enthusiastic about maintaining and constructing library buildings. They are also the least enthusiastic of any age group about the importance of libraries in a digital future.

THE GULF BETWEEN THE LIBRARY'S LEADERS AND THE PUBLIC

How are we to reconcile the differences between the aspirations of the library's leaders and the public perceptions of what a library is and should be? First, the survey results of the Lake Research poll need to be examined more closely.

Perhaps the most significant outcome of the survey is that for a vast majority of Americans, public libraries are a highly valued institution, even with the virtually unrestricted access to information from one's home computer. Although computers are increasing in popularity and familiarity, Americans are in no way prepared to abandon their libraries in favor of their personal computers. This is good news, obviously, for librarians who believe they are providing an important service. The great strength of the American public library is that it is a loved and respected institution in the community.

A majority of those responding to the survey believe that the library will continue to be important in the future, even though they recognize that digital technology is stimulating profound changes in the way we learn, work, and experience new ideas. Interestingly, though, the respondents who own personal computers said libraries would become less important in the future. As individuals grow more comfortable with their personal computers, it seems that they feel more secure about their ability to navigate through electronic information sources to find what they need. Librarians, to them, do not seem to be so essential.

What becomes dramatically apparent from the opinion poll is that the public sees the public library first and foremost as an institution that benefits children. There is a strong sense that the public library is a safe, educational, and generally "nice" place for children to frequent. Communities are expected to support this kind of environment for its next generation of citizens. But the library's leaders are far more interested in providing the electronic infrastructure to support a much wider range of community needs. While children's services are important to most library visionaries, the technological investment is clearly meant to support more sophisticated information provision schemes.

The "average" adult, however, does not necessarily expect these more advanced services from the local public library, and it is not clear at all that he or she is prepared to pay the bills for them. The respondents to the survey did not think of the public library as the place they would expect to learn how to use the new technology, and they were not prepared to pay higher taxes to build such a capacity in the library.

The respondents support using library budgets to preserve and erect library buildings, placing this activity third in the poll's rankings of library services that they would spend money on. A total of 65 percent indicated this was very important, and an almost identical number, 62 percent, thought this should be a library priority. Significantly, women are much more likely to support this activity than men (71 percent contrasted with 58 percent). Minorities, especially African-Americans, registered the strongest support for spending money in this way.

Clearly, the American public agrees wholeheartedly with the library's leaders that the American public library building is an intrinsic part of the library's identity. It is important to note that support of this function comes only after purchasing new books and computers and having computer access.

CONCLUSIONS

These two studies—the informal case studies by the Council on Library Resources and the public opinion poll commissioned by the W. K. Kellogg Foundation—underscore the need to understand how public libraries have developed and how they have been maintained in this country. We have found that citizens of specific communities consider the local public library to be "their library." The library's staff is most often proud of the ability to provide networked, electronic resources and services. Members of the community are happiest about the number of people who frequent the library; the use made of it by the community's children; and the combination of neutrality (no judgments are made about what the individual chooses to read) and accessibility (library staff will help individuals find the resources they need, wherever they happen to be located) represented by the institution.

Most often, we have discovered that the users of the public library depend upon its physicality. They need to know that a *place* is there for them and their children. This need presents an interesting dilemma for the librarian who is valiantly attempting to raise money to purchase computers, servers, and related equipment so that the library can be the community's on-ramp to the information superhighway. But the road that users are traveling is a dual-laned (or multi-laned) expressway. Terminals are important, and everyone wants to be "connected." But the books and the library building are important, too, and the place the community calls the library still serves to draw the community to it and to pull the community together.

The Council began looking at public libraries by asking how technology is being used in innovative ways to provide new services to communities, but it sharply redefined the question as it gained more experience—and more insight—from the site visits to public libraries around the nation. More precisely, the emerging picture has prompted a multitude of questions: how do libraries balance the many demands made of them by the heterogeneous citizenry of the community? How does the library make choices between collections of children's books and electronic access to business information? Between expanding the literacy classes that are held in the library and purchasing enough equipment for every branch library in the system to be part of the network? For the public librarian, the jarring questions are concerned with priorities in the face of overwhelming need.

It is in the public library, more than in any other type of library, that we see the delicate balancing act between the social purposes, the information-providing purposes, and the cultural purposes of the institution. Each community has defined its priorities in specific ways, often based on the funding that the governed are willing to provide.

The leadership within the professional associations and many of the leaders among the practitioners' ranks believe technology holds the transformative power needed by a public library that has become tarnished and worn by time. It is not uncommon to hear politicians describe the day when every schoolchild in America will be able to do his or her homework by consulting the resources of the Library of Congress on the computer screen. The empowering message contained in that image is a persuasive one for many community groups that have been waiting "their turn" for the equalization that seems to be integral to the technology. Other political leaders are more concerned about costs, and they point to the opportunities for many to have access to information without the local library system having to buy it. By providing access to

Internet resources, they take delight in saying that they can provide all the information anyone could want—and all free of charge.

The history of public libraries suggests that something more than a reliance on the world of information available through the Internet will be required and that the costs of providing information cannot simply be transferred to the black hole of cyberspace. Communities need public libraries for something more than just data and more than just electronic connections. In many places, the public library continues to be the symbolic center of the community, the place where people come together, the place where an information nexus occurs—an information exchange, if you will, that must offer access to past knowledge as well as linkages to the electronic wonders of the future. What the case studies show is that libraries are responding to their communities just as the old Carnegie libraries, established nearly a century ago, reflected their communities' needs at the turn of the century.

It is important that libraries throughout the nation receive nearly all of their support from their local communities. People like libraries, and they are in many places willing to show their support through commitment of tax dollars to maintain public libraries. The future holds great promise, but it also carries with it some very real dangers. Technology alone is not the sole answer to our information needs; nor is it the thing that will transform libraries into pure information deliverers. As the past reveals, technology does not always mean progress. If we are to enter the information age with purpose, we must not fail to see that libraries will remain very important places and, as institutions, will continue to depend on local financial support if they are to do adequately their jobs of serving their own communities. How that is accomplished and how the balance is maintained among the heterogeneous needs of the community are questions that remain to be answered.

We can achieve progress through technology. To do so, however, will require innovation and experimentation. It will require setting priorities and making choices. It will require looking at the information age not exclusively as one of hardware and software, but rather as one of information as a broad category of intellectual sustenance and knowledge. It will require all of us—the Council on Library Resources, other professional groups, and Americans who have an abiding interest in their communities—to redefine public libraries as we would like them to be rather than as what they have been in the past. It will also require us to redefine the library professional—the new public librarian of the information age—in light of the changes that are occurring at breakneck speed in all libraries, great and small. In turn, the educational enterprise that produces the information professionals will be forced to make changes to assure a cadre of well-trained new librarians, or knowledge workers. Inside public libraries, the professionals now at work must be retrained and redirected if they are to make the best use of available technology and continue providing the best possible level of service to the community.

The new technology allows for building a community among individuals who have not found a common meeting ground with others in a physical place. The key to this expanded definition of community depends upon public librarians realizing that the institutions for which they have responsibility offer a physical as well as a virtual meeting place. Both types of space are important and must be nurtured. Funding for the two must not be separate but interdependent, just as the two types of space are mutually reinforcing. And it is the expansion of this definition that allows for more individuals, now outside the social framework that has been created by physical places alone, to participate in the life of the community and to find solutions to some of their problems that have kept them isolated.

So it would seem, based on what the Council has recently seen in its visits to public libraries around the nation and what a number of studies, including the Lake Research survey, are telling us about how Americans perceive and value their libraries, that Robert Putnam's provocative portrait of a country that is fragmenting into its individual parts and forsaking its social capital is not precise—at least not for the moment. One might still raise a concern, as Putnam does, for the future of America and the tendencies of its citizens to become increasingly solitary in their activities, but at the same time one should look to the public library to see how an old institution, in some places battered and frayed, is taking on a new life at the very center of so many communities and is becoming a force in drawing communities together. In this sense, if Americans are "bowling alone," as Putnam maintains, they are also coming together at the library—the real one and the virtual one. The future is not set in stone, however. Libraries face tough challenges and must travel some rough roads ahead. But it is a hopeful sign that public libraries in this country are trying very hard to maintain their vitality within and for their communities. With continued effort, and with the right kinds of support, the public library will become a thing of the future, not a thing of the past.

ENDNOTES

[1] Robert D. Putnam, "Bowling Alone: America's Declining Social Capital," *Journal of Democracy* 6 (1) (January 1995): 65–78.

[2] Alexis de Tocqueville, *Democracy in America* (London: Saunders and Otley, 1835).

[3] Lake Research conducted the library survey among a national sample of 1,015 adults (504 men and 511 women) eighteen years of age and older and was completed during the period of 18–21 April 1996. The demographics by which the results were tabulated were: sex, age, region, race, household income, household size, number of children in the household, and education level. The margin of error for the survey was ± 3.1 percentage points.

In the end, it is the human qualities of the professional that will determine his future role. To the extent that the aspirations of individual professionals continue to encompass both the accretion of human knowledge, and its application to particular problems, each professional remains a unique resource. The double motivation that leads a person to want to make an individual contribution to the stream of knowledge, and also to apply that knowledge for the benefit of other human beings strikes a responsive chord in the individuals or groups for whose benefit it is applied, so that they can see their professional advisers as whole human beings, relating all their talents to their clients' needs.

For the professionals themselves there will be increasing tensions between the two roles. On the one hand, they will have to learn more and more to apply detailed knowledge from one smaller area by analogy to other areas, to use sophisticated knowledge banks with sophisticated judgment, to apply statistical measures of success and failure to norms of professional performance, to consult fellow experts without giving up their overall responsibility to the client. On the other hand, they will have to learn to work more effectively with groups of clients, and as members of teams of professionals. They will have to learn to listen more attentively and to explain their diagnoses and their strategies more fully to their colleagues (including colleagues on the other side of professional boundaries), to their clients, and to the general public. And they will have to find new ways, not yet dreamed of, to live with their dual roles.

Adam Yarmolinsky

From "What Future for the Professional
in American Society?"
Dædalus 107 (1) (Winter 1978)

Susan Goldberg Kent

American Public Libraries: A Long Transformative Moment

O NE SUNDAY MORNING, as I read the *Los Angeles Times Sunday Magazine,* I came across an article entitled "Beyond 2000—The Jobs of the Past, the Jobs of the Future,"[1] and between sips of coffee and a few twinges of paranoia, I learned once again that my job as a librarian was "on the way out." Why was I not surprised? The author, Emily Gest, reported that "computers have already replaced their beloved card catalogs, and soon may replace libraries as we know them. Despite the thrill of physically browsing through books, ultimately we'll forget about the traditional library. . . .instead we'll simply message a librarian to send the book over the Internet." The article then goes on to list ten jobs "on the way in," a list that included both the "cyberlibrarian" and the "answer network technician." The cyberlibrarian, according to the article, "will no longer work in service centers hoarding scarce reference information. . . .instead. . .librarians will act as filters, distilling the flood of available information to a trickle people can cope with."

Ah, I said to myself, at least when we get to the future our successors will not be hoarding anymore. On the downside, however, we will have become a sort of "info-coffee maker," a kind of info-source filtering system where the turgid waters of the Internet will be purified and poured clean through the wiry fingers of "cyber answer network technicians."

This report was only the latest of an occasional series of reports from the so-called front line of technology on the demise of the public library. I have heard the story often enough to counter

---

Susan Goldberg Kent is City Librarian at the Los Angeles Public Library.

those twinges of paranoia with the librarian's version of Mark Twain's famous quip: reports of the death of the public library are greatly exaggerated!

And yet, what is it about libraries that makes people like Ms. Gest believe librarianship will change to the point where the job of the present-day librarian will evaporate and an entirely new kind of profession will emerge?

Throughout the almost thirty years that I have worked in public libraries, librarians have had to respond to continual challenges— from futurists, from technologists, from elected officials, from trustees, and from funders—that the public library was going to disappear. The assumption has been that the more the world changes, the less likely the need for public libraries. And the latest symbol or leading cause of the public library's demise is almost always the silicon chip, the holy grail of the information-starved. Are the new machines with their silicon injections of speed really going to replace people *this* time?

The recurring theme of the obsolescence of the public library, encountered regularly by most librarians, should be challenged more than ever before. While the cybercynics have already written off the need for libraries, most librarians, not unsurprisingly, see a strong future ahead in what will perhaps be the most important era in the long and proud history of the American public library. Those of us "in the know" understand the radical changes that have occurred in public libraries over the past decade. Those who do not "know" are waving their Harry Houdini capes over the library disappearing act.

Is the tradition of neutrality and modesty that in some ways has characterized librarianship somehow exacerbating this common misunderstanding? The rhetorical questions keep coming, and we continue to struggle to answer them. Why build new facilities if every library can be replaced by one small computer chip? Why train librarians, teachers, and information professionals if their knowledge and expertise can be traded in for a personal computer and a client server? Why publish books, why educate people to read and analyze, to do math, to understand history and world affairs if the entire body of knowledge is going to be readily available and accessible on the microchip?

From my vantage point, the more we digitize, the more we miniaturize, the more we technologize, the more we need to provide assistance, mediation, instruction, and analysis. In his recent book, *The Myth of the Electronic Library*,[2] William Birdsall asserts the following propositions:

- Librarians should not accept the inevitability of a technologically dominated information society.
- The library will continue to serve as a crucial social institution providing a place for social interaction, communal and cultural authenticity, and sensory and intellectual stimulation.
- Librarians should be identified with a broad concern for the collection, organization, and dissemination of knowledge rather than a narrower focus on information.
- Librarianship's commitment to client self-sufficiency should be promoted in the context of the library serving as a bridge between community and individualism, reinforcing ligatures and providing options with the social objective of promoting life chances for all members of society.

What underlies Birdsall's apt formulation can be found in the nature of the *publicness* of public libraries. It is curious how quick some cybercynics are to forget about "public" and to talk instead only about "libraries." In my view, the primary role of the public library is, essentially, *a place to provide equity of access to information and the world of knowledge.* This role can be looked at from three perspectives: the library as a physical, architectural place; the library as a terminus on the information superhighway; and the library as a catalyst for converting information into knowledge.

First, public libraries exist in physical space; as long as human beings exist within bodies that have their care and maintenance grounded in the physical world, people will relate to buildings and hand-held objects like books, paper, chairs, and tables. Actually, the suggestion that libraries hoard space, as well as information, reveals a kind of cynicism about the need for human, public life. If the virtual world of the silicon chip becomes the gold standard by which human activity is measured or regulated, then the nature of social and cultural life associated with the word "public" will have indeed not only abolished public service work like librarianship, but it will have radically altered what it has meant to be human. The nature of our humanness has been built upon our dual needs to be both individual persons and members of groups in society. The nature of our humanness has been built, also, upon our ability to pass on to others the useful and required information for living. In addition, the activity of hunting down and gathering together such information has its own rewards and pleasures, and these collections of the useful information, the legislated and unspoken laws and rules of society, and the wise essentials of life are made available for all people to find and digest in the public library.

Also important in the nature of the public library has been librarianship's professional imperative to serve all people, and the newest technologies have become an available and convenient means to help fulfill this responsibility. As a result, instead of having to catch up to technology, librarians have been consistently out in front in terms of the new technology. In reality, libraries and librarians have been on the leading edge of change for many years, change that has been quietly transforming the public library. In fact, the American public library has been going through a trans-formative moment, albeit a long transformative moment, for at least the last ten years.

The silicon chip plays an important but not all-consuming role in this second perspective. That is, it takes its proper place in the context of what libraries are, rather than the other way around (in which the library will be subsumed by machines). If public librar-ies are important as physical places—places for study and educa-tion, places for finding information, places for social and commu-nity interaction, places for quiet and contemplation—then, most importantly, the library has to be a place where all members of a community can have equity of access to information, an ideal for many public librarians. Toward this end, the silicon chip is not an end but a means, a tool, like a wrench that will open the pipes to make universal access to information possible.

The technologies that are transforming our everyday lives have, in large measure, already transformed the library. No longer are libraries individual institutions whose users are dependent solely on their own limited resources. Rather, they are connected to the world of information through the Internet and the World Wide Web.

While the general public is now becoming more conversant with bar codes and automation, T-1 lines and URLs, facsimiles and scanners, multimedia personal computers and HTML, public libraries have been using these new telecommunications technologies and electronic equipment for many years. Long before each can of tomato sauce and every loaf of bread carried a bar code, libraries were using bar codes to identify their borrowers and to keep track of their collections. Whether in a large urban area or a small exurban township, the public library usually has the most advanced and most sophisticated technology infrastructure and sometimes the only viable and publicly accessible electronic data bases. In the mid-1980s, facsimile machines were used to enhance document delivery between libraries, and scanners were used to increase access to collections. Hypertext was a common topic for discussion at library seminars, and libraries became the places where the public could have their first experience using a computer. The advent of these new technologies has been embraced by public librarians, first by a few and then eagerly by more and more, as they began to see the benefits for the users and the library.

A decade ago, someone entering a public library could expect to find books, magazines, and some audiovisual materials in the building. The collection was determined by the size of the building, the local budget, and that particular library's collection focus. The library user was also limited to what he or she could expect from that library facility and, with a few exceptions through interlibrary loan, could only use the resources contained within its four walls. Today, that same person entering many of the public libraries in this country will expect and demand global resources, immediately and directly. Many American public libraries have been transformed during the past decade from a finite space with finite resources to a finite space with infinite resources. For some, this transformation is taking place right now; for others, the transformation is still on the horizon.

Long before there was an information superhighway, the public libraries of this country were the information main streets, the information rural roads, and the information freeways. *Public* is the word that is most often forgotten by those who claim that there is no future for the public library. Public is the underpinning of the American public library, public in terms of its definition: "of, concerning or affecting the community or the people; maintained for or used by the people or the community." No other educational or cultural institution in America serves everyone—regardless of gender, race, ethnicity, cultural identity, sexual preference, age, or economic condition. The *public* library is a public good, maintained and used by the entire community. And, as a public good, the public library has willingly accepted the responsibility of being on the cutting edge of technology, making the latest types of information available, advancing the notion that access to information is every person's right in this country, and maintaining the best of its historical and traditional resources and services while offering a chance to use the new products of the digital revolution.

Technology has created all sorts of formats, from books to CD-ROMs and now the Internet itself, through which information has been stored. Public libraries make information available. But creating meaning out of knowledge is, in the third perspective, both a private and a public necessity. While only the individual, the library user, can create meaning or knowledge from information through the struggle of learning, it is a public good when individuals become intelligent, wiser, happier in their pursuits through that creative process. Information and knowledge are not the same thing. The assumption for centuries has been that when people learn, when they transform information into meaning and knowledge, the personal transformation itself amounts to a societal benefit. We live in a world that is, ultimately, not machine made; finally we return to our social identities as members of the largest group we can think of—humanity. In this sense, public libraries are completely human institutions, dedicated to helping all people in their personal searches for information and knowledge.

Now, all the above notwithstanding, the public library may have itself contributed to the many predictions that it is a disposable and outmoded institution. Public librarians have, for the most part, kept quiet. We do not sing our own praises loudly enough. We do not tell our stories compellingly enough. We do not take credit for our achievements, and we certainly do not assert our position as the very public heart and soul of the information age.

What must libraries do to survive and prosper? One answer is solid and sound leadership. Leadership is something everyone talks about. We search for it, give seminars on how to achieve it, and take surveys of who has it. What is leadership, and how do you get it? Leadership is often perceived as a "star quality," but it is difficult to shine in environments where the emphasis is on each person having an equal voice. In many public-sector fields like librarianship, the norm is to be equal to everyone else, to work together in teams, to understand and value differences, and to achieve consensus. While these forms of acceptable behavior are valuable, sometimes it is critical, even imperative, to have someone figuratively step forward and emerge as the leader. It is neither easy nor popular to be the one to speak out and try to resolve differences. It is neither easy nor popular to tell people that you disagree with their ideas, that you have some other ideas that they might consider. It is often very difficult to volunteer to serve as a leader, to bring people together and implement new ideas. While I am not advocating dictatorship, benevolent or otherwise, it is clear that the American public library needs reasoned, outspoken, and well-articulated leadership if it is to flourish in a digital future.

Leadership is most difficult in situations where the leader is expected to be an "agent of change" in an institutional culture that abhors change, which is not an uncommon situation in many public libraries today. We mouth words like, "Yes, public libraries are valued by the public they serve—look at all the surveys and polls we have taken," "Yes, for the most part, government officials and funders think libraries are good institutions to have in their communities, even if funding is rarely at the 'right' level," or "Yes, public libraries give good service, try their hardest to keep up-to-date, add computers whenever there is money available, and are caring and responsive to the needs of children, teenagers, and senior citizens."

But it is no longer enough to be mom, apple pie, and boy or girl scouts rolled into one! It is not enough to be esteemed by politicians only to be funded at the minimal level, to be admired for giving good service but devalued as anachronistic and outmoded. Slogans such as "Americans can't wait" and "Libraries change lives" sound good, but what do they change? We know the potential of public libraries. We know what we must do for the communities we serve. We know what we must do in the future, at the very least, to keep abreast of all of these changes and to assist in the transformation not only of libraries but of society itself.

What we do not do aggressively enough is assume a key leadership role as the major player in a society that is now based on information and knowledge. More important than the physical space, the technology, or the collection of information and knowledge are the people who work in and manage public libraries. Public libraries are always going to be about people—the connection of people to resources, the connection of people to technology, the connection of people to people. Without people who are excited about the possibilities for the future of public libraries—staff, users, elected officials, trustees, the general public—the future may be grim.

The public libraries that have been the most successful in transforming themselves are those institutions that have had strong and visible leadership. Public libraries need leaders who can passionately and forcefully articulate a vision for the future coupled with a cogent assessment of the critical factors that American public libraries must now confront if they are to have a successful future. Public libraries need leaders who will address the major transformative issues for American public libraries.

When transformation occurs over time rather than instantaneously, it sometimes loses its impact. Public librarians have become so familiar with the changes wrought by technology that these changes may seem obvious and familiar, and their significance may be ignored or disregarded. If the American public library is in a long transformative moment, as I believe it is, the pivotal nature of the transformation and its effects mean the beginning of a new era for public libraries.

The major transformative issues that should be considered are as follows:

CONNECTIVITY AND CONTENT

The American public library can no longer stand alone. While we have a long and proud history of cooperation and collaboration on many fronts, connectivity by simply pointing to each other's bibliographic data bases is, for the future, an easy but unsophisticated and unsatisfactory solution. Our users want "information," and they want it now. Frankly, most of them do not care which library owns which book. They are unconcerned with how many copies of *Crime and Punishment* or the latest *Sunset Western Gardening Book* exist in a city, region, or state. They want the book in their hands as soon as possible. They do not care where the information comes from, they want the information they need; they do not want "more" information, they want the "right" information.

In a recent study, *California Local Libraries Statewide Survey of Information Needs,*[3] conducted for the California State Library by the Institute for the Future, the survey found that "as technology and information appliances become cheaper and more readily available, library users may begin to substitute library visits with these new alternatives. The desire for easy access to relevant information in a timely manner may draw current users who are experimenting with technology away from the library in the future. Californians do not necessarily want more information—there is more than anybody can possible use already—but they do want quality information in the form that will solve their problems most directly."

For many years, we have talked about networks, the connectivity of bibliographic data bases from one library to another. Bibliographic utilities such as OCLC have done a major portion of that type of network connectivity. Today, search the Internet and you will find library data bases—public, academic, technical—everywhere in the world. The key for us now is content—and the Web and the Internet are, if nothing else, full of content, constantly changing minute by minute; more importantly, so are library-created and vendor-created data bases. Newspapers and journals in full text, reference books, financial and business resources, census and demographic files, health and scientific information, biographic directories, works of literature, children's books, and indices in every subject area are now available on-line. This type of connectivity—to *content*—is the most exciting and important aspect of the library of the future.

MAINTAINING AND UPGRADING INFRASTRUCTURE

Future library building programs must accommodate future changes, some as yet unknown, and the buildings should be designed to be flexible, adaptable, and focused on the fact that change is the only constant. Older facilities need to be assessed for adaptability to the new technological and telecommunications environments and re-tooled if necessary. Furniture and equipment will need upgrading as well. Library buildings and the technologies employed by librar-ies must be constantly upgraded. Wiring, electrical connections and power, telecommunication services, hardware, software, and peripherals are keys to the transformation of the American public library.

Investments in technology and telecommunications are not one-time investments. They are ongoing, and that is a financial issue that is often unfamiliar to governing authorities. While most local governments understand the need to buy a computer, they have not yet come to terms with the continual need to purchase newer, faster computers so that new information software can work. Public libraries have gone from using the first Kaypros and Macs to working with 286s, 386s, 486s, multimedia PCs with CD-ROM drives, and so on very quickly—in fact, much more quickly than most governmental entities are amortizing these as capital equip-ment.

Even more problematic is the need for funding authorities to understand the issue of "leasing" information as opposed to buy-ing it. A book, once purchased, is owned by the library. It is an object one can hold, feel, and see; it is real. A leased data base exists somewhere in cyberspace or on a CD-ROM. It has no obvious tactile qualities. You cannot grab onto it unless you print out a few pages. The library does not own it but pays for its use only for a period of time. When the time period is over, you have to pay for it again. How is that explained to the purchasing agent, the taxpayer reform group, the mayor?

RADICALLY CHANGING EXPECTATIONS OF LIBRARY USERS

Remember the person walking into a public library ten years ago and then again today? That person has very different expectations of what the public library can do for the user. The library user of today, particularly one who has heard about or read about the revolution in technology and the information superhighway, wants information delivered on demand, as quickly as possible, as current as possible, and free of charge (if at all possible). Just recently, I overheard a library patron complain to a staff member at a reference desk that she could not understand why she had to wait thirty minutes to have a back issue of a magazine retrieved from the closed stacks when she could access a specific article "from out there in cyberspace" through the library's computer network in thirty seconds. Good question, I thought; now what do we do to change our service delivery patterns?

Of course, people still want books, videos, hard copies of magazine articles, children's story times, and interlibrary loans. But they have come to expect, from the constant exposure in the press and through the electronic media, that a simple silicon chip will bring them everything they need with immediacy. The full contents of the Library of Congress—sure, they insist, you can get it for me now. In actuality, they are coming to realize that public libraries are truly their "on-ramps" to the superhighway they have heard so much about. Now, public libraries must aggressively prove their ability to deliver.

RECRUITMENT, TRAINING, AND RETRAINING OF STAFF

To return to the traditional public library, staff members were educated and trained for their jobs. Professional librarians understood bibliographical resources, reference sources, collection management, and information referrals. They knew how to locate the right book from which to answer the library user's question. They usually knew where the book could be found, the color of the cover or binding, whether or not it had an index, and an overview of its contents. They would also know if the resources in their collections did not contain the sought-after answer and could often direct the patron to the right resource at another library. Thus they could say either, "Yes, we can answer that for you," or "No, I am afraid we cannot help you with that question."

Today, in the transformed library, things are not quite so simple or so clear. Instead of the yellow book on the third shelf in the biographical directories, staff members in public libraries also have to be aware of what exists in cyberspace to assist in answering reference questions. They know that there is probably or possibly an answer out there in the universe. They know that through the Web or through their own extensive holdings of electronic information they should be able to answer the question. But where is the answer, how should we begin, how long will the search take? And, when or if they find the answer, is it reliable, is it up-to-date, will the same data or new data be available tomorrow? Training, more training, hands-on experience, 'Net surfing—all of these methods of learning about resources are essential.

Not only do professional librarians now have to admit that they no longer keep the secrets about how to find information in the library's collections, they now have to assist users who are doing their own searching on the library's computers with data bases that are new, unfamiliar, or unfathomable.

Looming even larger is the question of developing a collection when some of the material, and an ever-increasing amount, is not owned but leased and constantly changing. Who has the archives, and who will keep the hardware to access the older forms of electronic information? When do you give up print or microfiche format in favor of electronic resources? There are no easy answers.

The library staff, in general, will have to constantly upgrade skills and knowledge, learn about using new technologies, and employ new techniques. Nontraditional library staff, such as technicians, network administrators, and software specialists, will have to be added to the staff complement, sometimes replacing outdated positions.

GOVERNANCE, STRUCTURE, AND FUTURE FUNDING

Almost all public library funding is local, usually coming from taxes paid by local residents for local services. Library governance, concomitantly, is also local. Whether appointed or elected, the governance structure usually includes a board of directors or trustees with either administrative and policy-making powers or an advisory function. Local elected officials provide oversight, some direction, and, most importantly, the majority of the funding. Most library service has been local, and over the past twenty to thirty years or more, through extensive reciprocal agreements and state-based systems, the local has often expanded to include all libraries in a particular area sharing resources and cooperative services. Recently, there has been a backlash from local taxpayers, in all areas of the country, who believe that their tax dollars should remain local and that library services, as well as other governmental services, should be provided *only* to those people who pay for them directly.

This new wrinkle is playing out in an environment that makes providing global access possible from a local library—and conversely means that "outsiders" can then access local library services. We are now facing situations in which access to global information is coming at a time when new barriers are being erected, figuratively, along jurisdictional lines. What will it mean when a city decides to restrict public library usage to their residents only and that city's library has a Web page with information readily available to the entire Web universe? Will the library have to restrict access to its Web site? Will it simply cease giving its own users global information because "global" users, those outside the city, are not permitted to use that library? Can we freely take information from "others" if we do not allow "others" to take information from us?

ACHIEVING INFORMATION EQUITY

In addition to the changing expectations of library users, changing demographics, continuing high levels of illiteracy, and the tremendous disparity in economic conditions all mean that public libraries should become even more relevant and more critically important than they have been during their two-hundred-plus year history in this country. The essential service that public libraries can provide better, and on a broader scope, than any other public or private institution is to become the platform for the achievement of information equity for every person in the United States. Equity does not mean equal, and it does not mean that every public library in every community must have the same resources. It does mean, however, that at every entry point to the global information infrastructure (i.e., at every public library), people have the ability to access the entire world of information. Right now, given the disparities that exist in telecommunications services and the implementation of new technologies from state to state, city to city, and rural to urban areas in this country, information equity remains a goal for the future. However, as the primary agency in helping to attain this goal, the public libraries of this country will be providing a basic and universal function, the delivery of global information services and equitable access to these services to everyone.

The transformation of the American public library will result in the rebirth of public libraries as essential and critically needed institutions, but *only if and only when* there is a coming together of the power, the means, and the commitment to make this happen. In nature, through the process of metamorphosis, the butterfly is the caterpillar's destiny. In terms of the life cycle of institutions, however, what can we say about this long transformative moment for public libraries? Ostriches do not become butterflies.

ENDNOTES

[1] Emily Gest, "Beyond 2000—The Jobs of the Past, the Jobs of the Future," *Los Angeles Times Sunday Magazine,* 20 August 1995.

[2] William Birdsall, *The Myth of the Electronic Library: Librarianship and Social Change in America* (Westport, Conn.: Greenwood Press, 1994).

[3] Institute for the Future, *California Local Libraries Statewide Survey of Information Needs: Preliminary Highlights,* Menlo Park, Calif., 6 October 1995.

Brian Lang

Bricks and Bytes: Libraries in Flux

THE LIBRARY AS MONUMENT

I S A LIBRARY A COLLECTION OF BOOKS, or is it a building? Historically, collections have needed buildings for storage, conservation, and access. The community has had need for a building—especially if it is a national library—to denote symbolically
as well as literally the existence of a national published archive,
announcing that the nation has a history of achievement, invention, exploration, and industry.

But do libraries still need buildings? It is apparent that our
politicians believe so, to the extent that they are willing to commit
very large sums of money to their construction.

The late twentieth century is a period of paradox for libraries.
On the one hand, the closing decade will be recalled, in Europe at
any rate, as a time of great new library buildings. The national
libraries of the United Kingdom, France, Germany, and Denmark
are all opening new buildings; some of them, as in Paris and
London, are monumental in scale, the largest public buildings of
the century in each country. On the other hand, libraries are living
through an information revolution, the fruits of which could suggest that centralized book repositories are redundant. The actuality is that demand for library reading rooms continues to rise.
Libraries house great treasures, whether these be medieval illumi-
nations or the latest treatises in thermodynamics, and their staffs
increasingly employ old and new technologies side by side. At the

Brian Lang is Chief Executive of The British Library in London.

221

British Library, librarians switch effortlessly between on-line and printed catalogs, and between CD-ROM and printed patent specifications; they provide information about services over the Internet and by printed brochure, whichever is more convenient and better meets the user's needs. And politicians understand this. They have shown themselves to be alert to the technological developments in libraries, partly because they are aware that wondrous things are happening all around them in telecommunications, computing, the provision of financial information, and the entertainment industry. So to the credit of both parties, librarians have been able to convince their political overlords to fund not only substantial new library buildings but also information technology programs, which insure that library users have less need to enter the new buildings to gain access to the collections they house.

Not that the requests made of government ministers for library buildings are necessarily straightforward. Library buildings can be controversial for the nature of their design or for the conduct of their construction. In London, for example, concern has been expressed at the cost overrun and the scale of the provision of new library facilities at Saint Pancras, rather than for the justification for the British Library's new building in itself. The building is widely regarded as essential. Heads may have been shaken over the delays, the inadequate provision of reader seats, and the need to correct faultily installed shelving; but as completion approaches, Saint Pancras is broadly appreciated as a fitting home for a great library.

The technological context within which libraries operate has been changing rapidly. The information revolution is well documented. Much more information is being produced, in a multiplicity of formats and accessible through a variety of means. The political context is also changing, though. National governments are taking a different attitude to public spending. They are increasingly reluctant to invest in public projects when private finance might be available to share, and sometimes underwrite, the financial "risk." So libraries are required to look for new ways of funding library and information projects, which involve revenue earning and partnerships with commercial organizations that regard information as a resource to be priced. Their experience has largely been that delivery of their public-good objectives and the earning of revenue to assist in fulfilling those objectives need not be incompatible.

Libraries deal with, and in, information. This may be regarded as being similar to a commodity with a value, which may be priced with due regard to costs and market forces. It is an unusual commodity, however. Information exists only through human perception. It can be shared, in that it can be reused and yet still exist for future use. It has the characteristics of a public good; more for you does not necessarily mean less for me.

Transnational government organizations, like the European Union, are challenging libraries to exploit new technology so as to collaborate internationally in ways that will question the notion of the "national" collection, and therefore that of the "national library."

None of these developments ought to cause us to question seriously the traditional responsibilities of libraries. Those responsibilities, broadly speaking, are to care for the recorded past and to collect publications about the present. Libraries catalog all of this data so it can be found quickly and easily, making it available to people who request it. This will not change. The transformation comes in *how* these activities are carried out and the scale on which they take place.

The national library is a noble institution. In 1784, Boulée, a French architect, said, "A nation's most precious monument is, beyond any doubt, that which is the repository of all the knowledge it has acquired." A new national library building is presently being completed in Paris, to open at the end of 1996, as a vast monument to the vision of the late president, François Mitterrand. In London, the new national library building at Saint Pancras will open in 1997, and in Frankfurt, a large new building is being constructed for the German national library, also to open in 1997. These buildings are designed primarily with printed publishing in mind, which is quite appropriate when we consider that these libraries house important historical collections that must be protected.

THE LIBRARY AS INFORMATION NODE

In Britain, Saint Pancras will account for only half of the British Library's activity. In London, the library concentrates on providing direct access to readers, usually through primary sources in reading rooms. Access is provided annually to more than five million items in this way. But from Boston Spa in Yorkshire, 250 miles north of London, the library supplies well over four million items to readers around the world, as well as to other libraries and workplaces, by fax, photocopy, traditional mail, and directly from computer to computer. This latter aspect of the British Library's activity has been growing the fastest. Over the past five years, delivery of items in London reading rooms has increased by 10 percent, while remote-supply fax, photocopy, and so on have increased by 24 percent. This gap is expected to continue widening.

Part of the information problem today is that so much information is being produced, and many publication formats are being used. It is very difficult to estimate just how much, but two anecdotal measures are relevant. The first is the suggestion that the amount of information and knowledge being produced in the world is now doubling every five years. The second is the estimate that of all the scientists the world has ever known, half of them are alive and working today. Output is therefore prodigious.

As for more quantified measures, this year the British Library will acquire, by legal deposit, purchase, or gift, over 2.4 million items. The collection grows annually by twelve kilometers of shelf space. While the vast bulk of this is in traditional published form—books, journals, newspapers, audio compact discs, and so on—there is a huge amount of *additional* information that is neither acquired by the library nor is recorded as having been "published." This mass of information is either not published as print on paper or appears in a form that we would not necessarily regard as truly "published."

Electronic data bases may be published off-line in the form of tapes or CD-ROMs containing current contents of data bases, which are delivered to customers and regularly updated. This type of publishing is, in principle, relatively easy to handle under existing procedures. But since the 1960s, publishers have also made data bases available on-line, with data being transmitted directly to the customer's own computer. In the United Kingdom, by the end of the 1980s, more than 350 on-line data bases were being produced. How many more were available in the rest of the world?

A great variety of material is now published on-line, such as cumulating on-line services analogous to traditional bibliographic, cataloging, indexing, and abstracting services. In content and alerting services, greater emphasis is placed on currency, and there are real-time transactional services such as financial data bases, which are updated from moment to moment. The United Kingdom's cartographic survey, the Ordnance Survey, will soon be available only as an on-line data base, updated every eight seconds or so.

What we face is a plethora of information being published, carried, and transmitted on a host of new kinds of technology.

THE LIBRARY AS LABORATORY

National libraries must persevere with their responsibility to acquire and care for the national archive. But it is very difficult to maintain a *comprehensive* archive in the absence of a statutory deposit of publications in new media. Few national libraries enjoy this right, despite the recognition of their need to nurture a comprehensive archive. One purpose is to produce a national bibliography. But this responsibility exists for reasons other than simply to provide employment for librarians. A record of a nation's intellectual output and access to the published archive are fundamental to scientific, technical, academic, and cultural development.

Broadly speaking, the organized pursuit of knowledge—and this applies in the humanities just as much as the so-called hard sciences—happens through laboratory research and experiment, through data gathering and comparison so as to develop and test hypotheses. At its most extreme, this can mean control or understanding of variables in a constant or controlled environment.

The experimental environment might be a scientific laboratory in a university or a library reading room. In my own case, as a social anthropologist, the research setting was a small town in East Africa. The researcher eventually publishes his or her findings, in pursuit of a variety of motives. One motive—we like to think it is the most important one—is to give an account to colleagues of a new contribution to knowledge in the subject area that they share. Other motives, understandably, are career enhancement, prestige, self-satisfaction, and money.

Findings may also be published in order to protect them from being tampered with, or claimed by someone else—at the most extreme they are published as a patent specification—so that intellectual rights as well as commercial rights are protected.

And this is what libraries accumulate; this is how the intellectual output of a nation is stored and recorded. Two fundamental principles of scientific progress are served. The first is that of replicability. It should be possible for others to replicate any experiment. The way a step forward was achieved—whether in the field of thermodynamics or in our understanding of sixteenth-century German verse—is described so its legitimacy is confirmed and the findings can be tested by others; this is subsequently built upon and taken further. So the store of knowledge in a library is the raw material for further progress as well as our assurance that progress to date has been reliable, that it can be depended upon.

The second fundamental principle, citation, is a corollary of the first. The earlier work that is being built upon and the evidence that is summoned to support new work—or earlier work that is being revisited for adjustment or refutation—has to be capable of identification, as part of the continuing cycle of experiment and replication. And here, again, there is a key role for the national library.

But why the *national* library? Why not university libraries, the libraries of oil companies, or even private collections? The reason is because we need to insure *comprehensive* collection and recording of the national published archive; hence legal deposit. This does not mean that the national published archive needs to be under one single roof. New technology means that the archive can be a distributed one, with shared bibliographic record creation and remote access, all over networks. But some organization has to take responsibility for insuring that all of this is properly coordinated, that the necessary legislation is in place, and that the system is properly understood by users and publishers as well as by librarians.

The other issue is that those responsibilities by their nature must be entrusted to an organization with a very long time perspective, planning for hundreds of years in the future. A commercial organization, with shorter time scales based on a return on investment, cannot give the near-absolute guarantees that a public body is better situated to handle.

In many respects, the national library is best suited to provide long-term assurance that information will remain available and to provide stability when technology is rapidly changing. While it is not possible at present to claim that national libraries are wholly fulfilling those roles, the objective of providing long-term availability for a comprehensive national published archive remains one worth striving for.

Fulfillment of that role requires that several key steps be taken. The most obvious one is to insure comprehensiveness of the archive, and hence of the national bibliography, by persuading governments to pass legislation on the statutory deposit of new media publications. Other steps involve the creation and linking of electronic catalogs, and the digitization of texts.

Some national libraries are digitizing items in their collections, and many have created digital catalogs, or commissioned commercial organizations to do so for them, and made them available over digital networks. Some European national libraries are taking part in a project that will allow them to search each other's on-line catalogs as if they were searching their own.

THE LIBRARY COMPROMISES AND IS COMPROMISED

Although such projects represent progress, substantial qualifications have to be made. The first is to accept that our collections will never be comprehensive. No library can possibly expect to collect comprehensively. It is already essential for libraries to share their collections, and libraries are putting less emphasis on acquiring information and more on knowing in which other library a required piece of information can be found. The idea of the library "collection" is changing. A collection may not necessarily be regarded as being under one single roof. Some "libraries" in the future may not actually contain any publications at all. The librarian then will not be someone who acquires books and cares for a collection, but rather a person who helps a researcher to identify where a particular piece of information is located and arranges access to it. In this context, networking of libraries is essential.

Sharing and joint-access agreements between libraries, data bases, and information stores of all kinds are essential. Mutually understandable catalogs are essential, and they must be capable of being queried quickly and easily from the other side of the world. Ordering and delivery mechanisms must share common standards. But in moving toward those goals we must also qualify our reliance on new technology, keeping it in its place as a means rather than as an end in itself.

For the time being, it appears that change in the near future for libraries is unlikely to be technology-led: the technology we are using seems to be in a fairly steady state. No sudden leap forward is anticipated; no breakthrough is expected that would mean a change in direction or pace of the kind that was brought about by, say, the personal computer or rapid facsimile transmission.

The advent of large mainframe computing in the 1950s led to the on-line availability of major abstracting and indexing services and to much more flexible searching. This was regarded pessimistically by librarians, who believed that they had become redundant because end users would conduct their own searches. But librarians continue to make contributions as different kinds of enablers. What seems to be happening now is an exploration of the possibilities and potential of the existing technology—networking, full-text delivery, and digital scanning. All of these are being developed by libraries, and there seem to be no serious technological obstacles about which we deeply worry. This does not mean that there are no technical obstacles whatsoever. There are still discrepancies in standards and protocols, and the finite storage lifetimes of digital media continue to cause concern.

It is arguable, however, that the most serious obstacles are not technological, but cultural, legal, and political. The cultural issues concern the acceptance, or lack thereof, of the way we gather, store, and distribute information. They are about attitudes to information systems and how they are used.

One example is the perception of the learned journal. This surely has been the key medium of scholarly discourse—a number of articles bound together and published at regular intervals. It has been extremely successful, and not only for the scholars and scientists whose work has been carried to those desks, laboratories, and libraries where the knowledge of seminal experiments and pieces of research can produce the greatest benefits.

The publishing of a learned journal involves a complex chain that includes peer review and hence quality control. Scholars, scientists, and technologists have for many years looked to the learned journal as a way to stay up-to-date in their fields. And in turn, the authors of the articles contained in the journal expect their careers to be enhanced by publication in such journals, especially the more prestigious ones like *Nature* or *Physics Review Letters*.

Publishing these journals is a veritable industry in itself. But the traditional learned journal, consisting of, say, eight or ten articles plus a few book reviews, is not the only way to publish research results. New technology offers many advantages over the traditional learned journal. A single article may be conceived, written, and refereed in very rapid succession, followed by circulation, or "publication," instantly over networks. And the reader need not also buy the other seven or eight irrelevant articles that in traditional form would have been bound together with the one in which he or she was interested.

Alas, the electronic journal, let alone the electronic single article, is not yet wholly accepted as a respectable, career-enhancing publication medium. Why is this the case, given the advantages of this new medium? One possibility is that scholars are not wholly used to the notion that their work is as accessible on-line as on the shelf. They may have been trained within a regime in which publication in certain key journals represents what they regard as the ultimate acknowledgment of acceptance within an elite, and they aspire towards membership in it. They may believe (with some justification) that "cyberjournals" do not guarantee immortality. Time will tell whether, how, and under what circumstances such attitudes will change.

LIBRARIES AND PUBLISHERS

As for the legal issues, it is unfortunate that the law lags behind developments in technology. While there is an urgent need for statutory deposit of electronic publications, the copyright law may also need amendment. The commercial and financial relationship between producers of information, publishers, libraries, and library users may also need to change.

This will require a considerable shift in attitude by publishers towards the way they exercise their rights over the information that they produce and control. Publishers have been wary about the implications of electronic storage and transmission. Their major fear is a loss of control over material in which they have a commercial interest and the loss of revenue that might result. It is therefore important that we come to an accommodation with publishers to insure that the maximum benefit from unimpeded access to information can be achieved.

Librarians cannot realistically proceed without the support of publishers, and they need a model for deposit and access that will provide some benefits to publishers. This will most likely involve giving assurances not just about the integrity of their publications (that is, that they will not be tampered with), but that access is granted under very clear and strictly applied circumstances. The Library of Congress has negotiated a complex set of agreements for access to legally deposited CD-ROMs; though the agreements are complex, at least they are in place as evidence that a library and publishers can agree on terms for legal deposit and access to this kind of material.

Librarians, then, need to compromise along with publishers. Perhaps as new means of storage and dissemination become more established, making possible greatly increased volumes of delivery, publishers will see an advantage in imposing lower royalty fees. Librarians and their clients will in turn need to become more comfortable with a regime in which charges are increasingly made for access to more kinds of information. In any case, we need to seek a new economic order for what used to be known as "the book trade" but is now about much more than "books"—an order in which the mutual benefits, and possibly the interdependencies, are explicit.

LIBRARIANS AS ENTREPRENEURS

Librarians are presently conducting negotiations, over a wide range of issues, with construction companies, publishers, computer and software producers, lawyers, their governments (of course), and—let us not forget them—their readers.

In the traditional print-on-paper setting, libraries have played a key role in the democratic process as well as the scientific process by insuring that information is universally available. The use of networks may make information more readily available to society at large if the Internet provides virtually equal access to all sources and types of information anywhere in the world. However, the Internet is unlikely to remain free of charge at the point of use forever. If exorbitant prices are imposed, libraries may have to exclude certain kinds of information. This could lead to a society divided into those who can afford to pay for certain kinds of information and those who cannot, those who have access to the technology and those who do not.

Getting the balance right between stability and innovation is not easy. There are activities—such as seeking legal deposit and extending our national bibliographies to include digital publications—that we must undertake as a matter of urgency because these are unique to national libraries. No one else will pursue them if we do not.

The traditional role of the national library as our collective memory must not change. But the library is not simply about the past; it is the basis for innovation and cultural stimulus. Invention tends to build on what has been done before. Libraries are indispensable stores of information for any researcher in any field of study. As such, they could be better recognized as key institutions within the economic as well as scholarly infrastructure, and they are also likely to be treated more sympathetically for public funding, assuming they do not compromise or neglect their responsibility to posterity. National libraries owe a duty of care, not just to those who are using the library in the present, but also to those people who many hundreds of years in the future will be consulting the information being gathered today.

The idea of the national library as a cathedral is likely to persist. The library building is too potent a symbol of civilization to fade as an ideal. But in terms of activities and serving users, both for the present and for posterity, an equally valid model could be a group of churches. The national collection will most likely be a distributed one, gathered, cataloged, and stored by a network of complementary regional libraries. This network's horizon will be international and reciprocal rights, and mutual access will have to be arranged on a worldwide basis. International organizations are already encouraging the development of infrastructure for this kind of library arrangement. The European Union is supporting numerous projects (at least one of which has a transatlantic component) in areas such as character-set recognition, name authority, and file labeling for electronic documents and other "meta-data" issues. The G7 group of major nations is encouraging what may be regarded as a "content" project, Bibliotheca Universalis, in which major documents in certain national libraries' collections are digitized.

The very fact of collaboration and cooperation between libraries in different countries is as significant as the projects themselves. Such collaboration is evidence of the inevitability of the evolution of the "library" into a set of networked institutions, on the basis of which complementarity can become a reality. In this sense, British libraries should in due course have no need to acquire, say, French publications because these will be readily accessible through French counterpart libraries, and vice versa. This process follows the logic of information technology: that collections will be increasingly digital, capable of transmission over networks, and that those networks will be global in operation.

Within this model, the rights of authors and publishers will need to be protected. Royalties and other fees, as appropriate, may be collected by mechanisms akin to what is already familiar for telecommunications accounts.

As for the national librarian, he or she will, doubtless to his or her chagrin, spend less and less time making collecting and service decisions and even less time in contact with readers. The national librarian is likely to become even more of an international "library trade" diplomat, attending countless meetings and dealing with copious e-mail in the task of regulating and organizing the flow of information among authors, publishers, libraries, and library users.

Librarians will also need to be even more entrepreneurial. Just as the role of information broker is intensified, so is the role of financial deal-making. As mentioned at the beginning of this essay, governments are decreasingly able or willing to fund library provision at existing levels from taxation. The relationship with publishers and information consumers, as well as with telecommunications companies and software and hardware houses, is bound to become more "businesslike." While libraries in the public sector must remain fundamentally "for the public good" in objective and "not-for-profit" in operation, the funding of their activities will require increasing availability of private-sector contributions. Among libraries, the British Library is the leader in terms of volume of revenue generated from its activities and the range of its priced services. As grant-in-aid from the government is less able to support the range of activities that the British Library believes is appropriate to the national library, and as it needs to find substantial sums to invest in new projects and new and replacement technology, its staff needs to talk constructively with private-sector partners.

And where lies the book? The notion of the demise of the book needs swift dispatch. The book will continue to flourish for many kinds of publishing and will coexist happily with electronic publishing. Libraries will continue to collect and care for books. National libraries will continue to care for large and varied collections of books and written manuscripts. Undoubtedly, some libraries will tend to specialize in books while others will specialize in electronic publications.

National libraries need to be expert in working with both kinds of publications and providing services from each. In the meantime, librarians are suffering the pains of an identity crisis caused by their uncertainty about where they stand in the midst of the information revolution. Augmenting this identity crisis is librarians' uncertainty as to just who it is they are serving. Library users may still be referred to as "readers," but just as often may be referred to as "customers" or "clients."

Perhaps the old certainties will never return. National libraries, however, ought to make it their major concern to *offer* certainty. An advertising slogan for Britain's national bibliographic service once asked, "Where can I be *sure* to find it?" This may need slight modification to cope with the future reality of distributed collections and networked access, but *"How* can I be sure to find it?" offers an equally valid, and equally useful, assurance. It is in that sense that librarians are "enablers" or "guides" within the dense information undergrowth. Library skills will still include cataloging. Librarians will still, ideally, be expert in specific areas of their collections and be capable of offering specialized advice based on a sound understanding of the research process. But their notion of their profession will need to be based on fresh legal and economic certainties and a lively sense of public good. The alternative is loss of public memory and a world in which once-great libraries become mere information supermarkets.

Peter Johan Lor

A Distant Mirror: The Story of Libraries in South Africa

SOUTH AFRICA. THE IMAGES THAT COME to mind are bittersweet: an inauguration; the tall and slightly frail figure of Nelson Mandela, statesman and saint from Robben Island, superimposed on an election; long, straggling lines of voters patiently waiting in the heat and dust to cast their ballots; and beyond that, now mercifully receding, a finger-wagging martinet, armored cars, uniformed men, and prostrate figures on the ground around the Sharpeville police station.

For a change, good news captivated millions of television viewers who watched a rainbow nation emerge into the light. Was it enthralling because it was unexpected? Or because of the hope it gave other fractured societies, to Africa? Suddenly South African "experts" were conducting master classes in peace and reconciliation.

Reality is more complex. In the aftermath of the liberation struggle, a high level of crime, continuing political violence, and the pressures of unmet expectations threaten our fragile democracy. It will take more than a saintly president and a democratic constitution to bring peace, respect for human life, and common courtesy to this traumatized society. We are in a state of revolution, the outcome of which is difficult to predict. We are closer to the situation in Rwanda than we dare to think.

Like South Africa, libraries are thought to be in transition. There are technological challenges: electronic networks, disembodied information, virtual libraries.[1] Libraries worldwide are chal-

---

Peter Johan Lor is Director of The State Library in Pretoria, South Africa.

lenged by economic and social forces.[2] The literature is replete with exhortations for the reconceptualization and repositioning of libraries, which must adapt to these changes or go the way of the dinosaurs.[3]

Thus, South Africa's libraries can be seen as being involved in two transitions. Along with libraries elsewhere, they are entering the white water of information technology. As social institutions they are molded by the forces at work in South African society. Our revolution brings with it massive changes in social relations, political power bases, governmental structures and financing, and in the clientele and conceptualization of social services and institutions. In this period of change, are South Africa's libraries at the forefront? Are they being dragged, kicking and screaming, into the future? Or are they quietly and benevolently being neglected? A further question arises. Does the story of libraries in South Africa have something to contribute to an understanding of libraries worldwide? Could America learn something from our experience?

BEGINNINGS

Learning from the American experience is something South African librarians have been doing for many decades. However, the earliest origins of our libraries can be traced to Europe, to the Netherlands, Germany, and Britain, countries that also contributed to American concepts of learning and scholarship. In the early eighteenth century private libraries were established at the Cape of Good Hope. The most notable collector was Joachim Nicholas von Dessin, who amassed a collection of over 3,800 volumes from the time of his arrival at the Cape in 1727 until his death in 1761. Von Dessin's collection was bequeathed to the consistory of the Groote Kerk, the Dutch Reformed Church of Cape Town, for the general public's use. He also left the church some money, the interest on which was used to extend the collection.[4]

The Cape of Good Hope passed into British hands in 1795 and was ceded to Britain in 1814. In 1818 the autocratic British governor, Lord Charles Somerset—who is remembered for his attempts to muzzle the fledgling press at the Cape[5]—established the South African Public Library in Cape Town. It was to be a free public library, financed by a tax on wine. Somerset's Proclamation of 1818 stated that it would be a public library that "...shall be open to the public, and lay the foundation of a system, which shall place the means of knowledge within the reach of the Youth of this remote corner of the Globe and bring within their reach what the most eloquent of ancient writers has considered to be one of the finest blessings of life, 'Home Education.'"[6]

The patrician Lord Charles clearly knew what was good for the settlers. In 1820 the Dessinian collection was deposited in the South African Public Library, which was officially opened in 1822. However, it did not remain a free public library for long. The wine tax was withdrawn in 1828, and the following year it became a subscription library.[7]

THE SOUTH AFRICAN LIBRARY CONFERENCE OF 1928

On August 20, 1928, a century after the South African Public Library lost its tax income, the state librarian of California, Milton J. Ferguson, and the chief librarian of the Glasgow Public Library, Mr. S. A. Pitt, arrived in Table Bay on a mission funded by the Carnegie Corporation of New York to study the state of libraries in what was then the Union of South Africa, Rhodesia, and Kenya Colony. The two men traveled throughout South Africa, visiting many of its libraries.[8] In their reports they noted that South African libraries were sadly lacking in most respects.[9] One of the main problems found to inhibit the development of libraries was the issue of race. Ferguson's comments on this topic are illuminating:

> The reluctance of the average South African to consider a wholly state-supported library system is to be explained more by the racial complications of the country than by any other consideration.... The South African is willing...for the native to cook his food, care for his children, keep his household in order, serve him in a personal way, carry his books to and from the library, but he would feel that an end of his régime were at hand if this same servant were permitted to open these books and to read therein. . . . Nevertheless, so far as the native is able to use books, they ought to be made available to him; though no sane person would advocate the circulation of the same books to all. . . . There can be little question that he has the sympathy of an active body of citizens who are working at all times

for his better and more reasonable development along lines best suited to his racial limitations.[10]

There is much unconscious irony in this text, which oscillates between liberal and crudely racist views. In hindsight, the qualifications implied in "[the native's] better and more reasonable development along lines best suited to his racial limitations" could hardly have expressed more eloquently the premises of what would later become known as "Bantu education."

The last town Ferguson and Pitt visited in South Africa was Bloemfontein, where a South African library conference was held from November 15 to 17, 1928.[11] This was a seminal event in South African library history. Ferguson and Pitt had formulated many proposals for the development of libraries in South Africa. These proposals were debated, and recommendations were adopted on various aspects of librarianship. Reporting on the conference, Ferguson noted that "the most heated debate arose...over the question involving service to the natives."[12] Nevertheless, some progressive, if racist, recommendations were made under the headings "General Library Services for Non-Europeans" and "School Library Services for Non-European Children."[13] An example is the recommendation in the latter section, which suggested that "these services be organized by the [proposed] central library system as in the case of European children, but the books be kept separate from those supplied to European children."[14] This probably reflects fears of the same nature as those that motivated the strict segregation of public toilets in South Africa and ironically echoes Ferguson's comment, cited earlier, that "no sane person would advocate the circulation of the same books to all."

PROGRESS AND RETREAT

During the subsequent decades, library development, which was initially slow, gradually accelerated. But development did not proceed at the same pace in all domains.

After the Bloemfontein conference the Carnegie Corporation continued to play an important role in library development in South Africa. In September 1929 the Corporation offered to establish an endowment fund for library development in South Africa, provided the Union Government and the City Council of Pretoria met certain conditions. Interest earned on the endowment would enable the State Library to serve as both a free public library for Pretoria and as the central library of South Africa, responsible for providing a national lending service, organizing library services throughout the country, providing in-service training for librarians, and promoting cooperation between all types of libraries.[15] After lengthy negotiations with the government and the City Council, the Carnegie Corporation deposited $125,000 in Barclays Bank in Pretoria to establish the endowment fund.[16]

The support forthcoming from the government was halfhearted. The State Library was brought under the State-aided Institutions Act, No. 23 of 1931, but the functions prescribed for it in terms of this Act failed to recognize it explicitly as a national central library that would extend public and school library services to all parts of the Union, as advocated in Bloemfontein.[17] This set a pattern of indecisiveness with respect to the national library infrastructure that has continued to this day.[18] The Great Depression and a catastrophic drought saw to it that little progress occurred for nearly a decade. In 1936 the Union Government appointed an Interdepartmental Committee on the Libraries of the Union of South Africa.[19] It looked like this committee would break the logjam, but before much could be done, World War II intervened. Nevertheless, an interlibrary lending system had been established in 1933 by the State Library. It grew steadily, and in 1941 the compilation of a union catalog of monographs commenced.[20]

The dominant theme during the 1930s and 1940s was the campaign for the institution of free public library services, particularly in rural areas. Into this campaign were channeled the idealism and drive of some of South Africa's leading librarians and many enthusiastic laypersons. A leader in this campaign and a pioneer in rural library extension services was a Scot, Matthew Miller Stirling, who was honored in 1936 by the Carnegie Corporation.[21] Although the free public library was an ideal shared with people of all persuasions, the campaign for it was probably not unrelated to the struggle of the Afrikaner for emancipation from political and economic dominance of the English-speaking establishment.[22] The outcome had legislation establishing free provincial public library services in all four provinces during the late 1940s and early

1950s.[23] These led to the replacement of the rural subscription libraries by free public libraries funded on the basis of a partnership between municipal and provincial governments, while the larger cities in most cases received provincial subsidies to help fund their own free public library services.

However, most of the free public libraries were for whites only. The story of library provision for black South Africans, long overshadowed by the success story outlined above, is a parallel but more protracted struggle against far greater odds.

Along with their South African colleagues, Ferguson and Pitt had taken it for granted that library facilities for blacks would be separate from those for whites. The Carnegie Corporation's funding for "Non-European" library services reflects a pragmatic acceptance of the racial attitudes then prevailing in South Africa. In addition to the endowment fund, the Carnegie Corporation had also made smaller grants for the development of library services for "non-Europeans." In each province private nonprofit committees ("Carnegie Committees") were formed to administer these grants. The Transvaal Carnegie Committee, which ran the Transvaal Carnegie Non-European Library, was the most successful. It supplied book boxes that by 1949, when it was renamed the Non-European Library Service, Transvaal, served about eighty centers. In 1941 it had instituted a Student Section assisting individuals who needed books for study purposes. In 1962 this service was taken over by the State Library, which then established its "Non-White Study Division."[24] It served black students throughout the country, providing them with books in support of private study and distance education. The service was extended to those who were physically unable to visit libraries, such as prisoners on Robben Island. One of these was Nelson Mandela.[25]

Patterns of segregation were already well established in South African society, in legislation as well as in custom, long before the National Party came to power in 1948 and proceeded to rigorously systematize segregation by means of legislation, such as the Group Areas Act, No. 41 of 1950, the Bantu Education Act, No. 47 of 1953, and the Reservation of Separate Amenities Act, No. 49 of 1953.[26] Together with other similar legislation, these laws had the effect of locking blacks into separate and inferior residential areas with inadequate commercial and cultural facilities and limiting their educational, vocational, and professional opportunities to those fields that were not perceived as threatening the position of whites.

The extent to which this directly affected the provision of library services to black people has been chronicled in detail by Kalley.[27] As free public libraries were established in the various provinces and cities, library facilities also came to be provided (separately) for blacks. But the provision remained glaringly unequal. A recent comparison of libraries in the black townships and municipalities with those of white municipalities shows that in terms of bookstock, membership, circulation, staff, buildings, and facilities, libraries serving blacks generally came in a distant second. Differences between the libraries serving the two groups accurately reflect the obvious discrepancies between the municipalities in respect to economic activity, income levels, living conditions, cultural facilities, and the political credibility of their institutions.[28] Separate educational institutions, separate municipalities, and separate homelands all served, among other things, to perpetuate inferior libraries.

In the meantime, the visit by Ferguson and Pitt bore fruit at the level of library procedures and techniques. Modern library ideas circulated. A number of promising young graduates were sent to the United States for postgraduate studies in library science. They came back to introduce American library practices and technologies: Dewey's Decimal Classification, the Library of Congress Classification, the three by five inch unit catalog card, the dictionary catalog, Sears and Library of Congress Subject Headings, Anglo-American cataloging rules, Library of Congress catalog cards, H. W. Wilson indexes and Bowker bibliographies, American library journals, and book selection tools. Open access university libraries became the norm. Reserve (or "short loan") collections were instituted. Some of the library school graduates became university librarians and started library schools at their universities, breaking with the British tradition of in-service apprenticeship. Modular library buildings were erected; Keyes Metcalf's book[29] became the undisputed bible for those planning academic library buildings. Microfilming, scientific library management, performance measurement, library research, information science, library automation, bibliographic instruction, on-line data bases, networks, library marketing—these and many more ideas, innovations, trends, and fads crossed the Atlantic and the equator to mold the practice of librarianship in South Africa. This is not to deny the British influence. While in this essay the American contribution is emphasized, South African librarianship can best be described as being Anglo-American in inspiration.[30]

Whereas notable progress also occurred in the development of school, university, and special libraries and the establishment of a national library and information network, increasing technical competence and resources were not always matched by intellectual and philosophical growth in the library community. Such a mismatch is illustrated by two significant events that took place in 1962. Both relate directly to the South African Library Association (SALA), which had been founded in 1930 as a result of one of the recommendations of the 1928 Bloemfontein conference.[31]

The first event was a major national conference intended to lay the basis for the further development of libraries in South Africa in much the same way that the Bloemfontein conference of 1928 had done. This national conference was the culmination of work done by a SALA Action Committee on Library Cooperation, which had conducted a survey and drafted a "Program for Future Library Development." The program was presented to a National Conference of Library Authorities, held under the auspices of the Minister of Education, Arts, and Sciences, in Pretoria on November 5 and 6, 1962.[32] The "Program," as amended and approved by the National Conference, was published in 1963. It dealt with the entire range of libraries in South Africa but put particular stress on national and regional structures for library cooperation. Included among the recommendations were the establishment of a National Library Council, a South African National Bibliographic Council and standing committees for bibliographic work, the national bookstock, and library research.[33]

The day after the approval of this forward-looking document, SALA held its seventeenth annual conference in Pretoria (November 7, 1962) where it took a regressive step that has haunted the library profession in South Africa ever since. The conference approved a motion that limited SALA's membership to whites and agreed to the establishment of separate library associations for "Bantu," "Coloreds," and "Indians."[34] The two events are not unrelated. Presumably those behind the motion were anxious to gain state support for the impressive but costly plans that had just been formulated. In addition, SALA was in the process of rewriting its constitution in the hope of gaining statutory recognition from the state.[35] No doubt the reasoning went that by falling into line with National Party policy, the prospects for SALA's otherwise well-intended plans would be improved.[36] Be that as it may, SALA's submissiveness fatally undermined the professionalism and moral authority of its member librarians and the library profession in South Africa in general.

The question arises, then, what went wrong? Why this dissonance between progressive library thinking and regressive social and political moves?

COLLABORATION, PALLIATION, AND PROFESSIONALISM

After SALA was closed to blacks, prominent members of SALA formed a "Consultative Committee for the Establishment of Library Associations for the Non-White Racial Groups," and separate library associations were created for the three racial groups as envisaged by the SALA annual conference of 1962: the Central Bantu Library Association, the Cape Library Association (for "Coloreds"), and the South African Indian Library Association. Of the three associations only the Central Bantu Library Association survived. Later renamed the Bantu Library Association of South Africa, it became the African Library Association of South Africa (ALASA) in 1972.[37] It remains an active association that plays a valuable role in South African librarianship, with a particular focus on problems of black librarians and the provision of library services to black people.[38] Although indirectly a creature of apartheid, ALASA inspires loyalty and pride in its own achievements.[39]

What is one to say of the motives of the SALA members who devoted a great deal of time to getting the new associations off the ground and assisting them? It is likely that many of these helpers were adherents of the National Party and supporters of its apartheid policy. They could have wholeheartedly underwritten the notion of "*reasonable* development along lines *best suited to* [the native's] *racial limitations*" as it was formulated by Ferguson in the passage cited earlier. Others, of white liberal persuasion, would have emphasized "sympathy" and "*better...development.*" For example, the work of the Committee of the (Carnegie) Non-European Library as described by Marguerite Peters[40]—not to forget the work of Peters herself—was a tireless labor of love. For some, it was also a form of resistance to library apartheid.

But such resistance as that existed was generally discreet and dignified. In part the quietness of dissent was due to a tradition of not raising one's voice. It was also due to an increasing clampdown on all nonorthodox thinking. As the pressure from within and without grew, the National Party stoked up a national siege mentality, invoking the "total onslaught" by the communists against South Africa in order to herd the South African public into a defensive laager. Christopher Merrett has evoked this period as follows: "Indeed dissidents who opposed the prevailing certainties, especially those who stepped over an invisible line of repressive tolerance, were actively persecuted leaving an embattled intelligentsia in the universities, Press, churches and professions; and a diaspora of anti-apartheid South Africans in exile."[41]

Of course, not all librarians were silent. Some liberals spoke out against apartheid and were "visited" by the Security Police, a frightening experience that would also count against them in obtaining employment in government and statutory organizations requiring security clearance. Threats were made. Some simply saw no future in South Africa and emigrated to Australia or returned to Europe. Some more radical activists went into exile less voluntarily; a few library workers were imprisoned.[42] Resource centers run by progressive organizations were subjected to harassment and, in at least one case, arson.[43] These cases barely merited a mention in the *Newsletter* of the professional body. It was an uncomfortable time to stand up for unpopular principles. Generally we in the mainstream of the library profession did not distinguish ourselves by heroic resistance.[44]

The general climate of intimidation explains, to some extent, the organized profession's failure to protest against increasingly restrictive censorship legislation and practices[45] and to speak out on the issue of library segregation.[46] In this context it is interesting to note that the American Library Association's "Library Bill of Rights"[47] and texts on intellectual freedom would have been required reading for students in most South African library schools. Why did this have so little impact on subsequent professional behavior? Most South African librarians in leadership positions would have had current issues of *Library Journal, Wilson Bulletin for Libraries,* or *American Libraries* circulated to them regularly, the academic boycott[48] notwithstanding. What impact did reporting of the activism of American librarians in the fields of civil rights, gay rights, women's liberation, and intellectual freedom have on these readers? From their vantage point at the embattled southern tip of Africa, most South African librarians gazed at the images of professionals waving placards proclaiming support for gays or the Equal Rights Amendment with mingled amazement and horror. Such activism was "unprofessional." This point of view was no doubt shared by many of their American colleagues. Nevertheless, it is a curious phenomenon that so many technical advances and management fads were rapidly adopted in South Africa through the influence of American library literature, while equally prominent social and ethical issues seem to have been filtered out.

By and large librarians appear to have sought refuge in a sanitized profession that emphasized library functions, technology, and organization structures. It was held that libraries should be politically neutral and that librarians should not become involved in politics. In the context of South African community librarianship, the case for political neutrality has been argued by R. B. Zaaiman as recently as 1988: ". . .libraries should preserve absolute political neutrality in order to maintain their credibility and acceptability to developing communities. They should be seen as neutral ground on which all parties can meet. Libraries that offer propaganda, no matter on whose behalf, will soon lose their legitimacy."[49] The political neutrality of a library is the responsibility of the librarian, who should carefully vet all material that may be considered propagandistic.

In the NEPI report on *Library & Information Services,*[50] the mainstream South African approach to librarianship is critically described as follows:

> The dominant mode of library and information work is characterized by a traditional approach to information "science" which ar-

gues that libraries are neutral agencies. This has led to a failure to recognise that the struggles in the workplace, schools, universities, and countryside of South Africa involve a contest over ideas and aspirations; and therefore that libraries are also sites of struggle.

This approach, which glosses over the connection between power and information, has resulted in a failure to engage with pressing socio-political and economic issues.[51]

The study reports that this "traditional approach" is of Anglo-American inspiration and is characterized by elitism, technicism, and an emphasis on professionalism and neutrality.[52]

These criticisms are borne out by trends within the organized library profession in the 1970s and 1980s. In 1980 SALA disbanded to make way for a non-racial professional organization, the South African Institute of Librarianship and Information Science (SAILIS).[53] The emphasis was on "professionalization."[54] Hence racial barriers were replaced by educational barriers. SAILIS membership was open to all who were professionally qualified, which automatically excluded many, if not most, black library and information workers. Was this deliberate, as critics would suggest,[55] or an unintended consequence of professionalization? In hindsight it is easy to condemn what to many was an ideal for which much time and energy were sacrificed.

Also during the 1980s many South African library schools dropped "Librarianship" or "Library Science" from their names, leaving only "Information Science" or "Information Studies." Curricula were revised to put more emphasis on information science and information management. A national library network, SABINET, was established, and issues of networking, technology, costs, and cost recovery became dominant themes in professional discourse.[56] But the profession's growing technical sophistication was not matched by intellectual and moral strength. Instead, librarians retreated into the safety of the politically neutral library where they busied themselves with library functions and technology.

REFORM: THE LIMITS OF THE OLD PARADIGM

Apartheid did not suddenly come to an end on February 2, 1990, when State President F. W. de Klerk announced the release of Nelson Mandela from imprisonment and the unbanning of the

ANC, the South African Communist Party, and other organizations that the National Party had regarded as its mortal enemies during the "total onslaught." On the one hand, apartheid has not yet ended completely. On the other hand, it had already started crumbling before that day as a result of economic and political factors that the Nationalists could not control.

The South African library profession was not left untouched by the changes that were in the air. From the mid-1980s two lines of thinking could be distinguished in the South African library community. In the mainstream of the profession there was a slow awakening to the inevitability of social and political change and a realization that libraries would have to adapt to it. This is reflected, for example, in an increased number of papers on this theme delivered at SAILIS conferences and published in the *South African Journal of Library and Information Science.*[57] To the left of the mainstream more radical thinking emerged, calling into question basic assumptions of South African library practice and demanding a radical reconceptualization of library services for South Africa.

By 1990 library apartheid was on the wane. Many major public libraries were open to all; some had been desegregated since 1974, when several local authorities in the Cape, Natal, and Transvaal had dispensed with library apartheid.[58] University apartheid was in retreat and university libraries were open to all. Government schools were still strictly segregated, but multiracial private schools were tolerated.

A major event in mainstream South African librarianship during the years leading up to de Klerk's announcement was the publication of a report entitled *The Use of Libraries for the Development of South Africa* by Professor R. B. Zaaiman and two colleagues.[59] Generally known as the Zaaiman report, it had been commissioned by SAILIS in 1986 and its final version was published in 1988, sixty years after the Bloemfontein conference.

The Zaaiman report was specifically concerned with the role of libraries in development, which was considered to have social, economic, and political dimensions.[60] It consists of twenty-four chapters, of which eighteen are devoted to public libraries. A great deal of attention is paid to the needs of and services to "blacks." This focus was something of a novelty in mainstream South African librarianship, and the report was regarded as an important document proposing "what seemed to many to be radical new service orientations."[61] It was widely disseminated and discussed in SAILIS branch meetings and workshops and is thought to have provided a significant stimulus for change in many libraries and library organizations.[62]

This said, Zaaiman and his colleagues seem to have unquestioningly accepted the status quo as a platform from which development can take place. This is most clearly illustrated by their use of Maslow's "hierarchy of needs." In chapter 3, which deals with "public libraries and social development," the report states:

> The applicability of information can be gauged according to Maslow's hierarchy of needs.
>
> A community whose needs are mainly at the lower levels of Maslow's hierarchy assigns a high priority to information that will enable its members to have food, shelter, safety, employment and good health. They will on the whole be less concerned with the insight into human nature afforded by Dante or Shakespeare, because the need for that kind of information is usually felt only after other, more basic needs have been satisfied.
>
> Public libraries should therefore determine (through research, not reflection) at what levels of Maslow's model the needs of their community lie. Once this is known, they should provide appropriate information for each level. If this is not done, the library will be out of touch with reality and cannot fulfill its purpose.[63]

At this point, the diagram shown in *Figure 1,* with the familiar pyramid shape, appears in the text.[64]

A deconstructive analysis of the diagram reveals elements that subvert and contradict its surface message.[65] For example, it embodies an opposition between vertical (upward) and horizontal forces. There is a predominance of horizontal lines, which suggest barriers to upward mobility. The horizontal lines divide the pyramid into a set of cells or containers into which people can be classified. The language of the diagram encourages us to think of top and bottom, upper and lower classes. Ultimately this suggests that to maintain a high intellectual level (at the stratospheric altitude where Dante and Shakespeare are read) we need a repressive system to keep the lower classes in their places, ensuring that the structure remains upright.

Figure 1. Maslow's Hierarchy of Needs as Reproduced in the Zaaiman Report.

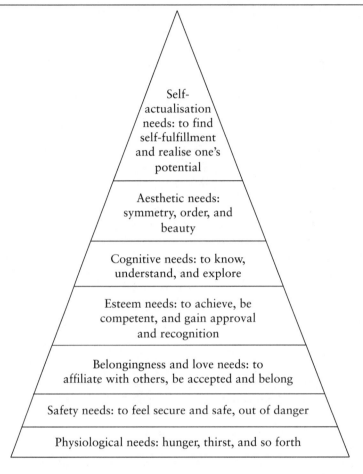

According to such an interpretation, the contradictions in this text reflect the tensions of establishment librarianship: aware of the need for change, but still caught up in the concepts and language of apartheid.

In 1988 more librarians were becoming aware of the inequality and injustice in the way South Africa's library and information resources were distributed. The initial response, conditioned by years of apartheid, was to provide more of the same facilities for "them." If "they" have their "own" facilities, "our" privileged professional environment remains unthreatened. Such a response perpetuates apartheid. It is also not affordable.

Another dimension of this mind-set is an emphasis on "upliftment," that is, bringing "them" up to "our" level. It assumes that the library and information facilities developed mainly for the use of white South Africans under the influence of the dominant American and British model of librarianship are appropriate to the needs of the whole population. Apart from being hurtfully arrogant, this response would impoverish South African librarianship by excluding the contributions of other models and specifically the insights of African librarianship. It is noteworthy that Zaaiman explicitly warns his audience about the dangers of a "paternalistic approach to users and their presumed needs," a model in which "gracious librarians" imbued with "notions of upliftment" impose services on "the grateful needy." Instead, a cooperative model of development is put forward.[66]

Africanization is dealt with explicitly in a brief section near the end of the Zaaiman report.[67] It is noted that library services to the "developing black communities" were based mainly on models derived from developed countries and that black librarians and library users were becoming disenchanted with such models. It continues:

> To provide acceptable services, the approach by libraries must be Africanised by being adapted to needs and conditions in this part of Africa. This might well result in library thinking and services that are diametrically opposed to present westernised principles and practice. . . .
>
> Librarians may find this transition to a new paradigm extraordinarily difficult. . . .[68]

An apt observation. The Zaaiman report mainly addressed an audience whose practice was firmly rooted in the assumptions of the old paradigm. A critical reading of the report uncovers many elements of the old "equal but separate" thinking that characterizes this paradigm. However, we must give the report credit for having stretched the boundaries of the old paradigm to the limit, in the process creating both an awareness of the need for change and a certain dissatisfaction that is very necessary for the paradigm shift that is now upon us.

Enthusiasm for the Zaaiman report was not universal. Whereas the Right was largely silent, perhaps hoping that the fuss would die down, Zaaiman came under fire from the Left. For example, Chantelle Wyley criticized the Zaaiman report for its uncritical and bourgeois use of the concept of "development" and for its silence on apartheid: "The social structures of apartheid are accepted, not to be challenged, and the political status quo is accepted as given, with no suggestion of change. The development of the subordinate social group is seen uncritically, according to the vision of the dominant group."[69]

This view illustrates the rift that had developed between the library establishment and what one might call left-wing librarians. The latter contributed not only a critique of establishment librarianship that was more fundamental and incisive than any that came from the reformers, but also an alternative vision of librarianship in South Africa—a vision that seems to have crystallized around the resource center model.

The emergence of resource centers has been linked to the rise of the Mass Democratic Movement (MDM). During the 1970s a variety of service organizations developed. In the 1980s this was followed by

> the mushrooming of services specifically devoted to information, education and resource provision. . . . The orientation of these resource centres derives from a situation of mass repression, a manifestation of which is the censorship of information, organisations and persons. Their main task has been to strengthen mass-based organisation through the provision of services otherwise withheld from, unavailable to, or inaccessible to, the oppressed.[70]

Stilwell has related the resource center movement to a variety of foreign and domestic antecedents and influences. American influences include the War on Poverty in the 1960s and the emergence of Information and Referral Services in the 1970s.[71] In South

Africa, she cites People's Education,[72] the emergence of groups stressing community democracy, the development of anti-apartheid networks and extra-parliamentary groups in the late 1970s and early 1980s, the Black Consciousness movement, and the example of consumer cooperatives as formative factors in the development of resource centers.[73]

Rapid growth in resource centers took place during the legitimacy crisis experienced by public libraries in black townships during the final years of the struggle. The public libraries (or "formal sector") were rejected by many as products of the apartheid state. They were perceived as having been established in a top-down manner without adequate consultation with the relevant communities, funded and maintained by government authorities tainted by apartheid, such as the discredited local authorities in the black townships, who were a prime target for those engaged in the struggle. Township libraries were criticized on account of underprovision, bias, and inappropriate resources, accommodation, and facilities.

The resource centers, on the other hand, were the result of voluntary action by the community and were controlled, owned, and sustained by the community. A community resource center differs from a public library not only in ideology and ethos but also in providing a far greater range of facilities and programs. These can include a library, activities hall, computer room, advice center, referral center, and study center. Programs, services, and training include career guidance, youth leadership, teacher reference resources, aptitude testing, job placement, computer literacy, life skills training, street law, and literacy.[74]

Further characteristics of South African resource centers are the relevance of their stock and organization in accordance with user needs, the accountable and democratic relationship between the resource centers and their users, democratic internal decision-making, their awareness of their role in society, their commitment to a new non-discriminatory, democratic, and united South Africa, and their involvement in the production of information as well as in its acquisition, storage, and dissemination.[75] They serve communities that are presently unserved and provide an in-depth and community-tailored service that will probably extend beyond the means of the public library networks. Resource centers have a

valuable role to play in serving as an alternative model of information service that can help to inspire the transformation of the
existing public library services.

The early 1990s saw the formation of resource center forums in
major urban centers as a means of providing mutual support and
sharing skills and experience.[76] During this period, too, what had
been relatively isolated and muted criticism of the library establishment blossomed into an articulate alternative library movement. In July 1990 LIWO was formed in Natal "to provide an
ideological and organisational home for progressive library and
information workers."[77] Unlike the other library associations, LIWO
has a clear position in the political spectrum and has aligned itself
with the "broad democratic movement." It played a key role in
ensuring that library and information issues were addressed in the
National Education Policy Investigation (NEPI), a project of the
NECC, and played a leading role in NEPI's Library and Information Services (LIS) Research Group.[78] LIWO has described itself as
presenting "a major challenge to the library establishment in South
Africa." Since many resist fundamental restructuring, this is as
important in post-1990 South Africa as before: "LIWO's task is
to challenge neo-apartheid and the new orthodoxy; provide a
home for those library and information workers wanting to compensate for the cowardice of their profession in the past; and play
a role in the debate about the future of South Africa, alongside
like-minded democrats seeking a just and humane social order."[79]

Criticism of establishment librarianship is a common theme. By
having in the past abetted the marginalization of people and cultures by the apartheid system, libraries have marginalized themselves.[80] The formal library sector generally is criticized for failing
to define their users and understand their needs; for subscribing to
elitist, racist, paternalistic, or patronizing philosophies; for being
culturally biased and biased in favor of literate users; for aspiring
to "neutrality" and ignoring the social, political, economic, and
cultural dimensions of information or failing to analyze these in
depth; for ignoring South African history and context, including
the reasons for phenomena such as illiteracy; and for being
"technicist" and over-emphasizing "professionalism," "standards,"
and "scientific" approaches,[81] the products of which are characterized by superficiality.[82] This is partly ascribed to a model of

librarianship (especially public librarianship) that is derived from Britain and to an uncritical adherence to First World traditions and international standards and systems for the organization of materials.[83]

What vision of the future do the radicals offer? Three alternative approaches are identified in the NEPI report: *1)* the structuralist or radical approach; *2)* African librarianship; and *3)* the "cultural life approach." The structuralist approach is derived from an Anglo-American reaction to the traditional paradigm. It is linked to the development of resource centers and associated with the concept of community librarianship. It is service-oriented, non-elitist, political, developmental, and critical. African librarianship is a reformulation of the radical approach to address the problems of limited resources, poverty, and illiteracy. The cultural life approach derives from Scandinavia and Eastern Europe. It particularly addresses the needs of workers, emphasizing relevance, empowerment, enrichment, and participation. These three approaches can be harmonized to create a paradigm more appropriate to South Africa's needs and conditions.[84]

Early policy-making exercises in which the radicals played leading roles emphasized the need to reconstruct South Africa's libraries on the basis of the "NEPI principles" of democracy, unity (a unitary LIS system), non-discrimination (non-racism and non-sexism), and redress of historic inequalities.[85] The vision was expressed as follows in a preelection ANC policy document on education and training:

> A government which serves and values the freedom and democracy of its people will treasure the empowering, liberating and educative role of ideas and information, and will commit itself to provide for the cultural, educational, economic and technological development through a national LIS [library and information services] system. On the basis of individual freedoms and rights. . .we envisage a society whose government provides every citizen [with] free access to information sources and resource-based learning facilities. Each LIS will be democratically developed and managed in co-operation and consultation with its users so that the collections and services are appropriate and relevant to the needs and diversity of the users.
>
> LIS workers will assume a pro-active, dynamic educational role in society through forums, networks, and the pursuit of joint ventures with educators, cultural workers and other sectors.[86]

The main thrusts of the policy proposals in the NEPI report were to emphasize free access to information, to link libraries and information conceptually to the education sector and administratively to the national ministry of education, and to institute central policy development, planning, coordination, and control through a hierarchy of democratically constituted boards and committees at national, provincial, and local levels.[87] Underlying the emphasis on central control was a desire to eliminate disparities in the availability and quality of library and information services in various parts of the country. It was feared, not without reason, that provincial, local, or institutional autonomy would shelter pockets of privilege, thus frustrating the ideal of free and equal access to information.

In subsequent policy-development processes[88] these ideas were refined or watered down, depending on one's perspective. Underlying the debates on the various policy documents that emerged from these processes is a struggle between the radicals who would break with the past and fundamentally transform or reconstruct the LIS system, and the conservatives who emphasize the value of the existing resources, institutions, and infrastructure and who would limit change to extending the system to reach the unserved.

A gulf still separates the two camps. If pragmatism gains ground in the policies of the new government, as appears to be the trend at the time of writing, radical librarians risk being left behind with little more than their ideological purity. On the other hand, the conservative camp, still trapped in its old paradigm, lacks the insight and imagination to create a system of library and information services appropriate to the diverse needs of a newly democratic nation. It would be a tragic outcome for South African librarianship if the opportunities for renewal that now fleetingly present themselves are lost because of mutual incomprehension.

CURRENT CHALLENGES

This account of the story of libraries in South Africa ends at a pivotal point where differences between library workers remain unresolved and a host of challenges await responses.

To a large extent the challenges are political and social. In the short term, administrative reorganization, such as the creation of additional provinces, has led to some disruption of library ser-vices.[89] However, a more general and fundamental reordering of national priorities, as exemplified in the Reconstruction and De-velopment Program (RDP),[90] is likely to have a more significant and lasting impact on libraries. Libraries are barely mentioned in the RDP document.[91] From the lack of references to libraries in other policy documents issued by various ministries, we can only infer that libraries are at best a low priority. Libraries are not seen by decisionmakers as contributing to national development; librar-ians agonize over the relevance of their institutions to the newly democratic nation.

At the same time, there is a real danger that libraries will be reinvented or circumvented. In policy initiatives launched in vari-ous sectors, assorted proposals are made for mechanisms such as information centers (some using glamorous information technol-ogy) to disseminate information to grass-roots communities. No-where in these proposals do we find a mention of a possible role for public or community libraries. The challenge, therefore, is not merely to extend library and information services to the unserved but also to reconceptualize libraries. The roles of libraries in a changing South African society—in serving historically disadvan-taged groups, celebrating our cultural diversity while promoting a shared South Africanism, serving communities in which oral cul-ture predominates and in which many languages are spoken, sus-taining a vigorous democracy, promoting literacy, enhancing the quality of education, and increasing the labor mobility and life-style options available to community members—urgently need to be clarified. This task is made much more complex by the apart-heid stigma that clings to many libraries and librarians and the related disunity of the library profession.

The challenges are also technological. South Africa's libraries exhibit a range of technological capacities. Such innovations as PCs, LANs, library automation, and access to on-line networks are taken for granted by library users and staff in libraries serving privileged communities. Libraries serving many other communities have to make do without electricity or telephones. This situation holds the danger that an information gap can arise between the sophisticated and unsophisticated libraries and between the his-torically privileged and disadvantaged groups they serve. Investment in information technology is impeded by the declining value of South Africa's currency. Hence a gap may develop between more and less affluent institutions of higher education and research. The Internet appears to offer low-cost solutions to overcome barriers to access, but as the connected elite increasingly rely on it for communication, the unconnected are all the more handicapped. Paradoxically, electronic technology has the potential both to eliminate barriers and to exacerbate the gap between the information-rich and the information-poor, within and between nations.[92]

In responding to these challenges, South African librarians and information workers need to empower themselves through networking. They must develop a greater political awareness and be prepared to participate in the political process by responding rapidly and effectively to relevant policy initiatives. They need cultural sensitivity and a willingness to question the paradigms that have constrained their thinking. Most of all, they need to communicate with one another across the boundaries that have divided them, build unity among themselves, and forge coalitions with library users and other stakeholders.

CONCLUSION

To a South African librarian the wealth of library resources in the United States is dazzling: the diversity of libraries, the rich collections, highly educated staff, powerful technology, and a multiplicity of cooperative systems and networks. South African library resources and facilities pale in comparison. The differences are arresting; the distance between the two countries seems vast.

At the conceptual level, however, the differences are not so pronounced. If one looks beyond the resources and facilities, one finds that librarians in both countries face similar issues. The most obvious is the challenge of modern information technology, which has a pervasive influence on intellectual activity and the production and dissemination of information. Although less obtrusive than information technology, economic constraints, political pressures, and cultural diversity are also modifying the environment of libraries. These challenges are as pronounced in South Africa as elsewhere.

As the opening of South Africa's markets to international players exposes the domestic market to more foreign competition, thereby threatening certain comfortable accommodations that came about during South Africa's isolation, the lifting of cultural and academic sanctions brings us back into the global marketplace of ideas. One of the benefits of this is that the connection between American and South African librarianship can be reestablished and strengthened. In the process, South African librarians will be able to learn a great deal from American librarians. Conversely, albeit on a modest scale, American librarians may be able to learn something from the way American ideas have taken root (or failed to) and evolved or stagnated in South Africa. In that sense, South Africa may hold up a distant mirror to American librarianship.

ENDNOTES

[1]See, for example, Kenneth E. Dowlin, "Distribution in an Electronic Environment, or Will There be Libraries as We Know Them in the Internet World?," *Library Trends* 43 (3) (1995): 409–417.

[2]See, for example, Neil MacLean, "Provision of Scholarly Information: The Economics of Supply and Demand," *Australian Library Journal* 42 (2) (1993): 94–97; John V. Nichols, "Using Future Trends to Inform Planning/Marketing," *Library Trends* 43 (3) (1995): 349–366; and H. K. Raseroka, "Changes in Public Libraries During the Last Twenty Years: An African Perspective," *Libri* 44 (2) (1994): 153–163.

[3]See, for example, J. E. Cox, "Can Dinosaurs Survive? The Future of Publishers, Vendors and Librarians," *Learned Publishing* 7 (2) (1994): 117–119.

[4]R. F. M. Immelman, "The History of Libraries in South Africa," in *Give the People Light: Essays in Honour of Matthew Miller Stirling* (Pretoria: State Library, 1975), 16–17.

[5]Anna H. Smith, *The Spread of Printing: Eastern Hemisphere: South Africa* (Amsterdam: Vangendt, 1971), 34–42.

[6]Proclamation cited by R. B. Zaaiman, "Die Stigting van die Suid-Afrikaanse Openbare Biblioteek en die Tydsgees van 1818, 1937 en 1990," *Mousaion Series 3* 9 (1) (1991): 11.

[7]A. M. Lewin Robinson, "National Libraries—Their History and Development with Special Reference to South Africa," in South African Library Association, *Papers Presented at the Conference, Johannesburg, 1978* (Potchefstroom: The Association, 1978), 419.

[8]P. C. Coetzee, *Die Carnegie-Biblioteeksending van 1928* (Pretoria: Staatsbiblioteek, 1975), 2–5.

⁹Milton J. Ferguson, *Memorandum: Libraries in the Union of South Africa, Rhodesia and Kenya Colony* (New York: Carnegie Corporation of New York, 1929); S. A. Pitt, *Memorandum: Libraries in the Union of South Africa, Rhodesia and Kenya Colony* (New York: Carnegie Corporation of New York, 1929). Both memoranda have been reprinted in Coetzee, *Die Carnegie-Biblioteeksending van 1928,* 69–102.

¹⁰Ferguson, *Memorandum: Libraries in the Union of South Africa, Rhodesia and Kenya Colony,* 10–11. It is not possible to discuss the history of South African libraries (or any other social institutions) without making use of racial categories. Their use here does not imply agreement with the classification of people in this manner.

¹¹Coetzee, *Die Carnegie-Biblioteeksending van 1928,* 9–14.

¹²Ferguson, *Memorandum: Libraries in the Union of South Africa, Rhodesia and Kenya Colony,* 15.

¹³Ibid., 18–19.

¹⁴Ibid., 18.

¹⁵Coetzee, *Die Carnegie-Biblioteeksending van 1928,* 18–19; Robinson, "National Libraries—Their History and Development with Special Reference to South Africa," 424–425.

¹⁶Coetzee, *Die Carnegie-Biblioteeksending van 1928,* 18–20.

¹⁷Ibid., 20–21.

¹⁸Elsewhere I have analyzed the tensions between centralization, coordination, and local autonomy in the inconclusive debates over a national infrastructure for library cooperation and resource sharing. See P. J. Lor, "Competing Models in the Development of the South African Interlending System, Part 1: Origins to 1961," *Mousaion Series 3* 6 (2) (1988): 77–95; and P. J. Lor, "Competing Models in the Development of the South African Interlending System, Part 2: 1962–1983," *Mousaion Series 3* 7 (1) (1989): 49–74.

¹⁹Interdepartmental Committee on the Libraries of the Union of South Africa, *Report of the Interdepartmental Committee on the Libraries of the Union of South Africa* (Cape Town: Cape Times, 1937). Its work has been evaluated by Clare M. Walker, "From Carnegie to NEPI: Ideals and Realities," *Mousaion Series 3* 11 (2) (1993): 58–83.

²⁰State Library, *Report of the Board of Trustees for the Year Ending December 31, 1941* (Pretoria: State Library, 1942), 6.

²¹Hendrik M. Robinson, "'Give the People Light. . .'; A Tribute to the Late Matthew Miller Stirling," in *Give the People Light: Essays in Honour of Matthew Miller Stirling,* 4.

²²The possible link between the free public library movement of the 1930s and 1940s and the Afrikaner emancipation struggle is a theme that to my knowledge has not yet been explored by South African library historians. Some evidence for such a link may be found in the participation in the library movement of Afrikaner cultural leaders such as S. H. Pellisier and in the dominant roles played by Afrikaner librarians in the fledgling provincial library services. Whether or

not such a link can be objectively established, it would be of particular interest to examine the parallels between the free public library movement of the 1930s and 1940s and the rise of alternative community libraries and resource centers during the anti-apartheid struggle of the late 1980s and early 1990s.

[23]Ordinances (laws) establishing provincial library services were adopted by the Cape of Good Hope (1949), Transvaal (1951), and Natal (1952). The Provincial Library Service of the Orange Free State operated under provincial regulations first drafted in 1950. Theodorus Friis, *The Public Library in South Africa; An Evaluative Study* (Cape Town: Afrikaanse Pers-boekhandel; London: Andre Deutsch-Grafton Books, 1962), 125–131.

[24]Marguerite Andrée Peters, "Historical Review of Library Services for the Non-White Peoples of the Republic of South Africa," in *Give the People Light: Essays in Honour of Matthew Miller Stirling,* 58–61.

[25]Esther Sibanyoni, personal communication, 1996.

[26]Jacqueline Audrey Kalley, *The Effect of Apartheid on the Provision of Public, Provincial and Community Library Services in South Africa with Particular Reference to the Transvaal,* Ph.D. thesis, University of Natal, Pietermaritzburg, 1994, 1–8.

[27]Ibid.

[28]Ibid., 223–237. Cf. Libby Dreyer, "Towards a New Public Library Policy," in *Structures and Roles of National Library Services in an Evolving Southern Africa; CNLSA Proceedings* (Pretoria: State Library, 1992), 101–112.

[29]Keyes D. Metcalf, *Planning Academic and Research Library Buildings* (New York: McGraw-Hill, 1965).

[30]This does not deny the importance of the continental European influences that reached us through such polyglot gatekeeper scholars as P. C. Coetzee (1905–1987) and H. J. de Vleeschauwer (1899–1986).

[31]*South African Library Conference held at Bloemfontein on November 15–17, 1928* (Bloemfontein: Executive Committee of the Conference, 1929), 12.

[32]Loree Elizabeth Taylor, "The South African Library Association," in *Give the People Light: Essays in Honour of Matthew Miller Stirling,* 75–76.

[33]"Programme for Future Library Development in the Republic of South Africa; as Adopted by the National Conference of Library Authorities, Pretoria, 5th and 6th November, 1962," *South African Libraries* 30 (3) (1963): 77–117.

[34]Taylor, "The South African Library Association," 78.

[35]Ibid., 77–78. The proposed approach to the state to enact legislation was never pursued.

[36]Another explanation is that the decision to exclude blacks was taken "in anticipation of government regulations to limit membership of professional associations by population groups." These regulations never materialized. Anna Louw, "Evolution from Occupational Association to Professional Institute," *South African Journal of Library and Information Science* 58 (2) (1990): 147–154.

[37]Taylor, "The South African Library Association," 78–80.

[38]Seth P. Manaka, "The African Library Association of South Africa: Its Role on the Black Library Scene," *South African Journal of Librarianship and Information Science* 49 (2) (1981): 76–80; A. W. Z. Kuzwayo, "ALASA Looks to the Future," *Cape Librarian* 37 (7) (1993): 22–23.

[39]A white outsider should not lightly criticize an organization such as ALASA as a creation of apartheid. Among its members it inspires pride and loyalty. It is something they have built up for themselves. This is illustrated by the reluctance of ALASA members to amalgamate their association with SAILIS after it abandoned the racial exclusivity of its predecessor, SALA, even though many joined SAILIS and now hold dual membership.

[40]Marguerite Andrée Peters, *The Contribution of the (Carnegie) Non-European Library Service, Transvaal, to the Development of Library Services for Africans in South Africa* (Pretoria: State Library, 1975).

[41]Christopher Merrett, "Human Rights, Information, and Libraries in South Africa: A Radical Perspective," in *A World Too Wide; Essays on Libraries and other Themes in Honour of Reuben Musiker*, ed. Joseph Sherman (Johannesburg: University of the Witwatersrand Library, 1993), 61.

[42]Cf. the case of Annica van Gylswyk, described by Christopher Merrett, "The Dark Hours: South African Libraries in a State of Emergency, 1986–1987," *Wits Journal of Librarianship and Information Science* 5 (1988): 124–132.

[43]Corda Berghammer and Jenni Karlsson, "A Resource Centre for a Changing South Africa," *Wits Journal of Librarianship and Information Science* 5 (1988): 8–20.

[44]This paragraph and some of those that follow contain generalizations based on my personal experience as a librarian since the late 1960s and those of friends and colleagues. My impressions will not necessarily be endorsed by all.

[45]Christopher Merrett has pointed out that one of the key censorship statutes, the Publications Act, relied "heavily upon the collaboration of librarians and booksellers, from whom, sadly, the State has received almost total co-operation." Christopher Merrett, "South African Censorship: A Legacy of the Past and a Threat to the Future," *Innovation: Appropriate Librarianship and Information Work in Southern Africa* (4) (1992): 3–6.

[46]Criticized, for example, by Philip van Zijl, "LIWO Challenges Library Establishment in South Africa," *Cape Librarian* 37 (7) (1993): 19–21.

[47]The American Library Association's "Library Bill of Rights" is cited, for example, in Jesse H. Shera, *Introduction to Library Science: Basic Elements of Library Service* (Littleton, Colo.: Libraries Unlimited, 1976), 55–56.

[48]A study of the academic boycott has shown that it had little effect on South African research libraries and served as "a nuisance more than anything else" and "more a symbolic gesture than an effective change agent." Lorraine J. Haricombe and F. W. Lancaster, *Out in the Cold: Academic Boycotts and the Isolation of South Africa* (Arlington, Va.: Information Resources Press, 1995), 112.

[49]R. B. Zaaiman, P. J. A. Roux, and J. H. Rykheer, *The Use of Libraries for the Development of South Africa; Final Report on an Investigation for the South*

African Institute for Librarianship and Information Science (Pretoria: Centre for Library and Information Science, University of South Africa, 1988), 244.

⁵⁰NEPI refers to the National Education Policy Investigation, a project conducted by the National Education Coordinating Committee between December 1990 and August 1992. It aimed to "explore policy options in all areas of education within a value framework derived from the ideals of the broad democratic movement." *Library & Information Services; Report of the NEPI Library and Information Services Research Group* (Cape Town: Oxford University Press, 1992), vii.

⁵¹Ibid., 5.

⁵²Ibid., 54.

⁵³Louw, "Evolution from Occupational Association to Professional Institute," 151–152.

⁵⁴C. J. H. Lessing, "Bydrae van die Suid-Afrikaanse Biblioteekvereniging (1930–1980) tot Biblioteekontwikkeling in Suid-Afrika," *South African Journal of Library and Information Science* 59 (2) (1991): 123–134.

⁵⁵Van Zijl, "LIWO Challenges Library Establishment in South Africa," 19. He states that "Most information workers are excluded from full membership of...SAILIS...because of rigid elitist membership requirements ('professional' qualifications)."

⁵⁶Such themes dominated the pages of the *SAILIS Newsletter* and the *South African Journal of Library and Information Science,* published by the South African Bureau of Scientific Publications and distributed to SAILIS members as part of their membership benefits. Christopher Merrett has stated that "a high proportion of contributions to conferences and journals has been notable for a paucity of intellectual rigour, analysis and academic content." Christopher Merrett, "South African Librarianship in Crisis: Alternative Viewpoints," *Wits Journal of Librarianship and Information Science* 5 (1988): 1–7.

⁵⁷For example, S. B. Brooke-Norris, "The Johannesburg Reference Library and the Crisis in Black Education," *South African Journal of Library and Information Science* 54 (4) (1986): 200–202; Mary Nassimbeni, "Libraries and Poverty," *South African Journal of Library and Information Science* 54 (2) (1986): 56–60; and S. Bekker and L. Lategan, "Libraries in Black Urban South Africa: An Exploratory Study," *South African Journal of Library and Information Science* 56 (2) (1988): 63–72.

⁵⁸Kalley, *The Effect of Apartheid on the Provision of Public, Provincial and Community Library Services in South Africa with Particular Reference to the Transvaal,* 5. A survey on the desegregation of public libraries, conducted by Patricia A. Stabbins, was reported in "Public Libraries: Comprehensive Investigation Undertaken," *SAILIS Newsletter* 10 (3) (1990): 14–15. This reveals that the tempo of desegregation increased from 1980 onwards. Nevertheless, the majority of responding libraries were still wholly or partly closed to blacks.

⁵⁹R. B. Zaaiman, P. J. A. Roux, and J. H. Rykheer, *The Use of Libraries for the Development of South Africa* (Pretoria: University of South Africa, 1988).

⁶⁰Ibid., 4.

[61]Clare M. Walker, "From Carnegie to NEPI: Ideals and Realities," *Mousaion Series 3* 11 (2) (1993): 58–83.

[62]Ibid., 72.

[63]Zaaiman et al., *The Use of Libraries for the Development of South Africa*, 22–23.

[64]Ibid., 23. The theory and diagram are derived from A. H. Maslow, *Motivation and Personality* (New York: Harper, 1954).

[65]This analysis has been described in P. J. Lor, "Maslow och Biblioteksbehov: Marginalanteckningar till en 'Progressiv' Rapport om Bibliotek i Sydafrika" ("Maslow and Library Needs: Marginal Notes on a 'Progressive' Report on Libraries in South Africa"), *Bis: Bibliotek i samhälle* (117): 6–11.

[66]Zaaiman et al., *The Use of Libraries for the Development of South Africa*, 226. The models have been derived from Edward French, "Beyond the Soup Kitchen: The Role of the Library in the Identification of Literacy Needs," *Mousaion Series 3* 3 (2) (1985): 62–82.

[67]Zaaiman et al., *The Use of Libraries for the Development of South Africa*, 232–233.

[68]Ibid., 232.

[69]Chantelle Wyley, "Philosophies Informing and Defining Library and Information Work in South Africa: The Transformation Imperative," *Innovation: Appropriate Librarianship and Information Work in Southern Africa* (6) (1993): 8–23.

[70]Cathy-Mae Karelse, "The Role of Resource Centres in Building a Democratic Non-Racial and United South Africa," *Innovation: Appropriate Librarianship and Information Work in Southern Africa* (3) (1991): 3–8.

[71]Christine Stilwell, *The Community Library as an Alternative to the Public Library in South Africa*, Master of Information Studies thesis, University of Natal, Pietermaritzburg, 1991, 74–88.

[72]Ibid., 34–73.

[73]Ibid., 275–277.

[74]Lindsay Lategan, *Developing Community Resource Centres: Some Ideas for South Africa* (Johannesburg: Read Educational Trust, 1989): 11–13.

[75]Wyley, "Philosophies Informing and Defining Library and Information Work in South Africa: The Transformation Imperative," 16–17.

[76]Stilwell, *The Community Library as an Alternative to the Public Library in South Africa*, 280–281.

[77]Wyley, "Philosophies Informing and Defining Library and Information Work in South Africa: The Transformation Imperative," 17.

[78]*Library & Information Services; Report of the NEPI Library and Information Services Research Group*, 30.

[79]Ibid.

[80]Carol Brammage, "Development and Diversity: Listening to the Silenced," *Innovation: Appropriate Librarianship and Information Work in Southern Africa* (5) (1992): 3–7.

[81]Wyley, "Philosophies Informing and Defining Library and Information Work in South Africa: The Transformation Imperative," 19–20.

[82]Christopher Merrett, "The Academic Librarian and Political Censorship in South Africa: Victim or Collaborator?" *Wits Journal of Librarianship and Information Science* 3 (1985): 17–37.

[83]Wyley, "Philosophies Informing and Defining Library and Information Work in South Africa: The Transformation Imperative," 19–20; *Library & Information Services; Report of the NEPI Library and Information Services Research Group*, 54.

[84]*Library & Information Services; Report of the NEPI Library and Information Services Research Group*, 54–56.

[85]Ibid., 3. A closely related vision was developed in Translis Coalition, Working Group 1, "National Library and Information Services Policy: A Discussion Paper of the Translis Coalition; 2nd draft document, 1993," Durban, the Coalition, unpublished.

[86]African National Congress, Education Department, *A Policy Framework for Education and Training, January 1994* (Braamfontein: African National Congress, 1994), 79.

[87]Ibid., 80–81.

[88]Following NEPI, the two most significant policy development exercises were those of the Library and Information Services (LIS) Task Team of the Centre for Education Policy Development (CEPD) and the Library and Information Services (LIS) Subcommittee of the Arts and Culture Task Group (ACTAG) of the Minister of Arts, Culture, Science, and Technology. The report of the CEPD's LIS Task Team was incorporated in Centre for Education Policy Development, "Implementation Plan for Education and Training," Johannesburg, CEPD, 1994, unpublished. The report of the ACTAG LIS Subcommittee was incorporated as part of ACTAG's report to the Minister, and also published separately as Arts and Culture Task Group (South Africa), Library and Information Services Subcommittee, *Report on Libraries and Information Services: Chapter Six of the Report of the Arts and Culture Task Group as Presented to the Minister of Arts, Culture, Science, and Technology on 31 July 1995...* (Pretoria: State Library, Department of Arts, Culture, Science, and Technology, 1995).

[89]J. M. Meyer, *Report from the Working Group Regarding Public Library Services in the Nine Provinces*, unpublished report to the Council of the South African Institute for Librarianship and Information Science, 29 November 1995.

[90]African National Congress, *The Reconstruction and Development Programme: A Policy Framework* (Johannesburg: Umanyano Publications, African National Congress, 1994).

⁹¹P. J. Lor, "The RDP and LIS: An Analysis of the Reconstruction and Development Programme from the Perspective of Library and Information Services," *South African Journal of Library and Information Science* 62 (1994): 128–135.

⁹²Cf. Brammage, "Development and Diversity: Listening to the Silenced," 3; and Peter Lor, "Information Dependence in Southern Africa: Global and Subregional Perspectives," *African Journal of Library, Archives and Information Science* 6 (1) (1996): 1–10.

One group of historians—broadly speaking the defenders of the colonial record—point to the colonial experience as a form of enforced modernization, painful at times, but necessary for the ultimate benefit of Africa. They draw attention to the impact of education in Western languages, to the contribution of missionary schools and hospitals, to economic growth with the opening of export markets and the exploitation of untouched mineral wealth. Especially in South Africa, the defenders of *apartheid* make much of the material well-being of the African population which is, though far worse off than the overseas Europeans, sometimes a little better off than some African populations in tropical Africa. Lewis Gann and Peter Duignan make a special point in favor of the settlers' Africa—that colonies with relatively numerous settlers experienced the most rapid economic development and arrived at the end of the colonial period with the highest per capita incomes. . . . The argument that material well-being resulted from European settlement mistakes correlation for causation; it's like blaming the police for traffic tie-ups because, at the center of any traffic jam, you find a policeman directing traffic. Having conquered all of Africa by the end of the last century, Europeans were free to choose where to place their investment, where their skill and technology would pay the highest dividends. By making the right decisions for their own self-interest, they went where the resource endowment was ripe for development. The greater wealth of settlers' Africa is therefore the result of men and capital following resources. Given their superior technology, it could be argued that they should have done far better than they did in comparison with countries like Ghana, where economic development remained largely in African hands.

Philip D. Curtin

From "The Black Experience of
Colonialism and Imperialism"
Dædalus 103 (2) (Spring 1974)

Affonso Romano de Sant'Anna

Libraries, Social Inequality, and the Challenge of the Twenty-First Century

L IBRARIES, ESPECIALLY NATIONAL LIBRARIES, constitute what are
known in the sciences as "reduced models" of their country's
social reality and ideological complexity. A few years back,
Peru's national library was closed because it was discovered that it
had become a hideout for members of the Shining Path guerrilla
movement. France's Très Grande Bibliothèque is both a reflection
of the Mitterand administration's cultural agenda and the cultural
heritage of a people who have long maintained a literary and
bookish relationship with reality. The US Library of Congress,
already housing some eighty million items and placing yet another
seven thousand on its shelves daily, is the product of a culture that
has dominated the world this century. The obsession with amass-
ing every single document ever published anywhere on the planet
sparked my amazement when I attended the 1992 International
Federation of Librarians Association's congress in New Delhi and
discovered that India's Library of Congress employs 115 staff
members exclusively to collect material produced in the country's
eighteen official tongues. On the other hand, only the Soviet communist regime with all its paradoxes could have produced a situation where—although the USSR once boasted 350,000 libraries,
containing some six hundred million works—the directors of national libraries around the world received desperate telegrams in
1991 from the then-director of the Lenin Library, asking us to
lobby Russia's rulers in hopes of averting the complete destruction
of that institute in the midst of the administrative chaos marking

Affonso Romano de Sant'Anna is President of Brazil's Biblioteca Nacional.

the demise of the Soviet Union. In Spain, to mention only one episode, the old Biblioteca Real fell victim to the historical devastation wrought by Napoleonic imperialism and was demolished by the invader Joseph Bonaparte. Only in 1896 did a new building open its doors to the public.

In Brazil, strangely enough, the Napoleonic effect was more positive. When Junot's troops invaded Portugal, King Don João VI headed to the tropics with a court of fifteen thousand, and among the institutes he created in his old colony was the Biblioteca Real (Royal Library), founded in 1810. That King Don João VI brought the Biblioteca Real with him to Brazil—albeit taking part of it back with him to Portugal years later—and emperors Don Pedro I, Don Pedro II, and other Brazilian rulers stocked it with rare documents explains why our library's holdings include, for instance, the Moguncio Bible, some two hundred engravings by Dürer, a thirteenth-century Book of Hours, sixteenth-century maps, illuminated parchments, and over forty thousand nineteenth-century photographs that belonged to Emperor Don Pedro II. It also explains why today we are considered the world's eighth national library, with a collection totaling some eight million items.

Between the sixty thousand volumes transported from Portugal and today's eight million works lies a long history, winding its path through a monarchy, a republic, dictatorships, and democracy. Slaves once routinely worked for our library and, following in a tradition dating back to Ashurbanipal, it was first headed by clerics, who were later replaced by writers and librarians.

But let me return to the notion that a national library can be taken as a microcosm of a country's culture—my point of departure for illustrating Brazil's current social inequalities and our perspectives for the twenty-first century.

Brazil is a giant laboratory. It stands among the world's ten largest economies and is also among the countries displaying the world's worst income distribution patterns. The existing social and economic inequalities can be accounted for in different ways. Many of our institutions are young—practically infants. During three centuries as a colony of Portugal we were prohibited from having our own industries, presses, or universities. Public libraries and publishing houses appeared only in the nineteenth century. To give some idea of how astonishingly young everything in Brazil is, it was only in 1934 that universities came to be organized along European lines. We are a nation where socially, economically, and technologically one portion of the population is getting ready to step into the twenty-first century, while another still lives in the nineteenth, yet another in the Middle Ages—and where we even find native peoples living in the Stone Age. We are, I repeat, a laboratory, perhaps a reduced model of what is happening throughout our planet.

In continuing to address the topic at hand, I would like to shift my focus somewhat. I will make use of the factual to ground a bit of practical theorizing, rather than detain myself with pure historical and academic speculation, and tell a series of "true parables" about what it is like to administrate a national library within a country plagued by tremendous social inequalities, one that nevertheless has exciting projects for the twenty-first century. I will contrast paradoxical or contradictory scenes whose dialectical nature becomes clear when viewed from a broader perspective.

SCENE ONE

I am seated in my office one morning on the fourth floor of our national library building, constructed in 1910, when I hear an exchange of gunfire coming from a neighboring street. I notice that the pane of a nearby window has been shattered and that a dumdum has met its end right next to me.

Assistants and other staff members leave their desks—arranged beneath high, wide domes whose design mixes the neoclassic with art nouveau—and anxiously rush over to see what has happened. A holdup at a nearby bank has left its mark, breaking into our daily work routine.

I immediately thought about how different this was from the life of my then-counterpart at France's Bibliothèque Nationale, Emmanuel Ladurie, whom I had just visited in Paris. Without a doubt, it was safer and easier to be the director of the Bibliothèque Nationale.

A military police captain came to my office to examine the bullet, and as he proceeded with his work, he engaged me in a conversation about the issue of violence in our city. He mused that the government, suffering from a guilty conscience for having failed to solve the problem of abandoned children, had passed a law applicable to teenage offenders that was so paternalistic that it deprived a police officer of the right to make an arrest in flagrante delicto. I suddenly realized I was discussing the country's grave social problems instead of addressing library matters related to cataloging or the restoration of rare works. But I also came to the realization that I could not discuss one without the other.

In any case, I asked that they retrieve the bullet—whose arrival was indeed a peculiar way of making a *depôt (il)légal*—and suggested that it too be cataloged as a sort of "rare work." This bullet is as important to Brazilian culture and society as the latest essay in sociology.

SCENE TWO

The atmosphere is festive in the Biblioteca Nacional's splendorous foyer. Its red-carpeted stairway splits into two as it rises towards the upper floors. High above, a cupola of colorful *belle époque* stained glass is pierced by the rays of the sun. Against this backdrop, and before hundreds of guests including a number of ministers of state and public authorities, we are inaugurating and exhibiting a project that will transfer thousands of scores from the library's music collection into a computer. At the same moment that the score appears on a computer screen, this piece of modern equipment—as if it were an orchestra—begins playing the Brazilian national anthem. The same computer then executes an unpublished piece by Ernesto Nazareth, composer of both erudite and popular music.

Some large screens are showing our visitors at the same time how this project to modernize our sound archive actually works. Library users will no longer need to leave their homes, cope with traffic, wait their turn in line, or consult card catalogs before finally having the score they want in front of them or before sitting down at the library's piano to study a composition. Now, right from their own homes via modem, users can access the library and view a reproduction of the score of their choice on their computer screen, be it in Barcelona or in the backlands of Brazil. And if the user's computer is near a piano, he or she will be able to play the score, even while it is stored at the Biblioteca Nacional. This is not tomorrow's plan, nor the next century's. It is happening right now. Close to two hundred works by Brazilian composers have already been stored in our computers. Our ideal is to soon have on-line, for instance, the scores of Mozart's first editions, brought from Austria in the nineteenth century by Princess Leopoldina, who came to marry Emperor Don Pedro I.

SCENE THREE

I am arriving home from the library one night, and as I get out of my car in the building's garage, an employee in charge of washing and parking vehicles comes up to me and asks a rather odd question: "Professor, do you think a town of twenty thousand deserves a library?"

His question was unusual from several angles and even more curious if we stop to think what a small town in this man's home state is like. Conversations with these kinds of employees generally tend towards soccer or the weather or some tragedy that has befallen a neighbor; libraries are not exactly a common topic. Still, ever since we initiated an effort to erase the image of the Biblioteca Nacional as an ivory tower, making it instead part of Brazil's day-to-day life, people on the street have often come up to me, displaying an animated interest in talking about ongoing projects or asking me in a somewhat intimate tone, "How's 'our' library doing?"

I soon realized that underlying this worker's question was another discourse; he was trying to give me a message. And so I let him get to his real point. He comes from a little town called Mulungu in Paraíba, a state in Northeast Brazil, and he wanted to know what kind of assistance might be available to help out the small local library. Before immediately getting in touch with his governor and mayor to make arrangements for such help, I thought about the fact that here was an ordinary citizen approaching a federal authority not to ask for a personal favor but instead seeking guidance on how to improve a public asset—a library. Following my narration, in a column that I write for the news daily *O Globo,* of the story of how this worker asked me to help out a library in his home state, many people joined in an action to collect and send books to the library in Mulungu.

SCENE FOUR

Five years ago, the president of Brazil along with governors, ministers of state, mayors, writers, members of the publishing industry, and other invited guests gathered in the foyer of the Biblioteca Nacional to hear a series of official announcements, including that of the creation of a National Library System and of a national reading incentive program known as Proler—literally translated as "pro-reading."

The Biblioteca Nacional thus became the leader of a national network comprising three thousand libraries. We are not only responsible for overseeing the country's holdings of rare works, conducting exchange activities, cataloging and restoring items, and carrying out other activities routine to national libraries, but in a country with Brazil's unique social features, the Biblioteca National is also the coordinator of a national library policy. We want to formally incorporate not only the Mulungu Public Library but all libraries around Brazil into one broad system. Brazil has about five thousand municipalities, some of which are larger in territorial extent than certain European nations. It is not enough to simply know how these libraries are doing—we must also promote them as centers of cultural action and social transformation. Our battle is to foster an active library, not a passive one, a library that goes after readers: taking the elderly books that they can read at home, inaugurating libraries and reading circles inside prison walls, and intensifying our programs involving "biblio-buses," "biblio-boats," and even "biblio-train-cars."

I was witness to an equally pertinent scene while attending a meeting of the Board of Brazilian University Presidents. Discussing the country's cultural problems as germane to our project "The Library—Year 2000," these college presidents emphatically expressed their agreement with us that Brazil's nine hundred university libraries should become part of our network and system. Universities like São Carlos, in São Paulo, or Rio's Castelo Branco have now opened their libraries to the public as a way of enhancing social and intellectual integration with their surrounding communities. And during the Southern Hemisphere's 1996 summer, the Board of Brazilian University Presidents sponsored a social drive in poor areas of the Northeast, in conjunction with the

Solidarity Program coordinated by anthropologist Ruth Cardoso, who also happens to be First Lady. Universities cannot be islands of excellence divorced from social reality. Moreover, dozens of joint-action agreements are already being signed between Brazil's largest library and the nation's university network. Reading programs, the issue of copyrights, restoration questions, and even strategies for opening college libraries to the general public are currently under discussion. Since we are like neither Denmark nor Sweden, where practically every neighborhood has its own library, we must open these nine hundred college libraries (with due precautions taken) to the community at large.

I must point out that in a country of continental proportions like mine, projects and intentions cannot be small in scale. We need to think big. And throw into the bargain that we are a culture of "latecomers" who will need to swiftly shortcut many stages of development if we are to reach the twenty-first century in a more uniform fashion. This means computerizing the greatest possible number of libraries so that a library in the Amazon region or along our border with Argentina can electronically receive the visual, textual, and numerical information it requires. In short, we must deploy the concept of a virtual library. One example of joint efforts in this area is Diadema's pilot project to computerize twelve libraries within that municipality, located near São Paulo. This experimental system affords the city's four hundred thousand inhabitants access to a gamut of information, including the Biblioteca Nacional's bibliography. The model is expected to be applicable throughout the rest of the country. A book or text need not be located physically at every library but should be available on a computer screen and be reproducible. We are working towards this goal now in conjunction with the Brazilian ministries of Science and Technology, Culture, and Education; the educational broadcasting network; and Brazil's state-owned telecommunications company, Embratel.

The Biblioteca Nacional has also opened its doors to the "Booknet," Brazil's first virtual bookstore. A pioneer effort undertaken jointly with a private institution, Booknet has received over one thousand purchase orders from throughout Brazil and abroad in a single day. The intent of this virtual bookstore is to help anxious readers and book buyers who cannot locate a certain work or who may not even have a library in their town of residence. Anyone can log into the network, consult a list of available books, and make a credit-card purchase. This way, Brazil's four thousand Internet users—as well as the millions of users abroad—can enjoy greater access to the world of reading and information.

SCENE FIVE

During a lunch break one day, as I was strolling through the library, I came upon a group of men and women in uniform, seated on the floor, listening attentively to someone reading a text to them.

These workers are members of our cleaning staff, and the person reading and commenting on the text is a member of our reading incentive program, Proler; he is known as a *leitor-guia,* or "reading guide." On this particular day the story is by Machado de Assis. When the guide has finished reading, one of the workers comments excitedly, "This text was written just for me!"

SCENE SIX

The reading guide mentioned above belongs to the Proler team located in the neighborhood of Laranjeiras, where the reading incentive program is housed in a beautiful mansion obtained and refurbished by the Biblioteca Nacional. It is here in the Casa de Leitura, or Reading House, that strategies are devised for implementing our national reading policy. Planned actions are grounded in the idea that a citizen can only fulfill his or her role in society by reading and having access to information. We must make the whole country read, for no country has ever achieved development without first learning to read. Reading is what makes it possible to improve a labor force. Reading is what makes it possible to increase productivity. Reading is what makes it possible to enhance the quality of life. A society that reads can better map its destiny. And a national library with our peculiarities, conscious of its social responsibilities, must interact with society as a whole. It is more than just safeguarding books; in addition to enforcing a national library policy, our library can and must turn its attention to the issue of reading and to the education of readers.

For these reasons, the Proler reading incentive program has already been inaugurated in three hundred municipalities around the country. In partnership with mayors and state governments, programs consisting of four progressive modules draw not only teachers and librarians but also engineers, doctors, members of the armed forces, lawyers—in short, people from all walks of life. Dozens of such seminars have already taken place, bringing together around five hundred people for events lasting a week or more, where participants' relations to reality are modified through reading.

One of Proler's basic mottoes is that we must "de-school" reading. In other words, instilling good reading habits is not a task to be entrusted solely to the school (a place where this activity is generally mismanaged and where students sometimes even learn to detest books)—it is also a form of social action.

Taking books and the act of reading into public parks, hospitals, and prisons and creating library train-cars, boats, and trucks are ways of disseminating not just books themselves but the socially interactive habit of reading. Research conducted among Brazilian laborers indicates that productivity can be linked directly to competence in reading a written text. This is not merely an issue of illiteracy but also involves the so-called functional illiterate—the individual who knows how to read but who does so poorly and has an even poorer understanding of what was read. Functional illiterates in Europe number fifty million, and the same figure applies in the United States. This is prejudicial not only to the health and lives of these individuals but also to a nation's economy. Looking after a society's reading habits means looking after its social and economic well-being, and the Biblioteca's efforts have already crossed our country's distant borders. With the support of the Latin American and Caribbean Regional Center for the Book (CERLALC), we have held a number of international meetings focusing on national reading policies, attended by Mercosur member-nations as well as our Amazon neighbors.

Our strategies for fostering the reading habit through Proler thus complement our strategies for forming an electronic library network through the National Library System. Viewed individually, a person working on a computer or reading a book is engaged in a solitary act. In the socially grounded act of reading, this person becomes a member of a group, engaged in an act of solidarity.

It is worth pointing out—digressing for a moment from these scenes of real life—that libraries and reading have a history of which many are unaware. At the beginning of time, back in the days of Ashurbanipal, for example, only a select few had access to books or reading, and the library belonged to the king. And although the world's oldest known library already existed in Ebla, Mesopotamia, as far back as forty-five hundred years ago, individual reading gained impetus only at the time of Pericles, in fourth-century Greece, when many books were reproduced either on papyrus or on waxed or gessoed tablets. In public readings, both in Pergamum and Rome, someone would walk about with a book, reading aloud from it. It was the fifteenth-century invention of the printing press and, principally, the eighteenth-century translation of the classics that made reading a more democratic, less elitist act.

Our task today is twofold: to broaden in range and number our books and libraries and to expand in scope the habit of reading, socializing and individualizing this act at the same time. To this end, Brazil's Biblioteca Nacional has stepped beyond its traditional role as caretaker and restorer of books to become a reading advocate, above all because we are a society of sharp social and economic contrasts, where a bullet fired during a holdup may come to rest next to the desk of the director of the country's national library, and where some of this library's employees are teenagers from Rio's poor outlying neighborhoods or hillside shantytowns, serving internships while they wait for a better chance in life to appear.

SCENE SEVEN

I receive a phone call from the Tocantins State Secretary of Culture. He invites me to attend the first Writers' Meeting to be held by this new state. Getting there takes nearly a day, since the plane must go through São Paulo and other cities. I look at my date book, crammed full of commitments that are both more urgent and geographically more convenient, and I think about politely declining his invitation this time around.

The secretary, however, is insistent, requesting that I go there to launch my latest book of poetry. Stalling for time, and hesitant to respond with a straight-out "no," I inquire how he intends to go about this and if he could ask some local bookseller to obtain the books for this launching when he breaks in, declaring "You'll have to bring the books yourself, because we don't have a bookstore here."

Shocked by this other side of my country, I decided right then to accept the invitation. I have to go, I thought, precisely because of Tocantins's challenging straits. Invitations from other capital cities that are already part of modernity could wait until later.

A bit of background: Tocantins is a new Brazilian state, created ten years ago. I suppose it is about the size of the Iberian peninsula. It was formerly part of the state of Goiás, home to our national capital, Brasília. The capital city of Tocantins, Palmas, is being built from scratch. When I arrived in Palmas, flying over the dusty construction yards, I was reminded of the building of Brasília over thirty years ago. Brazil has always been like this, constantly rediscovering itself since 1500, pulling cities out of nowhere, constructing within a vast territory a future that bit by bit becomes our present.

Construction of the university in Palmas was nearing completion, but so far, emblematically, only the governor's mansion was finished, radiant in the midst of the dust, a scene from magical realism. But the writers were there, as was the will and the need to make the book part of daily life.

If Palmas is a nineteenth-century Californian setting, the site of a new westward march and devoid of bookstores, Brazil is a whole country waiting to be conquered. This is why for strategic purposes Proler and the National Library System have created an interactive network of continental proportions. Maintaining programs in the farthest reaches of the country—as I pointed out in an October 1994 debate with Stiftung Leseng, in Frankfurt—is tantamount to Spain's Biblioteca Nacional maintaining programs in Madrid along with programs in Finland, Greece, and Moscow. And all of this, it goes without saying, happens within a meager budget hardly commensurate with such daunting responsibilities, let alone with our dreams.

SCENE EIGHT

We are in Frankfurt now, far from Palmas or Mulungu. Brazil is the 1994 Frankfurt Book Fair's theme country. On display here are the latest, most sophisticated resources in publications and materials for libraries, including a large sector dedicated to the electronic library. Within Brazil's area at the fair, the Biblioteca Nacional marks its presence in several ways: two large exhibits on the evolution of Brazilian literature (one of which later went on to visit other European nations); a series of foreign-language publications disseminating information on Brazilian culture; and news of our annual program offering fifty grants for the translation of Brazilian authors. Meanwhile, dozens of Brazilian writers are traveling around Germany giving lectures and launching books. The German press is forced to devote space to Brazil—but this time not to report on the burning of the Amazon rain forest or the murder of street kids. The country of Brazil has a culture, and it has a literature boasting exceptional writers as well.

How odd, some might think, that this is the role of a national library. But that is the way things are in this most unique of countries called Brazil. And perhaps it is best like this, for the very institute that is expanding a national system of libraries and working to instill the reading habit may be the one that in turn can help export Brazilian literature, thus coming full circle in its activities. Our library is concerned not only with books and reading but also with the writer, and its roster of activities includes programs and sponsorships meant to solidify this triad: book, reader, writer.

A consistent cultural project must forge links between the rural countryside and the world beyond our national borders, between the arid *sertão* and the big city, between Brazil and the world. This explains our efforts at the Bogota Book Fair, where Brazil was also the theme country in 1995, and at book fairs from Bologna to Guadalajara, from Buenos Aires to Tokyo.

Within this same realm of international connections between book, reader, and library, it is likewise important to look beyond the immediate context of Brazil and underscore the role of ABINIA, the Association of Ibero-American National Libraries, headed until 1995 by Virginia Betancourt, director of Venezuela's Biblioteca Nacional. I have now replaced Virginia as General Secretary of

ABINIA and am endeavoring to expand our common projects. For instance, we recently received extensive support from the University of California at Berkeley and Harvard University for a project to improve exchange programs with those institutions' Latin American departments.

Something new is happening in this continent's twenty-two national libraries, which through ABINIA have joined together with Spain and Portugal. Real efforts are being made to recover our history and explore our future. Countless practical results have come already, with many supported and approved, especially by Spain, against the backdrop of the commemoration of the quadricentennial of the discovery of America. One ensuing achievement is that we have opened the eyes of Latin America's rulers to the role of books, reading, and libraries in our societies; as a consequence, in many documents signed at meetings of Latin American presidents, the terms "library" and "reading" appear more and more explicitly as part of a government strategy. It is commendable that Argentina has inaugurated a new national library, that Mexico has expanded its own, that Venezuela has finished a new building, and that Brazil has restored its Biblioteca Nacional and invested in a fabulous annex located along the city's docks; it will also soon start construction of the long-awaited Brasília Library.

In speaking of the libraries in this region, mention must also be made of the work carried out by the Latin American and Caribbean Regional Center for the Book (CERLALC), headquartered in Bogota. CERLALC promotes a wide range of programs, from reading advocacy among Latin America's underprivileged populations to consulting services for the organization of libraries and publishing houses to the issue of copyrights.

CONCLUDING COMMENTS

After this brief sequence of clips where I have shuffled scenes from Brazilian reality with news on current library projects, I would like to close the circle. I began by suggesting that libraries, especially national ones, can be seen as reduced models of their surrounding social reality. I then offered some examples of problems and solutions found along the road to our project "The Library—Year 2000."

In closing, I think it appropriate to ask what libraries will be like at the end of the twenty-first century. For instance, at an international seminar held in the year 2095, what might the directors of our planet's libraries be thinking, on the threshold of the year 2100?

This is an exciting question, especially now when the threat of an atomic apocalypse is behind us and electronic technology is constantly triggering a succession of revolutions that previously took centuries to unfold.

In similar fashion, but retroactively, it is a didactic exercise to wonder what it might have been like had such a meeting been held in 1895 and to imagine what library directors back then might have been envisioning for the future of their institutes in 1995.

Although one hundred years ago most of our national libraries had already been founded, there were as yet no pocket-size books, no digital books, no virtual restoration processes, nothing like what the computer has made possible through data banks, scanners, and the Internet. Our nations had many more illiterates, and libraries were—as perhaps they still are in some areas—sacred places.

I think about these things first of all in order to relativize our position today, casting ourselves within a framework where the vectors of time and technology are fundamental; and secondly, in order to situate ourselves within a moment of transition, underscoring the role we must play between yesterday and today—for our libraries do not belong to us, even though they may temporarily depend on our administrative policies.

That said, I would like to recall a statement made by Hipolito Escolar in *Historia de las Bibliotecas*:

> The essential lines of library tasks were defined 4,500 years ago: the cataloguing of material, the writing of classificatory codes on the spines of tablets to facilitate their localization, and shelves where materials are placed in order by size and by content so as to preserve them safely and locate them rapidly.[1]

Perhaps it is that the entire technological revolution engulfing us is nothing more than a revolution in back-up support rather than in content; that the cathedral library's revolving tables that allowed a reader to consult several books at one time were forerunners of the CD-ROM; that the embryos of photocopying and reprographics can be found in the craftwork of thirteenth-century scribes who copied texts for students; that since the time of the Sumerians, the library—serving as an archive known then as a "house of tablets"—constituted that era's data bank as well as its school or, as we would call it today, free university.

It is therefore possible to foresee that such a meeting held in 2095, while unpredictable from a technological angle, would most likely not reveal much variation in substantive terms: the ultimate destiny of a book is each person's reading of it—reading as pleasure, as information, as a path to individual and social transformation.

Libraries have indeed undergone transformations. From temples where librarians were members of the clergy, they have steadily moved into the hands of the laity. The twelfth century's cathedral libraries were joined by university libraries starting in the thirteenth century and by subscription and lending libraries in the nineteenth century. And now some libraries, like Brazil's Biblioteca Nacional, interact with public and university libraries, welcoming a heterogeneous public because we cannot afford to close our doors to those who as of yet have no way to do research or enjoy the pleasure of reading in their own neighborhoods or cities.

On a final note, I will say that the profession of librarian as custodian and manipulator of information should constitute one of the most highly esteemed occupations in the coming century. The librarian will be a kind of "information engineer," not just a simple keeper of books, a classifier, or a teacher displaced from the classroom. As an object, the book has changed. Library buildings have changed as operational spaces. The role of reading in a computerized society has gained new recognition. Librarians, as information engineers with broad humanist backgrounds, must of necessity change their way of thinking if they are to meet the challenges of the twenty-first century.

ENDNOTE

[1]Hipolito Escolar, *Historia de las Bibliotecas* (Madrid: Fundacion German Sanchez Ruiperez, 1987), 22–23.

Brazil lives simultaneously in a number of historico-social epochs. Some scenes recall the relations of the colonizers and conquerors with the natives; others abound in the turbulent activity of an industrial civilization with all the characteristics—both national and foreign—associated with it. Against this backdrop, ethnic or racial relations and the significance of color in human life manifest themselves in different ways. The Brazilian racial dilemma may be characterized most succinctly by the situation of the Negro or mulatto in the city of São Paulo. Although the percentage of Negroes and *métis* in São Paulo is among the lowest in the urban centers of Brazil, the city is significant for other reasons. On the one hand, it is situated in the last region in Brazil where slavery played a constructive role in the long cycle of economic prosperity that began with the production and export of coffee. On the other hand, it was the first Brazilian city that exposed the Negro and the mulatto to the vicissitudes of life that are characteristic of and unavoidable in a competitive economy in the process of expansion. It, therefore, permits one to analyze objectively and under almost ideal conditions why the old racial order did not disappear with the abolition and legal interdiction of the caste system, but spread out into the social structure that emerged with the expansion of free labor.

Florestan Fernandes

From "The Weight of the Past"
Dædalus 96 (2) (Spring 1967)

Jean Favier

The History of the French National Library

F RANCE, LIKE MANY COUNTRIES with a long history, has grown older without realizing it. The French National Library, located in a building primarily designed during the nineteenth century, had been the model of an open library, welcoming researchers among whom no distinctions were necessary. As the registration of copyright extended to all public and private publications, the library offered rich collections of manuscripts, engravings, and geographical maps that well complemented its collections of printed books and periodicals.

Slowly, however, the drama unfolded. Fifty years ago, there was already some concern about the need, generated by a growing population, to modernize the library's equipment and expand the library's collections and services. The number of readers who wanted access to the library increased, particularly as universities developed shorter education requirements (shorter postgraduate studies, shorter doctorate theses). At the same time, the increase in leisure time and the lowering of the retirement age created a new clientele of well-educated people, temporarily or finally liberated from their professional responsibilities. As reading rooms became more crowded, restrictions had to be imposed—an unfortunate result in many ways. The proliferation of printed publications crowded storage areas. Increasing diversification in collections of non-printed matter—photographs, manuscripts, contemporary literary correspondence, and musical scores and materials—also contributed to the saturation of these storage areas.

Jean Favier is President of the Bibliothèque Nationale de France.

Surely, these developments are not unique to France. But some aspects set France and its capital city apart. The first characteristic relates to the extensive centralization that has deeply marked French literary and historical tradition, the patterns for obtaining access to knowledge, and the distribution of research instruments. Decentralization, a recurring item on the government's agenda for the past twenty years, has not changed a situation steadily reinforced throughout the last seven centuries. Paris is one of the few capital cities that is at the same time the political headquarters of a still heavily centralized country, a metropolis of ten million people, and the most important university city in the country. With three hundred foreign diplomatic missions, 360,000 students in twenty universities, and some one hundred *grandes écoles*; hundreds of thousands of professionals in middle and senior management involved in politics, public service, liberal professions, or business management; and millions of individuals in the general public—all potential library patrons—it is clear that to find a reasonably comparable match of the community's needs, one would have to combine London with Cambridge and Oxford, Frankfurt with Heidelberg, Rome with Florence and Milan, or Washington with New York and Cambridge. Of course, this does not mean that one is superior to the other; it is merely stating a fact.

The second defining characteristic relates to the strength, and also the burden, of an institution that is almost six centuries old. The first royal library dates back to the middle of the fourteenth century; continuity in administration has been maintained since the sixteenth century. The structural configuration of the library as we know it today essentially dates back to the nineteenth century. In other words, any modernization must respect this heritage to the highest degree. Yet undertaking renovation while at the same time ensuring continuity is easier to define in concept than it is to realize concretely. The public got used to its own demands and its own ways of approaching the library. Although awkward, it is possible to train a staff to understand that learning new methods is their responsibility; however, it is much more difficult to convince the public of the urgency of the adaptation that they must themselves undertake. To take only two examples: it has been difficult to make some top researchers understand that typing a call number on a keyboard is no more difficult than dialing a phone number, and it would be impossible to replace the extremely complex book classification system with a system of continuous classification, which would make unreadable all the references found in the notes of books published over the last one hundred years. (This would be the case even if a computer could match the call numbers from one system to the other within a few seconds.)

This heritage carries its deficiencies. Compensating for them is sometimes only a matter of financial capacity, yet one must contend with painful arbitrations between competing needs. Under the leadership of the scholars who directed the library from the sixteenth to the twentieth century, the institution progressively lost its encyclopedic character. While writers, researchers in the social sciences, or university professors in literature can often be found in the reading rooms, this is not true of doctors, physicists, or mathematicians. With time, erudition withdrew into itself. Restoring encyclopedism is a necessary step towards the creation of a system encompassing universal knowledge.

Only one thing was certain: a new building was needed. It was absolutely impossible between the seventeenth and twentieth centuries to expand extensively beyond the occupied areas north of Palais-Royal. The problem would be the same in London, Vienna, or Florence. Ancient palaces—the French National Library has occupied the palace of Cardinal Mazarin for more than three hundred years—are not indefinitely expandable, and the possibilities for interior remodeling are also limited. Considering the prohibitive cost of land and buildings in the city center, expanding into neighboring quarters would prove too expensive; it would also presuppose changes in the physical organization that public opinion today, unlike a few decades ago, would no longer tolerate. Indeed, our contemporaries have become aware of the heritage represented by historic neighborhoods, and moving even one stone nowadays triggers a general outcry. This positive reaction to the unfortunate consequences of a vandalism that still raged not so long ago makes it extremely difficult to conduct any large-scale operation to keep alive the historical centers of old cities and prevent them from becoming sleepy museums.

What was possible, however, was to construct a new building in a neighborhood undergoing complete transformation. Across from the Seine riverbank at Tolbiac, over seventeen acres of land were available not far from the city center. Here, the new library would be close to the downtown area—being equidistant from the Châtelet or the Champs-Elysées roundabout—and at the same time offer enough space, once the idea of building towers as the means of gaining that extra space was accepted. (The presence of ground water not far below the riverbank surface prevented construction from going too deep, and the cost of land did not allow building horizontally beyond the space available, which is roughly equivalent to the surface area of the Place de la Concorde.)

Carrying the burden of its centralizing past, the library is confronted with a new reaction that started twenty years ago—decentralization—in the implementation of its ambitious projects. Since it cannot rely on strong public support for its financing demands, the library must take into account the new commitment to decentralization. In other words, a large institution that happens to be located in Paris, which people in the provinces expect to find in Paris, cannot be at the service of Parisians exclusively. An expense borne by the entire country cannot sustain an information monopoly for the benefit of the writers and researchers of the Parisian intellectual elite, for people in the provinces visiting Paris once in a while, or for university organizations in the Paris area.

As centuries passed, the world of the readers changed. It became extremely difficult to distinguish a professional researcher from an enlightened amateur. With the progress of democracy in cultural areas and in education, it is impossible to restrict nonaffiliated researchers from accessing a national library. There is therefore an unavoidable conflict between the elitism of a high-level research library and the ever-present demands of a democracy for wider access to knowledge.

Solutions were probed in different directions. For the reasons given above, the idea of a unique library open to all was quickly abandoned; it would have immediately overwhelmed the researchers and, in the long run, damaged a historic collection that would gain nothing from being consulted abusively. Therefore, what was instead adopted was the idea of two superimposed libraries that would be managed jointly, yet would have a different audience—and, most importantly, different collections. On the lower level of this rectangular base, at the garden and Seine level or *rez-de-*

jardin, a research library will house the twelve million books and three hundred thousand copies of periodicals that constitute the current heritage. This will occupy half of the four hundred kilometers (about 248 miles) of available shelves. The remaining half will hold future acquisitions resulting from copyright registrations of French publications or from exchanges and necessary purchases of foreign material. Only researchers entitled or otherwise authorized will be allowed access to these historic collections. In short, the garden level will be reserved for the original French National Library, now bigger and modernized; at the higher (or *haut-de-jardin*) level, the other library will be open to all adult readers and will house a rich collection of four hundred thousand books bought especially for that purpose, with a capacity of up to eight hundred thousand books. The libraries will share the same documentation management and computer systems and will conduct a joint policy of cultural development.

Innovations will be quickly implemented so that the new library, without repudiating its past, can keep abreast of the needs of the next millennium. One innovation is the return to encyclopedism, which nineteenth-century administrators, led to extremes by their scholarly education, had somewhat lost sight of. While the French National Library is one of the world's leading libraries in French literature and historic research, the same cannot be said for its collections in the physical sciences, law, and economics. At a time when new encyclopedias are springing up in the form of exhaustive collections or CD-ROMs to provide the diversity of knowledge our patrons are expected to have, it was time to compensate for such deficiencies.

Another innovation also returns to the sound practices of the early days. Thirty-eight catalogs have been created since the time of Guillaume Budé, that most influential French humanist who encouraged the study of Greek in France and contributed, in the early sixteenth century, to the creation of the "royal lecturers," the future Collège de France. Each has its own description rules, if any, because classification was done well before the notions of system, norms, and rules came into play. Of all these research tools, only the latest are computerized. A reverse conversion of these catalogs is currently under way and essentially completed.

Soon the reader will have to deal with only one computerized catalog.

Building up collections also calls for a conciliation between the older and newer forms of thought memorization. It is important not to repeat the mistake made in the sixteenth century when manuscripts were still preferred to prints, which they considered a less noble product; or when the manuscript or correspondence of a contemporary historian had less claim to shelf space at the French National Library than medieval manuscripts and collections of copies from scholars or ancient original pieces, a mistake made well into the twentieth century. For the forthcoming third millennium, we will have to ensure the continuity of manuscript collections as well as that of printed books and periodicals, knowing that the recent expansion in the diversity of technical means of reproduction makes it impossible now to characterize a printed publication immediately. In addition, we must take into consideration the new types of documents, currently found under two categories—audiovisual and computerized—that involve digital technology.

The problem here is not specifically European in nature. It is rather that the reactions of professionals—and, even more, of the European public—reflect customs and value judgments going too far back to be ignored. However psychological some of these "blocks" are, they are nevertheless obstacles to overcome. The fact that today a distinguished sixty-year-old professor claims to be unable to type his name and call number on a keyboard, bitterly deploring the passing of the index card upon which he used to write the same information with a pen, reflects habits and mental processes that probably exist in every country, but most particularly in Europe. There is a well-known difference between the American, who shows a visitor the newest buildings in his city, and the European, who takes his visitor to see the oldest church. The point here is that while modernization is welcomed by many, both young and old, for others it represents an upheaval of the world as they know it.

For the Europeans, the surprise came with the introduction of technology into their lives, which for a long time had characterized the New World. Until the 1950s, Europeans returning from the United States usually brought their families products that were still impossible to find in Europe. Today this no longer applies. The surprise came so suddenly to the Europeans that they are now ready for anything. Since everything changed in less than a generation, everything can change again. Beyond what is available to-day—computer data entry in one's native language, immediate processing of bibliographical queries, multiple remote consultations, computer-aided reading, and a host of other developments—European librarians, as well as their client readers or archivist colleagues, know that tomorrow will continue to bring revolutions in our relationship to information. They do not know what kind of information or what means of access to information they will be expected to provide; they only know that they will be asked for not only what today has yet to be requested, but what is not even conceivable. Because they had to react quickly, they expect every-thing from the best to the worst. They know that people talk, rightly or wrongly, about the paperless office, the book without an editor, even the book without pages. They have seen too much in their lifetime to be surprised.

This does not, however, prevent them from worrying. Book preservation, one of the most serious concerns of librarians and archivists, is currently undergoing a peculiar mutation. For many centuries, books preserved themselves; the only threat hovering over them was abusive consultation, from which books were pro-tected by the greatly limited access to a high-ranking library. Two factors came to disturb this relatively comfortable situation. The first is the increased fragility of the media—from acid paper and other sensitive media to short-lived magnetisms. The idea that a work never consulted is a work that preserves itself has slowly become erroneous, and professionals in the field perceived the acceleration of the phenomenon as a brutal assault.

The second factor relates to the tremendous increase in simple access to library collections. For an institution such as the French National Library, the transition from its current six hundred seats to the two thousand seats that will be available in the new research library is enough to indicate the change in scope. The creation of a new type of university studies—two- to five-year degrees, instead of the twelve to fifteen years required for the old thesis—has brought an increase in the number of scientific readers. The in-crease in leisure time has created a group of readers who are not motivated by research but expect the library to provide intellectual enrichment and a cultural activity. All this contributed to accelerate the aging process of books consulted more than ever before. As a result, professionals switched gears. Restoring the damage already done now appears a lost cause; we should not have waited for the books to become damaged before worrying about their preservation. Means of prevention therefore take precedence over means of repair. Of course, restoration will always be needed, but it is better to intervene before the damage occurs. In the past ten years, preservation and maintenance have become a high priority at the library.

The recent wave of decentralization led an old centralized country like France to adopt policies of complementarity that until then were totally foreign to its traditions. What remains from its centralizing legacy is the fact that decentralization is being conducted by a ministry, the Ministry of Culture, and by a national public institution located in Paris. It would occur to no one that things could be different. Yet, around the French National Library institution, a whole network has begun to develop. This network is not only a "building site" for a collective catalog that will incorporate all the information on the existence of rare or foreign books available in any given library in France. It is also a system of associated centers sharing their acquisitions based on the excellence demonstrated by some libraries already well-known in a given field. Indeed, city and university libraries often have rich collections of original works, making them the single owners of books that are unavailable elsewhere. These include estates of monasteries and seminaries whose possessions were confiscated in 1789 during the French Revolution or in 1905 when the separation of church and state was declared; private collections that the library somehow received that were acquired in France or abroad, outside of the normal channels that supplied the royal, imperial, or national library; and finally, collections created more recently, following the development in a particular city of a specialized research center. These collections often provide a wide array of foreign books unavailable under a copyright registration system necessarily limited to French publications. Only a few years ago, it took flair and enormous endurance to find one's way through these local treasures. Today, technology allows the collective consultation of these disseminated resources and encourages access at the lowest possible cost, by eliminating the need for costly multiple acquisitions.

There is a political interest at stake here: France now only reluctantly accepts large public investments for the exclusive benefit of Parisians. The capital city needed, and still needs, to win forgiveness for its national library. It is therefore important that non-Parisians have equal access to the library. And they will, by reserving a seat and books for a date convenient to them, currently through the Minitel system (the French home videotext service) and in the future through their personal computer—all without wasting a lot of time in going to the library, looking for the call number, and waiting for the book to be brought to them. They will have access to it after first consulting—at home, at their university, or at their town library—a catalog that will help them organize their work.

Finally, they can one day expect to see the actual text of the book on their computer screen. While techniques of telecommunication and computer-assisted reading have been mastered, there are still problems to resolve concerning works that are not yet widely available in the public arena. These problems are mainly due to the fragile economic predicament of the specialized publishing houses, which no one wishes to seriously hurt. Technology obviously does not represent a threat to general literature because there will always be people who prefer reading novels, essays, or poems in a more comfortable format; however, the opportunity for researchers to consult works of reference on the computer screen could harm small editors. Although the fundamental problem is the same in all the countries that try to apply technology to books and images, the approach to the problem differs according to the legal system, cultural heritage, and mentality prevalent in each country.

The French National Library shares with all libraries the ambition of meeting the needs of our time. Its original characteristics are rooted in the mental and institutional structures of a country forged by a long history. It needs to take into account two millennia at the same time—one coming up and one coming to an end—and this is not always an easy task.

Translated by Mireille M. Dedios

For a writer like Borges, the library is the landscape of human drama; it is experience, tragedy, social history. Among our own writers, satire and parody and mimicry are directed to a mind that must itself be richly aware of banalities, old movies, literary texts, conundrums, puns, a torrent of references. Ellipses, allusiveness, disconnection, are to be filled, identified, connected by the imagination and knowledge of the reader; otherwise the creative effort, so detailed, so mindful of tone, will have been in vain. "Description of physical appearance and mannerism is one of the several methods of characterization used by writers of fiction," John Barth says in an early story. "But to say that Ambrose and Peter's mother was pretty is to accomplish nothing." This asks of the reader a contemplation of physical description in narrative; it also, perhaps, asks him to smile—*knowingly*.

Proust left a short book titled *On Reading*. It says, of course, many beautiful things about himself, about decoration (William Morris), Carlyle, Ruskin, the Dutch painters, Racine, Saint-Simon—on and on. And then somewhere in the pages he notes the insufficiency of reading and says that it is an initiation, not to be made into a discipline. "Reading is at the threshold of spiritual life; it can introduce us to it; it does not constitute it."

Elizabeth Hardwick

From "Reading"
Dædalus 112 (1) (Winter 1983)

Vladimir Zaitsev

Problems of Russian Libraries in an Age of Social Change

W ITH THEIR IMMENSE INTELLECTUAL potential and comprehensive holdings of world culture, Russian libraries comprise an integral part of the international library community. They perform a mission of enlightenment at a defining moment in Russian history, contributing to the development of science and education within Russia and providing access to information required by users in other countries.

They vary dramatically in size, ranging from some of the world's biggest collections to tiny facilities providing for the country's remotest areas. The most important ones in Russia are the two national libraries—the Russian State Library in Moscow, with holdings of 40 million bibliographic units, and the National Library of Russia in St. Petersburg, the oldest library in Russia. Among other major collections are the Library of the Russian Academy of Sciences (with 20 million bibliographic units) and the state science and technology libraries in Moscow and Novosibirsk (with over 10 million volumes). There are more than three thousand libraries in the system of higher and secondary education—at universities, academies, institutes, and colleges. The most extensive and ramified is the Ministry of Culture library network, encompassing fifty-five thousand libraries in all regions of this vast country, ranging from national libraries for the republics integrated in the Russian Federation down to minor rural services.

Vladimir Zaitsev is Director of the National Library of Russia and President of the Russian Library Association.

Multiple libraries are in operation at factories, plants, trade unions, culture centers, schools, and a host of smaller local institutions.

Recent years have witnessed radical transformations in Russia; political turns have caused dramatic changes in the status of libraries in the country. What then are the factors governing their development on the eve of the twenty-first century?

THE IMPACT OF STATE REORGANIZATION IN THE USSR

Until recently, the map of the world featured a huge country, designated for over seventy years as the Union of Soviet Socialist Republics—the USSR. Today, the USSR exists only in history, replaced with a multitude of sovereign, independent states. Among them is the Russian Federation, spread from the Arctic Ocean to Kazakhstan and Mongolia, and from the Baltic to the Pacific—containing more than 115,000 libraries of different sizes and functions.

During the Soviet period, libraries were entrusted with the tasks of public ideological education and promoting the policies of the ruling party—in addition to the more typical responsibilities of cultural education and administering the functions of science and technology centers. The state maintained a centrally-coordinated regulation of the country's library service, supporting the existing libraries and establishing new libraries.

The USSR operated a rigid, centrally organized and directed library system structured along branch/territorial principles. Additionally, however, there were coordinating bodies for all library systems and departments. The most important among them were the State Interdepartmental Library Commission under the USSR Ministry of Culture and the All-Union Library Council—nominally a public organization, but in essence an administrative body. The libraries were subject to hierarchical relationships and responsibilities, with some having all-union functions (e.g., the USSR State V. I. Lenin Library, the USSR State Science and Technology Library, and the central agriculture, medicine, patent, and other functional-area libraries), acting as consultative centers for the corresponding libraries in the union republics. During this period the state was wary of national-library functions, regarding them as manifestations of nationalism. Such a view also informed decisions as to the linguistic origin of works held in the libraries; publications in Russian were prevalent. Irrespective of their location, Russian libraries generally acquired all the publications needed to provide service to their communities; the republics were quite closely interlinked in scientific, economic, and cultural spheres, yielding an integrated information space.

On December 31, 1991 the Soviet Union ceased to exist, and each of the union republics emerged as a sovereign state. This caused dramatic changes in the library sphere. The collapse of the Soviet Union broke nearly all the links that had tied the library system together; the exchange of publications among the former union republics actually stopped, and the once-broad information space was narrowed down to the scope of each particular state. The isolation of information of the former partners was even more evident from the West's perspective. The situation seemed paradoxical: In an age of information resources integrated on a worldwide scale, it was easier for Russia to acquire publications from distant lands than from neighboring states that were now foreign countries.

Recognizing the great losses suffered by science and culture here, some efforts have been made recently to restore information links. National libraries have revived their direct contacts, reestablishing publication exchanges on contractual principles. The Interparliamentary Assembly of the Commonwealth of Independent States (IPA CIS), established to coordinate activities of the new states, considered and adopted a legislative instrument entitled "On a Uniform Policy in the Sphere of the Legal Deposit Copy of Documents," also approving a draft agreement "On the Interstate Exchange of Legal Deposit Copies of Documents of state-members of the Commonwealth of Independent States." With a view to reestablishing the lost contacts between libraries, an international public organization—the Eurasia Library Assembly—was founded in 1992, seeking to promote partnership contacts between national and other libraries in the former union republics. Their coming together is a positive process, even though progress has been inhibited by economic hardships.

CHANGES IN THE SYSTEM OF NATIONAL LIBRARIES

The state-political reorganizations within the former Soviet Union, and the transformation of many of the union republics into sovereign states, triggered the strengthening of national library functions. Each of the former union republics created national libraries from what had been their state republic libraries.

The Russian library system has been likewise subject to change. In particular, the period of social changes brought about a growth in national consciousness among the member-entities of the Russian Federation. All the republics encompassed by the Russian Federation have reorganized their regional libraries as national ones, proposing to collect and store the written memory of their nations. These libraries are currently functioning in twenty republics of the Russian Federation.

In parallel with branch libraries, major USSR libraries, previously in union subordination, have now come under the jurisdiction of Russia. Changes occurred, for example, in the status of the former USSR State V. I. Lenin Library. This institution, proclaimed in February 1925 as the All-Union (i.e., national) Library of the Soviet Union, was reorganized in accordance with new Russian state library regulations approved by the government of the Federation, and on August 2, 1993 gained its current status as an all-Russia national library. Thus, as a result of state reorganization in Russia, there appeared another national library—the Russian State Library, or RGB. The situation has grown out of the country's historical process and was formalized as such by a Federation law, "On Library Service," adopted in late 1994. One should bear in mind that Russia already possessed a national library—the Saltykov-Shchedrin State Public Library of the Russian Soviet Federated Socialist Republic, which has, since its founding in 1795, functioned in the role of Russia's national library, the title by which it is known today. A special decree of the president of Russia, "On the National Library of Russia," of March 27, 1992 confirmed its status. A similar situation occurred in Germany with two national libraries—the Deutsche Bibliothek in Frankfurt am Main and the Deutsche Bücherei in Leipzig—after the reunification of the German Democratic Republic and the Federal Republic of Germany. These were, however, integrated into one library, designated as Die Deutsche Bibliothek.

One can perceive a certain meaning in the new names for the two national libraries in Russia. The first to be established was designated as the "National" library, in an attempt to emphasize the right of seniority; the other, by being designated as the "State" library, made clear its relationship to the government.

The existence of two national libraries in the country imposes the need for new approaches to the organization of their functions. There is a need to seek an organic interaction on the principles of equity, with no discrimination between the two. In the many years of their existence, the national libraries have always maintained certain links and a degree of collaboration. With the changing situation, the nature of collaboration between them has likewise changed. In each of the situations, the metropolitan libraries (be it the Imperial Public Library in St. Petersburg—presently, the Russian National Library—or the USSR State V. I. Lenin Library in Moscow—now, the Russian State Library) held key positions by definition. Today, the two libraries are formally equal in rights, though one should not fail to realize that de jure status and de facto reality are never the same.

The Russian State Library (RGB), functioning for many years as the Soviet Union's main library, is still anxious to maintain its leading position, often extending its all-union functions to the territory of Russia. It is in a more favorable geopolitical situation than the Russian National Library (RNB). It is located in the capital and has greater material resources in addition to well-developed international contacts. All these would contribute to the RGB's retaining its leading position in library service.

Nevertheless, the RNB has been functioning as Russia's national library for the whole of its history. In consequence, it has stronger ties with the country's regional libraries, acting as a leading research and methodology center within the Russian Federation. It holds the richest collection of national literature and pre-revolutionary Rossica and offers a better-developed catalog system. All these would justify the library's leading position in library service as well.

The existence of two leaders provokes scrutiny as to whether there is a distinction between them and whether the country needs two national libraries. In tackling these questions, one should first note that the status of national libraries is generally established by a formal decree, yet it is not a decree that determines the essence of a national library. National libraries cannot be established spontaneously; rather, they are products of a prolonged historical period, growing along with their countries, collecting the most-valued monuments of domestic history and culture and becoming monuments of culture in themselves. The emergence of two national library centers in our country is, on the one hand, a result of the complex history of our state and, on the other, evidence of the immense intellectual potential in our culture and the Russian community's social demand for the institutions. Their necessity and unique nature have been confirmed by the decrees of the president of Russia that named both national libraries among the most-valued features of the cultural heritage of nations within the Russian Federation, thus placing them in the top protection and registration category involving special forms of government support. There can be no question of the wisdom of having two national libraries rather than one. There is little point in destroying what has been built up by generations.

Of course, the existence of two national libraries necessitates a line of demarcation between their functions, which indeed are largely similar. It cannot have been otherwise, considering the libraries' history. Analysis of the functions of these two institutions indicates frequent overlapping: some of them, associated with in-house activities, the libraries can manage independently, while others ought to be strictly coordinated. On the other hand, each of the libraries has a specificity whose priorities can be taken into account in drawing the line.

Sitting in November of 1995 to discuss the RGB's activities as the country's national library, the Federation's Ministry of Culture Board voted the organization of work in this direction a failure. The judgment is, of course, of a temporary nature and can be revised in the near future. The Board advised the national libraries of Russia—the RGB and the RNB—to work toward an agreement of collaboration and division of functions.

On this basis, the libraries themselves, in a fairly short time, worked out the "Agreement of Partnership and Cooperation between the Russian State Library and the National Library of

Russia," signed at the end of May 1996. The agreement provides for cooperation between the two national libraries in developing and storing the national library stock, ensuring access (through bibliographic records, cataloging, improved library-bibliographic classification, automation and services), scientific research and science-based methodology, and international activities. Work on the document indicated the possibilities of successful cooperation between the libraries in sorting out their functions.

The situation with the national libraries has been complicated by the fact that in our country some of the typical national library functions—legal deposit, current bibliographic records, and state archivation of printed matter—are entrusted to the Russian Book Chamber (RKP), an institution specially founded for this purpose. The RKP has suggested a collaboration with the two national libraries in creating national bibliographic records. This would not be a short-term arrangement, but rather a sustained effort over a fairly long period requiring a balanced analysis of the division and coordination of activities between the national libraries and their collaboration with the Book Chamber.

This small example helps to illustrate a larger point: the number of problems demanding solution in the library service of Russia is so large that it is only with the united efforts of the two national libraries and other institutions that even a portion can be handled.

CHANGES IN THE SOCIAL ROLE OF LIBRARIES IN THE COMMUNITY

The social changes occurring in Russia in recent years can be regarded without exaggeration as revolutionary. In the last decade the society has become more dynamic, enterprising, and open to the acceptance of new ideas. The sphere of human effort and energy has been greatly extended, with new structures emerging in politics and the economy as well as increasing democracy in all areas of public and social life. The whole of public life has been changing.

The most vivid manifestation of these processes were the political transformations that opened the way for dramatic change in the community's spiritual life and which in turn initiated the many-sided (and frequently contradictory) process of democratization. These caused manifold changes, both on the community scale and in terms of library service.

Among the more profound changes is the new social role of culture and libraries in the country. As has been mentioned, culture in the Soviet period was an instrument supporting the policy of the party; hence, the state controlled the libraries' activities, seeking to make them promoters of party policy. In return, the state took responsibility for the libraries' material welfare, constructing buildings and making allocations for book and equipment purchasing. The result was a tremendously ramified system of cultural institutions, which encompassed practically all the functions of libraries.

Political changes in Russia resulted in the elimination of the party's monopoly and the declaration of the principle of political neutrality for libraries. This in turn led to the deideologization of their activities, rejecting unified state control in determining the content of activities for cultural institutions. The character of stock development likewise changed; libraries came to acquire publications without regard to the author's ideology or book content, and the Rossica and Sovietica holdings were expanded to include foreign acquisitions previously strictly regulated.

Restrictions regarding the service provided to users were also lifted, with access to information extended, censorship abolished, restricted-access stocks opened, restrictions for political or religious considerations eliminated, and the scope of lecturing and exhibition subjects expanded. Profound changes are evident even in bibliographic activities: the Library-Bibliographic system of cataloging is being updated, and the scale and range of recommendatory bibliography has been altered.

By and large, there have been fundamental changes in the general orientation of library service—from the propaganda and promotion of the policies of the Communist Party of the Soviet Union toward developing the ideas of humanism and national and universal values. There has been a revival of the original mission of libraries—to accumulate and communicate knowledge, information, and cultural values to the broadest possible audience, meeting the users' demands. The country is witnessing an increased demand for library service, with a growing reading public, increased library attendance, and expanded circulation.

There are several reasons for the resurgent popularity of libraries in Russia. It is rooted primarily in the need for information to evaluate the past, present, and future, a demand that generally increases in periods of radical change and grandiose reforms. Another reason is the changing curricula of both the existing and rapidly emerging new educational establishments. New textbooks being insufficient, particularly in the humanities, users are more frequently forced to turn to the primary sources held by libraries. Yet another important factor is a significant rise in prices for printed matter (by many times over) with a general decline in living standards for most of the public. Libraries in present-day Russia are actually the only seat of both free education and entertainment, providing access to cultural and intellectual property.

An undeniably positive result of these trends is that librarians are striving to orient their activities toward public needs; they are, figuratively speaking, turning around to face the reader. This aim has changed some library structures. For example, there used to be strict distinctions, at least in urban areas, between adult and child services; now "family reading libraries" are being established. Similarly, an increasing number of libraries are focusing on specific segments of the reading public—women, youth, handicapped persons, connoisseurs, entrepreneurs, and many others.

There is a new understanding of libraries as cultural institutions and public authorities. Culture has ceased to be an instrument supporting state policy and catering to the demands of government bodies; it has thus ceased to be necessary for the authorities. This could not but affect the status and economic situation of libraries; at present, they are suffering grave financial hardships in maintaining their functions. At the same time, culture and libraries are attractive as an object in political games; an important dimension of election campaigns involves the use of culture-saving catchwords, which helps culture survive in many critical periods of the country's development.

The situation of library service in Russia is thus still complicated and contradictory. However, there have been some obvious changes for the better. While in the early 1990s Russia maintained a totalitarian-state library system in a state of crisis and decay, today there is a rapidly developing library environment in a new, open society. In the process of building up the society, libraries are in the avant-garde.

DEVELOPMENT OF THE PUBLIC-PROFESSIONAL LIBRARY MOVEMENT

In the period of major social changes in Russia, the library community gave serious support to the idea of developing a public-professional movement to intensify the role of libraries in the community, promote their interests, and establish and maintain professional contacts. With these goals in view, the Russian Library Association (RBA) was established in Moscow in 1994 and set itself the task of uniting the public to contribute to the development of the library sphere in Russia and the social protection of librarians' rights.

The RBA represented the reestablishment of an all-Russia public library movement. The earliest library-bibliographic associations in Russia emerged more than a hundred years ago. Since then various forms of professional public movements have come and gone, but the idea remains. The rigid central organization of all spheres of public life from the 1920s to the 1970s destroyed public library organizations. Coordination of library activities was implemented by administrative public bodies; the All-Union Library Council, with its Bureau, held plenary sessions; and interdepartmental library commissions were universally established under the USSR Ministry of Culture, under corresponding ministries in union republics, and by culture administrations in territories, regions, towns, and districts. This limited the possibilities for the public to influence library service, inhibiting lower-level librarians' initiatives. The situation began to change during the period of *perestroika* in the late 1980s, and a whole series of associations, societies, and unions emerged on the regional level. However, attempts at creating an efficient public organization for librarians within Russia proved a failure.

Establishment of the RBA was an act of necessity to enhance the public library movement, uniting the efforts and coordinating the actions of not only societies and associations, but also library staffs of all levels, types, and specializations, bibliographic and information facilities, educational institutions, and other services and public organizations, in the interest of maintaining and developing library service in Russia.

The basic strategies of the RBA were defined in a general form:

- To contribute to the development and implementation of federal and regional library policies and professional programs;
- To assist in the social protection of librarians, and enhance the status of libraries in the community;
- To organize multilateral professional contacts and to assist in the professional development and training of all levels of library staff;
- To represent and defend interests of the library community of Russia on federal and international levels.

Since its founding, the RBA has carried out a number of activities directed toward the attainment of these goals. During the preparation of federal laws on library service and legal deposit issues, RBA members actively participated in their development and discussions. Approval of these laws by government bodies was hindered by a series of objective and subjective factors: both were submitted twice for the consideration of the Supreme Soviet, the State Duma, and the Presidential Administration of the Russian Federation but failed to obtain a final decision. When the laws had passed the State Duma and were submitted to the Presidential Administration for the third time, the RBA sent a direct appeal to President Yeltsin requesting his support for the laws as the basic instruments ensuring the functioning and growth of libraries in Russia. Both laws were signed on December 29, 1994. A more recent signal event in Russian library life was the establishment, on application of the RBA, of the All-Russia Library Day by decree of the president of Russia of May 27, 1995. This celebration coincided with the bicentenary of Russia's first public library.

The RBA Board has now specified a range of problems requiring federal-level developments. The foremost concerns the need to establish, through appropriate laws and administrative ordinances, a clear definition of the responsibilities of state and local governments for the protection and development of library services on the one hand and the libraries' responsibilities before the community on the other. Another important goal is the definition of a uniform recommended format of machine-readable records for libraries in Russia in order to create an integrated electronic catalog eventually with links to all the regions. The RBA Board has also pointed to research in the preservation of the book holdings as representing nothing less than the preservation of the common memory of Russia.

Particular emphasis is placed by the RBA on establishing contacts with government structures. To familiarize the public with the problems faced by libraries, the RBA initiated publication of the *RBA Information Bulletin,* containing official federal, regional, and international documents; information on major professional activities; and news from library communities, associations, and libraries in the country. At present, two issues have been published, and a third is in preparation. Since June 1995 the RBA has been sponsoring publication of a special supplementary sheet to the journal *Biblioteka* (Library) discussing activities of the International Federation of Library Associations (IFLA); systematic information has also been published by the secretariat of the IFLA Russian Committee and the IFLA information center in Russia. These publications provide our colleagues with information on major professional problems faced by librarians in Russia and the world library community, contributing to a better recognition of the need for joint efforts among library staffs.

In implementing the planned professional programs, the RBA collaborated with the RGB and the RNB to hold, with the assistance of the IFLA, an international seminar on authority files, inviting the participation of major specialists from Germany, the United States, the United Kingdom, Finland, France, Slovakia, the Czech Republic, Poland, Byelorussia, Lithuania, and Russia. This meeting was convened in St. Petersburg in October of 1995. At the moment, the RBA is working on finding ways to implement the "Russian Libraries on the Internet" program, which extends to the country's major libraries. A series of actions is being taken under the library collections preservation program.

RBA activities are not limited to the top echelon of the RBA Board. Many RBA regional members carry out a range of public-professional activities that deserve attention and distribution in other regions. In particular, mention should be made of the Moscow Library Association, the St. Petersburg Library Society, the Association of Librarians in Kurgan, and the Ryazan Library

Society, among others. Fruitful efforts have also been made by the Eurasia Library Assembly, represented in the RBA by a Russian branch recently accredited as an observer at the CIS Interparliamentary Assembly. In addition, the RBA's headquarters has received numerous requests from libraries and public organizations concerning the establishment of roundtables and subject panels on various issues in library life, thus proving their growing interest in, and hopes for, RBA activities.

At the same time, many regions of Russia have shown no signs of developing a public library movement. Library staff in these areas can see either no reason or no means of applying their efforts to the activities of professional associations and so acknowledge no reason for their establishment. This indicates that the RBA should look for new forms of public cooperation among librarians to arouse public activity. The first step toward this goal was the festivities surrounding the celebration of the first All-Russia Library Day, the theme of which was to honor the initiative of librarians, their roles as contributors to the development of science and culture, and their work promoting knowledge among the general public. This will certainly be followed by other efforts.

THE IMPACT OF THE NEW ECONOMIC CONDITIONS ON LIBRARIES

The new economic structure in Russia has influenced many aspects of libraries' activities, reflecting the broad impact of economic changes throughout social life—in publishing, book trade, transportation and communication costs, customs and tax regulations, and in the general decrease in living standards.

The transition from rigid governmental control to the market, from a centralized line of command to a greater emphasis on the local authorities, has also seriously impinged on the life of libraries.

All this led to the need for library directors to pay more attention to economics; as a rule, they presently devote most of their time to dealing with such questions, a significant change from the usual work of library directors just five years ago.

In the way of financing, little has changed. As before, federal libraries get their money from ministries and regional ones are provided for by local authorities. However, the regulation of expenses and the distribution of income have undergone drastic reform. Formerly, all expenses were outlined well in advance and could not be revised at a later stage; there were no additional possibilities to search for more income. Library budgets were allocated by officials, and any money collected in excess of these revenues went to the state. By contrast, libraries today plan their own economic activities and may raise funds at their own discretion. Quite recently, in something of a reversal, we have seen new attempts to impose a greater degree of governmental control over library fund-raising activities.

The financial standing of the libraries is greatly influenced by the attitude displayed by local administrations. In order to function, libraries have to prove that they are essential; they must fight for whatever they can get. On the whole, there exist prospering Russian libraries while at the same time quite a few can hardly make ends meet. Many have simply closed down.

The federal libraries also feel the severe crisis in the domestic economy. For instance, during early 1996, they did not receive the minimum necessary to pay salaries. Even the national libraries are financed at barely 10 percent of what they really need, and if this situation continues, the consequences will be grave. Fearing this, libraries are attempting to lobby the legislative and executive branches in an effort to reverse a dangerous trend. Ultimately, however, the new economic order may well influence positively the financial standing of libraries—if the state clearly defines, and then carries out, its obligation to support them.

Recent social changes in Russia have brought a variety of new problems for libraries. It is impossible to list them all in the space of a brief report, to say nothing of examining the particulars. Along with the complications that have emerged in the everyday life of the libraries, however, they have acquired new possibilities for carrying out their social functions. They still remain the source of a great cultural influence. Many have begun extensive technical modernization efforts, introducing computers and developing Internet access. International cooperation has also increased significantly, in both directions. All this leads to a sound basis for optimism on the future of Russian libraries.

Klaus-Dieter Lehmann

Making the Transitory Permanent: The Intellectual Heritage in a Digitized World of Knowledge

THE RISING TIDE OF KNOWLEDGE

S CHOLARLY TEXTS AND INFORMATION have long since ceased to be identified exclusively with printed publications on paper. To an increasing extent, information is being provided and disseminated in digital form, whether on physical media, such as floppy disks, magnetic tapes, or CD-ROMs, or in nonmaterial form as networked publications.

Today even the print media rely largely upon electronic word processing as one of several possible modes of issue. Ultimately, the decision to utilize a particular form of issue and distribution is dictated by market factors and the level of acceptance among users. We can be certain, however, that users—especially those involved in scholarship and research—will opt for contemporary methods of generating and disseminating information.

More than sixty million people all over the world now communicate through the electronic network. On the Internet alone, the volume of data transmitted in a single day is equivalent to five hundred thousand books of two hundred pages each. The Internet continues to grow by 10 to 15 percent each month. This massive exchange of data and information on a global scale is unprecedented in our history. While it is true that the majority of data transferred is intended for communication purposes, rather than

Klaus-Dieter Lehmann is Director General of Die Deutsche Bibliothek in Germany.

for publication, and although the classical publishing houses do not yet regard the Internet as a medium for publication, the Internet is rapidly establishing itself as an alternative academic medium—a development influenced in part by changes in relationships among authors, publishers, and libraries.[1] The pace of this trend varies from one academic field to another and depends upon a particular discipline's need to maintain currency, the number of publications it produces annually, its international stature, and its relative size within the academic community.

The supply of digital information encompasses much more than new publications and presentations of recent research results, however. Academic communication through data networks has now become such a dynamic force that programs for the retrospective digitization of large library collections are now being planned and implemented in increasing numbers. From a national standpoint, the process of digitizing older literature is regarded as an undertaking of strategic significance for both the academic community and the economy. Not only will it affect the quality of access to academic information and opportunities for research, it will also alter the quantitative relationship between print and digital media in the medium term. The programs now being carried out in the United States and France illustrate just how ambitious such measures in support of digital libraries have become. Within the framework of a national digital library, the Library of Congress will have digitized five million items of Americana by the year 2000. Congress has approved expenditures of $15 million for this effort. A total of $24.4 million in grants has been provided by the National Aeronautics and Space Administration (NASA) and the National Science Foundation (NSF) to six universities for the purpose of developing and optimizing suitable tools for virtual digital libraries. France is pursuing the bold objective of offering one hundred thousand digitized books and microfilms through the Internet on the occasion of the opening of the new Bibliothèque Nationale de France in 1996–1997 and expanding this digital library to include three hundred thousand books by the year 2000. Upon completion of its new building in early 1997, Die Deutsche Bibliothek will have an information infrastructure at its disposal that will enable it to begin digitizing its collections, an effort intended both to supplement existing approaches to the preservation of library holdings and to make them available to users in digital form. A modest pilot project to be carried out in conjunction with the Börsenverein des Deutschen Buchhandels will be devoted to compiling a canon of German-language publications, fiction and nonfiction, according to qualitative criteria: *1,000 books—A German library.* The collection is to be digitized and offered through the Internet. The Deutsche Forschungsgemeinschaft has provided an important planning instrument, "Neue Informations-Infrastrukturen für Forschung und Lehre."[2] This essay calls for the immediate establishment of a decentrally-organized library of digital research collections. To support the development of such a distributed research library in Germany, the author recommends the institution of a special funding program with the federal and state governments' participation through the Bund-Länder-Kommission. It is suggested that funds be made available for the improvement of hardware facilities within the framework of the "Hochschulbauförderungsgesetz" (law regarding university construction, or HBFG). The intention is to accomplish rapid implementation of innovative application systems through pilot projects.

Of particular interest is the recommendation to combine the efforts of the federal and state governments and the Deutsche Forschungsgemeinschaft under a joint promotion concept in support of new information infrastructures, thus consolidating both resources and specific measures.

THE POOR MEMORY OF DIGITAL PUBLICATIONS

The fact that academic information doubles in quantity every ten to fifteen years and that the high cost of production, combined with falling numbers of copies sold, make print media increasingly and disproportionately expensive underscores the need for new solutions with respect to academic publications. Digital publications can offer an alternative in this regard, at least in some areas. The new and appealing characteristics of digital publications have a favorable effect on this development: unlimited availability, a range of different options for provision to users, flexible access (selectivity), easily updatable versions, interactivity, and short cycle times.

Because of the potential to integrate digital library collections into the working environment, thereby expanding resources and accelerating access, we can expect to see an increased willingness to digitize older collections. However, this positive attitude towards digitization also harbors a danger—namely, that aside from using digitized texts and information for the benefits that their innovative qualities offer for academic work, digitization may come to be regarded as a panacea for all of the real and imagined problems libraries now face in connection with the preservation of physical collections: the growing need for storage space, the deterioration of books due to acid paper, and the rising costs of library operation. Libraries are not merely streamlined service centers; books are more than containers of text. They are cultural and intellectual indicators of the first order. Therefore, scholars and librarians must join in developing strategies focused upon specific rather than generalized solutions—strategies that ensure books their proper place and approach the use of digital forms in an appropriate manner without regard to ideology.

The political demand for the creation of an academic workplace without a media break strikes me as a rather more technocratic articulation of the problem. I would welcome a media break that reflects the quality criteria and working methods of users.

The shining vision of global communication tempts many people to regard libraries as old-fashioned. Communication is not merely a global phenomenon, however. We should seek out and promote local and regional solutions, which can then be linked with global resources. The information society must not be allowed to replace historically-established spheres of human communication. We should strive, therefore, to promote libraries for the good of the public. Libraries must remain centers of intellectual stimulus and human encounter in addition to their role as nodes in a global network.

Without doubt, digital publications not only improve the conditions of production in economic terms but also offer new qualities capable of influencing the process of scientific discovery in a decisive manner and accelerating it as well. Their widespread use involves risks, however, especially when it is not guided by an critical, discerning approach.

The way to the information society has already been paved. For missionary computer gurus and incorrigible pessimists alike, one thing is above dispute: the new knowledge, in its predominant form, is short-lived, transitory knowledge. Although information itself is theoretically indestructible, the medium in which it is stored is anything but. Long-term availability is an essential criterion for sources of information and should be given careful consideration. The following characteristics and circumstances pose the greatest danger to the long-term availability of digital publications:

Physical deterioration of digital information. Given the present state of digital storage media, information can be preserved for a period of between five and thirty years. Magnetic media, from the floppy to the digital audio tape (DAT), may lose some portions of their information in just a few years. CD-ROMs have a life expectancy of fifty years. At present there is no storage medium in sight that would eliminate the need to recopy.

Changes in coding and formats. Information retrieval requires an internal character-coding structure and a data format for the recognition of coded substantive content. This structure changes every ten to twenty years. The current state of development does not offer much hope for achieving permanently applicable standards and rules in the foreseeable future. It is this rapid evolution of information technology itself that offers the greatest potential for further development.

Changes in software, operating systems, and hardware. Hardware and software—the keys that provide access to coded information—are changing constantly; developments in this area are fully capable of rendering existing collections of information obsolete. In addition, marketing strategies are often designed deliberately to exclude both forward and retroactive compatibility by means of inaccessible core components of operating systems, hidden objects in software programs, or protective mechanisms in processors.

System-based causes. By their very nature, hypertext documents cannot be reproduced or stored locally, as their linkage systems exist only within the network itself. Coded instructions provide options with respect to the interrelationships among the various parts of a document; the user is free to create new publications by combining document segments.

Economic limitations. In modern society, information diminishes in value within a very short period of time. Publications in some fields are out of date after only a few years. This fosters the attitude that such publications represent throwaway materials.

Radical delocalization of processing and decentralization of data bases. As a rule, data is made available where it originates but can be downloaded from any other location whenever it is needed. This arrangement does not provide a framework for a binding commitment to long-term availability. Networking leads to a reduction in the geographic distribution of information. In extreme cases, a digital publication may be stored on only a single server in the global network. The decision as to how long it is to remain available on a particular server is made on an individual basis. This leads to uncertainties with respect to both long-term availability and, in light of their inadequate reference-ability, the authenticity of digital publications.

These are a few of the most notable features of digital publications. They are cited here as evidence of the transitory nature of knowledge recorded and stored in this manner and on these media, and they illustrate the difficulties we face with respect to long-term preservation.

The large-scale use of new technologies places the cultural and intellectual heritage of an entire epoch at risk. Is our society to become a faceless one?

THE INTELLECTUAL AND CULTURAL INFRASTRUCTURE

Umberto Eco was once asked during a reading how a person of average intelligence could be expected to stay ahead of things in the information society.[3] Increasingly vast bodies of knowledge are becoming inaccessible to people with average educations; increasingly exotic fields of knowledge are asserting their own languages and forms of presentation. Eco replied that he did not believe we faced a future of boundless, incomprehensible knowledge, but rather an epoch of forgetting in which human memory would survive only in fragments. It would become increasingly easier, he thought, for people with very little knowledge to impress others.

Both of these positions—resignation in the face of the tidal wave of knowledge and fear of a world culture full of blind spots—represent opposite sides of the same coin. No matter how all-encompassing and tightly woven the global data network becomes, doubts will continue to grow as to whether this exchange of knowledge is built upon a lasting foundation.

Libraries have always been an essential component of the cultural and intellectual infrastructure. They are treasure houses, cultural tools, and service institutions. Their value lies in their capacity to preserve sources and provide access.

They do not belong to a single generation alone but instead link the past and the present. In their long history, libraries have witnessed a number of technical changes, but none so radical as the current one. It seems that, at a time in which the vision of a global virtual library can become a technical reality, libraries have begun to dissolve, particularly where they exist only on servers distributed throughout the network and their users navigate freely over the global network as electronic nomads.

In dealing with digital publications we are now concerned with more than identification, selection, and administration by libraries. The preservation of intellectual property is also at stake. If libraries fail to take an active part in shaping this aspect of their role, they will soon lose their function as providers of information and as the objective memory of our cultural heritage. The immediate issue is not the libraries themselves, however, but their users. In our culture, libraries guarantee users unlimited access while providing the framework for the growth of relationships between an individualized society and the cultural tradition and its historical dimension. I would like to think of this as the economy of culture. It is expressed not only in marks or dollars but also in the acceptance of values. It is this field of responsibility that libraries must continue to preserve and develop. As Goethe once observed, "A library that is not kept up soon grows old."

Although Goethe surely did not have digital publications in mind, his comment is applicable to our own situation. Paper is not a suitable criterion for an exhaustive definition of library responsibilities.

Why is long-term preservation so important in this context? What is its particular value? Publications are expressions of our cultural and intellectual activities and endeavors. Every culture relies upon a heritage nurtured throughout its history, not as a cult of the past, but as a lasting and durable bond between tradition and the constantly-changing present. Conventional publications are no longer an adequate source of information for a segment of the academic community. On-line data bases, on-line reprints, and CD-ROMs provide viable alternatives, and to a certain extent progress in scholarship and research is taking place in precisely these digital media.

When gaps and defects begin to appear in our intellectual heritage—and this will happen if we fail to provide for preservation on a large scale and include digital publications in our efforts—our culture will be at risk or, at best, will have diminished in quality. And that is saying a great deal.

THE DIGITAL DEPOSIT LIBRARY

Just as important as our commitment to books is the realization that digital publications are also a part of our library collections and that we must intensify our efforts in this regard.[4] If libraries were to exclude certain information media in the future, we would soon find ourselves faced with a variety of barriers to access. The obligation to preserve print collections for the benefit of future generations, a commitment embraced by nearly all major countries of the world, should naturally be extended to include digital publications as well. Although the form of issue is not the same, the content and purpose of such publications is in no way different from those of printed materials.

The fact that the long-term preservation of digital publications is likely to cause considerable problems should hardly influence the decision about whether or not to pursue the objective. Instead, it should provide the impetus to develop appropriate methods. In many cases national libraries have been assigned a role as deposit libraries. They are responsible for the comprehensive collection of all publications issued in a given country; they prepare the national bibliography and guarantee the authenticity of publications through preservation and cataloging, thus providing protection for intellectual property. As a rule, collection takes place in accordance with provisions of the law. In the future, such laws should be amended to cover digital publications as well.

Die Deutsche Bibliothek is required by law to collect all publications (text, image, and sound) appearing in Germany and all German-language publications issued abroad, to index them in accordance with the principles of the national bibliography, to preserve them on a long-term basis, and to make them available for public use. Today, Die Deutsche Bibliothek is present at three locations: in Leipzig with the Deutsche Bücherei, in Frankfurt am Main with the Deutsche Bibliothek, and in Berlin with the Deutsches Musikarchiv.[5]

The foundation for the consolidation of collections comprising fourteen million books and the continued operation of these three great cultural archives at their original locations was established with the reunification of Germany in 1990. Based upon a redefined system of task distribution, a new, future-oriented organization was formed; its achievements have clearly surpassed previous performance levels.

The most important cornerstone was laid in 1991 by the first unified German parliament (the *Bundestag*), which approved the construction of a new library building in Frankfurt am Main. This decision represented a response to the profound changes in the library and publishing environment, brought about by new information and communication technology, and to the recognized need for long-term preservation and accessibility of digital publications. Thus, the new library will be equipped with complex computer and network technology, making it both a house of books and an electronic archive. Operations in the new building are scheduled to begin in 1997.

The enhanced potential for cooperation with the large German libraries, particularly the state libraries in Berlin and Munich, will then be put to even more productive use. Structured according to the principle of federalism, Germany has always had several different centers of intellectual and cultural activity. For this reason, the concept of the national library in Germany clearly departs from the centralistic approach; it is based upon decentralization and cooperation. While Die Deutsche Bibliothek carries out its mission as the general archive of German-language publications and the national bibliographic center, the libraries in Munich and Berlin offer large international collections. Die Deutsche Bibliothek is a partner in international networking, particularly in its cooperation with national libraries abroad. The new building comes at the right time and to the right place. Die Deutsche Bibliothek will begin operations in its new headquarters at the same time the new facilities for the British Library in London and the Bibliothèque Nationale de France in Paris are completed, thus fulfilling an essential requirement for effective cultural dialogue in Europe.

Not only will the new building for Die Deutsche Bibliothek provide sufficient book-storage capacity for the decades to come, it will also be equipped with the innovative technology required to meet the needs of the twenty-first century. Thus, the library will be able to expand its collection mandate in a consistent manner to include digital publications as well. The currently applicable law covers publications distributed in physical form, i.e., print media, printed music and music publications, sound recordings, and electronic publications on data media (CD-ROM, floppy disks, etc.). Publications must be defined with reference to content, however, rather than to the medium on which they appear; thus, it makes little sense to distinguish between on-line and off-line publications. This distinction is ultimately made by producers based upon marketing policy considerations and often leads to the issue of parallel versions of a publication on different media. Die Deutsche Bibliothek has a binding obligation as a legal deposit library to collect digital publications, regardless of the medium on which they appear.

The current state of technology and the new forms of publication production and distribution that derive from it demand that the existing law be amended. A draft version of the new law is scheduled for presentation to the legislature during the current session. A number of different national libraries are either already operating under amended laws designed to cover new forms of publication or are preparing drafts for such legislation.

Having joined in a concerted effort to produce the framework of the Telematics Program of the European Commission, the European national libraries sponsored a study concerned with the most important aspects to be considered in preparing legislation regarding the preservation of digital publications.[6] The results were discussed and approved by publishers and librarians participating in a workshop conducted in Luxembourg in December 1995. The study provides a sound basis for national legislative initiatives and contains concrete recommendations for specific projects to solve problems of information technology and organization. The following specific topics were considered: the necessity of long-term preservation; the responsibilities of legal deposit libraries; cooperation between national libraries and publishers; collection guidelines; technical infrastructure; national bibliographic records; and availability. The study was conducted by the Dutch consulting firm nbbi (John S. Mackenzie Owen and Jan van de Walle). The steering committee was comprised of the directors of the British Library, Die Deutsche Bibliothek, and the Royal Library in The Hague.[7]

Participating librarians and publishers followed the study's recommendations, particularly with respect to the principle of assigning legal deposit responsibilities for digital publications to the national libraries. Publishers and representatives of the national libraries agreed to cooperate closely in developing concepts and experimental models. A joint task group has been established for the purpose of defining and managing mutual project activities, which will receive funding under the two-year CoBRA + program. CoBRA + is a concerted undertaking on the part of European national libraries within the framework of the Telematics Program of the European Union and is concerned primarily with issues such as metadata, bibliographic control, and the long-term preservation of digital publications. Results are to be made available to all interested libraries.

In its recommendations contained in the paper entitled "Elektronische Publikationen im Literatur- und Informationsangebot wissenschaftlicher Bibliotheken" ("Electronic Publications as a Part of the Collection of Literature and Information Provided by Academic Libraries"),[8] the Deutsche Forschungsgemeinschaft also cites the urgent need for long-term availability of digital publications that are capable of being referenced. The authors also emphasize the necessity of establishing legal deposit regulations for digital publications that would include measures devoted to ensuring long-term preservation. According to their findings, Die Deutsche Bibliothek is well-suited to assume this responsibility, and they point out that expanding the mandate for long-term preservation will also guarantee that the national bibliographic processing of digital publications actually takes place. Bibliographic data generated in this way should be made available on a national and international basis; this would apply as well to the indexing and navigation instruments required, which, like printed materials, should be designed to meet data-sharing needs at the regional and local levels.

Once established in its new building, Die Deutsche Bibliothek will have the technical platform it urgently needs in order to meet its expanded responsibilities. Specific measures in support of this infrastructure will be initiated in cooperation with German academic libraries and closely coordinated with publishers. Close cooperation with the European national libraries is also assured.[9] As the conditions governing electronics technology change so rapidly, it will be necessary to give all decisions thorough consideration. Every decision made will involve substantial capital investments as well as the allocation of personnel resources, a strong willingness to accept innovation, the testing and use of complex communication interfaces, and a further commitment to international cooperation.

COLLECTION GUIDELINES

It would appear wise to choose as general a definition as possible for the collection mandate at first, in order to provide for future developments. The guidelines should then be made more specific through the process of excluding certain publication forms. Finally, a strategy for practical implementation, permitting a step-by-step approach to this complex field of applications, should be developed. Based upon these premises, collection guidelines could be formulated in the following way: The publication must be available in digital form and intended for distribution—it makes no difference whether it appears on a physical medium or as a networked publication; parallel versions in printed and digital form must both be submitted; and, as a rule, data base entries are to be treated as copies in accordance with the definition contained in ARTICLE 16 UrhG (German Copyright Law). The following items should be exempted from the collection mandate (for example): *1)* public communications and news (e-mail, NetNews, listservs); *2)* messages, forums; *3)* advertising and publications that serve purely commercial, business, or corporate purposes; *4)* computer games; *5)* distributed publications (hyperlinks); *6)* media containing no data in the form of text, images, or sound; *7)* publications subject to very frequent updating; *8)* parallel issues of different digital versions; and *9)* publications not amenable to controlled preservation within the existing infrastructure of the legal deposit library.

Certainly, the collection guidelines will have to be made more precise in order to insure that there is a strategic concept available to meet the very complex requirements of the task—"beginning with the easy and proceeding to the difficult." The long-term preservation of digital publications is frontier country. Thus, selection must take place in such a way that risks remain calculable and experience can be gained step-by-step. Initially, publications that employ established technical platforms and appear on physical data media should be selected. Exotic structures should be excluded. Classical publishing houses should be given first consideration as suppliers in order to insure that we have stable, bug-free products (electronic periodicals and books) with which to work. Expansion can then take place gradually. Dynamic publications should be collected in chronological increments, whereby one could store only the first and most recent issue or opt for longer intervals, such as a year.

Neither data format nor data media should be used as criteria for the selection of digital publications. The library must be free to convert publications to the form it regards as most appropriate for preservation purposes. We must accept the fact that a growing number of dynamic or distributed publications will not be stored in the digital deposit library. In this context the library can act only as a reference server, citing publications by means of addresses.

The efficiency of the library's deposit function depends to a significant degree on the willingness of publishers to cooperate. Thus, in addition to the collection guidelines, agreements in support of the goal of long-term preservation should be established between the library and publishers:

- Digital publications should be stored together with all supplementary materials (documentation, manuals, etc.) with which they are ordinarily sold and used.

- Where given publications are accessible only in conjunction with proprietary hardware and software and sold in combination with them, these accessory hardware and software items must be submitted as well.
- Where identical versions of a digital publication are available on different media (floppy disk, CD-ROM), the library should have the option to choose the medium it regards as most appropriate for storage purposes.
- In view of the anticipated need to convert a commercially available digital form to a form more suitable for storage, publishers must grant the library the right to reproduce all publications intended for preservation.
- Digital publications must be submitted in impeccable condition and be suitable for use. In the case of publications found to be incomplete or defective on arrival or at a later date, the library must be granted authorization to produce a new copy free of charge.
- In view of the shared responsibility of publishers and the digital deposit library with respect to the preservation of the intellectual and cultural heritage, both partners should be prepared to commit themselves at the outset to forming joint task groups for the purpose of developing and implementing standards and methods to be employed in future stages.

Consideration should also be given to the matter of extending the submission requirement to include data base providers and gateway operators alongside publishers and producers.

ARCHIVING AND LONG-TERM PRESERVATION

An essential precondition for the ability of the digital deposit library to fulfill its responsibility is the long-term preservation of acquired digital publications. From the very beginning, however, preservation efforts must take the issue of access into account. Long-term preservation will succeed only if reliable technology can be harnessed in service of a thoroughly consistent archiving concept based upon the reformatting and conversion of publication forms available for sale and use. We should plan to implement a central server concept using a rapid local network connected via open communications interfaces (Z39.50, an international communication standard) to the wide area network.

Digital publications not only contain text but may include language, music, images, and other components in a single application. The system architecture must therefore be designed to store, transport, and display the various elements within the system itself. The digital publications to be preserved by Die Deutsche Bibliothek in the future include digital publications on physical data media; publications available on-line (networked publications); converted digital publications; and transformations of analog materials.

The wide range of materials should be transferred, to the extent possible, to a homogeneous storage system. Such a storage system would have to meet the following requirements in particular: *1)* insure long-term preservation in conformity with state-of-the-art technology; *2)* provide as much forward compatibility as possible in anticipation of future developments; *3)* provide publications for use, regardless of the specific properties of the original data medium; and *4)* provide quality-control procedures for reproduction, conversion, and migration.

Having thoroughly examined all available storage technologies, Die Deutsche Bibliothek has given preference to optical data media. In our opinion, the CD-ROM qualifies as a comparatively durable and uniform storage media for multimedia data. According to recent prognoses, magneto-optical media capable of providing long-term storage for periods of over one hundred years will be available within five years. These storage media currently serve as benchmark standards.

It is possible to imagine a scenario based upon the assignment of publications to one of five different use-form categories. These categories would be defined in terms of relative frequency of use and the spectrum of demand.

- CDs are copied onto hard drives. Multiple users can then access the hard drive copies of CDs at the same time. This method of providing access to information is especially well suited for frequently used "reference libraries."
- Frequently used CDs that do not qualify as "reference books" are made available in specified CD drives in dedicated CD servers or in CD-ROM subsystems.

- CDs are made available in jukeboxes.
- CDs held in the archives can be provided to the user on request for access at a special workstation (equipped with a CD-ROM drive) or as a virtual drive. Where statistical evaluations show that CDs in this category are used with particular frequency, they can be reassigned to one of the categories listed above.
- CDs containing built-in retrieval software but incapable of network operation can be provided to the user on request for access at a special workstation (equipped with a CD-ROM drive). Emulation software can also be supplied, enabling the user to access the CD through the network.

A high-speed network will be used. From the backbone section to the distribution points only Asynchronous Transfer Mode (ATM) components, the new standard for high-speed networks, will be employed. An open, modular system architecture comprised of five function blocks is to be used: terminals and multimedia workstations; system administrator; export system; object server (facilitates the control of transaction between terminals and the media server); and media server. The media server is the actual archive where digital objects that are available for use are stored either temporarily or permanently. Technical equipment and facilities for refreshing, formatting, conversion, and migration will also be required.

Unlike original forms of print media, digital media cannot be preserved as originals or artifacts because of the diversity of distribution forms and the related variety of hardware and software; the library would soon become a museum of technology. Faced with the necessity to choose between artifact and content, we will have to opt for content, even though in certain cases this will result in the loss of interactive, dynamic components present in the original publication form.

But even then the library will be unable to ignore the need to make continual adjustments. The library's own information structure changes every five to ten years. The introduction of a new computer or operating or data base system does not always guarantee compatibility with existing preservation and access systems. Thus the issue of appropriate planning with regard to migration must be addressed as well.

Reference was made at the beginning of this discussion to the transitory characteristics of digital data records. Our understanding of these problems allows us to derive specific measures designed to avoid data loss. The physical deterioration of digital information can be prevented by refreshing information to a new medium of the same type or converting it to a different, more stable medium. While the retroconversion of such data to paper may seem an attractive alternative at first glance, it is not really recommendable since important multimedia features can be lost in the process.

Nevertheless, there is one variant worthy of note in this context that allows problems of long-term preservation to be solved with the aid of traditional media. Many institutions have converted their archives to optical digital storage media, which are incompatible with new software applications. For such cases Kodak offers the Digital Science Document Archive, with which extensive digital collections can be converted to microfilm and thus to long-term storage media capable of outlasting entire generations of digital systems. This process is intended primarily for documents originally printed on paper and later digitized in order to save space or provide more convenient access. No multimedia features need be taken into account in dealing with documents of this kind.

In mid-1995 a US task group, formed in response to an initiative of the Commission on Preservation and Access and the Research Libraries Group, presented the conclusions of their study and described measures in support of long-term preservation.[10] The US study proposed a migration concept that goes far beyond the system of preservation based upon refreshing and conversion. Migration comprises a bundle of measures that can be used to transfer digital materials periodically from one hardware or software configuration to another, or from one computer generation to the next. The study provides persuasive evidence in support of the contention that the long-term preservation of digital publications is not merely a matter of optimizing existing techniques but is in fact a process that requires a strategic approach. What is needed is a genuine infrastructure capable of insuring long-term preservation of our cultural heritage. The task group places responsibility for migration in the hands of designated digital deposit libraries. However, it appeals to publishers to assume responsibility as well: appropriate prerequisites for acceptable long-term preservation—technical platforms, compression mechanisms, and coding methods, for example—must be taken into account even during the production phase.

As designated repositories for digital publications, digital deposit libraries should be equipped with two major mechanisms. First, they should be given official certification as digital deposit libraries. Although this would not produce immediate, direct economic benefits, the evaluation process would contribute to the development of values and confidence with respect to measures taken in support of the preservation of collections. Second, as the task group emphasized, digital deposit libraries need a comprehensive mandate for long-term preservation. This could best be accomplished through legislative measures. Appropriate legislation would enable the library to take an aggressive approach to its preservation function as well as underscore the cultural importance of its role in a convincing manner.

Without official certification and a firm foundation of the preservation mandate in law, the maintenance of a digital cultural heritage will be left to the whim of market forces. In this case, fiscal and economic considerations would likely take precedence over the interests of the public and the academic community. The US study does not confine itself to general statements but instead goes on to propose specific initiatives, studies, and pilot projects.

It is surely too early to render a final judgment about the opportunities and risks, the effort, and the methods involved in the technical migration of large quantities of data. Digital deposit libraries should carefully analyze the development of technology with respect to its impact on library responsibilities. In doing so, they should not only observe long-term evolutionary change but also identify and respond to radical, short-term changes as well.

An alternative to migration is discussed in an essay that appeared in *Scientific American* and in a paper written for the December 1995 Luxembourg workshop.[11] In this case, the authors propose the use of emulators for the conservation of digital publications. Emulators are systems capable of simulating obsolete hardware and software environments in new system environments. As we know, digital information remains incomprehensible until the proper program containing necessary instructions can be installed in a suitable system environment. Special programs make it possible to simulate the behavior of out-of-date hardware on computers of more recent vintage. This software-based system reproduction is known as an emulator. The specific hardware types themselves need not be preserved for posterity; it is enough to store documentation on the type of hardware in an independent form.

A new type of software now under development in the network will pose new problems for preservation: the Java software from Sun (Microsystems). Java consistently applies the network philosophy of the virtual computer, familiar to us as it relates to documents, to software as well. It is no longer necessary to install complete programs on a hard drive; instead, small program modules are written for each specific purpose. These so-called objects—Java refers to them as "applets"—are available on various computers within the network and can be downloaded as needed and combined to perform a particular task. An interpreter simulating a second computer on a PC insures that the different browser programs understand the applets. The interpreter runs the applets as soon as it receives them.

If Java becomes the Internet standard, and that appears likely to happen, the software structure will produce not only distributed documents but distributed programs as well. Considerations of this kind show how important it is for digital deposit libraries to take such developments into account as soon as possible, to initiate experimental phases and projects, and especially to examine the economic ramifications of all possible alternatives.

The diversity of migration strategies clearly suggests that long-term preservation will involve substantial expense and effort and remain subject to considerable uncertainty. Even if we can imagine that standards and migration processes will one day enable us to build a more uniform structure for digital collections—in the form of object-oriented or relational data bases, for instance—we will surely have to deal with nonstandard formats for some time to come. In practical terms this means that, regardless of our collection guidelines, the digital deposit library will be unable to ignore the question of cost when choosing techniques and technologies for long-term preservation.

In taking the selective approach dictated by these circumstances we must still strive for a representative collection of the various digital publications and insure that authors, publishers, disciplines, and user groups are fairly and appropriately represented.

BIBLIOGRAPHIC CONTROL

These remarks on collection guidelines and long-term preservation describe only half of the task that lies ahead. Indispensable to the fulfillment of our responsibilities is adequate bibliographic control—that is, processing and cataloging procedures suited to the requirements of the media in question. Without them, collections lack order, identifiability, and a comprehensible system of access. In light of the diversity of digital publication forms, the related conversion and migration processes, and new developments with respect to user requirements, it will come as no surprise to anyone that a simple bibliographic title citation will not suffice. Physical media (CD-ROM and floppy disks) are still the most amenable of all digital forms to this kind of bibliographic processing. But they also require the inclusion of an additional information component that is gained through the installation of the respective data medium, providing technical data pertinent to the publication. Thus, it appears sensible generally to follow the cataloging procedures used for printed publications, with respect at least to bibliographic elements; it would be advantageous to seek the greatest possible degree of conformity with the Anglo-American Cataloging Rules (AACR). The phenomenon of global networking must be reflected in rules as well, therefore standards for the necessary metadata should be established as soon as possible.

New "index services" or search engines for networked publications have now been developed more or less within the Internet. These include WebCrawler, Alex, Lycos, and Yahoo as well as WWW pages with specific subject structures. They offer very simple and convenient access. "Auto indexing" in networks is likely to experience strong growth, not least of all because of the speed and efficiency it offers.[12]

Nevertheless, I am still convinced that digital deposit libraries must perform bibliographic indexing for networked publications as well; the European and US studies also share this view. Bibliographic citations establish a clear correlation between bibliographic information and an authentic publication. Publications are documented in keeping with copyright laws and protected against textual manipulation; comprehensible, standardized modes of access are established, and the status of networked publications as sources of scholarly value is enhanced.

In the interest of better access, bibliographic data—like the documents themselves—can be provided in a hypertext markup language (HTML) structure. Alternatively, bibliographic data fields could be defined for digital publications on the basis of rules for descriptive cataloging and the appropriate data formats (MARC). Other data elements would include descriptive information pertinent to digital characteristics. These could be generated using sources such as the opening screen, metadata from the publication, supplemental material in electronic form, and other supplementary material (information included in the product package).

The following data will also be required:[13]

Access data. This information must be included in the title data record. It functions more or less as a location number.

Structured descriptive information (metadata). No uniform specifications are currently in force. Standardization is needed with respect to defining elements, formats, and forms of presentation as well as relationships to the documents.

Archive data. This information describes the different states in which the document appears as it passes through the migration process, including the document in its original format, the current status of the publication as provided for use, and the form in which the document is archived.

The significance of bibliographic processing goes beyond the issue of meeting the local needs of digital deposit libraries; it is an indispensable element oi the national bibliography. We should accordingly adhere to the principle of including every digital publication in the national bibliography. This not only serves the purpose of documenting national intellectual production but also provides a mechanism for linking bibliographic description, including metadata, with original digital publications.

In preparing the national bibliography the digital deposit library should not restrict itself to its own collection. It makes sense to supplement data using other sources precisely because of the wide distribution of publications and the difficulty involved in allocating them to national production.

CONCLUDING REMARKS

The conceptual scheme outlined above, which is certainly in its infancy with respect to specific requirements, offers possible avenues of approach to the issues of long-term preservation and access to digital publications. Concrete steps must follow if it is to become a genuine process capable of providing real solutions. Such solutions should be open ones, developed as far as possible through international cooperation in order to foster the growth of global networking.[14] Although the effort required is great, we simply cannot ignore our obligation to pass on cultural experiences and insights, nor can we be content to plan only one day at a time. Making the transitory permanent and turning publications of the moment into publications for the ages are important and worthy goals for libraries.

ENDNOTES

[1] *Die unendliche Bibliothek—Digitale Information in Wissenschaft, Verlag und Bibliothek* (Wiesbaden: Harrassowitz, 1996).

[2] Deutsche Forschungsgemeinschaft, "Neue Informations-Infrastrukturen für Forschung und Lehre," *ZfBB* 43 (2) (1996): 133–154.

[3] *Frankfurter Allgemeine Zeitung,* 6 December 1995, p. 37.

[4] Klaus-Dieter Lehmann, "Networking and the Challenges to be Faced," proceedings of the European conference, "Library Networking in Europe," Brussels, 12–14 October 1994 (London: TFPL Publishing, 1995), 365–375.

[5] Michael P. Olson, *The Odyssey of a German National Library: A Short History of the Bayerische Staatsbibliothek, the Staatsbibliothek zu Berlin, the Deutsche Bücherei, and the Deutsche Bibliothek* (Wiesbaden: Harrassowitz, 1996).

[6] European Commission, *Telematics for Libraries, Report of the Workshop December 18, 1995: A Study of the Issues Faced by National Libraries in the Field of Deposit Collection of Electronic Publications* (Luxembourg: European Commission DG XIII-E/4, February 1996).

[7]John S. Mackenzie Owen and Jan van de Walle, *A Study of Issues Faces by National Libraries in the Field of Deposit Collections of Electronic Publications,* ELDEP Project, version 2.0, November 1995.

[8]Deutsche Forschungsgemeinschaft, "Elektronische Publikationen im Literatur- und Informationsangebot wissenschaftlicher Bibliotheken," *ZfBB* 42 (5) (1995): 445–463.

[9]Klaus-Dieter Lehmann, "Langzeitsicherung digitaler Medien durch Die Deutsche Bibliothek," *ZfBB* 42 (2) (1995): 214–219.

[10]Commission on Preservation and Access (CPA) and the Research Libraries Group, *Preserving Digital Information: Report of the Task Force on Archiving of Digital Information* (Washington, D.C.: CPA, May 1996).

[11]Jeff Rothenberg, "Ensuring the Longevity of Digital Documents," *Scientific American* 272 (January 1995): 42–47.

[12]Glenda Browne, "Automatic Indexing and Abstracting, Conf. Indexing in the Electronic Age," Robertson, New South Wales, April 1996, Australian Society of Indexers, <http://www.zeta.org.an/~aussi/browneg.htm.>

[13]Bill Moen, "Metadata for Network Information Discovery and Retrieval," *Information Standards Quarterly* 7 (2) (1995): 1–4.

[14]European Commission, Telematics Application Program 1994–1998, *Telematics for Libraries* (Luxembourg: European Commission DG XIII, 1995).

Books, magazines, and newspapers are not about to disappear. Their functions and forms may change a great deal, especially those of newspapers, for the instantaneity of electronic media affects them in particular. But as Anthony Smith argues persuasively in *Goodbye Gutenberg,* they have changed before and will change again to survive in a fluid world. There is no basis for predicting that, because books, magazines, and newspapers will face new competition from new media, and become partly electronic media themselves, a hundred years hence there will be nothing around that looks like a book or journal, or that people will have stopped reading. Nonetheless, my contention in this essay is that, for reasons of convenience and cost, publishing is becoming electronic. Using computer logic on arrays of bits, large and complicated patterns can be edited, stored, transmitted, and searched with far more flexibility than is possible with ink records or paper. Millions of words can be searched in seconds and transmitted across the world in minutes. Up to now, however, those conveniences were bought at a price. Electronic text handling was good, but expensive; paper records were cheaper. That is reversing. It is becoming cheaper to handle words electronically than to handle them physically, to the point where the latter may soon become too expensive for ordinary use.

Ithiel de Sola Pool

From "The Culture of Electronic Print"
Dædalus 111 (4) (Fall 1982)

Hermann Leskien

Allocated Parts: The Story of Libraries in Germany

T HE LIBRARY SYSTEM IN GERMANY is somewhat complicated and sophisticated. To fully understand the contemporary situation, one needs to go back in time and consider the outlines of the German constitutional tradition. In Germany, the states (*Länder*) and the local authorities (*Gemeinden*) are primarily, and almost exclusively, responsible for cultural affairs. States are parent bodies of academic and scholarly libraries, whereas almost all larger public libraries are defined as belonging to a local authority. As a result, it is often impossible to make or negotiate comprehensive and concerted overall plans, or at least it is rather difficult to put them into practice.

TYPES OF LIBRARIES AND THEIR HISTORY

The Nineteenth and Early Twentieth Centuries

The German nation achieved its political union as a nation-state quite late, not earlier than 1871. Since then, Germany has had a federative constitution, and now after reunification the sixteen *Länder* take pride in their cultural independence. Many of the regional and state libraries have their roots in the tradition of the old court libraries. Over the past centuries these libraries have played a pivotal role in the development of the modern service library.

Hermann Leskien is Director of the Bavarian State Library in Munich.

Owing to these historical and constitutional facts it is not surprising that there has been no room for establishing a comprehensive national library. A certain break was made in 1913 when in Leipzig the Deutsche Bücherei was newly established as a library responsible for all publications printed in and about Germany.

More or less separated from the history of scholarly libraries, German public libraries lived a life of their own. The movement of middle-class enlightenment, the churches (especially the Roman Catholic Church with its related associations) along with the labor and union movements fostered the development of the public libraries. Correspondingly, they have always been carriers of public education and social ideology. But initially, the dissemination of pure information was not their primary function.

The Nazi Period

The orientation of German public libraries towards public education made them susceptible or even favorably inclined toward totalitarian influences. It is not surprising, therefore, that the Nazi propaganda machine used the public libraries for its own purposes.

As far as scholarly libraries were concerned, the effects of the Nazi period were less intensive in the long run than one might have expected. The reasons are simple: The Nazi regime was only marginally involved in scientific affairs; the peace period after World War I was too short for any substantial reform of longstanding institutions such as libraries; and during World War II there was no interest in restructuring the library system. Thus, the most striking effect of the Nazi period was the loss of library buildings and holdings, caused to a very large extent by bomb attacks as well as by the consequences of countless recovery moves. (A number of German libraries are still missing hundreds of thousands of volumes, which can be found today predominantly in Russian and Polish libraries.)

Two Germanies

After 1945, with the division of Germany, the situation changed again. The Berlin Library was split between two countries—it became two institutions in two different worlds. After a long period of consolidation, the Western part of the library returned to

Berlin and has been located since 1978 in a building near the Berlin Wall, whereas the Eastern part of the library remained in the renowned Unter den Linden building, acting as the State Library of the German Democratic Republic.

Because the Leipzig library was situated in the German Democratic Republic, West Germany founded a counterpart in Frankfurt in 1946. Both libraries claimed the same goal: to collect all books produced in Germany as well as all books about Germany that are published abroad. The process of decentralization had been drastically intensified.

In the field of public libraries things ran quite differently. As a result of the communist principle that every citizen should have comfortable access to a library, a large number of libraries existed in the German Democratic Republic, created as parts of a coordinated system. In relation to the former status, after reunification the number of libraries was reduced by 30 percent—mainly by the loss of firm libraries (*Werksbibliotheken*) and union libraries (*Gewerkschaftsbibliotheken*). In terms of substance, this loss is not as important as the sheer number may suggest because in most cases the holdings of the libraries were extremely uniform and dedicated to the purpose of public education—and not immune to infiltration by the Communist Party.

The Contemporary Library System

The contemporary situation in Germany cannot be assessed without mentioning the *Bibliotheksplan* (Library Plan) of 1973, which was revised in 1993. It was a plan not so much for action as for orientation, attempting to squeeze the historically-grown contemporary situation into a functional system. Essentially based upon the historic regions and the libraries with an older tradition, after reunification the West German patterns have been adopted by the whole country. The system is structured as follows:

As already mentioned, there is no national library in an all-embracing sense. Nevertheless, a trio of large libraries have jointly assumed various functions of a national library, each one contributing its services in a well-defined field. Libraries that fall into this particular category are: the German Library in Frankfurt and Leipzig (Die Deutsche Bibliothek), the Berlin State Library (Staatsbibliothek zu Berlin-Preussischer Kulturbesitz), and the Bavarian State Library (Bayerische Staatsbibliothek) in Munich. These libraries provide service in the fields of archiving and delivering literature through in-house use as well as by document delivery and interlibrary loan, making available in Leipzig and Frankfurt German literature published since 1913 (6.9 and 4.4 million volumes, respectively), particularly older German editions, and foreign literature and special holdings in Berlin (8.9 million volumes) and Munich (6.8 million volumes).

Central subject libraries are listed separately. The Technical Information Library (Technische Informationsbibliothek) in Hanover, which is in charge of technology and applied sciences (1.5 million volumes), the Central Library of Medicine (Deutsche Zentralbibliothek für Medizin) in Cologne (0.9 million volumes), the Central Library of Economics (Zentralbibliothek der Wirtschaftswissenschaften) in Kiel (2.4 million volumes), and the Central Library of Agriculture (Deutsche Zentralbibliothek der Landbauwissenschaft) in Bonn (0.4 million volumes) collect literature in their respective fields and render their services on a national basis.

The next substantial group of libraries are the approximately eighty university libraries, which offer their services primarily to the members of universities with which they are affiliated. There are no longer any differences between the former West and East German library systems, since the Western principles and programs have been adopted by the reformed Eastern universities.

The older and more important university libraries—approximately thirty in total—do not have a strictly centralized library system. In all these traditional universities, the central library is supplemented by a great number of institute and faculty libraries. Nevertheless, their total riches are crucial, and their respective holdings are similar to those of the largest German libraries: Berlin Freie Universität, 7.8 million volumes in 124 libraries; Frankfurt/Main University, 7.2 million volumes in 156 libraries; and Göttingen, 7.1 million volumes in 148 libraries.

In the 1960s and 1970s, when new universities were established, completely different elements made inroads into the German library scene. The novel systems were conceived as centralized systems with a strong central library for purchasing, cataloging, information, and literature (dedicated to loan), surrounded by only a few faculty libraries (for in-house use). In time, the overall holdings of the newly established universities (*Neugründungen*), approximately fifty in total, have met the mark of three million volumes.

Owing to the lack of regional libraries within their respective states, quite a number of university libraries—older as well as newly established ones—also serve as regional libraries; they often are referred to as university and regional libraries (*Universitäts- und Landesbibliotheken*). The most spectacular unification took place in early 1996, when the two libraries in Dresden combined to form the Sächsische Landesbibliothek—Saxonian State and University Library.

Predominantly maintained by the sixteen *Länder,* regional libraries and other research libraries with regional responsibilities function as service institutions for literature and information. The German library statistics puts the number of these institutions at about forty. They often have similar histories but differ greatly in size and contemporary importance. Libraries of national and international character are, for example, the Württembergische Landesbibliothek in Stuttgart (2.5 million volumes), Niedersächsische Landesbibliothek in Hanover (2.0 million volumes), Badische Landesbibliothek in Karlsruhe (1.4 million volumes), and Herzog-August-Bibliothek in Wolfenbüttel (0.8 million volumes with excellent older collections). The holdings of the smallest libraries of this type do not exceed fifty thousand to one hundred thousand volumes.

Most of the citizenry's needs are met by the 13,500 public libraries, which even today in Germany are very strictly separated from academic and research libraries. Only two thousand communities out of sixteen thousand have libraries with full-time librarians at their disposal. They represent 4,700 institutions altogether. Libraries are more numerous (with a coverage ratio of more than 90 percent) in communities with at least twenty thousand inhabitants. The number of libraries decreases with the size of the community. In rural areas, especially, they are supported not only by local but also by church bodies.

Institutions of National Importance

Apart from the different types of libraries and their parent bodies, there are a number of supraregional organizations of importance for librarianship. Among them, the German Research Society (Deutsche Forschungsgemeinschaft, or DFG) is regarded as the most essential and acknowledged institution for patronage in the library field (their annual budget for library purposes is approximately DM 35 million). The DFG is jointly financed by the federal government and the *Länder*. It is the authoritative, central, autonomous organization in German academic life. Its main functions include financial support for all disciplines, improvement of the research infrastructure (including the promotion of research libraries), the counseling of parliament, and other scholarly matters.

According to the general principle of the DFG, the library department only supports cooperative projects between research libraries, central institutions within the library field, new developments in technology, and organization or individual library projects of special interest for research. However, the DFG is not responsible for the permanent funding of maintenance costs and equipment (with one exception). Various measures have extended the improvement and modernization of library services, especially in the field of electronic data processing.

In terms of foreign literature, at the end of the 1940s and the beginning of the 1950s the DFG established a cooperative system in order to provide the research community with sufficient resources (*Sondersammelgebietsplan*). Today, approximately one-third of all expenditures of the German Research Society is devoted to this program. A ratio of an additional 25 percent of the costs of purchase and the total expenses for personnel are contributed by the eighteen libraries, which together with the DFG support this system as a collaborative task.

Like the DFG, there is another institution that is supported by the federal government and the *Länder*. Its focus is library affairs, including the responsibilities and duties of public libraries. The German Library Institute (Deutsches Bibliotheksinstitut, or DBI) in Berlin has been operative since 1978, with 150 employees now and an annual budget of DM 18 million. Its main tasks are advice and information services in addition to hosting some very substantial data bases, such as the "Zeitschriftendatenbank," with more than eight hundred thousand periodical titles and 3.2 million local holdings, and the union catalog of machine-readable data, which includes 26 million entries (last edition 1995). After reunification two institutions in the GDR that were similar to the DBI—Zentralinstitut für Bibliothekswesen and Methodisches Zentrum für wissenschaftliche Bibliotheken—were merged into one institution, the expanded DBI.

THE GERMAN NEED FOR COLLABORATION

The most striking effect of the decentralized structure of Germany is the awareness that cooperation is crucial—and it is often successfully achieved. Foreigners tend to be rather bewildered by the fact that most of the more extensive and important ventures in Germany have been cooperatively structured and managed. No library has the resources to carry out a project of national importance or size at its own expense. But partners are available who are convinced to be as strong as any other library—and feel often in a better position either because of more holdings, holdings of better quality, or staff with more skill and expertise. This is the reason why German libraries have considerable experience in collaboration and, it should be added, with intricate patterns and repeatedly changing coalitions. To give only a few examples:

The *Verzeichnis der im deutschen Sprachbereich erschienenen Drucke des 16. Jahrhunderts,* which since 1969 has gathered all German imprints of that period, is a common enterprise led by the Bavarian State Library in Munich and the Herzog-August-Library in Wolfenbüttel. The coalition for a similar undertaking for the seventeenth century, which started in 1994, is comprised of Berlin, Munich, and Wolfenbüttel. The well-established authority file for corporate names is run by the virtual national libraries in Berlin, Frankfurt/Leipzig, and Munich under the technical assistance of the German Library Institute in Berlin. After a period during which the German Library Institute hosted this data base, the revised project of the *Personennamendatei* is now supported by the German Library Frankfurt/Leipzig, the Berlin State Library, the Bavarian State Library, and the Library Network of North Rhine-Westphalia.

Since 1989, under patronage of the Volkswagen-Stiftung, an attempt has been made to create a coordinated, but allocated, retrospective national library for the period before 1913, when the Deutsche Bücherei was established. Partners in this project are the Bavarian State Library, Herzog-August-Library in Wolfenbüttel, State and University Library in Göttingen, City and University Library in Frankfurt, and the Berlin State Library.

BASICS OF THE DIGITAL AGE

In 1995, the Library Committee of the DFG, as the first of the supraregional bodies, published an official statement concerning the impact of digital media on the services of scholarly libraries. Its intent is twofold. First, the paper offers some guidance for librarians on how to solve related problems. The second aim deals with supportive measures of the DFG, which have led to a specific program that is open for application. In the meantime other papers have been published. The most prominent themes of general interest discussed in German papers at present are as follows.

Paradigm Shift

Electronic media offer absolutely new capacities, which mainly focus on very high storage, disembodiment of media, ubiquitous availability, and the floating nature of documents. All of these features add up to one very remarkable outcome: that a fundamental alteration of paradigm is to be recognized—the shift from physical ownership of information and its related data carrier to the valid and effective facility of getting access.

This change is presumably of specific importance to German libraries. The history and entire orientation of German libraries focus on strong holdings. The greatest libraries were founded at times when it was most fashionable to gather antiquities. In accordance with this pattern, for centuries German librarianship has concentrated on purchasing and cataloging books with regard to an appropriate balance between their long-standing intrinsic value and the expected short-term demand. In this respect German libraries have not shared the Anglo-American approach to society, where rendering immediate services is the prevailing part of the mission.

So up to now the importance of a German library has been defined by the quantity and quality of its holdings: the more comprehensive the holdings in both respects, the higher the rank. Old libraries also have a notably high reputation because it has proven exceedingly difficult to build up large holdings retrospectively. In the era of the printed book, strong holdings have not easily been surpassed, so a balance has been struck between the given budget and the need to satiate the public's appetite for information. In the electronic era the changes are dramatic because the strict differences between buying, providing, and storing information are shifting and sliding. Everyone knows that not all books bought by librarians are really used.

On the contrary, as opposed to the proclaimed intention, a considerable number of books are outdated before they are requested even once. The loss of physically coded and visible information makes every librarian feel weak and helpless. The traditional guidelines of book and periodical selections are put into doubt and cannot be transferred to the electronic era.

Specific Information Profiles

The majority of librarians and researchers in Germany believe in and underscore the fact that every discipline has its own intrinsic need for information, a specific information profile. Consequently, there is a wide variety of approaches to meet these demands. It is not, or at least not merely, a question of the customers' being or not being familiar with the new media. Rather it implies an underlying and distinct style of working.

First, consider the position of a chemist who does research in the field of a certain compound. Only the most recent publications are of value to him; he knows that each contains only a few pages that will interest him and that there is a precise, internationally agreed-upon indexing method. Due to the existence of electronic services, he is able to identify the information he needs quickly and order the relevant copies.

Second, imagine a folklorist engaged in, say, the history of Bavarian rococo. No matter when and where and in what language they have been issued, all publications, unpublished reports, and pictures are of interest, as are items directly linked to the subject or that have an indirect relationship to it. Most of the pertinent and substantial information is found in print publications; this will not change during the next decade. The community of researchers in this field is too limited and the topic too nation-specific to make effective electronic services or the conversion of existing information affordable.

Admittedly, these are two extreme examples. But extreme examples always help in focusing on the crux of a problem, in this case, to illustrate the complexity of the contemporary information environment. After juxtaposing and analyzing both examples it is important to differentiate each position very carefully. In the foreseeable future, we will have both paper-based and electronic-based research—each a method with its own validity. As a result, library services ought to be traditional as well as digital. More diversification in operation is needed to satisfy the needs of the researchers' community. Furthermore, librarians of the future will have to grapple with a much broader variety of media, tools, and methods, always with an eye to the specific demands of their distinct patrons.

The Impact on Library Organization

The impact of the digital age on library organization is another theme to which attention should be drawn. Traditionally, we are used to the classical scope of functions like acquisition, cataloging, and reader services. They constitute individual departments, although, of course, there is a lot of variation. These divisions, however, are not suitable for dealing with electronic media. To find information one needs to find the path to it; recording the location of this path amounts to a sort of cataloging system. Often by finding information we are beholden to buy it; the mere inquiry might put us under an obligation. The patron who needs information calls on the full services of a library and is involved in a kind of sale and purchase process. Not only will the sequence of operations change; they will take place in quite different contexts and combinations. Although no perfect and all-embracing solutions are within sight, half of the solution is to see the situation as a problem that must be sorted out.

The loss of physical possession influences the entire mentality. Every librarian, no matter what department he or she works in, will feel like a member of reader services. When the daily work is done, nothing tangible of the workers' efforts remains. The work done in an electronic era grows to be more and more fluid and transitory. The bare knowledge of what kind of information is available and where suffices to satisfy a client. Carrying out this job quickly and properly is our task in the future; to be in full command of the information landscape is the secret of success. Meeting the needs of the customers requires qualified staff regardless of the source that the demanded information comes from, with the actual transmission taking minutes or seconds. In other words, as far as the digital media are concerned, a good library of the future is determined only by the quality of its service.

Within the scope of managerial issues the cost issue attracts particular attention as a matter of presumable change. In the electronic age, a direct relationship between costs and use has become real while at the same time mirroring all other activities. At least in the case of net publications and in terms of the prevailing pay-as-you-go-scheme, the costs connected with a distinct operation are fixed and steady in relation to the usage itself. Accordingly, librarians find themselves tempted to share fees and other costs completely with the customers. The decision as to what kind of information should be purchased and what kind should only be available on the basis of intermediation is more or less a result of economic calculation. Even though we cannot afford the overall costs and even if we cannot continue providing information free of charge to the customer, there must be a well-defined limitation to splitting the costs. A scholarly clientele is not in the position to pay all the fees and market costs out of its own pockets. And it should not be overlooked that libraries traditionally invested their budgets in both required and non-required information. Adapted to the electronic age, library participation to cover some of the costs of needed information must be regarded as a fair deal.

COMPETITION AND COOPERATION

Since the publication chain has been broken, competition will increase but so too will cooperation and partnership. However, mathematicians, physicists, chemists, and information scientists, discontent with their publishers, are taking their fate into their own hands. Given the long time they have waited for their essays to be published and given the high costs of the journals, they feel that they are in a position to help themselves. It is also fair to say that, in Germany in the past, fate has not exactly smiled upon authors in the fields of science, medicine, and engineering, who used libraries devoted to the general public. Too often a strict division between libraries and documentation centers has been observed. Libraries carry the journals, but efficient indexing services are missing; documentation centers offer information services, but they are not in the position to deliver articles. For these reasons, scientists often deny the useful role of libraries and dream of new systems. In their scenario, authors are not merely competing with publishers and librarians, but they are bypassing all of the links of the publication chain and are eagerly working to regain control of their information channels.

While authors are thinking of how to eliminate publishing houses and libraries, librarians—not accustomed to being competitors in a service market—have to face the fact that the scenery will change in the near future and various new information agents will be on the market. On the other hand, libraries have the chance to balance their losses of the past because they can now offer information services, which are produced outside of libraries, to their clients and combine them with the advantages of having the original sources. Imported information services and a delivery service based upon strong holdings—that is a recipe for success.

Libraries without walls are theoretically open 24 hours a day, and the location of the library is no longer important. The convincing success of libraries with an effective service, like the Document Supply Center of Boston Spa, has supported this theory even in paper-based times. The better, more attractive service will substantially influence the decision of the client as to which library he or she will use. A shortage, however, will jeopardize even the traditional links between the customers and their regular library. If libraries are not alert to these fundamental facts, in a figurative sense, some of their beautiful buildings might collapse like a house of cards because there is no longer any demand for their services.

As important as competition will be in the future, widespread cooperation—between specific libraries, publishing houses and libraries, booksellers and libraries, and faculties or learned societies and libraries—should also be seriously considered. Cooperation in the future may not have the same meaning as it has in the past. It is reaching the point of resembling a close, joint venture. For example, it is a thing of the past that librarians were able to design cataloging and indexing rules without firm contact with their customers. If their information tools are not accepted by their clientele, they will fail. And because they are not able to rely exclusively on their own material—the material is not free—they have to rely on the service of another participant in the information market. This could be another library, but it could also be a publishing house or a host.

Reliability under those circumstances, however, is only guaranteed if there is a clear restriction to a specific field of activity. To put it in other words, the result of widespread cooperation will certainly lead to a narrowing and specialization of services in a distinct library.

MEASURES AND PROGRAMS

The DFG-Program Allocated Digital Library

Faced with the problems of electronic publication and digital media, the DFG is willing to play an active role. Focusing on electronic publishing in the narrower sense, in 1996 a completely new program endowed with almost DM 1 million annually was initiated to integrate electronic publications into currently available information resources for academic or applied research. The intention is to promote the development, implementation, and testing of new organizational and structural procedures to attain the supraregional availability and use of digital publications. The main aspects to be considered in this context are: *1)* provision and supply of digital media; *2)* development and enhancement of reference and indexing tools for specific media and subjects; *3)* navigational procedures; *4)* integration of electronic publications into the range of currently available information resources; *5)* methods for the production and provision of university publications (especially dissertations) in digitized form; and *6)* long-term availability of electronic media, including archival purposes.

A second grant will support the digitization of printed material. This program, the "Allocated Digital Library" (*Verteilte digitale Bibliothek*), will start in early 1997. Guidelines for the type of literature to be converted will be worked out by the fall of 1996. To avoid conflicts with publishers' rights, documents of special long-term national importance will constitute a certain focal point. The program provides DM 3 million for the first year with a possibility of greater funding for the following years.

The third program, to commence in 1997, is devoted to basic research for digital libraries and puts an emphasis on joint ventures between research institutions and libraries. Working with libraries, information scientists are invited to find solutions for digital-related problems in activity centers of research. Specific fields have not yet been circumscribed since endorsement depends on how worthwhile and efficient the proposed projects are judged to be by the approving committee. Applications for grants are expected by the end of 1996.

These three interrelated new programs will continue for a period of at least five years. Subsumed into one figure, roughly DM 40 million will likely be available for the digital future from DFG sources alone.

Document Delivery and the SUBITO Project

For seven decades interlibrary loan has been a traditional service of the German library system. The paths used today are not very different from those used in 1924. Scholars in particular are likely to grow impatient and organize themselves or accept foreign services offered by an increasing number of commercial agencies. It is our hope that the implementation of information highways, which is now taking place in Germany, will enhance the electronic services of the libraries.

Under the label SUBITO a joint initiative has been set up by the federal government and the Standing Conference of the Ministers of Cultural Affairs of the *Länder* to establish a novel, electronically-based document delivery service. SUBITO is primarily a library network, scheduled to start in early 1997. It contains a complete electronic catalog of more or less all of the periodical holdings (the already mentioned Zeitschriftendatenbank), with electronic document ordering as well as electronic and traditional delivery devices. The delivery, or a message that an article was not able to be delivered, will be provided by the standard service within a maximum of three workdays. The basic fee is expected not to exceed DM 5 per article. Quicker services, delivery by post or fax, nonelectronic ordering, and other services are subject to additional charges. Specific compensation for publishers has been denied, with their approval, for a period of three years during which time all order information will be available to the publishers. After this time span, negotiations should lead to an agreement.

Concentration of Networks

In the 1970s, German librarians decided to establish regional networks according to the federal structure of cultural affairs. All of the seven operating networks have applied identical cataloging rules (RAK) and have agreed to use identical data structures. Nevertheless, they have developed independently of each other and have failed to communicate. During the last five years there has been a growing intention to alter this unsatisfactory situation.

When PICA, from the Netherlands, was selected as the software of choice in the northern states of Germany, a coalition of four remaining regional networks settled for a tender. In the summer of 1996, the surprising decision was that besides PICA only one other software would reign in German library networks of the future: Horizon, from the American Dynix Company. Despite Germany now having sixteen *Länder* instead of the former eleven, the number of network centers will not increase but will remain at a maximum of five.

For the time being, the differences between the existing networks are being bridged by strong efforts from both sides (Project DBV-OSI). As a result, with the help of the Z39.50/SR interface, searches are executed under a single surface in external data bases containing library networks as well as in bibliographical data bases like Medline or STN. In a further step, links will be extended to the document ordering and library loan services.

UNSETTLED QUESTIONS OF MAJOR INTEREST

A Multiple Approach is Needed

German libraries—particularly libraries not specializing in distinct subjects—are accustomed to performing their tasks in a more or less uniform manner. In other words, a book is a book irrespective of its contents. Since there is no supraregionally accepted indexing system, considerable human resources are invested in indexing. Verbal indexing methods compete with classification systems of more local or, at best, regional pertinence. The information world is divided into two parts: One concerns the librarian who is busy with indexing books as a whole, and the other, the world of information specialists, covers the field of documenting periodical essays.

The novel issue is that automatically supported indexing systems are successful and efficient only if they are built on very specific vocabularies. It is absolutely feasible to get valid indexing terms out of the context of title pages and table of contents. As a consequence, the overall concept of indexing methods must be abandoned and the individual disciplines be treated with distinctive tools. In this connection another fact must be mentioned. Some disciplines, particularly in science and medicine, prefer the English language, while the social sciences, law, and the humanities cannot do without German terminology. Thus, even the language issue influences the choice of indexing methods.

Intellectual Property Rights

Discussions about intellectual property rights are widespread in Germany, like elsewhere in the world. With regard to digital documents and the Internet, it is obvious that it has not been available long enough to solve all the problems involved. Even though everyone knows that we are in a period of transition and flux, opposite positions are difficult to reconcile.

On the one hand, publishers say that their investment has to be protected, and until that is the case they are not willing to invest money in spreading on-line data. They fear that unprotected services could lead to expropriation, or legalized piracy, as a noted publisher calls it. On the other hand, librarians demand free and unlimited access to all kinds of information. Hence at the moment a risky lack of innovation and activity is evident in Germany.

The struggle is exacerbated by a legal case concerning document delivery services. The Technical Information Library in Hanover is involved in a test case of whether or not it is legal to deliver electronic copies of periodical essays. In Germany the operator of a photocopy machine is liable for duties on a fixed average basis determined by the specific kind of copying activities. It depends on the capacity and on the distinct purpose (administration, library, manuscripts, or prints) of the respective copy machine. It is not related to the number of copies made of a specific document or a distinct copy event as it is in the United States. Compared to the Anglo-American level, duties are rather low (DM 120 for a small machine annually).

In the long run, a fair solution must be achieved for all parties involved. However, at the moment nobody knows how to find it (with the possible exception of SUBITO, described above).

Archiving

Legal deposit has a long-standing tradition in Germany. On account of the regional character of German history, the regional aspect of legal deposit prevailed for centuries until 1913, when the Deutsche Bücherei at Leipzig was established. Since then, theoretically every print publication has been collected there or in Frankfurt. This national function does not preclude the second network of legal deposit based on a regional scheme. For example, for reasons of legal deposit, a book published in Munich in 1996 can be found in four German libraries: in Frankfurt and Leipzig, in the Bavarian State Library in Munich (on behalf of the State of Bavaria), and in the University Library in Munich (on behalf of the region of Upper Bavaria).

The German pattern of legal deposit cannot be applied in the electronic age. Accordingly, serious proposals have been made as to how to coordinate the difficult and expensive task of archiving. Since not every library will be in a position to afford all of the necessary devices, the logical application of the traditional pattern might lead to a completely novel agreement on resource sharing. One of the proposals is to store information permanently only at the national level (i.e., Die Deutsche Bibliothek), granting at the same time limited but nevertheless permanent access to other right-holders.

German librarians are convinced that they play an indispensable part in storing electronic information. The more time that passes, the more scientists and publishers seem to approve of such a concept and—opposed to their ways of providing and procuring information—agree with the principle of storing information independently of publishing houses or publishing institutes. From the librarians' point of view, this approach is the only realistic one. Hence they deny the willingness and suitability of other participants in the publication chain, knowing that learned societies will shortly solve this problem for themselves.

All partners involved have to learn and conceive viable solutions for the archiving process, but by tradition German librarians feel predestined that they will come up with a better approach than other participants in the information market. Until now, we have been lacking both in the necessary technical tools and in internationally accepted concepts. It is obvious that these aspects have assumed a global dimension, and the need to invent technologies and develop patterns of shared responsibilities is urgently felt. What has been invented and accepted in one country should be shared with other countries all over the world.

The Role of Libraries as Publishers

German universities and other public bodies normally have their research results disseminated by publishing houses in the private sector. Therefore, publishers have a watchful eye on the activities of public institutions. They look for the smallest signs of interest in electronic publishing or in converting printed books to an electronic data carrier. Whenever publishers and librarians meet, this topic is always on the agenda, and their discussions tend to involve fundamental clashes and quite often are rather harsh. Publishers insist on their inviolable right to publish what they deem is fit to be published. Librarians claim that all publishers' activities must be judged with caution.

Nonetheless, the majority opinion of librarians does not call into question the predominance of private publishing houses. They are aware that in Germany the public sector has to accept its own subsidiary role in cases where services or products can be offered better or at least equally by the private sector. But from their point of view it can hardly be disputed that there are fields that do not interest publishers because they earn very little profit. This particularly applies to specific information that only a very limited number of book-buyers is interested in—regardless of its being novel or republished on a different data carrier.

Borders Must Be Further Opened Up

Strong evidence points to a growing awareness that concentration and cooperation, even beyond German borders, are vital for the future of the library. Library leaders increasingly favor stronger international data exchange and the adjustment of cataloging rules and data formats. What five years ago seemed absolutely impossible is now—under the pressures of efficiency and performance— a universal theme: sensible reduction of quality and maximized uniformity down to the limit patrons are willing to tolerate. Why not mix and mingle American cataloging records with reconverted low-level items and genuine German entries, perhaps supplemented by key images like title pages and tables of contents?

For leading library managers, reduction of cataloging efforts is the only means to cope with shrinking personnel resources. German librarians are devising options for national and transborder data flow alike. Even if the entire community of librarians is not yet aware of it, it seems that the international transfer and exchange of bibliographic data must be decisively increased. This is the only way to reduce the need for human resources, freeing them up for more patron-oriented jobs.

In Germany, much still remains to be done in this respect. But since we have specific national cataloging rules (RAK) as well as a national data format (MAB), the national border at times has proved to be a real obstacle. For example, establishing a name authority file in our times is unthinkable without close cooperation with the Anglo-American Authority File. But the rules and format have been incompatible so far. Only time will tell whether large-scale achievements can be realized.

OUTLOOK

German reunification implies that historic tradition and long-lasting developments will guide the German library system of the future. It is easy, therefore, to prognosticate that all participants of future developments are well-known even today. The only question is how successfully the existing libraries—based upon their distinct traditional character and actual service outline—are prepared and capable to cope with the new challenges.

Fulfilling demands for open access to information is not considered to be equally paramount in America and Germany. In Germany, it is seen as an important good, of course, but not as an absolutely essential, indispensable prerequisite for democracy like in the United States. Therefore in Germany, public libraries are more widely regarded as intermediaries of reading pleasure or as cultural centers in the context of leisure activities. In discussions and conferences of public librarians, fears have been voiced that multimedia might jeopardize democracy because of their predominantly uniform information channels.

However, most librarians are willing, even keen, to offer their patrons electronic media. But in truth the local authorities, as the most frequent parent bodies of public libraries, are not in a position to invest the sums necessary to offer these services. Especially for on-line services with a sufficient scope, funds are lacking to an extent that raises concern. The main reason for this problem is the exceedingly high telecommunication costs. The range of costs for a connection with a bandwidth of 2 Mb varies from DM 70,000 (network termination point) to DM 250,000 (main attachment) a year—too costly for smaller institutions.

Furthermore, the subsidiary support of the corresponding states for public libraries has been decreasing for years and does not amount to more than approximately 5 percent of the overall costs. The strategies of several libraries are entirely determined by the bare struggle for survival. From the librarians' perspective there is little room for innovation as long as the funds do not cover the costs for printed books and periodicals.

In the field of research and academic libraries, in Germany—like in other countries—universities and *Fachhochschulen* (applied science universities) are forerunners in the use of electronic media.

Whereas these institutions have been sufficiently promoted, regional and state libraries are in a significantly worse position. The situation is exacerbated by the fact that, because of their proximity to the advanced institutes, university libraries are in a better situation to have employees with sufficient skill and experience in modern data processing, an indispensable prerequisite for initiating projects and experiments and realizing achievements in this field.

To conclude, libraries of all types wait in front of electronic media gates that are not yet open, and nobody knows who is going to open them. The divided world of academic libraries and public libraries in Germany constitutes an additional problem of its own. For the time being, it seems that some libraries will lose the game and remain electronic have-nots or at least electronic paupers. One-person libraries, libraries in small communities, smaller regional libraries, and libraries that are not connected to networks may face a gloomy future. They are apt to find themselves in competition with more efficient and more competent larger libraries, and therefore their chances to sell information may be limited. Perhaps their last opportunity lies in specializing as competence centers for printed material. As the number of German imprints increases annually by more than the GDP, it could be a recipe for survival.

The majority of German libraries seems to stand a fair chance for further development; owing to their traditional mentality, they are specifically prepared and accustomed to acting as partners in cooperative systems. The fate of having such a complicated history may prove to be a favorable factor for German libraries in the long run—as a gift for collaboration with allocated parts.

BIBLIOGRAPHY

Bibliotheken während des Nationalsozialismus, 2 vols., ed. Peter Vodosek and Manfred Komorowski (Wiesbaden: Harrossowitz, 1989–1992).

Christine Bossmeyer, "Unimarc und MAB—Strukturunterschiede und Kompatibilitätsfragen," *Zeitschrift für Bibliothekswesen und Bibliographie* 42 (1995): 463–480.

Bundesvereinigung Deutscher Bibliotheksverbände, *Bibliotheken '93* (Berlin: Strukturen, Aufgaben, Positionen, 1994).

Gisela von Busse, *Libraries in the Federal Republic of Germany,* rev. and enl. (Wiesbaden: Harrossowitz, 1983).

Deutsche Forschungsgemeinschaft/Bibliotheksausschuss, "Elektronische Publikationen im Literatur- und Informationsangebot wissenschaftlicher Bibliotheken," *Zeitschrift für Bibliothekswesen und Bibliographie* 42 (1995): 445–463.

Deutsche Forschungsgemeinschaft, "Neue Informations-Infrastrukturen für Forschung und Lehre," *Zeitschrift für Bibliothekswesen und Bibliographie* 43 (1996): 131–155.

Eberhard Dünninger, "Öffentliche Bibliotheken in den neuen Ländern der Bundesrepublik Deutschland: Ausgangslage und Neuorientierung," *Die neue Bücherei* (1991): 13–124.

Jürgen Eyssen, "The Development of Libraries in the Federal Republic of Germany," *IFLA Journal* 9 (1983): 91–101.

Franz Georg Kaltwasser, "The Bayerische Staatsbibliothek (Bavarian State Library) as Part of the Library System of the Federal Republic of Germany," in *International Librarianship Today and Tomorrow: A Festschrift for William J. Welsh* (Munich: Saur, 1985), 65–79.

Klaus-Dieter Lehmann, "Die Deutsche Bibliothek: Germany's National Library and National Bibliographic Agency," *Alexandria* 5 (1993): 161–174.

Michael P. Olson, *The Odyssey of a German National Library* (Wiesbaden: Harrossowitz, 1996).

Der Rat für Forschung, *Technologie und Innovation. Informationsgesellschaft: Chancen, Innovationen und Herausforderungen* (Bonn: Bundesministerium für Bildung, Wissenschaft, Forschung und Technologie, 1995).

Wolfgang Thauer and Peter Vodosek, *Geschichte der öffentlichen Bücherei in Deutschland* (Wiesbaden: Harrossowitz, 1978).

Hans-Peter Thun, *Eine Einführung in das Bibliothekswesen der Bundesrepublik Deutschland* (Berlin: Deutsches Bibliotheksinstitut, 1995).

Die unendliche Bibliothek, *Digitale Information in Wissenschaft, Verlag und Bibliothek* (Wiesbaden: Harrossowitz, 1996).

Dwarika N. Banerjee

The Story of Libraries in India

ONE OF THE OLDEST CIVILIZATIONS and the seventh largest country of the world, India has a kaleidoscopic variety of people and a rich cultural heritage. It has a population of approximately 800 million, of which only 50 percent could be considered sufficiently literate. This fact has to be kept in mind while discussing the role of libraries in India.

In ancient India, knowledge was disseminated by a teacher to his students; through this practice, knowledge was passed on to the next generation. This continued to an extent even after the practice of writing on stones, leaves, skin, papyrus, and finally paper was made known. Until such time, knowledge was communicated from mouth to mouth from one generation to another, without any major lapses in the system.

In medieval times, India's rulers and elites became caught up in a love for books—primarily manuscripts, mostly illustrated, and often written in oriental languages. They amassed monumental libraries, of which quite a few are still accessible to researchers.

Librarianship began to be considered a mission with the arrival of the British in India; librarians came to be viewed as integral to the process of education, and education was the principal forerunner of modernization. Library development was placed on the agenda of nationalist movements and was accepted as the people's movement. It was not merely by coincidence that the annual meetings of the All India Public Library Association (AIPL) used to be held in conjunction with sessions of the Indian National Congress.

Dwarika N. Banerjee is Director of the National Library of India at Calcutta.

353

In 1811, Lord Minto, then governor general of India, stressed the need for libraries in the educational system; this theme was echoed by a later incumbent, Governor General Lord Auckland, in 1839. The Hunter Commission in 1822, the Raleigh Commission in 1902, and the Sadler Commission in 1917 all noted the lack of library facilities in educational institutions and suggested suitable remedial measures.

The Press and Registration of Books Act of 1867 made it compulsory for every printer in India to send copies of their books to the government. The quarterly list published on the basis of these receipts was practically a national bibliography.

Most of the preconditions for progress were present in the country when India became independent in 1947. There were universities, colleges, schools, and national level scientific agencies such as the Indian Council of Medical Research, the Indian Council of Agricultural Research, the Council of Scientific and Industrial Research, the Indian Standards Institution, and the like. These institutions supported varied levels of library facilities, from very good to almost nonexistent. In addition, the National Library of India, which traces its origin to the Calcutta Public Library established in 1836, already had a rich and scholarly collection. Although the public libraries were few and far between, those in the states of Andhra, Baroda, Punjab, and Bengal functioned satisfactorily.

The passage of the Delivery of Books and Newspapers (Public Libraries) Act in 1954 greatly increased the number of works published in India that were collected by principal Indian libraries. It entitled the National Library of India at Calcutta and three other libraries in the cities of Delhi, Madras, and Bombay (in the north, south, and west) to each receive one copy of all the publications published in India. This made possible the publication of the Indian National Bibliography (INB).

Professor S. R. Ranganathan, a mathematician turned librarian, played a major role in all spheres of library activity in postindependence India. A pioneer in the cause of library legislation, Ranganathan presented and campaigned for library acts for all the Indian states. Yet despite his efforts, today only ten of India's twenty-five states and seven union territories have implemented library acts. In the Indian constitution, libraries are listed under the state subject heading; this means responsibility for libraries falls not directly under the government of India (the federal government) but under the control of the individual states within the Indian Republic. Although a library act of national scope has long been thought essential in a developing country like India, it is difficult at best to shape a single act for such a diverse nation. A comprehensive National Policy on Library and Information Science has recently been finalized, and it is soon to be sent to the Parliament of India for approval.

Since education is a process of interaction between learners and information sources, the library serves as a learning resource center. Education itself has been continuously updated through new developments in information technology, thereby requiring libraries to keep up-to-date with modern technologies. Ensuring the integration of library services into educational activities is the most challenging task of library management in present-day India. Library professionals have understood the importance of library support for technological innovations in education. Such technological revolutions demand numerous attitudinal changes in transforming traditional libraries into automated systems. The impact of these revolutions has been felt by all organizational sectors of libraries—the library authorities, the library clientele, and, most importantly, the library staff.

There are many important organizations in India that handle information in a modern sense; some are described below.

THE INDIAN NATIONAL SCIENTIFIC DOCUMENTATION CENTER

The Indian National Scientific Documentation Center (INSDOC) in New Delhi, established in 1952 with technical assistance from UNESCO, is a premier science and technology (S & T) information organization in the country. With three regional centers, INSDOC provides such services as document procurement and supply, preparation of specialized bibliographies, translation, reprography, printing, selective dissemination of information, and current awareness services. It has a number of publications to its credit. Its fortnightly, *Indian Science Abstracts,* reports on the contributions of Indian scientists by scanning through about seven hundred periodicals, and it lists more than thirty thousand items annually. The National Union Catalog of Scientific Serials in India, also supported by INSDOC, lists thirty-six thousand titles available in nearly nine hundred S & T information centers in the country. INSDOC has introduced on-line information retrieval facilities for indigenous data bases and has launched programs for the creation of S & T data bases, network based on-line services, and a National Information Resource Center.

THE NATIONAL INFORMATION SYSTEM FOR SCIENCE AND TECHNOLOGY

India's technology policy statement of 1983 covers a whole range of issues relating to technology development, assignment, forecasting, impact and absorption, adaptation, and further development. The seventh and eighth five-year plans of the country (1985–1990 and 1990–1995) envisage the integration of science and technology into socioeconomic and rural sectors to fulfill the basic needs of water, food, nutrition, health and sanitation, shelter, education, energy, clothing, and employment. Towards this end various organizations were set up and schemes were drawn. One such organization was the National Information System for Science and Technology (NISSAT), established in 1977 with a view to creating Sectoral Information Centers based on the priorities of the Indian government in such areas as food, leather, drugs, textiles, and chemicals. The overall objective of NISSAT is to interlink and coordinate existing systems, sources, and services into an effective information network. It is being implemented as a decentralized network involving standardized and mutually compatible systems for the collection, storage, and dissemination of information.

With a mandate to facilitate provision of broad-based information services in the country, NISSAT took the initiative to design and develop metropolitan library networks beginning in 1985. The Delhi Network (DELNET), the Calcutta Library Network (CALIBNET), and other city library networks have either begun service or are in the pipeline.

Computers arrived in India much later than in many countries of the world. The Indian Statistical Institute at Calcutta installed a computer in 1955; this event marked the beginning of computer literacy in India. Nearly thirty years later, in 1984, the Department

of Electronics of the Indian government announced a new computer policy, which envisaged large-scale computerization as an
effective way to solve the problems of India in the information
field. Still, the major advances in the development of data networks in India took place rather late. The Indian government's
policy to support such programs resulted in the establishment of
many networks:

I-NET: The Department of Telecommunications has established
a nationwide public packet-switched data network called I-NET.
I-NET provides international connectivity to important data net-
works outside the country through the Videsh Sanchar Nigam
Limited (VSNL), India's overseas communication service at Bombay,
Madras, and Delhi.

NICNET: The National Information Center's network utilizes
almost exclusively satellite-based communication, using low-cost
rooftop micro-earth stations to connect 450 district headquarters
all over the country and thirty-two state and union territory capi-
tals with a central hub at Delhi. NICNET is principally meant to
be used by government departments and has a potential for use by
the library and information community. Medical and biotechnol-
ogy information systems are also being successfully operated by
NICNET.

INDONET: INDONET is a commercially distributed computer
network that provides access to the computing and software resources of CMC Ltd., a public sector company in India.

INFLIBNET: A particularly ambitious effort—one that has received substantial financing, though not an amount that is likely to
prove adequate for the magnitude of the project—is the Information and Library Network (INFLIBNET).

Realizing the importance and necessity of linking the resources
of university and other research and development (R & D) institutions in the country, the University Grants Commission (UGC), an
autonomous body funded by the government of India, convened
an interagency working group to examine the feasibility of developing an information and library network. This group's report,
popularly known as the "Blue Document," envisaged a computer-
communication multiple function network connecting the libraries
and information centers in about two hundred universities, over
7,200 colleges, and some four hundred R & D laboratories and

other scientific organizations. It would be based on a computer network, headquartered at the Gujarat University campus in the city of Ahmedabad, and would piece together all existing and forthcoming information resources in a standard machine-readable form and make it accessible to facilitate specific information searches from almost any place in India.

INFLIBNET is envisaged as a cooperative venture and depends for its success on the cooperation of all its participants. It will use modern technology and techniques: computers, telecommunication, micrography, and document delivery. It is being structured as an economic tool in the current environment of budgetary constraints, rising document costs, and decline in the value of the Indian rupee. It will avoid the duplication of costly resources and create a favorable situation for resource sharing. The major objectives of INFLIBNET are to evolve a national network, create an on-line union catalog, provide access to data bases, establish resource centers, encourage shared cataloging, and implement computerization.

INFLIBNET as conceived is undoubtedly a bold initiative. But the scheme, which has followed a typically top-down approach, could not take into account the realities throughout the country. The participating institutions vary from a few years old to 150-year-old libraries. The methodologies adopted by these institutions for classifying and cataloging their documents are greatly varied and diverse. Another difficulty confronted by INFLIBNET has been the different kinds of libraries involved, as well as the tremendous variations in the collections of participating libraries—varying from more than two million titles to a few thousand. The catalogs of these institutions have been built over a few decades with various kinds of rules and classification schemes. Converting this cataloging data from existing methods to a standard record format in machine-readable form poses a problem that is being handled in a confident and systematic manner.

Finding money for this ambitious project, and indeed the sheer size of the plan, leads one to wonder whether it might not have been wiser to start small and slowly build up the whole program. Coordinating a well-defined group of libraries with shared interests would probably have been more feasible and manageable than coordinating a heterogeneous group of libraries of this vast subcontinent. To meet the information challenge India must provide the means of accessing and presenting information and organizing local area networks, with a view to linking to national and international networks. The costs of information in absolute and strategic terms have to be computed. Attempts should be made to think of regulating the information industry to make sure that information is secure, copyright is protected, and privacy is not infringed upon. Finally, it must be decided whether the country needs a national directive on the freedom of information.

LIBRARY EDUCATION

Inroads were made during the early part of this century to impart training for persons working in libraries. The Madras University, under the guidance of Professor Ranganathan, started a university-level training program in 1931; today, India has nearly one hundred institutions training library and information-science professionals.

Changes in the structure of the library and information profession as a consequence of developments within the professional field are being accounted for in the library education programs of India. Master's degree programs at nearly forty-five universities are adapting to new innovations. A curriculum balanced between core concepts and specialization is being worked out. INSDOC, together with the Documentation Research and Training Center (DRTC), an institution founded by Professor Ranganathan, took upon themselves the task of training their graduates in the use of computers in their courses; both courses are heavily loaded in favor of information technology. The graduates of INSDOC and DRTC are considered specialists in information science and are preferred for senior positions in information centers in the country.

NISSAT has also funded several training programs that have played an important role in improving awareness of new technologies and their potential. Various continuing education programs conducted by professional associations and library schools have helped working professionals to update their knowledge and skills.

PUBLIC LIBRARIES IN INDIA

The public library in India is considered to be a living force for education, culture, and information and seen as an essential agent for the fostering of peace and spiritual welfare through the minds of men and women. The country has had public libraries for nearly two hundred years, but public library development has not come up uniformly and systematically all over the country. The library movement in India is now eighty-five years old; yet in spite of that duration, except for ten states, library legislation is not in operation to provide "free book service for all." Public libraries are still not effectively integrated in the educational and cultural development of the nation. Rural public libraries have not developed into centers to create awareness about education, information, recreation, and culture.

The objectives of a rural public library are construed to be concerned with rural reconstruction. Such libraries are required to serve various sectors of the population. Apart from rural populations, the public libraries should serve disadvantaged people, which includes tribal people. Such libraries should develop special collections including tribal histories, material culture, early ethnographic records, and tribal traditional customs, as well as the histories and oral records scattered in tribal belts. Tribal archives may also be developed along with the library. Seen in this light, library and information needs fall into two areas. The first need is for library services for all ethnic groups; the second is for specialized informational needs unique to tribal populations as a whole. The goal of library service, whether in the cities or in rural communities, must be to provide increasing awareness of, and access to, books, documents, and other library materials and to store and disseminate information.

Another important sector that public libraries must develop more fully is that of women's studies. Women form almost half of the population of India. All efforts are being made to educate them through massive literacy programs. To keep literacy alive, steps have to be taken to provide reading material of interest. The tremendous increase in research and action relating to women's issues in the country must be reflected in library collections. A library's service, in such cases, should also include particular forms of information sources. Public libraries must emphasize the needs of women as users of the libraries as well as the needs of those interested in evaluating and developing women's studies.

The impact of new technology on public libraries in India is insignificant. However, the Indian government plans to extend information technology facilities to some selected public libraries. The national policy on library and information science, when implemented, will introduce new technologies in the functioning of those public libraries.

CONCLUSION

The library profession in India must assess and reassess the constantly changing library environment as we near the threshold of the twenty-first century. Higher education, scholarship, technology, and economics are all interrelated, and they play major roles in the library infrastructure of the country. New technologies will call for organizational changes in the traditional libraries.

The present period of transition will probably last for a long time. Libraries will be in ceaseless transition, and the library environment will be perpetually changing. This situation will place considerable demands on staff, requiring a vast range of knowledge as well as a high degree of flexibility.

At one end of the spectrum the country can boast of a highly specialized information retrieval system, but at the other end stands the common man who has no access even to basic reading material or advice because of the lack of a public library network spread throughout the length and breadth of this vast country. While there is an "information flood" in some places, there is an "information drought" in many others.

Information in India has to be provided to the illiterate and neoliterate masses—quite a formidable segment of the country's population. Illiterate people also have the innate urge for information, which can be satisfied by a well-knit public library system in which the libraries are not only book-oriented but have a multimedia approach and oral information service through audiovisual aids.

Like power grids, library and information personnel can, by joining together, build up a power base to supply the right information to the right person at the right time.